PAPERS

of the

NEW WORLD ARCHAEOLOGICAL FOUNDATION

NUMBER SEVENTY

Colonization, Warfare, and Exchange at the Postclassic Maya Site of Canajasté, Chiapas, Mexico

By

MICHAEL BLAKE

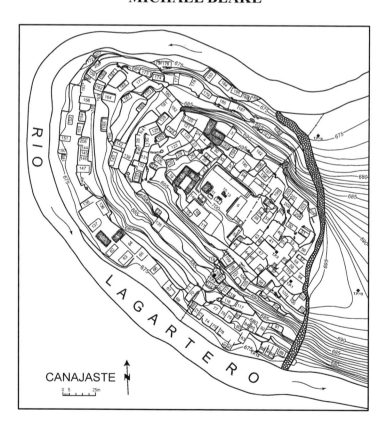

NEW WORLD ARCHAEOLOGICAL FOUNDATION

BRIGHAM YOUNG UNIVERSITY

PROVO, UTAH

2010

Colonization, Warfare, and Exchange

at the Postclassic Maya Site of Canajasté,

Chiapas, Mexico

PAPERS

of the

NEW WORLD ARCHAEOLOGICAL FOUNDATION

NUMBER SEVENTY

Colonization, Warfare, and Exchange at the Postclassic Maya Site of Canajasté, Chiapas, Mexico

By

MICHAEL BLAKE

NEW WORLD ARCHAEOLOGICAL FOUNDATION

BRIGHAM YOUNG UNIVERSITY

PROVO, UTAH

2010

VOLUME EDITOR

MARY E. PYE

Printed by
BYU PRESS
PROVO, UTAH
2010

FORWARD

This volume is an in-depth study of the small archaeological site of Canajasté, a defensively positioned, walled town nestled in a bend of the Lagartero River in the Chiapas Highlands of southern Mexico. Michael Blake selected this site for his doctoral investigation because it appeared to have been the political seat of a small, independent polity, most likely a secondary state. Because the formulation and implementation of this research took place in the 1980s when archaeologists were especially concerned with understanding the systemic processes that underlie social change, Blake planned his research to investigate exactly what social processes were responsible at this location for the formation and perpetuation of this particular form of sociopolitical organization. Blake's training at the University of Michigan meant that his research was explicitly problem oriented, theoretically grounded, and with the issues to be investigated laid out clearly, along with the predicted archaeological expectations that would either support or refute them. Consequently, the resulting dissertation, as well as the present volume, which is an updated version of the dissertation, is an example of exceptionally well-crafted archaeological research.

Although Blake's theoretical interests evidently guided his choice of Canajasté as a research site, this decision had additional beneficial consequences for our understanding of Maya prehistory, since that ancient community occupied both a space and a time that have been notoriously neglected in archaeological studies of the ancient Maya. Canajasté is located within the Maya Highlands, a region that has been seriously understudied, especially in comparison with the adjacent Maya Lowlands. In addition, the Canajasté polity was extant during the Late Postclassic Period, the last major unit of time in Mesoamerican prehistory prior to the arrival of Europeans, when the consequent social upheaval ruptured all native systems of social organization. Similarly, this late, pre-contact time period has been much less

studied compared with earlier times, especially when compared with the antecedent Classic Period. Thus, at the time Blake's dissertation appeared it was notable not only because it was an exemplar of modern archaeological research but also because its focus helped fill gaps in the archaeological record of Maya prehistory. Now three decades on, the significance and importance of this study has not dimmed, although of course some archaeological progress has been made in the interim.

When Blake initiated his field research, Canajasté, located very close to the international border with Guatemala, was isolated in a remote, peaceful, rural area. However, this tranquil setting was soon ruptured by the arrival of dispirited, frightened, and disease-ridden Guatemaltecos who had crossed into Mexico as refugees from the disastrous civil war that was raging in their country. Their temporary camp near the archaeological excavations became a magnet for aid workers, Mexican government officials, and other concerned individuals, all of whom changed the local atmosphere from bucolic to chaotic and added substantially to the challenges facing Blake and his crew. Not the least of these challenges were infectious diseases, and the fear of possible cross border attack by the Guatemalan military or paramilitaries. This was the extremely tense situation when I paid a visit at one point during the five-month field season. Despite the unforeseen setbacks, Blake persevered and was able to complete his investigations at the site. Accordingly, this landmark study is not only a paragon of archaeological research, but also it testifies to one archaeologist's ability to overcome considerable hardships without detriment to the quality of his research project.

It is especially laudable that this study is being published in the Papers of the New World Archaeological Foundation where it will get the readership exposure that it fully deserves. The volume will be of great interest for those readers who are concerned with understanding the dynamics of social change, for those who

admire the cultural achievements of the ancient
Maya but want to know about the full range
of their cultural experience, and for those who
simply take pleasure in a well-designed and
well-written scientific study.

Barbara Voorhies
University of California, Santa Barbara

PREFACE

Some 30 years have lapsed since I began my archaeological investigations at the Postclassic Maya site of Canajasté in the upper Grijalva region of southern Mexico. The research was undertaken as the central part of my doctoral dissertation project at the University of Michigan and completed in 1985…a mere 25 years ago! While by no means a detailed site report—the dissertation aimed to present an archaeological case study of the ways in which secondary states emerged, expanded, and transformed—it contains a fairly complete discussion of the site's layout, ceremonial architecture, house features, and the artifacts and other data recovered during the excavations. Recently, John Clark, the director of the New World Archaeological Foundation, suggested that it would be worthwhile making the dissertation available as a monograph in the Papers of the New World Archaeological Foundation series since it still represents one of the most detailed discussions of a Postclassic period settlement in the upper Grijalva region of Chiapas. In taking him up on his generous offer, I have tried to resist the temptation to revise the original work—after more than two decades, such an update would entail entirely new sets of analyses and a substantial, if not complete, rewriting of the book. Instead, I've opted to update a few sections of the study in order to benefit from the recent publication of the region's ceramic sequence (Bryant, Clark, et al. 2005) and detailed settlement surveys (De Montmollin 1995). In addition to the present work, I am currently preparing a detailed monograph describing the excavations and artifacts from the site and comparing Canajasté's material record with those from Postclassic sites in neighboring regions and beyond.

Although there has not been much new archaeological research on the Postclassic archaeology of the Grijalva River region in Chiapas nor in the western highlands of Guatemala during the past 25 years, a few new publications have appeared. One is a chapter by Lynneth Lowe and Carlos Álvarez A. (2007), in a recent volume in honor of Gareth W. Lowe, describing excavations at the site of Los Cimientos de las Margaritas located 45 km to the north of Canajasté. This site, along with the many sites surrounding it, is in the Tojolabal Maya region and was likely closely related to the Chuj Maya communities of western Guatemala. As I discuss below, I think Canajasté was most likely a Chuj community and so its residents could well have been closely related to the Tojolabal Maya of Los Cimientos de las Margaritas. The architecture, settlement layout, and artifacts from Los Cimientos de las Margaritas are all very similar to those at Canajasté, supporting the Tojolabal-Chuj connection—and Canajasté's identification as a Chuj colony.

Another important new study is the publication of the Postclassic period archaeology of the Chantuto region of Pacific Coastal Chiapas, approximately 140 km to the southwest of Canajasté. Barbara Voorhies and Janine Gasco (2004) describe in detail the survey and excavations, artifacts, and architecture of this densely occupied zone within the larger Soconusco region. Their detailed work shows that the Postclassic Soconusco, at least as it is represented in the vicinity of the main center of Acapetahua, was only broadly similar to Postclassic Maya communities of the upper Grijalva region. In spite of the general "Postclassic" nature of the material record, there are many specific differences in the settlement layout, architecture, and artifacts between the Soconusco sites and Canajasté and its neighbors. This may be partly due to the cultural and linguistic differences between the Maya of the upper Grijalva and the Mixe-Zoque speakers of the Pacific Coast.

For those readers who wish to situate the present study within the larger picture of Postclassic Mesoamerica I recommend the following works which represent just a few of the excellent new studies dealing with the archaeology of Maya and Mesoamerican communities that were occupied during the three centuries prior to the Spanish Conquest: (Fox 1987; Kowalski and Kristan-Graham 2007;

Masson 2000; Smith and Berdan 2003; Taube 1992). In the newly released second edition of her text *Ancient Mexico & Central America: Archaeology and Culture History*, Susan Toby Evans (2008) has written several chapters that provide clear and thorough overviews of Postclassic Mesoamerican archaeology. Finally, for a recent overview of the Late Postclassic, Spanish Conquest, and the Early Colonial periods I highly recommend *The Legacy of Mesoamerica: History and Culture of a Native American Civilization* edited by Robert Carmack, Janine Gasco, and Gary Gossen (2007).

ACKNOWLEDGMENTS

Funding for this research was generously provided by the Social Sciences and Humanities Research Council of Canada (Doctoral Fellowship), the Horace H. Rackham School of Graduate Studies at the University of Michigan, the New World Archaeological Foundation of Brigham Young University, and the Wenner-Gren Foundation for Anthropological Research.

Mexico's Instituto Nacional de Antropología e Historia (INAH) granted permission to carry out the archaeological excavations in 1981-82. For their support I thank Professor Gastón García Cantú, then Director General of INAH, Archaeologist Joaquín García Bárcena, President of the Archaeology Council, Archaeologist Ángel García Cook, Director of Prehispanic Monuments, and Licenciado Juan José Solórzano, Director of the INAH Regional Center in Chiapas, and members of the Archaeology Council for granting the excavation permit.

The research was carried out under the auspices of the New World Archaeological Foundation (NWAF). Generous support was provided by Gareth Lowe, its Director, and Thomas A. Lee, Jr., its Field Director. Tom Lee was the cornerstone of this entire effort and has helped see it to completion in literally every possible way. I benefited greatly from the constantly stimulating atmosphere provided by other members of the NWAF—Gareth Lowe, Susanna Ekholm, Pierre Agrinier, John Clark, and Douglas Bryant were always willing to share with me their years of experience in helping to understand Chiapas archaeology.

Joyce Marcus, Jeffrey Parsons, Henry Wright, Aram Yengoyan, and John Eadie, my dissertation committee members at the University of Michigan, saw to it that the research project maintained a fruitful direction and did not stray too far down less productive, though tempting, paths. I especially thank Joyce Marcus who sparked my interest in Mesoamerican archaeology and ethnohistory and guided the theoretical and practical development of this research from its inception to its final presentation.

My interest in Mesoamerican archaeology began in 1977 when Brian Hayden invited me to participate as a member of his Coxoh-Maya Ethnoarchaeological Project (1977-79). Brian's unfailing encouragement, support, as well as endless stimulating conversations and debate created the intellectual foundation on which this project was built.

Several people labored on the project above and beyond the call of duty. John Clark's support by way of detailed argumentation and constant, thoughtful comments and criticism has added to the project at every stage. He not only analyzed the obsidian but helped me to analyze all of the other excavated materials as well. John's comments on the initial draft of this report are much appreciated.

Special thanks are due to Ben Nelson, who helped with the ceramic analysis; to Paul Minnis, who analyzed the botanical remains; to Olivier de Montmollin, who willingly shared information from his own doctoral research in a neighboring valley; and to Barbara Voorhies, who shared her unpublished data and ideas as well as made detailed comments on this manuscript. All four of these scholars have been sounding boards and sources of much inspiration.

I thank many other individuals who commented on the various written and verbal stages of this work, and I am grateful to them for their generous efforts and valuable ideas: Mark Aldenderfer, Carlos Álvarez, Douglas Bryant, Robert Carmack, Roz Chrenka, Michael Deal, Robert Egbert, Manuel Gándara, Patricia Gilman, Mary Hodge, Gloria Jiménez, R.G. Matson, Michael Moseley, Margaret Nelson, Hector Neff, Tomás Perez, Susan Pollock, Don Rice, Susan Scott, Michael Smith, and Sonia Rivero Torres.

Several archaeologists have helped to carry out specialized analyses of the materials collected. I am indebted to Kent Flannery and Patty Wattenmaker for analyzing the faunal collections, to Fred Nelson for determining the obsidian sources, and to Hector Neff for examining the plumbate ceramics.

The fieldwork was carried out with the permission of the municipal authorities of La Trinitaria, and Las Delicias, Chiapas—and I thank them for their support of this work. I am especially grateful to all of the men from Las Delicias who worked painstakingly to complete the excavations: in particular, Hilario Hernández, Alberto Zamorano, and the two men on whose land the site was located: Margarito Aguilar and Fidel García. I would also like to acknowledge the good-natured support of the many families from the pueblo of Chacaj, Guatemala, who, beginning in 1982, were forced to take refuge in and around Canajasté during their country's civil war. Under harsh and trying circumstances they showed constant bravery, ingenuity, and civility.

I am forever indebted to my trusty assistant Artemio Villatoro who is a superb excavator, field and lab supervisor and analyst and who translated my idea of organization into one that worked. Alejandro Sánchez and Vicente Pérez helped set up the camp and take it down, and they worked with Tom Lee on the excavation and consolidation of Structure 9. Josefina Gasca Borja generously helped with the fieldwork for two months, and Irma Paniagua kept the sherds

clean and the crew fed. Jean-Pierre Courau helped to make some preliminary modifications to Kristi Butterwick's excellent original site map.

Elizabeth Ross and her assistant, Alonso Méndez, cheerfully applied their artistic skills to the artifact and map drawings, and Ray Scippa skillfully photographed the artifacts. I also thank María Elena Fernández Galán R., of the Centro de Investigaciones Ecológicas del Sureste in San Cristóbal de las Casas, for making available several publications in the Center's library. I am grateful to Michael Moseley and the staff of the Field Museum for making available their collections and allowing access to their library.

I would also like to thank the NWAF staff for the production of this volume. BYU students, Megan Wakefield digitized the illustrations and developed the the volume layout, while Arlene Colman did the final copyediting. As NWAF series editor, Mary E. Pye edited the volume and John Clark did the final review. Funding for the student work and printing costs was provided by the David J. and Edloe Rust Memorial Fund.

Finally, I thank my wife Susan for her help, laughter, and support during every stage of this project.

CONTENTS

FIGURES

TABLES

CHAPTER 1

INTRODUCTION

Spanish conquistadors who entered the Maya area of Mesoamerica at the beginning of the 16th century encountered dozens of small competing kingdoms (Figure 1.1). The ease with which they were able to conquer these native kingdoms was due, in part, to their shrewd ability to exploit existing political rifts by allying with one group against another. Even one of the largest Maya kingdoms, the Quiché in highland Guatemala, was relatively easy to overthrow, as Pedro de Alvarado discovered in AD 1524 (Alvarado 1924). He enlisted the help of the Cakchiquels who, at the time, had been encroaching rather successfully on the Quiché's domain. They leapt at the opportunity to align themselves with a foreign power in order to subjugate their long-time neighbors and enemies. This inter-polity conflict characterizes the nature of Postclassic Maya politics. Gerhard (1979:4-5) has summarized the area as one which:

> …was occupied by a great many autonomous native states, most of them with diminutive and well-defined territorial limits. While there were regional confederacies and hegemonies, and states allied through dynastic ties or trade, there was also a good deal of inter-community warfare, and (with the exception of Xoconochco's inclusion in the Aztec empire) the political structure at first European contact was fragmented: there was no cohesive force, no great imperial center.

Excluding the Quiché, this description applies to the entire Maya area. One particularly apt description by Landa gives the flavor of the Preconquest political relations in northern Yucatán (Tozzer 1941:40):

> Between the three great princely houses, namely the Cocoms, the Xius

and the Chels, there were great strifes and enmities, and they exist even today although they have become Christians. The Cocoms said to the Xius that they were foreigners and traitors who had assassinated their natural lord and stolen his domains. The Xius answered that they were as good as they and of as old a family and as princely; and that they were not traitors but liberators of the country by putting the tyrant to death. The Chel said that he was as good as they in lineage, since he was the grandson of the most esteemed priest of Mayapán; and for himself personally, he was greater than they, since he had been able to make himself as great a lord as they were.

Ethnohistoric documents have allowed anthropologists to reconstruct partially the social and political organization characteristic of these societies at the time of conquest (Carmack 1981; Roys 1943; Thompson 1970). For the most part they were highly stratified societies with two classes—hereditary nobility and commoners. Within each was a series of ranked lineages, the ruler being chosen from the senior noble lineage. The commoner class included slaves and their children; some of the slaves were prisoners of war who survived the first few years of captivity. These basic divisions were present in the smallest political units, even though the range of the nobility's control might extend over a territory of no more than 100 to 200 sq km. At the other extreme, as in the case of the Quiché kingdom, the ruler exacted tribute from hundreds of small and large polities alike, ranging over a zone of many thousand square kilometers and incorporating more than one million inhabitants (Carmack 1968:77; Fox 1978:4). The organization of the Quiché state at its peak was, of course, much different

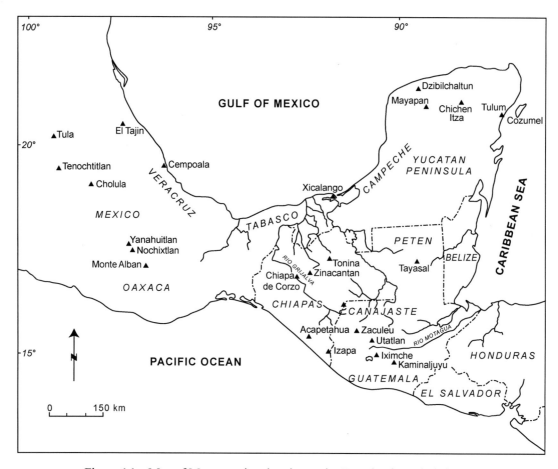

Figure 1.1. Map of Mesoamerica showing major Postclassic period sites.

than it had been when it started out 200 to 300 years earlier (Carmack 1981). When it began it consisted of no more than a few warriors who took over a relatively uninhabited territory in the highlands of Guatemala. They expanded their political control gradually through conquest, trade and marriage alliances, and direct colonization. When the Spaniards arrived, many of the subjugated regions were busy revolting against the central Quiché state: for example, ". . . the Cakchiquel, the Rabinal, and the Aguacatec revolted and initiated rival systems" (Fox 1978:4). Much the same thing had taken place in Yucatán when Montejo set out to conquer that province. As Tozzer (1941:62, n.292) notes:

> It was not until after the fall of the city [the Cocom capital of Mayapán] that these lords or *halach uinics* were independent of any

central authority and ruled, each sovereign in his own state, the condition found in the country by the Spaniards.

The pattern that emerges is one of small-scale states, sometimes politically independent of one another and, at other times, joined into large territorially expansive states administered by an elite stratum. The question of how these small-scale states evolved after the Classic Maya collapse remains to be answered.

In many ways these individual polities resemble stratified chiefdoms known from Polynesia (Goldman 1970; Sahlins 1958) in that they were relatively small (compared with the Aztec or Tarascan states, for example), unstable, and had small, unspecialized administrations. Nonetheless, most of these Postclassic Maya polities had the historical legacy of being descended from past greatness, and this ideology underwrote a complex stratified society. In other words, although diminished in size, the smallest Maya city-state had within its structure the "code" for growth and political elaboration—a legacy from the Classic period states. This was embodied in myth, legend, and written history, as well as the living remnants of past social structures. Not only did these societies have the impetus of their own past to encourage and maintain statehood, but they also interacted with large-scale states in Central Mexico, such as the Toltecs, and later, the Aztecs. They were flanked in time and space by state-level political organization and ideology. As such, they can be considered secondary states (Fried 1960, 1967; Service 1971, 1975).

Secondary states, in this broad sense, develop in the wake of already existing states. They are either descendants of former states or states reconstituted in the political vacuum following the collapse of a former central state. The handful of primary or pristine states, which have been the subject of a great deal of archaeological study around the world, justifiably absorb the attentions of most researchers interested in the origins of civilization (Wright 1977). But the question of why and how these first archaic states persisted, with such tenacity, to spawn hundreds of secondary states over the centuries and millennia is also a worthwhile evolutionary question. It is not enough to reconstruct their past structures and organization; archaeologists must also attempt to understand the processes whereby they evolved.

The project reported here has two main aims: (1) to integrate ethnographic, ethnohistoric, and archaeological data in developing a methodology for monitoring the evolution of Postclassic Maya secondary states between about AD 1100 and 1525; and (2) to use that methodology to evaluate the relative importance of four specific processes or factors that anthropologists have suggested are important in explaining secondary state evolution: (a) interregional exchange, (b) warfare, (c) elite colonization, and (d) complete colonization by all population sectors of entire

polities. Each of these, sequentially or in various combinations, is described in the native Maya and Early Colonial period ethnohistoric sources. They are also well represented in examples from many other states in different parts of the world. One of my goals is to see just how well they can be documented in a single archaeological case in order to determine their relative contributions, as specific processes, to the long term changes in the social, political, and economic organizations of archaic secondary states.

The study focuses on the Postclassic Maya site of Canajasté, one of many small centers in the uppermost reaches of the Grijalva River Basin in southeastern Chiapas, Mexico (Lee 1975). Although no ethnohistoric documents describing Canajasté at the time of the Spanish Conquest are known to exist, archaeological fieldwork shows it to have been the center of a small territory and perhaps the capital of its region. Its size, location, settlement layout (especially its defensive nature), residential features, ceremonial architecture, and surface artifacts all pointed to the ancient community's vigorous relations within the regional territorial organization.

The site is located on a meandering stretch of the Lagartero River in a small pocket valley that almost straddles the Mexico-Guatemala border. Figure 1.2 shows a recent Google Earth satellite image of the site, illustrating how the central residential and civic-ceremonial zone is surrounded on three sides by the river— forming, in essence, a moat. Although the river is slow moving, it is both wide (12 to 16 m) and deep enough (up to 3 m) in most spots to make crossing it difficult unless one is prepared to swim (Figure 1.3). The exposed "neck" of land unprotected by the river was protected by a massive stone wall creating an impenetrable fortress (Figure 1.4a-b). More residential structures were dispersed outside the walled zone on both sides of the river. Reconnaissance of the site, including preliminary testing and surface artifact collections, showed that it was restricted to a Postclassic occupation and that some of the artifact classes—particularly those made of obsidian—were imported from distant sources. As such, Canajasté appeared to present

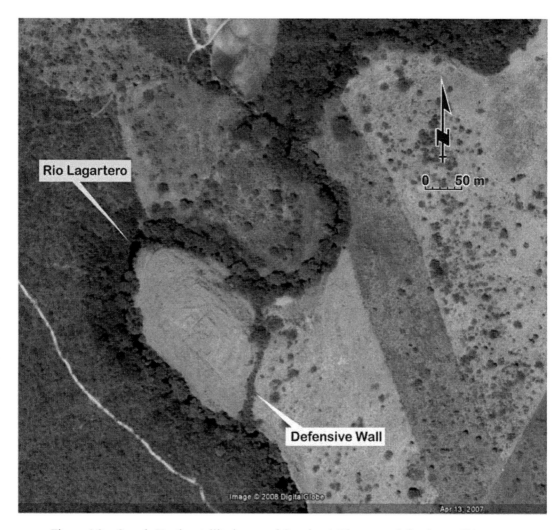

Figure 1.2. Google Earth satellite image of Canajasté. The stone defensive wall is
visible as it cuts across the "neck" or meander of the Lagartero River.

a perfect case study to examine the effects
of the above-mentioned specific processes in
secondary state development.

The approach used here is that each of
the four processes under consideration will
influence, in predictably different ways, the
evolution of hierarchical relationships among
social units within a polity. Hierarchical social
and political relationships within and between
communities undergo significant changes as
states evolve. Ethnographic and ethnohistoric
literature on secondary states in several parts of
the world shows that households are social units

sensitive to these changing relationships. The
answer to the question of why households should
be sensitive to these changing relationships
rests on theories of the way elites perpetuate
themselves, as well as the way they distinguish
themselves from non-elite. In most complex
societies, including Prehispanic secondary
states in the New World, claims to elite status
were based upon principles of inheritance.
Claims to positions within the political and
economic structure rested on hereditary rights
and relationships that were largely defined by
membership in a household and the status of

Figure 1.3. Susan Blake and Hilario Hernández crossing the suspension bridge over the Lagartero River. This illustrates how difficult it is to gain access to the site from the opposite side of the river.

one's household within the community. The individuals who comprised the elite stratum would have learned many of the appropriate behaviors, customs, beliefs, and symbols of their elite status within the context of social relations defined by the household (G. Marcus 1983:17). The same would be true for members of non-elite social strata. Therefore, the relations among the social strata would, to a large extent, be embedded in relations among elite and non-elite households. Some of the relations could have been direct ones, such as simple exclusionary behavior—whereby the non-elite households would be presented with regulated differences

in consumption rituals between themselves and elite households. Other relations might have been more indirectly mediated by way of institutions, such as military or religious orders, which had their own restricted rules of recruitment and training, some of them only indirectly related to household membership.

The main processes underlying changing social structure and organization should each have their own unique and distinguishable impact on the social structural and organizational changes. At the household level, these differing processual impacts will manifest themselves in the way households in different

a

b

Figure 1.4. Views of the massive stone defensive wall that protected the principal residential and civic-ceremonial center of Canajasté: a) shows the intact wall near the summit of the site; b) shows the collapsed south end of the wall close to river level.

social strata modify their relations with each other.

Based on ethnographic, ethnohistoric, and ethnoarchaeological sources, I develop a model that specifies the effects of these distinct processes on four major classes of archaeological information derived from house remains: (1) household features, (2) domestic artifacts, (3) subsistence refuse, and (4) community settlement pattern. In addition, I trace the impact of these processes on community-wide features, such as ceremonial structures, fortification features, and regional settlement pattern.

In 1981-82, I began a detailed archaeological study of Canajasté in order to identify and trace changes in the relationships among social units within the community, and between Canajasté and its neighbors over the course of its occupation span. The kinds of changes I was able to observe in the relationship between elite and non-elite households allowed me to evaluate the changing importance of the various specific processes at work in the community's evolution from a small to a large center.

As an example of the way each of the four specific processes differentially affects material remains of the community, let's briefly examine variation in house styles. Intercommunity exchange relations may encourage the elite of one polity to emulate the styles of another stronger polity (Friedl 1964; Pollock 1983). By exchanging wives in marriage, for example, local elites may be encouraged to build residences that imitate the palace styles where their wives came from, thereby enhancing their own status in the eyes of the local population (Hodder 1979:448). Similarly, local non-elites may attempt to emulate their own local rulers and, thereby, contribute to the process of stylistic change within the community. In contrast to this, during periods of intercommunity conflict when warfare is the dominant mode of interaction, emulation of nonlocal styles decreases (especially emulation of the enemy's styles) (e.g., Hodder 1979:447, 1982:114). In this case local house styles may be elaborated using traditional patterns in

order to distinguish between the conflicting communities.

When nonlocal elites take over the political, religious, and economic upper stratum of another society, there would be an abrupt introduction of a range of new styles that duplicate the pattern in the homeland. These should be restricted to the elite and may involve a complete discontinuity with earlier forms (Fox 1978:8; Kubler 1961). Elite houses may be built in entirely new locations or may be built on the razed foundations of earlier elite residences. The more distant the elite and the greater the cultural differences between them and their new subjects, the greater the discontinuity between old and new house styles.

When entire polities move into a new area, colonizing it and displacing or absorbing the local population, there would be a complete break with earlier styles and traditions, and the local patterns should all but disappear (Kubler 1961). Houses in this situation would be built according to the traditions in the homeland, in as much as local environmental conditions permitted. Any differences in styles among the various strata of the society would be part of the pre-existing, nonlocal social dynamics.

By monitoring and comparing the different trajectories that elite and non-elite houses went through during the course of a society's history, it should be possible to determine the relative importance of the four specific processes or mechanisms of change. In Chapter 2, I will introduce the study of secondary states and take a closer look at the processes operative in their evolution. Chapter 3 presents an outline of the concepts I use to look at how these processes affect the relations between elite and non-elite. In it I will also examine the way these relations are likely to be symbolized and how changes in the relations between the two classes require changes in their symbols. In addition, I present more detailed arguments for why changes in households and their remains provide a particularly productive avenue of archaeological inquiry into the evolution of states. This is especially true when household information is wedded with other lines of information, including changes in regional settlement patterns and civic-ceremonial architecture.

Chapter 4 outlines my specific expectations for the effects of these four processes on a number of artifact classes. I will specify how each class of artifacts (as well as architecture and settlement patterns) might differ between elite and non-elite segments of the community, and even more importantly, how those differences are affected by each of the specific processes.

In Chapter 5, I present an introduction to the environment and archaeology of the upper Grijalva region of the Grijalva River Basin. Chapter 6 presents analyses of house architecture, Chapter 7 details the analysis of the household artifacts, Chapter 8 discusses the mortuary remains—primarily infant burials, Chapter 9 describes the analysis of subsistence remains, and Chapter 10 presents the analysis of settlement pattern data and civic-ceremonial architecture.

The ultimate goal of this endeavor is not so much to reconstruct the organization of a prehistoric state but, rather, to contribute to an understanding of the processes whereby ancient states changed. In other words, this research attempts to study states by examining their transformations, not their structures. Chapter 11 sums up the results of the study in terms of this goal and discusses the implications of this research.

CHAPTER 2

PROCESSES OF CHANGE IN SECONDARY STATES

STUDYING PROCESS

Understanding cultural variation and change are central aims of both anthropology and archaeology. The temporal dimension allows archaeology to concern itself with variation over time and therefore concentrate on change. The question of why and how cultural change takes place must necessarily focus on the underlying processes and their interrelationships. In this respect, it will be useful to briefly consider the nature of both general and specific processes of sociopolitical change.

In the broadest sense, processes are sequences of events or changes unfolding through time, with no restriction on the span of time involved. Nonetheless, in traditional approaches to the study of emerging social complexity and state formation, the processes normally considered are transformational in nature and take place over the course of centuries or millennia. They are often stated categorically such that: A must take place before B can take place, or A transforms into B. In this sense almost any aspect of society can be considered in its processual dimension. Here, I will make the distinction between two levels of process: (1) general, and (2) specific. General processes apply to all systems and result from combinations of specific, lower-level processes, the exact combination of which depends upon the particular system. Examples of general processes are: growth (increase in size), development (increase in numbers of parts), coherence (increase in numbers of linkages among parts), centralization (increasing hierarchy among linkages), and specialization (functional differentiation of parts).

Specific processes vary depending upon the particular system in question. They include the mechanisms by which individuals and groups interact with both their social and natural environment. I include under this category: exchange, conflict, subsistence, and technology. Some confusion might arise here since each of these processes or mechanisms of interaction can be considered in its synchronic aspect and be described as though it were static. Since none of processes is ever static, it makes more sense, especially in archaeological research, to study them diachronically. They can, simultaneously, be considered as mechanisms enabling general level processes to take place. They can also be considered as social strategies. In this latter aspect, specific processes are manipulated by individuals or social groups. Thus, they are short-term processes. However, in the former context, specific processes can be seen to operate over the long run and have unforeseen influences on each other and on general processes. I prefer to consider them in their diachronic, processual aspect since it is both their short-term strategic dimension and their long-term changes that must be understood in order to eventually explain the general processes of sociopolitical change.

Stages of Cultural Evolution and Process

Understanding changes from one "level" of socio-cultural integration to another (Service 1971:30) has traditionally been attempted by determining the characteristics of societies at level A and comparing them to those of level B. The changes in characteristics and the timing of their changes are used to test hypotheses concerning the processes underlying the shift from one stage to the next. For example, the transformation from chiefdoms to states can be studied in terms of the processes necessary to bring about the characteristics of states that were not present in the preceding chiefdom stage.

Discussion in the previous section suggests, however, that it is not necessary to restrict ourselves to examining only the diachronic variation between two different, synchronically described stages. Instead of studying the process of changing social structures, it is possible to develop a method for studying the structure of changing social processes. To do this it is necessary to characterize changes in the specific processes and their influences on one another, and then monitor the evidence for their effects on long-term general processes. Specific processes of political or economic interaction may lead, for example, to changes in general processes such as increasing growth, complexity, and specialization (Flannery 1972a). Understanding the relationship between the two levels of processes lies at the heart of explaining long-term sociopolitical change. This study will present a method for monitoring several specific processes and characterizing a secondary state by the way these processes change through its history. I hope to demonstrate that it is possible to examine the larger problem of sociopolitical change by focusing on short-term processes within a given level of socio-cultural integration. When more cases are studied it should eventually be possible to examine the broader-scale shifts in the emergence of complex society.

Archaeological Evidence for Specific Processes

There are many ways of studying the processes of secondary state evolution and many types of data that could be brought to bear upon the problem. Archaeology, however, allows access to data that are unique in that they provide evidence for both specific and general processes that operate in states. Although archaeological data often do not provide the same kinds of sociological and political detail as ethnographic or historical sources, archaeology does provide the most complete information, of any sort, that can be firmly anchored along the dimension of time. These data are comprised of the material remains of past societies, not the documented sequence of political events themselves. This leads to a major obstacle: how does one find evidence of *process* in the archaeological record?

In order to answer this question I have relied on one main approach to studying material culture that allows statements to be made about the processes involved in socio-cultural change. It is that material culture, technology in the broadest sense, is more than just a reflection of the society that made and used it (Hodder 1982). Material culture is a complex system of active symbols (Douglas and Isherwood 1980). As Hodder (1982:12) has argued: "symbols do not 'reflect' but . . . they play an active part in forming and giving meaning to social behavior." Whereas material culture may simply "reflect" some past process from the point of view of the archaeologist or anthropologist, in its symbolic role in an ongoing functioning society, material culture was part of an active communication system.[1] It is this dynamic, symbolic aspect of material culture that provides one key to studying process directly.

In bringing the notion of material culture as active symbols to the search for change in the archaeological record of past societies, we can look for and find evidence of sociopolitical processes on a much finer scale than ever before. This study will explore the implications of the symbolic approach to material culture as it bears on the changing sociopolitical and economic organization of a secondary state. Before proceeding with an introduction to the study of processes in secondary state evolution, I will first introduce the approach that this study will take.

I am taking as given that material culture can serve symbolic functions (Hodder 1982; Wobst 1977). Based on this assumption, we can ask the question: how does this approach allow one to discover evidence for processes of change? The main answer is that it requires a different emphasis on the description and interpretation of parts of the archaeological record that might normally be treated as reflections of some past process. The general form or model of this shift in emphasis is presented below.

Changes in sociopolitical organization, such as would take place in secondary states, involve the alteration of relationships among sub-units or institutions of society. Flannery (1972a:409), for example, outlines two general processes that lead to such altered relations: segregation and centralization. These processes, in turn, alter the character of relationships within and between whole polities. As they do so, there must also be alterations in the symbolized relations and, thus, in the material culture made and used for that purpose. In other words, as sociopolitical relationships change, then so too must the symbols of those relationships. They must either be physically modified or their meanings must be redefined. These physical modifications of material symbols provide the raw data for the archaeological investigation of process. Specifically, different processes should have different effects on changing social relationships. These differences should result in distinct patterns of change or in distinguishable sequences of modification in the material symbols of the social relationships.

Following this idea, the present study will wed the archaeological goal of detecting and explaining processes of sociopolitical change with the concept that, whatever else material culture may be, it is its symbolic dimension that can be most fruitfully explored in our attempts to understand such change. At this point I will turn directly to the central research question: what specific processes lead to change in secondary states and how can they be studied archaeologically?

CHANGE IN SECONDARY STATES

Secondary states are political organizations that inherit their complexity from earlier forms or neighbors that had already reached the state-level of organization (Fried 1960, 1967; Price 1978:179). The question of how state-level societies came into being in the first place has captivated generations of anthropologists, archaeologists, and historians (cf. Service 1975; Wright 1977). No less interesting is the history of secondary states. Processes that influence the way states develop are not restricted to the question of origins alone.

As already mentioned, there is a tendency in archaeological research to concentrate on explaining change from one stage to another stage (for example, from chiefdom to state) and confining research within a given stage to the reconstruction of social, political, and economic organization. But the processes at work in social evolution do not stop once cultures cross some evolutionary watershed. They continue to operate, and societies whose ancestors reached levels of complex organization, sometimes centuries or millennia before, continue to evolve. To be sure, subsequent changes may not be as gripping as the ones that initiated the initial emergence of pristine chiefdoms or states, but they can provide exciting evidence for the interplay between specific and general processes (Kottak 1972; Price 1978).

Fried's (1983:470) distinction between pristine and secondary states stresses that different processes are at work in the *origins* of each. This may be true. But what must be pointed out is that pristine states result from specific processes that operate in pre-state forms of society. Once in existence, pristine states are obviously no longer pristine, and the processes at work in their ongoing transformations are the processes that shape secondary states.

Interestingly, the specific processes that are said not to be "prime movers" in state emergence are "secondary movers" in continued state development. Trade, warfare, agricultural intensification, population growth are examples of processes that are universal in complex societies. The first two seem to be present in some form or another in all human societies— including ones that never developed hierarchical institutions (Service 1975:308). Processes of inter-polity relations, such as trade and warfare, seem to become more important once state forms of government are put in place (Flannery 1972a; Service 1975; Wright 1977). Let's look at the example of warfare and its role as one of the dominant sociopolitical forces in secondary state development.

Warfare

In small-scale, pre-state societies warfare may never lead to increased complexity because, as Carneiro (1970) points out, special sets of social and natural environmental conditions must be necessary for it to propel societies in that direction. Depending upon these conditions, which he has described as social and environmental circumscription, the nature of warfare can vary greatly. It can vary from punitive raiding for the purpose of defending territory or gathering booty to conquest for the purpose of subjugating other communities. The range in the types of warfare and the goals of the participants must be considered in order to understand the role it plays in the development of states. This may also help in avoiding the trap of considering warfare as only either a cause or a consequence of state evolution.

Warfare is not simply an exogenous variable, a condition in the social environment that must be dealt with. Instead, it is itself a process that can be actively manipulated by segments of society to achieve particular goals. Some of these goals are: subjugation, tribute, acquisition of land, plunder, trophies and honors, defense, and revenge (Otterbein 1970:4-5). The nature of warfare will depend upon the nature of the goals which, in turn, depend upon the overall conditions of the society.

Otterbein (1970:17), in a cross-cultural study of warfare, has shown that the more politically centralized a society, the more efficient are various aspects of its methods of waging war, such as "military organization, subordination, initiating party, initiation of war, diplomatic negotiations, tactical systems, weapons, armor, field fortifications, cavalry, fortified villages, siege operations, and causes of war." The scale of warfare varies from a few individuals in raiding parties to hundreds of thousands of people arranged in highly organized armies. But more important than scale is the degree of specialization. Otterbein (1970:19-23) finds specialization most closely associated with complex societies. Centralized societies (chiefdoms and states) are most likely to have a professional military apparatus.

They are the only kinds of societies which can support such an expense. Gorenstein (1966, 1973) has reached similar conclusions with respect to military organizations in Prehispanic Mesoamerica and Peru. Nevertheless, she argues there were significant differences in the degree of specialization between the Aztecs and the Inca. They both had full-time, professional military forces, but only the Inca had worked out an efficient means of provisioning distant garrisons and maintaining fortresses (Gorenstein 1966:46-47). The Aztecs had a much harder time maintaining troops and preferred to fortify towns and let some of the citizenry double as soldiers in times of conflict (Gorenstein 1966:56-58). Even among states there is a great deal of variation in warfare, suggesting differences in importance, efficiency, and even organization.

Despite their differences, it is clear that both the Aztec and the Inca states relied on warfare to maintain their very existence, even when they were under no serious threat of being conquered themselves. For these secondary states, warfare was a process of both internal and external specialization, the main goal of which was the maintenance and expansion of the state. An indication of the internal importance of warfare to the Aztecs is illustrated by Gorenstein (1966:62):

> The Spaniards, who knew that secure political domination meant complete centralization of power, wondered why Moctezuma permitted the Tlaxcalans to flourish in his own backyard and asked why he had not conquered them. His reply, "we could easily do so, but then there would be nowhere for the young men to exercise themselves without going a long way off."

This leads to another necessary set of distinctions that must be made with respect to warfare. Warfare did not occur on only one level of interaction, i.e., between one fully developed state and another or between one town and its neighbor. Several levels of warfare were present at the same time, and all had different goals. An example from Mesoamerica illustrates the different degrees of inclusion that war might take between one lord and his retinue and another lord and his retinue. Spores's (1967:14) ethnohistoric study of the pre-Conquest Mixtec of Oaxaca has shown that "there was a rather well-developed pattern of warfare." There were skirmishes between neighboring communities as well as between distant communities where each was a relatively autonomous kingdom. In addition, they all fought intruding Mexican armies, sometimes alone or allied with each other and even with the Zapotecs. Spores lists the following as reasons for warfare: boundary disputes, contested royal succession, extension of tributary dominion, taking of slaves, and to counter Mexican expansion. All these reasons for war can be traced specifically to goals of the elite segment of society. Depending upon a given elite's goals there are likely to be several kinds of warfare in secondary states:

1) Intracommunity conflict over succession or control of political structure or economic resources.
2) Intercommunity battles for territory, resources, tribute, slaves, and booty.
3) Regional defense (multi-community alliances) against a powerful aggressor state.
4) Conquest by a powerful aggressor of smaller communities and weaker regional states.

These aspects of warfare may all be operative at roughly the same time, but some are likely to take precedence over others. For example, a conquered region is unlikely to engage in the first two types of warfare since the conquering state can try to impose its own system of governance on its new dependencies. Another possibility is that one elite faction can initiate intercommunity conflict in order to defuse intracommunity conflict (see next section).

In Chapter 5, I will look at the effects of particular kinds of warfare on changes in material culture.

VARIATION IN SECONDARY STATE DEVELOPMENT

Instead of going through the spectrum of processes that are involved in state-level societies, I will examine several general dimensions of their ongoing functioning. This section will look at two African secondary states and point out how each developed through different combinations of processes. Many specific processes simultaneously contribute to secondary state evolution, each to a greater or lesser degree in individual cases. Secondary states have unstable interactions with neighbors. If they are not dissolving, they are either incorporating or being incorporated into neighboring political units. Territorial divisions and spheres of political influence regularly fluctuate, depending upon the success or failure of inter-polity alliances. Sometimes conquest, or trade, or continued warfare formed the basis of interstate relations.

A simple conquest or diffusion model of secondary state formation does not explain how states formed prior to their embarking upon a program of expansion (Kottak 1972). If a nonlocal elite conquered a region then it could either have been extending the domain of its existing state or reorganizing the local polity. In order for the colonizing elite to be able to assert control, the local population must already have some form of complex socio-political organization. Of interest here is the question of how conquest may affect the rate and kinds of state growth and the internal reorganization in the conquered polity.

A contrast of two African states will show how different specific processes can be important in the development of secondary states. Interregional trade, defensive military activity, and, subsequently, offensive military action were key factors in the emergence and continued growth of the Ganda state (Kottak 1972). For the Nyoro state, trade and warfare were also important. But a key element of its shift to statehood involved the immigration into Bunyoro of a non-local elite who were able to reorganize and redirect political activity (Beattie 1960; Mair 1962).

Kottak's (1972) analysis of state development in Buganda shows the interplay of warfare and trade on an existing stratified society. He summarizes the key elements in Ganda state formation as follows (1972:375):

> The slave and ivory trade had at last reached Buganda and had plummeted this stratified society into state formation. The

introduction of these trade goods is the most attractive explanation for Buganda's advance. The developed Ganda state owed its existence to reinforcement of the traditional stratified system through inclusion within an externally oriented trade network and to the introduction of a foreign currency. He also notes that the Ganda state developed by way of internal manipulation of the subsistence base, control of interregional trade routes, and the military change from a defensive posture to offensive expansion (1972:373).[2] The Ganda trajectory of state development contrasts with the case of neighboring Bunyoro, where oral histories claimed that the ruling Bito clan was descended from Nilotic peoples from the north (Beattie 1960:39-40). This is not to say that the Nyoro state was formed when conquerors invaded and assumed control over the local population, forming a higher stratum that controlled the regional political organization. Instead, it implies that, if indeed the Bito rulers are an elite immigrant class, they took over an already ranked, if not stratified, society. The Bito clan may have either been able to control and exploit existing internal factional strife or, perhaps, were invited into the society in order for one of the factions to bolster claims to power by means of an alliance with an external political force. This process then would have been *an option* for one group of locals who may have been competing at a disadvantage with another group already manipulating interregional exchange to further its political goals. In some ways, elite conquest may be thought of as an "importation" of a nonlocal and high-status system of organization and symbols that allows one faction to maintain or to increase its edge over its competitors. If successful, then oral histories and genealogies would be promulgated in order to consolidate the new group's status. The only way to investigate the sequence and importance of the specific processes in each case is through archaeology. In this way historical documents and oral history can be compared with the physical evidence for the emergence and development of Ganda and Nyoro states.

Warfare, trade, elite immigration, and intensification of agricultural productivity are manipulated as part of political strategies both on the within-polity and the between-polity levels (Swartz et al. 1966). Determining the specific processes involved and their relative importance in particular historical cases may help in understanding the processes of state development in general. I will now turn to an examination of some Mesoamerican states. Specifically, I discuss the interplay of internal and external political relations in the context of documented Mesoamerican states. The aim of the next section will be to consider several specific processes of secondary state development in Mesoamerica. It attempts to place them in the context of broader "civilizational processes" without either reducing the arguments to single variable explanations (e.g., Athens 1977) or restricting the study to the question of origins of pristine states and broad stages of development (Ribeiro 1968).

INTERNAL AND EXTERNAL RELATIONS IN SECONDARY STATES

Several themes of political interaction emerge from both the early native histories of Mesoamerican states and, also, from recent ethnohistoric studies of them. These "themes" can be boiled down to several processes of inter-community relations that operated among and within most Postclassic Mesoamerican states. The first of these is that the elite in different communities were bound together by exchanges of goods and marriage alliances (Marcus 1976, 1983a; Spores 1974). Second, tribute exaction was the main form of economic integration within political units—the extent of a polity was defined by its range of tributaries. Third, the reality and threat of military action initiated and maintained the networks of tribute relations.

Before discussing the dynamic nature of these processes I should first note one key aspect of Mesoamerican societies. There were two basic social classes or strata: the elite or nobility, and the non-elite or commoners. This basic division was probably present by the Middle Preclassic period in many parts of Mesoamerica (Blanton et al. 1981:225-226). It was constantly expanded upon and elaborated after the initial emergence of chiefdoms and subsequent transition to states. By the time of the Spanish Conquest there were dozens of different styles and degrees of complexity in the basic system of stratification. The Mexica, at one extreme, had the largest and most complex system of social and political organization. Their capital at Tenochtitlán is estimated to have had 150,000-200,000 residents (Calnek 1973:192; Parsons 1976:234), but their direct control spread several hundred kilometers beyond their borders (Gibson 1964) and included several million people. The areas over which their "influence" was felt included most, if not all, of Mesoamerica; however, within the Aztec "Empire" were incorporated many previously independent states, each with different histories, types of political organization, and degrees of complexity (Hodge 1984). Aztec society exhibited an enormous range of differentiation within each of the main social strata as well as indications of new emergent groups such as merchants (Adams 1966:164).

We can contrast the Aztec empire with contemporary and relatively autonomous city-states in eastern Mesoamerica. For example, there were small kingdoms like Zinacantán and Chamula in the highlands of Chiapas, which had no more than five or ten thousand inhabitants, located in a few small centers and scattered over the surrounding countryside (Calnek 1988; Vogt 1968; Wasserstrom 1983a, 1983b). Even so, there still existed the basic division of nobility and commoners and several gradations of status within each. There were also specialized priests, warriors, and religious functionaries (Calnek 1988). But the scale and many aspects of the organization of these mini-states were clearly different from states in Central Mexico. The link between these two vastly different kinds of states—the Aztec on the one hand and the highland Maya of Chiapas on the other—is the way they used their external relations to modify and change their internal relations.

This is one of the main characteristics of states that sets the stage for the kinds of specific processes that lead to their continuing evolution: the interplay between internal and external sociopolitical relations (cf. Swartz et al. 1966). Specialization for the purpose of successfully manipulating these relations is what some have concluded is the hallmark of state-level political organization (Wright 1977; Wright and Johnson 1975).

Some examples of Mesoamerican states at the time of conquest will illustrate how the internal manipulation of external relations was a recurrent process that looms large in the ethnohistoric sources. The tale of the banishment of Quetzalcoatl from Tollan (Tula) is a good example. Quetzalcoatl, the ruler or co-ruler of Tula, was forced to flee in humiliation after losing an internal power struggle with Tezcatlipoca, God of the Night and the North (Porter Weaver 1972:204). He and his followers migrated to the Gulf Coast where they founded new capitals. Not long after, Yucatecan Maya sources note that Kukulcan (their name for Quetzalcoatl) arrived from the west (Thompson 1970).

Whether or not an actual historical individual and his followers indeed migrated to this region, the central point is that conflict within Tula led to the out-migration of a group of elite. Furthermore, for a few elite to be able to enter a series of existing states in the Gulf Coast and Yucatán regions, there must have already been strong relationships between the Toltecs and both the Gulf Coast and Yucatecan Maya (Carmack 1968, 1981). Clearly, it was in the interests of some factions of local Maya society to welcome and align themselves with the vanquished Toltecs—in ideology if not in person. If exchange relations were already in existence, then the Maya who controlled exchange with the Toltecs may also have been the ones who welcomed the Toltec elite.

Certainly the Toltec elite, no matter how elevated their status, could not have expected to travel to a distant Maya state, belonging to a people with a different culture and language, and expect to conquer them and introduce a whole new ideology. For example, we are told that, after the fall of Tula (by one account many years after Quetzalcoatl's departure), Huemac, one of Tezcatlipoca's successors, finally abandoned the city and fled to Chapultepec in the Valley of Mexico. There he did not found a new bud-off state nor did he take control of a local population. Instead, the histories say that in AD 1156 or 1168 he committed suicide (Porter Weaver 1972:205). Interestingly, two other points help to interpret this: first, Huemac is said to have left after violent attacks from northern "barbarians" who destroyed the city, and, second, Toltecs remained in Tula for 15 or so years after Huemac's departure. These facts suggest that there was both internal struggle—between two or more competing sets of elites, just as there had been earlier during Quetzalcoatl's eviction—and external conflict between the Toltecs and neighboring states to the north.

Here, we have a case where warfare was manipulated by one faction of the state to strengthen itself against Huemac and eventually oust him. The outcome was the expulsion and demise of a leader. In the earlier case of Quetzalcoatl, his expulsion did not result in his death but in the purported conquest of several other distant states. In those states the process of adopting the migrant Toltec elite must have resulted from internal conflicts, not unlike those which Quetzalcoatl fled. One or another faction of the local Maya elite probably allied itself with the famous Toltec or, more likely, his noble followers, and used that alliance to consolidate its own power and internal control.

The idea of elite colonization of neighboring or distant regions is, then, part of a two-fold process. On the one hand, it is started by the out-migration of unsuccessful elites who either lose or are avoiding internal power struggles (Mair 1962:125, 132). On the other hand, they are accepted (unless they commit suicide as did the unfortunate Huemac) by one or another faction of neighboring or distant elites who are themselves engaged in internal power struggles. I will be concerned here primarily with the part of the process as viewed from the recipient end. From this perspective it may matter little whether the migrating elites are actually received or it is their symbols and ideology and exotic exchange items that are received.

Webb's (1965) study of secondary state formation in Hawaii clearly illustrates this process from the point of view of the receivers. He was not looking at elite migration or colonization so much as conflicting elites taking advantage of new opportunities on the horizon. The Hawaiian King Kamehameha II was able to exploit new trade relations with Europeans, to manipulate internal symbols of power, and to bypass and undermine his competitors. He abandoned traditional taboos and protocol and accepted Christianity, thereby defining the rift between his followers and those of competing nobles. The abandonment of traditional mores took place in the context of a new king attempting to maintain control over a political domain that included the whole island group just recently united by conquest. The process of internal conflict was determined by new outside opportunities that allowed the power struggle to take place and enabled the king to create a new political order that transformed the existing political structure. The relations between the king and other nobles, and between all nobility and commoners, changed. The reason for the change was Kamehameha's emulation of Europeans and, especially, their Christian religion. By emulating Europeans and adopting their ideology, and controlling trade with them, the king undercut the authority of traditional priests and advisors and freed himself from the traditional restrictions on his efficient control of political action (Sahlins 1981:56-57; Webb 1965:32-34). By trading with the Europeans, he could back up his challenge to the traditional system by continuing the inflow of metal and arms, as well as huge quantities of exotic, nonlocal items.

We can compare this example of change in Hawaii with similar changes in Mexico. The Quetzalcoatl migration myth can be seen as the defeat of the "traditional" ideology in both Central Mexico and the Maya region. Paradoxically, the defeat of Quetzalcoatl by Tezcatlipoca represented for Central Mexico "...the shift away from sacerdotal or divided leadership toward the ascendancy of militaristically inclined leaders responsive to deities more appropriate to their outlook"

(Adams 1966:136). The paradox lies in the effect that the transmission of the Quetzalcoatl cult had on many parts of the Maya area:

> The *object* of the cult was an archaic, agricultural, at least formerly peaceful, deity. But its new social content, unlike its form, was the rationale of a warrior aristocracy who, if they failed to construct a durable, politically integrated realm, nevertheless were successful as independently organized military parties in imposing themselves over widely scattered Mesoamerican peoples (Adams 1966:134).

To various elite factions in Maya polities the adoption of this ideology and manipulation of its symbolism must have allowed them to bypass traditional restraints on their growth. The proof is in the rapidity and scale of the spread of this ideological system from Central Mexico throughout the Early Postclassic Maya area. Interestingly, its military aspect was stressed and this continued for several hundred years, in fact, until the Spanish Conquest.

This leads to the problem of distinguishing local elites emulating nonlocal patterns from the actual adoption of a nonlocal elite as the new heads of state. Both processes allow a shift in relations between competing factions of local elites, particularly when one side can ally with outsiders to gain control over insiders. Either of these possibilities may take precedence over the other option: that of allying with other inside factions against the encroachments of outsiders. This latter process is another for which there are many ethnohistoric examples and one that will be examined shortly. Before doing so, I will outline the differences between the processes of elite emulation of nonlocal patterns and the actual in-migration of nonlocal elites.

In the first case, elites engaged in internal power struggles may find it to their advantage to identify with a powerful distant state and its ideology, just as the Hawaiian king did. In the second case, representatives of those distant elites may be invited to take up residence in, and titular control over, a society, especially when it is to the advantage of a local faction to control that alliance. Over time, however, it may become a matter of historical record, and thus open

for dispute, whether a particular elite lineage was actually related to or simply emulated the distant power. In the arena of ongoing conflict, and over the course of several generations, rulers may find it in their favor to claim descent from some god-ruler from a distant land, such as Quetzalcoatl. They may try to do this as a justification and rationale for their claim to power. In the same way they can manipulate their knowledge of elite symbols, dialects, and rituals—whether or not representatives of the distant elite ever really were in control of the society's political organization.

This overall process can be seen in the ethnohistoric studies of the Quiché Maya of highland Guatemala. Carmack (1968, 1981) has argued persuasively that the Quiché noble stratum was formed by a group of warrior nobles who originated in the Gulf Coast region of Mexico and migrated up the Usumacinta River, eventually inhabiting the highlands around their present home. They set up fortified settlements in the mountains and from there attacked and conquered local communities. The local populace provided wives and tribute. The Quiché lords, in turn, provided protection and went on to expand their territory, eventually conquering much of the highlands. The mechanism by which they expanded into neighboring areas merged several specific processes: (1) conquering distant provinces by warfare and then sending young nobles, who could be a potential threat, out to rule over them, and (2) marriage alliances and trade relationships to link the elite in communities within the realm. Both of these processes had many variants and subprocesses, which had differing impacts on communities, both within and outside the Quiché state. Fox (1978) has traced the effects of conquest on settlement patterns and determined the extent to which various regions were brought under the direct control of the Quiché.

Both Carmack's and Fox's work provide good archaeological and ethnohistoric examples of four specific processes of state expansion: (1) exchange relationships, including marriage alliances, and tribute exaction (i.e., the exchange of tribute for protection); (2) warfare, including conquest and raiding for the purpose of setting up exchange relations and tribute exaction; (3) direct colonization of an area by building new communities in previously unoccupied or only lightly occupied regions; and (4) elite colonization of neighboring and distant polities by "exporting" nobles to ally with and rule over them. All of these relied upon the clear distinction between elite and non-elite but were driven by the processes of conflict within elite social units or "dynamic contentiousness" (De Montmollin n.d.).

De Montmollin (n.d.) has analyzed Quiché political histories from the perspective of internal conflict and has concluded that the structure of the organization was conducive to both ramifying and lineage cross-cutting strife. Many of the processes discussed above were ways for the highest ranking lineages to maintain and increase their political control in the face of constant contentiousness. According to Webb (1965:30), in pre-state societies this very conflict would probably have prevented the emergence of controls that could have superseded the community level of organization:

> Indeed, even the most cursory review of the political situation in Hawaii before and during the rise of Kamehameha I to power shows that precisely this kind of inescapable, legitimate rivalry and "disloyalty" among the various closely related members of the ruling senior kin groups or ramage "core"—generally cousins, and often brothers or even father and son—was not only a leading cause, or at least mechanism, of the aboriginal failure to achieve the consolidation of state power and thus full civilization, but was also the chief hindrance to state formation after the advent of the Europeans.

Nonetheless, in states, this internal contentiousness can provide the motivation for political expansionism that eventually leads to conquest states. The idea is that conquest of neighboring polities allows the political faction leading the military endeavor to consolidate power at the expense of rivals—or at least to undermine their support, if not divert their attention. The end product, if the endeavor

is successful, is that the ruling elite and their supporting nobility expand their sphere of influence and at least temporarily consolidate their control over internal rivals.

MONITORING INTERNAL COMPETITION AND EXTERNAL RELATIONS

The changes that take place within evolving secondary states can be very difficult to monitor archaeologically. This difficulty lies in not being able to identify all the competing social units that would have existed, let alone specify their relations with one another. Even so, there are some approaches that can be taken and that are likely to yield positive results. The first is to concentrate on the processes that are most likely to be observable in the archaeological record. The second is to focus on an archaeologically visible social unit for study. That is, a unit below the level of the whole region or community and one that has spatial constancy and an archaeologically preservable and visible existence.

The processes under consideration have already been selected. Also, I mentioned in Chapter 1, some of the theoretical reasons why households are social units upon which these specific processes are likely to act. Additional social units include: social strata, neighborhoods or wards, moieties, clans, and lineages. In the archaeological record, however, these are not always directly observable and their specific existential symbols may not always be clearly associated with particular locations. Households, on the other hand, are both visible and regularly recurrent in the Mesoamerican archaeological record (Flannery 1976). This unit has the added advantage that it is often subsumed within these other larger-scale groups and, therefore, can indirectly provide information about them.

Prehistoric Mesoamerican households varied a great deal. They ranged from single nuclear families to extended families to multiple family patrilineages. The extensiveness of the co-residential bonds was directly related to the status of the household within its community. The higher the social rank the larger and more inclusive the household. One general correlation that holds true in many societies is that high status households were both wealthy and had more members (Netting 1982:657). Part of the wealth is generated by the household's own labor (Sahlins 1972). But, in high-ranking households belonging to the upper or noble class, an additional portion of their disposable resource base is generated through claims to tribute and labor from low-ranking households. This, in a nutshell, defines an important dimension of the relations between elite and non-elite households. This is the very relationship that fluctuates with the varying importance of the external relationships in which the community is engaged. If we can monitor the changing relationships between elite and non-elite households we should be able to determine the internal and external processes affecting those relations. The following two chapters describe a method for doing this.

ENDNOTES

1 Although it can be argued that material culture passively reflects information in the same sense as a mirror, that information is always created and interpreted according to the overall symbolic system of the observer. Even a "mirror" is created and used for social purposes and, accordingly, changes made to a "mirror" result from social action. Different kinds of changes should result from different social processes.

2 This is similar to the development of primary states (Wright 1977). However, I would maintain that since the Ganda state developed in the context of exchange with foreign states, it was a secondary development. Even so, the general and specific processes involved illustrate that the "post-emergence" processes are the same in both secondary and primary states.

CHAPTER 3

HOUSEHOLDS, PROCESSES, AND SYMBOLS

Households are appropriate units of study for understanding problems of both synchronic social organization and diachronic change in the organization of past societies. One view is that archaeology has as its most important goal the understanding of how societies change. Another often stated goal is to reconstruct or to discover the range of variation in the organization of past societies. These two goals are traditionally seen as complementary. Normally, archaeologists first attempt to reconstruct societies during segments (i.e., phases) of the past, and then use their reconstructions to explore questions of changing social organization between segments. I argue here that the first step contradicts the second step: the study of change does not depend upon a prior reconstruction or paleo-ethnography of past society and is actually hindered by such an endeavor. This is because subsystems of society change at different rates and in response to different specific processes. This can be illustrated by looking at ceramic change.

Cooking wares used in domestic food preparation activities change at a slow rate compared with the rate of change in decorated serving vessels used in food consumption. The processes underlying change in food preparation implements operate primarily at the intra-group level while the processes underlying change in food serving implements operate regularly at the inter-group level. In order to understand the types and importance of the underlying processes ceramic vessels have to be tracked during the course of each subsystem's history. To do this a unit of analysis must be used that allows the monitoring of temporal variation in subsystems below the level of the reconstructed community and within the temporal span usually defined as an archaeological phase.

By looking at households and their houses as units of analysis I hope to demonstrate this

point; however, I will defer my discussion of the implications of choosing to study process over reconstruction until the final chapter.

THE HOUSE AS A SYMBOL OF SOCIAL RELATIONSHIPS

As stated above, changing sociopolitical organization is, from one point of view, constituted by changes in the relations among social units. In archaeological contexts it may not be possible to recognize all social units in a past society, but there are some that can be recognized. And, more importantly, the changes in their relationships can be monitored. This is because some, such as the household, symbolize their social relations in a concrete way.

In most societies, in most parts of the world, and certainly since the beginning of sedentary communities, groups of individuals have lived in houses. In a sense, the group of people who live together are *held* together in social relations with each other in a house: they are a household. Recent ethnographic studies of the household as a social unit have emphasized their highly variable nature and the difficulty in characterizing their attributes (Netting et al. 1984:7). But, in spite of this difficulty, there is and has been, since the time of Lewis H. Morgan's work, recognition of the close relationship between houses and their social contents. Morgan (1965:63) makes this point clear in *Houses and House-life of the American Aborigines* when he describes households in societies where the "gentile" organization prevailed:

> They erected joint tenement houses large enough to accommodate several families, so that, instead of a single family in the exclusive occupation of a single the [sic] house, large households as a rule existed

in all parts of America in the aboriginal period. This community of provisions was limited to the household; but a final equalization of the means of subsistence was in some measure affected by the law of hospitality. To a very great extent communism in living was a necessary result of the condition of the Indian tribes. *It entered into their plan of life and determined the character of their houses.* (italics added)

For Morgan, the house structure was determined by the social relations among community members. As such, co-residents symbolized their social relations with each other by living communally in a house.

The house structure can be seen on two dimensions: emically it symbolizes a particular group of individuals to other members of the community, etically it is a clue that anthropologists can use to understand the organization of social relations. Most anthropologists are fully aware that the first dimension has two implications: first, that the house structure represents the relations among the house occupants and, second, that it represents the relations between that group and the rest of the community. Morgan used both implications in his discussions of cultural evolution. In citing James Adair's (1775) *History of the American Indians*, Morgan (1965:55, 68) twice pointed out the following passage "and when one of them [Cherokees] is speaking, either of the individuals or habitations of any of his tribe, he says, 'he is of my house,' or 'it is my house'." Household members have relations individually and collectively with other social units and other individuals, and it is these relations that their house symbolizes. The relations between two or more groups of individuals is the relationship between two abstract concepts that are by their very nature ephemeral. Before groups can interact with one another as groups they must symbolize both their existence and their potential relations (Cohen 1979:102-103).

Away from the domestic domain there is very little apart from the house itself that could be used to stand for the household. In societies where the individual is not distinguished from the household then what better referent to use in discussing oneself or one's lineage than the actual house? Individuals grouped in households can symbolize their present and future relations with other households comprised of other groups of individuals by means of their house. Glassie (1975:116) sums this up quite nicely by saying that

> without leaping willy-nilly into the unfathomable the student of past architecture knows that the house functioned somehow within the structure that relates one person (the house's inhabitant) to the other members of his community (those who will see the house).

We can take this even further by realizing that houses are not simply symbols of the *individual* inhabitant but of the group of occupants collectively called the *household*. As Rapoport (1969:47) has said,

> The forms of primitive and vernacular buildings are less the result of individual desires than of the aims and desires of the unified group for an ideal environment. They therefore have symbolic values, since symbols serve a culture by making concrete its ideas and feelings.

The utility of houses as symbols of the household lies in their ability to give permanence to a transitory group with respect to that group's interactions, both among themselves and between them as a whole and all other subgroups within the community. In addition, the house can stand for relations between households in different communities. But on this level other symbols, such as ceremonial buildings or pan-community clothing styles, perhaps better represent the community as a whole and stand for its relations with other larger social and political entities.

A particular household may be simply a "household" to other households, but at the same time may be "our household" to a resident; a subject household to the village headman; a taxation unit to the state bureaucracy; the residence of "my wife's family"; the largest household in a neighborhood or ward; a potter's or a butcher's or some other specialist's household; a new household just begun or one at the end of its cycle, and so forth. In other words, a household is both a real and an abstract group of people embedded in a matrix of social relationships with other social units, all of which, on different levels, can be symbolized by the house. The house helps make these relationships observable and predictable and thus workable. Without the house the household in its relations with others could not transcend the limits of time and space. It stands for the relations, represents those relations, can be used to express them publicly and, in some cases, to manipulate them. Furthermore, the house itself is a physical entity that is produced by the labor of a group of people—usually a group larger than the household itself. It thereby comes to represent the relations among the groups of people who built it and who had it built.

Innumerable examples from societies around the world are not necessary to convince the reader that the house is more than just a shelter (McGuire and Schiffer 1983; Rapoport 1969). The strictly functional nature of the house and the materials available for building it is, of course, an element in house structure variation that cannot be denied (Gilman 1983:47; Rapoport 1969). Nonetheless, I would like to stress that the materials do not constrain symbolism and are not crucial when comparing changes through time and within a single region. A quick perusal of Duly's (1979) *The Houses of Mankind* demonstrates the possibilities for stylistic manipulation of houses regardless of the particular materials used.

Using this idea of household representation via the house and its symbolic dimensions, one can begin to trace changes in social organization. One such study was carried out by Flannery (1972b) who examined the social implications of the shift from round structures to rectilinear structures with increasing sedentism. Ethnographic analogies provided clues to the kind of social organization that could have been operating in the past communities at different points in time and, therefore, suggested the kinds of changes that must have taken place.

The next step is to develop a method of determining the underlying processes involved in social change. This step requires a model that links change in the symbols of the evolving social relations to the different possible kinds of processes responsible.

INTRACOMMUNITY HOUSEHOLD RELATIONS

Following other anthropologists and archaeologists (Netting et al. 1984; Wilk 1983:100), I draw a distinction between *households* and *houses*. A household is a group of individuals, often related by way of kinship (but sometimes not), who regularly live and work together; in other words, the group of people held by a house. The "house" refers to the whole range of dwellings and other structures used by the social group. This may be one structure encompassing all necessary functions or it may include several separate structures each with a more or less specialized function, such as kitchen, storage rooms, or altar.

There are several reasons why households are an appropriate social unit of analysis and why houses, therefore, are ideal units of observation for the archaeological study of process. First, the household is the basic social grouping above the level of the individual that has both a spatial and temporal dimension. The household provides a vantage point from which we can observe, on a lower level, relations among individuals, and on a higher level, the relations among supra-household social units. In this latter instance, it is because households participate in relations with other households, and with other levels of society, such as neighborhoods, wards, moieties, clans, classes or castes, economic unions, and political and religious organizations, that they must also participate in intercommunity processes. In other words, within-community processes and between-community processes affect each other. To be more precise, the four specific processes under consideration here may be initiated or amplified by the conflicts between households and the goals of groups of households. Similarly, these processes may put in motion re-alignments of the relations among households.

I mentioned in a previous section the point of view that I am using towards material culture. Specifically, material culture is viewed as an active set of symbols (Wobst 1977). The question naturally arises: symbols of what? This can best be answered in the context of households. Besides functioning as tools for shelter and storage, houses function as material representations of their occupants, the occupants' world view, and their relationships with other social units in the community (Donley 1982; Duly 1979; Glassie 1975; Rapoprt 1969). It is this last "function" of houses that is crucial to the arguments that follow. Members of a household are a social group. Households, like any other social group, must have symbolic forms in order to give meaning to the abstract relations among the group members and with other groups. These symbols may take the form of rules of behavior and etiquette, or ritual among group members (Cohen 1979). An individual, such as the eldest male, may represent the household and as such stand for the aggregate of household members. In this same way the house and associated structures and features symbolize several aspects of the household's social existence. As a cosmological symbol the house communicates to the household their own social worth and place within the broader society, and it communicates this same information to other households. As a status symbol the house is a statement of the relationship between the household members *as a group* and other similar groups. Part of this information may be transmitted simply by house location and its placement with respect to other houses or ceremonial structures. Another part of this information may be transmitted by house style and layout, ornamentation, quality of building materials, and size. Still more information may be transmitted by the quantity and types of tools and other items located in and around the house. All of these things display the nature of the interactions or relationships between the household and other households.

In many societies at different levels of sociopolitical integration and complexity, the term "house," as well as the actual building itself, stands for a larger social unit such as the lineage or clan (Carmack 1981; Rapoport 1969; Richards 1940). For example, Richards (1940:88), speaking of the Bemba of Zambia, discusses how social groups within clans are recognized:

> These have no distinct name; though the Bemba often refer to them as 'houses' (*amaianda*, sing. *injanda*) of the same clan. Such a house consists of the direct descendants of one particular ancestress traced back to three or four generations.

Although all members of the lineage do not live under one roof, that the group is symbolized as a "house" indicates that the physical structure of a house evokes, to community members, the nature of the social group and its expected relations with other groups.

CHANGE IN SOCIAL RELATIONS AND THEIR SYMBOLS

In a synchronic study of a living social system one may actually observe social relations, i.e., the interactions between distinct social units. In such a study, though, it is not possible to observe the long term processes whereby social relations change. The relations may be visible: a member of household X marries a member of household Y; household A gives goods to household X, who then gives them to the village headman; all the members of a household work in their fields and bring their produce back to their house; the adult male members of a group of households gather together for one week to help build the headman's house, and so on. All of these relations manifest themselves in ongoing, real events that can be symbolized by houses.

When the relations change and evolve from year to year and from generation to generation, then either their symbolic form or the meaning of the symbols must change. As the symbols change and differentiate, then so must the social relations which they express. Symbols are powerful because they are ambiguous and abstract representations of social relations and often communicate intended meanings at the unconscious level (Cohen 1979:103). Control of the symbols is essential for the control of social relations, especially in power relations. In many societies if a group tries to manipulate symbols of status or prestige in ways that are prohibited by law or consensus, they are punished. This is because they are saying in a public way that, in their opinion, their position within the social structure and their relations within the organization are changed or should change. In other words, physical symbols, houses included, are models of past, present, and future relations.

Houses communicate two things: first, how the household members who are responsible for creating the physical symbol view their relations within the community and, second, how the rest of the community views their relations with the particular group of people represented by the house. In many stratified societies, such as 18th century Korea, Late Postclassic Aztec and Maya, and even 14th century France, there were laws prohibiting the architectural emulation of the rulers by the nobles or the nobles by the commoners.

Some examples from 18th century Korea are revealing in this regard. Hulbert (1906:250-251) gives several examples from Korea and outlines the house modifications that would have been particularly offensive to the royalty:

> A private citizen would be arrested and punished severely if he presumed to paint his house. It would imply an assumption of royal privilege. The same would happen if he should leave the posts of his house round instead of squaring them. This also is a royal prerogative.

There were also sumptuary laws against building houses of more than one story tall as both Morse (1897:7) and Kang (1931:129) mention: "Only the king at Seol could have a two-story house by law." Roof materials were also clearly limited by class. Hamel (1918:139-140) put it this way:

> The houses of the Coresians of Quality are stately, but those of the common sort very mean; nor are they allowed to build as they please. No Man can cover his House with Tiles, unless he have leave, so to do; for which reason, most of them are thatch'd with straw or Reeds.

These rules do not originate only from the top of the social hierarchy. As Wilk (1983:112) points out for the Kekchi Maya, the egalitarian ethic in this agrarian peasant community ensures that anyone who builds too large or "fancy" a house is accused of witchcraft.

> Though Kekchi houses vary a great deal in size, they are very uniform in construction, external appearance, and function. This standardization is imposed by very strong social sanctions which the Kekchi level against village members who do not conform to the community standard. While many could afford to build houses with cut lumber, tin roofs, and wooden floors (and privately express a desire to do so), they will not. Houses are a potent symbol of community solidarity and equality. Though wealth differences exist, it would invite envy and witchcraft to publicly display those differences.

The house in this case is a symbol of egalitarian social relations, and one who modifies the symbol is making an unacceptable statement about how he wishes to modify relations. The treatment of witches in many societies is a clear statement of the community's perception that those who manipulate symbols improperly are trying to change social relations. Consequently, those who try to change social relations improperly are not fit to be part of the society and should be removed.

When a house is modified beyond the changes required by growth of the household during the domestic cycle, then it can be inferred that the household's social relations are changing. The particular kinds of modifications in particular kinds of social relations depend, in turn, on the specific processes involved. Those processes may be larger scale inter-societal relations such as exchange or warfare between two polities. Or they may be ecological relations, such as intensification of agricultural production systems with concomitant environmental shifts.

CHANGING SYMBOLS AS CLUES TO PROCESS

Here, I will give a brief example of how we might proceed directly to studying change, but, before I do, a key distinction must be made. Determining changes in the *meaning* of symbols is quite a different task from simply monitoring the physical *changes* in symbols. I will focus on interpreting the meaning of changes and not the changes in the meaning of the symbols themselves. Glassie's (1975) study of 18th and 19th century Virginian folk housing attempted to do both in order to understand some of the structural principles and ideas underlying early American society. His work was successful but relied on historical documents to give meaning to the symbolism of houses. The houses alone could not have generated his interpretations. As Glassie points out (1975:185-188), far-reaching national and international historical processes impinging upon the community led to changes in the symbolism of houses. Without interpreting the specific meaning of the symbolism, it still would have been possible for him to track the evidence for these broader diachronic processes that influenced the region.

In archaeology this is most often done in the realm of mortuary analysis (Brown 1971). Mortuary studies provide invaluable information on the ranges of social personae and, thus, status categories within societies for any given phase (Peebles and Kus 1977; Saxe 1970, 1971). This has proven effective in "reconstructing" hypothetical social hierarchies for phases, each phase usually spanning a century or more. Yet the question remains: is it possible to proceed from a static reconstruction that characterizes a phase to the dynamic processes that may have waxed and waned during the phase? In most mortuary contexts each burial event is unrelated to other events, and, therefore, it is not possible to track the shifts in relations among the social units who sponsor and carry out the mortuary ritual. When mortuary remains are deposited in stratified contexts, processual interpretations become easier to make. For example, sequential burials of chiefs in mounds can provide a clear

record of the changes in the relations between chiefs and the rest of the community. Or, when burials are placed below house floors, and it becomes possible to sort out their relative chronological position, the type of information necessary to study process can be obtained. But then, once again, the household and its remains become the analytical unit (e.g., Winter 1974).

Sanders's (1974) study of the development of complex society at Kaminaljuyú, Guatemala, provides an excellent example of the type of analysis I am proposing for household remains. He noted that changes in modifications to pyramid-mortuary mounds yielded evidence for changes in the processes of emerging complexity. The analysis in no way depended upon an interpretation of the meaning of the symbol itself. Instead, he relied on an interpretation of the meaning of the *change* in the symbol (the pyramid mound). Specifically, increasing the volume of construction of a mound upon the death of a chief or ruler symbolized an increasing ability of that person's lineage to exact tribute labor for the display of its status. Three Verbena phase increments to mound E-III-3 were about the same as one increment to contemporary mound B-III-1 (Sanders 1974:103). Then, in the Arenal phase, mound E-III-3 underwent two successive increments many times larger than the five previous ones combined. At the same time, mound B-III-1 had an additional increment no larger than its first. The comparison in the trajectories of change between the two mounds allowed Sanders to conclude that significant differences between the social groups responsible for building each of the two mounds was emerging. He hypothesized that, "political power of the level required to organize really major architectural effort [i.e., the ability of the leader to amass labor for ceremonial construction] was not available until Arenal times." He goes on to say: "It would be extremely interesting and revealing to be able to compare the histories of construction of each of the 14 plaza complexes at Kaminaljuyú, relative to each other and in terms of overall chronological phasing" (Sanders 1974:103).

This is exactly the approach that would allow archaeologists to monitor changes in the relations between particular social groups, each symbolized by their temple-funerary mounds and associated ceremonial structures (Hodder 1979:450). It also allows consideration of civic-ceremonial structures as part of a political system and not as a static reflection of particular stages of sociopolitical evolution (cf. Kaplan 1963:399-401). Even more important, changing social relationships can be studied by making only the broadest interpretation of the meaning of the symbol itself within the aboriginal ideological system. That is, large-scale construction can be viewed as an expression and display of the lineage's status within the community and the wider polity. At least initially, it would not be necessary to concentrate on the emic and structural implications of the symbolism. Finally, the question of how subtle changes in differences between the various plaza complexes are related to both intra-and interregional processes could be explored.

The above example shows how the symbols of mortuary ritual are particularly suitable for this type of analysis. However, one problem with mortuary remains is that they seldom preserve sequences of change that show how a single social unit evolved over periods of time shorter than a single phase. While a chief or ruler may be placed in an elaborate monument that covers earlier similar monuments, people of lower status may be placed in cemeteries, courtyards, or dispersed locations outside the community. Therefore, in lower-status social groups, rarely would it be possible to trace sequences of change that indicate their relation to other groups—especially within a single archaeological phase. This is probably one of the reasons that mortuary analyses in archaeology are often aimed at reconstructing the range of social variation and status differentiation within communities and within phases. Seldom are

mortuary data available that permit the study of short-term shifts in social relations. As a result, they often yield little information about the processes of change. Instead, they usually only document the gross stages of change or the range of variation within a stage. Even when the data are available, such as at Kaminaljuyú, they are not subsequently manipulated to explore the underlying processes of change. What processes underwrote the increasing ability of the mound E-III-3 lineage to construct larger and larger monuments to its illustrious ancestors? Was it control over interregional or local exchange, or was it through effective marriage alliances with other lineages within the community? Did conquest or even sporadic warfare play a role in the increasing social differentiation? At present, it would be difficult to answer questions like these with mortuary remains alone—even though Kaminaljuyú has good evidence for changes in elite mortuary symbols.

More effective ways of approaching questions like these—aimed at determining the underlying processes of cultural evolution— require the use of all lines of available evidence. Mortuary remains combined with ceremonial and residential architecture, ritual and domestic artifacts, and community and regional settlement patterns all can be collected and studied from the perspective of their histories or trajectories of change. These histories of change can then, as Sanders suggested, be compared for each social group in order to illuminate their processual underpinnings.

In the next chapter I will examine the effects of specific sociopolitical processes on the trajectories of change in symbols of households, social classes, and whole communities underwent during the course of a secondary state's history.

CHAPTER 4

FOUR PROCESSES IN SECONDARY STATE DEVELOPMENT

Anthropologists have presented and discussed a wide range of processes in their attempts to understand both long-term and short-term sociopolitical change. Nonetheless, four specific processes emerge as dynamics that structure the relationships both within and between individual polities. Exchange, warfare, elite colonization, and colonization by whole polities are ongoing processes that occur and recur in the historical record of every known state. Their changing relative importance and impact on society both determines and is determined by social, political, and economic action. By this I mean that these processes present opportunities and limitations for the society as a whole, for smaller sub-units, and for individual members of the society. Before continuing, I should point out there are other processes of state evolution that could and should be studied. For example, population increase and agricultural intensification are two processes that have been debated at length in the anthropological literature on the origins of complex society. I avoid dealing with them in this research, however, in order to restrict my focus to a set of political processes that are at the heart of sociopolitical change as seen in secondary states. Both population increase and agricultural intensification can be used for political ends and can be manipulated to achieve the goals of a complex political organization. They are, though, brought into play after or at least in the context of the four main processes outlined above. In order to continue the discussion of just how inter-polity relations operate in state evolution I will briefly define their use below.[1]

(1) *Exchange.* I will use exchange in the broadest sense to include transfers of goods, services, and information. This study will distinguish between two types of exchange: (1) long-distance inter-polity exchanges, and (2) local exchange, including tribute flow, within a single state's political domain.

(2) *Warfare.* Warfare can be defined as organized armed conflict between polities (Chapter 2). It may involve raiding to obtain booty or to avenge some previous injustice. It may also involve large-scale battles, with the goal of conquest to set up new exchange relations or to initiate colonization. I will be concerned here mainly with the effects of warfare between small neighboring states.

(3) *Colonization by elites.* In the historical record of many polities there are examples of external elites moving into an area and dominating the local political and economic structure. In some instances this process of elite colonization involves the forcible replacement of existing elites, perhaps in the aftermath of war. In other cases it involves the invited replacement of local elites by outsiders who are perceived to be of higher status. This may be brought about by imbalances in interregional exchange relations or evolve out of marriage alliances between polities of markedly different sizes.

(4) *Colonization by whole polities.* This process is one whereby new communities bud-off and expand into a vacant or marginally occupied area. It results from internal dissension and conflict within the source state. Colonization by whole polities also involves the conquest of existing polities in a region and often results in the incorporation of their members as a subservient class.

These processes are all modes of interaction among political units. Modes of interaction such as exchange and warfare are, of course, not restricted to states, nor even to chiefdoms, but operate at all levels of sociopolitical organization. Exchange, in the broad sense, both on the local and regional levels, is carried out by all types of societies. But some types of exchange, for example, the exchange of tribute for the privilege of maintaining an alliance or for protection, are found exclusively in chiefdoms or states. Warfare is present among hunters and gatherers organized at the band level of integration; however, the scale, strategies, and goals of warfare change drastically as the size, complexity, and goals of society increase (Otterbein 1970). But colonization by elites and wholesale colonization may be more common among the most complex form of sociopolitical organization: the state. My goal here is to see how state-level societies use these four processes to attain their political ends and how they lead to sociopolitical change.

How does each of these four processes affect the organization of social, political, and economic relations within a secondary state? And, conversely, how do the political groups within a state use these four processes to achieve their goals? Any attempt to answer these questions using archaeological data requires a model that describes the relationship between social process and material culture. Since the questions direct attention to temporal change as the primary dimension of variation, the perspective outlined in the previous chapter must be built into the model. Namely, the symbolic use of material culture is an essential part of the very processes under consideration. Changes in material culture are caused by and help to facilitate the process. The social meaning of the material remains themselves may never be known, but the processes involved in their *changes* can be inferred.

To do this it is first necessary to choose the unit of society in which the specific processes operated. As set out in the previous chapter, the household is an appropriate social unit, and its remains provide a comprehensive unit of archaeological analysis. Many archaeologists have argued for the increased study of households (Wilk and Rathje 1982). In Mesoamerica, archaeological houses have been studied for many years and have provided a great deal of information about the range of social variation and economic activities in given societies and at particular times (Diehl 1974; Fauvet 1973; Flannery 1976; Flannery and

Winter 1976; Healan 1977; Ichon 1975; Kurjack 1974; Wauchope 1934, 1938; Winter 1974).

The reasons for the utility of household level of analysis are: (1) the relations among households become more complex along with other aspects of sociopolitical organization; (2) these relations are expressed symbolically in the house and associated structures and are often preserved archaeologically; (3) a wide range of other material items associated with the household's social, economic, and political relations within the community find their way into the archaeological record (floors, patios, middens, and so forth); and, most importantly, (4) in many situations houses are maintained and modified through generations of occupants, thus preserving a record of its changes. This is not to say that other aspects of the archaeological record should be ignored or are not valuable for studying the processes I have mentioned. Obviously, as many lines of evidence as possible should be studied, including burials, settlement patterns, sculpture, ceremonial structures, and all other preserved portions of the archaeological record.

ARCHAEOLOGICAL EXPECTATIONS

In order to interpret the material changes that took place during the history of Canajasté, I use secondary and some primary ethnohistoric sources describing similar changes among the Quiché of highland Guatemala, the northern Yucatecan Maya, and the Tzotzil and Tzeltal of highland Chiapas. Occasionally, I also use examples from other parts of Mesoamerica, such as the Mixtec and Zapotec of Oaxaca. My approach is to look for the kinds of changes that took place when one or another of the four specific processes (exchange, warfare, elite colonization, and complete colonization) was dominant. I examine five categories of archaeologically observable variables to see what information is available for each. And, where possible, I observe the differences between the two main social classes (elite and non-elite) in the kinds and rates of change.

My goal is not to find correlates of these social classes in the archaeological record. The ethnohistories of most, if not all, of Mesoamerica make it clear that these were the basic social structural divisions, played out in terms of descent, alliance, and ethnicity (Carrasco and Broda 1976). Given these divisions, how do differences in the way each line of evidence changes through time allow the interpretation of the operative processes of inter-polity interaction? Based on a reading of the various sources it appears that each of the archaeological variables will form a distinct pattern in the way it changes, depending upon the relative importance of the various underlying processes. To be more precise, some of the variables will shift to a nonlocal style or pattern while others retain a local or traditional pattern. The change cannot always be reduced to a local/nonlocal distinction, but I will begin with it and then elaborate it to account for other types of changes. A simplified diagram of the differing effects of the four processes of inter-polity interaction on the changes in the two main social divisions is presented in Figure 4.1.

Figure 4.1a illustrates that, under conditions of intense intercommunity exchange, the elite emulate nonlocal styles in order to maintain their social distance from the non-elite. In this scenario, I expect the non-elite to also emulate the elite, causing major shifts in "local" styles. Nonetheless, in this situation sumptuary rules, greater scale (amount), and shortened periodicities of consumption can be invoked to slow down, if not stop, the commoners from displaying pretensions (Douglas and Isherwood 1980). Hodder (1979:448) cites Cohen's (1974) study of Hausa ethnicity to demonstrate that competition for control over long-distance trade with other ethnic groups led to a deepening of "their cultural identity and exclusiveness" (Cohen 1974:92). The Hausa maintained and symbolized their control of trade by way of a "distinctive material culture" (Hodder 1979:448). Presumably, as their control of trade increased, the differences between them and rival ethnic groups also increased.

Figure 4.1b illustrates the expected trajectories of change when the dominant form of intercommunity interaction is warfare. Here, the elite and non-elite may maintain a certain stylistic distance from each other, but the elite do not do this by emulating nonlocal patterns. Thus, whatever the traditional local elite/non-elite distinctions are, they will be preserved and elaborated. Part of this is due to decreased access to exchange networks and, therefore, nonlocal elite symbols—but part would also derive from a need to actively maintain intercommunity differentiation in styles. In Hodder's view (1979:450):

Artifacts play an especially important role in symbolizing and supporting social relations when those relations are under strain. When tensions exist between groups, specific artifacts may be used as part of the expression of within-group corporateness and "belongingness" in reference to outsiders. Spatial distributions of exchanged items may show plateaus of similar frequencies within groups and sharp breaks at the edges.... Tensions between hierarchical, age, and sex groups within societies may also be expressed in the structure of artifact associations.

Based on Hodder's conclusions, I argue that when between-polity tensions increase (as a consequence of increasing warfare) there arises a need to downplay within-polity divisions. An increased emphasis on within-polity material symbols of solidarity could accomplish this. It is exactly the opposite of what I would expect if exchange, and not warfare, was the primary specific process of inter-polity relations.

When nonlocal elites colonize a polity I would expect changes to develop as shown in Figure 4.1c. At the time of colonization the elite segment should be distinctly different in almost all respects from the local population. Through time, however, the non-elite emulate the new elite styles. If, subsequently, the new elite control interregional trade, then the tensions and differences between the two social strata would deepen (Cohen 1974; Hodder 1979:448); however, if the new elite become embroiled

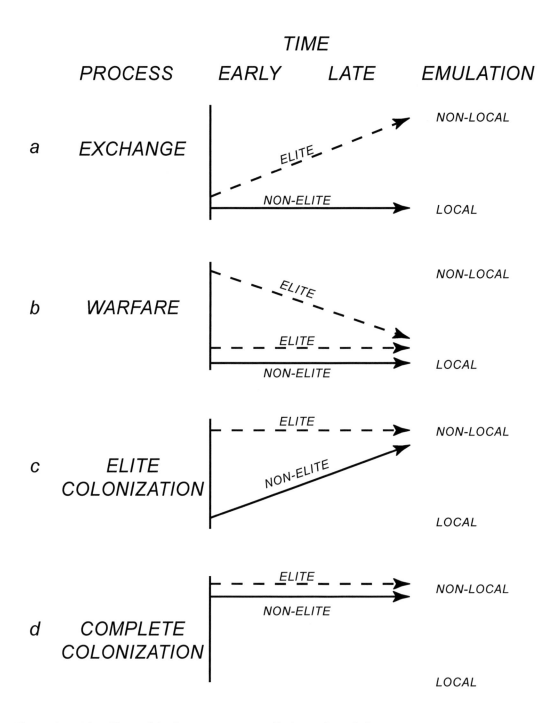

Figure 4.1.   The effects of the four processes on elite/non-elite relations.

in increasing inter-polity warfare, they would reduce intra-polity divisions and lessen the differences between themselves and the local non-elite.

Finally, when the entire community begins as or is replaced by a colony we would expect both elite and non-elite to exhibit nonlocal styles and patterns (Figure 4.1d). Through time the elite would maintain a distance from the non-elite by their continued use of styles and symbols based on their nonlocal traditions. These eventually come to be the "local" pattern, but the specific patterns of change from the point of establishment of the community would depend upon the relative importance of the three previously mentioned processes.

This overall model of monitoring change is useful as a starting point in searching for patterns of change in the archaeological data. But it is only a starting point. The actual history of any community or polity would be much more complex than any of these four simple diagrams. In all likelihood, the real situation would be a mix of the various processes and, conceivably, one could be tacked onto another with a historical sequencing or mixing of all four processes. Still, the value in initially approaching the data with simplified models such as these is that they allow the integration of as many archaeologically observable variables as possible and allow the specific processes of political interaction and their interrelations to be observed and interpreted.

The following sections will present the expected effects of each process on the archaeological record. Where possible I will draw on ethnohistoric, ethnographic, and archaeological examples of the relationship between the four processes and the following classes of material culture:

    (1)   Household features.
    (2)   Household artifacts.
    (3)   Subsistence goods.
    (4)   Settlement pattern.
    (5)   Civic-ceremonial structures.

The approach used below is rather eclectic in that it draws supporting examples for my expectations from a wide range of sources. The main goal was to obtain a range of cases that

showed how material culture was influenced by the broader processes. In many instances, though, I found no specific examples and the expected change is merely a hypothesis.

EXCHANGE

Household Features

Inter-polity relations dominated by exchange would lead to increasing stylistic differentiation between elite and non-elite (Hodder 1979:447-448). As the elite emulated their exchange partners, i.e., the elite of neighboring states, then their internal status or prestige would be symbolized by their exclusive use of nonlocal styles (Donley 1982; Pollock 1983:21-24). The elite's ability to control nonlocal exchange relationships, in effect, demonstrates and legitimates their superiority over the non-elite. Therefore, as the exchange process increases in importance, stylistic differences in household features between the two classes become increasingly pronounced.

Under these conditions, different house styles for the elite—particularly styles similar to high-status elite in neighboring states—are a direct indicator of two sets of social, political, and economic relations at the same time. First, house styles show how members of the elite households may be similar to nonlocal elite, thus reinforcing elite solidarity that cross-cuts community lines. Second, they show that members of elite households are different and distinct from the non-elite, thus serving to reinforce the division between elite and non-elite.

The relation between housing and internal social disunity is illustrated by an example from India. Rapoport (1969:58) points out that the strong caste distinctions in Cochin, South India, "results in a low community spirit in these villages." Not only are the house styles of each caste distinctively different, but their locations within the community are also quite separate. This rift is maintained because the elite have access to nonlocal symbols and display those nonlocal symbols in a local context (Douglas and Isherwood 1980; Peebles and

Kus 1977; Pollock 1977). Inasmuch as houses are appropriate social contexts for the display of these nonlocal symbols, elite houses will be different from non-elite houses. Differences will increase as the intensity or importance of nonlocal exchange increases.

I would expect there to be a major dichotomy in the kinds of household features that would be selected as appropriate domains for the display of nonlocal styles. Highly visible features will be the ones to change first and change the most: construction styles (shape, layout), building materials (walls, roof, platform), layout of the house group, external decoration of the walls. Features less visible to other members of the community will be the last to change and will change less: floors, patio, hearths, indoor or buried storage facilities, indoor decoration, offerings or caches, and burials. Hodder (1982:204-205), however, gives contrary examples from tribal societies in Africa.

Naturally, any argument that a community was engaging in increasing levels of exchange with other regions will have more direct evidence of exchange than simply changes in house styles. And ideally it would be desirable to have a broad base of comparative house style information from neighboring regions in order to see if the elite were indeed emulating nonlocal elite (e.g., Donley 1982). But it is often impossible to make detailed comparisons with other regions because the data simply do not exist. In such cases it is still possible to rely on the expected trajectory of changes within a given community and to assess the relative importance of exchange by observing if the differences between elite and non-elite houses increase, stay the same, or decrease. If they increase then it would be worth looking for other evidence of increasing exchange.

Examples

Glassie (1975:88) discusses an example of the introduction of the Georgian house style into the Middle Virginia area around 1760. Middle Virginia "was knotted into nets tying it into the thought of eastern Virginia and, ultimately London." Exactly how the new style

was introduced is difficult to say but, as Glassie (1975:88) explains, it was likely first used by:

> members of the community whose personal bent or wealth or mobility or nonagricultural occupation places them in a peripheral position so that they may accept outside novelties, but whose primary affiliations are internal so that they may become local advocates for those novelties. A local builder may have traveled to the East, there to see a house, or, more likely, many houses. Possibly an Easterner or a new arrival from England requested that an alien house be built. A book carrying plans and elevations may have been bartered for some barrels of Indian weed. However it happened, a local man perceived a new form—the Georgian house type.

The first example of the Georgian house style in the region was the Parrish mansion—one of the most elaborate houses in the whole county and definitely belonging to one of the members of the economic and social elite of the region (Glassie 1975:87). There was a fifty-year lag before it was emulated by other builders in the region, and gradually the style became merged with local styles. It became a symbol of interaction with the nonlocal elite of the Eastern U.S. and not with London (see the section on warfare's impact on house styles for further discussion of this case).

An excellent example of the differentiation between elite and non-elite house styles with trade as the major interregional process comes from Donley's (1982) work in Kenya. Coral houses built in Lamu Town on the Island of Lamu by the Swahili trader-merchants are completely different from those in native villages on the mainland opposite the island (Donley 1982:63-65). The Swahili or wa-Amu lived in coral houses and controlled trade with Arab merchants who traveled along the east coast of Africa. The Swahili of Lamu use the style and layout of their houses to express and maintain the closed nature of their community. The houses also demonstrate that the elite class is inaccessible to the non-elite villagers. Control of active interregional trade allows the elite to maintain their dominance in the region's economy and thus underwrites their elite social status. Elaborate houses allow them to maintain their control of trade by symboling to traveling Arab merchants that they are part of the same social system, share the same religious and political values, and are thus trustworthy trading partners (Donley 1982:65). Their different house styles are an essential part of their ability to remain elite by demonstrating "eliteness" to themselves, to the local native population, and to their long-distance trading partners.

It would be difficult for the mainland non-elite groups to emulate the elite houses and lifestyles because their access to Lamu Town is restricted and entrance to houses prohibited (Donley 1982:65). The boundaries between the elite and non-elite are, in fact, pervasive ethnic differences that increase with the elite's control of trade. House styles are a central element in the maintenance of these ethnic boundaries.

Household Artifacts

The process of exchange, both local and interregional, will have a large material impact on the household level. The greater the importance of exchange, the more frequent exchanged items will be within the community in general as well as within each household. When imports become more frequent in households, then their remains will also become more frequent in the archaeological remains of the household. Households controlling this exchange, and whose prestige within the community increases as exchange increases, should have increasing amounts of nonlocal exchange items. Also, they will have progressively larger quantities of local goods produced for exchange out of the community. I expect higher frequencies of nonlocal exchange items in elite households for two reasons. First, the elite were in control of external relations that resulted in incoming goods. Second, displaying and using these goods symbolized their very "eliteness" and social distinctiveness (Douglas and Isherwood 1980).

Examples

Webster (1977:361), in discussing the implications of the economic relations between Teotihuacán and Tikal, says:

It seems very likely that the establishment of Teotihuacan commercial influence at Tikal further stimulated the development of that center in a number of ways. It provided the emerging local elites with exotic status symbols and strengthened their managerial functions insofar as they effectively manipulated a lucrative foreign trade and allowed some of its products to trickle down to all levels of society.

Controlling foreign exchange relationships such as this would allow the elite to increase their differentiation from the non-elite, which in itself would confer prestige. Networks of allied elite lineages in Tikal's secondary and tertiary centers would build upon their mutual similarities to distinguish themselves from the non-elite. Strong interregional and local exchange relations would cause the chain of emulation to break between social strata within communities but remain strong across communities.

In Mesoamerica, there is ethnohistoric evidence that exotic imports were used as currency, and in this sense the elite would have had the greatest access to these items. For example, Gaspar Antonio Chi wrote in 1582 (Tozzer 1941:231) that among some Maya states in the Yucatán:

The money which they used was little bells (of copper) … and they were valued according to their quantity or size; … (also certain) red (shells) which they bring from outside these provinces, (of which they make strings like) the beads of a rosary. Likewise they used as money … (those) grains like almonds of what they call cacao, of which … (they make) their drinks.

The material produced by the community for exchange to other communities could come under elite control in two ways. One is the production, in non-elite households, of goods which are then traded or given as tribute to the elite. The other is the specialized production of goods in the elite households themselves. These two possibilities will be clearly distinguishable archaeologically. In the first case, the implements and debris of production concentrate in higher frequencies in non-elite households. In the second case this material will be found in the elite households. In either case the finished products accumulate and are consumed in the elite households. Both of these possibilities become more pronounced as intercommunity exchange becomes a more important part of the local elite's means of maintaining political control within their own community.

In terms of overall stylistic similarity among neighboring states, the more frequent their interaction and the less competitive, the more similar they will be. Hodder (1982:114) describes an example from the Lozi of Zambia where tribal differences have almost completely broken down:

> Generally there is little past or present evidence of conflict between the tribes within the kingdom, or of competition over resources. In the past, the presence of the king also helped to remove competition by providing an economic, administrative and juridical umbrella.
>
> It is suggested here that, since each member of each tribe is involved in an exclusive symbiotic and non-competitive economic system, there is little need to express tribal differences symbolically. Rather, there is an advantage in demonstrating symbolic and cultural similarity with others in the same system. Thus the various Lozi and Ila-Tonga tribes are indistinguishable culturally and their tribal identities have become blurred.

Although he does not mention it, house styles would also be subject to the same processes of homogenization.

Subsistence Goods

With increasing importance of interregional exchange there may be some evidence that the elite had greater access to imported plant and animal foods. Any nonlocally produced plants or animals should be first consumed by the elite who may also have procured them. Therefore, there should be more remains of nonlocal plants and animals in elite house deposits than in commoner households.

Examples

That the elite consumed nonlocal foods as a means of displaying their status is revealed in several cases. Landa (Tozzer 1941:40) says of Yucatecan groups who were fighting with one another that:

> they caused each other's food to be insipid; since the Chel, who lived on the coast would not give fish nor salt to the Cocom, making him go a long distance for it; while the Cocom did not permit the Chel any game or fruit.

The exchange of fish and salt for game and fruit was interrupted by the Chel elite in order to break off political relations with the Cocom. This, in turn, led to intensified warfare between the two groups.

The acquisition and consumption of these goods was necessary for the elite to symbolize interclass exclusionary principles. They consumed these exchanged foodstuffs as part of the status validation process and this distinguished the elite from the non-elite.

The elite also consumed larger quantities of high protein food. Haviland's (1967) study of stature differences between elite and non-elite of Tikal suggested that male rulers, at least, had a more nutritious diet during both the Early and Late Classic periods. If the Maya elite had even a portion of Moctezuma's daily fare, (as described by Bernal Díaz del Castillo [1912]), then they would have had, through both local and interregional exchange, a veritable smorgasbord.

Settlement Pattern

Exchange between regions can be expected to have a profound effect upon regional settlement patterns. The more important exchange is in the economic structure of the society, the more likely settlement configurations will evolve or change to accommodate exchange. Particular kinds of exchange relations should result in particular settlement patterns (Haggett 1965:21-25).

Within a single region encompassed by one polity and over a relatively short period of time, the increasing importance of exchange could lead to growth of communities that controlled the exchange. Specifically, I would expect the communities at the top of the hierarchy to remain there, regardless of the original reason for their location. If a community site was originally chosen for overriding defensive reasons and eventually came to be the administrative and ritual center of a state housing the highest ranking elite, then with increasing exchange the location would probably not be changed. However, new smaller centers might grow up in indefensible locations where previously there were simply small hamlets. This would contrast with the situation where the threat of warfare remained high. In the latter case all important communities would remain located in defensible locations. I would expect, then, that evidence for growth of communities in places most advantageous for exchange and not for defense would indicate the relatively more important role of exchange in interregional political relations.

To the extent that exchange is based on the efficient exaction of local tribute from subordinate communities, then the settlement pattern might exhibit a clustering around the center (Steponaitis 1978). Steponaitis argues that this takes place in complex chiefdoms in order to reduce the costs of transporting tribute and in order to lower the costs of administering the outlying communities. Settlement clustering may not be significant enough to distinguish between exchange and warfare, however, since under both processes tribute would be exacted from subordinate communities.

The community-level settlement pattern may not change with increasing exchange. Nevertheless, one possible change that I will hypothesize is that with increasing exchange, especially combined with decreasing threat of direct attack, the community may be able to grow beyond its defensive features.

For example, a community may be able to expand outside of a walled zone, or from the top of a hill down to the surrounding flats. In this situation, features that were at one time defensive can come to symbolize elite versus non-elite social divisions (Webster 1978). A wall, moat, hilltop community, or community located on a sharp bend in a river, originally for defensive purposes, can, with increasing exchange, be used to separate the nobility from the commoners (J. Marcus 1983b).

Therefore, in cases where exchange replaces warfare, several changes in the community settlement pattern will take place. First, there will be an increasing separation of elite and non-elite, with a previously defensive barrier becoming, instead, primarily a social barrier. Second, there will be an elaboration of the demarcating or protective feature. During times of decreasing warfare and increasing exchange, a defensive wall may become an elaborate plastered and possibly painted structure. Another change might be the general spreading out of the community and the increased spacing between households.

Examples

At the time of the Spanish conquest, the Tzotzil Maya community of Zinacantán was one of the most active market centers in highland Chiapas (Díaz del Castillo 1912; Vogt 1969:109). Zinacantecos were heavily engaged in exchanging a wide range of commodities with surrounding regions. Zinacantán's renown as a market center was so great that the Aztec sent disguised *pochteca* traders among them to gather information about the region in general (Vogt 1969:15). McVicker (1974), who has studied the Late Postclassic Zinacantecan settlement patterns, draws an interesting comparison between them and the Postclassic Chamulans, also Tzotzil Maya speakers. The Chamulans apparently did not involve themselves actively in trade and, instead, were intent upon warring with neighboring highland groups.

In fact, most of the highland Tzotzil communities were much more belligerent than Zinacantán (Godoy 1858:467). When the conqueror Marín and his cohorts invaded the highlands of Chiapas they quickly obtained an agreement from the Zinacantecos to become allies. Díaz (1912:305) reports that the Chamulans, in contrast, made no such agreement and, thus, prompted the siege of Chamula. McVicker (1974:554) makes the point that the Zinacantecos had a more open community located in a much more vulnerable position and that this was related to their open political and economic relations with their neighbors. The Chamulans had a more defensible settlement pattern with a fortress that, according to Diaz's (1912:306-307) account, was undeniably formidable. Perhaps because they lacked the economic opportunities that the Zinacantecos enjoyed, they used warfare instead of exchange to maintain their territory and political system.

It would be interesting to know more about the relations between these two polities. At the least it appears that Zinacantán was not under a continuous threat of attack from Chamula. It also appears that Zinacantán's battles were fought away from the community, primarily in the vicinity of Ixtapa, the source of salt supplies for the region and whose control was frequently contested by the Chiapanecs on the Grijalva River (Calnek 1988; McVicker 1974; Navarrete 1966; Ximénez 1929-31, II:360).

An archaeological example of the effect of increasing exchange and decreasing warfare on the community settlement pattern comes from the Yucatán. Webster (1980:835-840) describes the fortified sites of Chacchob and Cuca in northern Yucatán, which were occupied during the Terminal Classic period. Apparently at both sites stone walls were hastily erected around the elite ceremonial core for defensive purposes. Later, the communities expanded outside the walls, especially at Cuca, but there was no dense settlement within the walled zones. Webster (1980:843) says that at both sites the walls were eventually "dressed up" with coats of plaster or more elaborate stone work as they came to symbolize the social distance between the elite and non-elite.

Civic-ceremonial Structures

Changes in civic-ceremonial structures are likely when exchange relations become progressively more important. The elite can increase their prestige locally by emulating foreign elites, and by incorporating nonlocal symbols in ceremonial architecture. This takes place only when the elite wish to emphasize their political and ideological alliance with a more powerful neighboring polity. Much as the structures of a household symbolize the relations that members of the household have with other groups, a community's civic-ceremonial buildings symbolize a wide set of relations that the community as a whole has with other communities. The architectural styles, construction, and layout of the buildings express those relationships. The way these structures are modified is a direct result of the internal and external political strategies of the people making the modifications. In the case of civic-ceremonial structures, rebuilding of the various structures would be directed and carried out by members of the nobility using corvée labor. Their decisions to use nonlocal styles in building construction would be a visible and lasting expression of the nobility's perception of their close relations with foreign elites. The more pervasive and extensive the exchanges between the nobles and those they are emulating, the more likely they are to embody their relations in architectural symbols. This not only demonstrates the nature of the nonlocal relations that the elite have, but it also underscores the status that the elite have within their own community.

With exchange as the underlying process whereby elite consolidate their position, gradual emulation of higher ranking, nonlocal elites is to be expected. This would contrast with the case where warfare was dominant. Under conditions of heightened warfare, I would expect nonlocal styles of civic-ceremonial architecture to be avoided and both a proliferation and elaboration of local styles.

The direction of emulation is analogous to the direction of "mentioning" higher-order centers with emblem glyphs among Lowland Maya during the Classic Period. Marcus (1976) has shown subject communities (e.g., secondary centers) erected stelae that mentioned primary or higher-order centers, using emblem glyphs representing those communities. High-ranking communities never mention low-ranking communities.

In the same way, I would expect lower-ranking or subject communities to emulate the civic-ceremonial architecture of their dominant political, economic, or religious center. These centers would not likely try to emulate low-level centers since there is little to be gained in terms of status or political power by doing so. Communities or centers at the top of the hierarchy who are equals and engaged in various forms of exchange could emulate each other or emulate some more distant and even higher-status center with which they could maintain exchange relations.

The important part of this hypothesized set of relations is that it allows a determination of whether or not exchange is the most important specific process of inter-polity relations, depending upon whether architectural change is an emulation of nonlocal patterns or a local elaboration. For the Postclassic Maya, who discontinued the use of stelae and carved glyphs, tracing patterns of architectural emulation could provide evidence of both the extent of states and of the processes underlying their regional influence (Fox 1978).

WARFARE

Household Features

Differences between elite and commoner households would change little or even decrease during a period of increasing warfare. The elite may elaborate local styles or emulate their allies, but I would expect them to differentiate their styles from those of their neighbors with whom they are in constant conflict. The reasons for this expectation are included in the following arguments.

First, elites will emphasize their distinctiveness from neighboring enemies during times of increasing warfare (Hodder 1979:447). This can be done by elaborating traditional styles within the community and prohibiting the use of neighboring styles.

Second, as the frequency of exchanges decreases, including exchanges of wives between elites from different communities, stylistic sharing between communities, especially in non-portable items, will decrease. Political rifts between communities can be expressed in stylistic dissimilarity also resulting from a decline in most interactions that previously would have allowed the observation of details of housing in other communities.

Third, the reason for emulating nonlocal elite will disappear. If emulation takes place in order to express a social similarity with a group believed to be of higher status, then, during periods of warfare with that group, stylistic differentiation would take place as a result of, first, the lack of desire to emulate that community and, second, the desire to actively mark social distinctiveness from the enemy (Hodder 1982:74).

These factors combine to increase the differences between elite and their nonlocal, hostile neighbors. But what would they do to the differences between elite and non-elite? If warfare is intense, then elite/non-elite distinctions may not be expressed as vigorously through stylistic variation in material culture. Non-elite households may be allowed to emulate the elite in the interests of community solidarity when warfare is more frequent (Hodder 1979:450). Under this circumstance the nobility would rely on local patterns for houses and household features, and the differences between elite and non-elite would change. The elite would still need to maintain symbols of their social superiority over the non-elite, but they can accomplish this with scale instead of style. For example, the two classes might have the same style of houses, but the elite would have larger houses or more of them. They might also have more expensive or durable materials and might more frequently refurbish floors, walls, and the like (Douglas and Isherwood 1980:121-122, 181).

The non-elite would be encouraged to emulate their own elite's household styles, while the elite maintained their differentiation and social distance by increasing the size of their houses and switching to more valuable construction materials. This way, internal cohesion is expressed in terms of stylistic similarity, but class distinctions are expressed in terms of large differences in the expense of the symbol (Rapoport 1969:58). A general hypothesis that would be worth testing cross-culturally is that in conditions of increased warfare, sumptuary rules should decline, and in times of dominant exchange they should increase.

Examples

A major question is what effect does the scale of warfare have on internal elite and non-elite differentiation? With conquest empires, such as the Aztec, continuous success in expansion might actually lead to increasing differentiation between social strata. As Adams (1966:142) points out:

> With the spreading conquests of Aztec armies and the consequent further accretion of strength to the king and the nobility at the expense of the traditional calpullec council, increasing social barriers in movement, dress, and behavior were erected not only between the nobility and the commoners but between the king and the nobility. Durán tells of elaborate regulations to this effect promulgated by Moctezuma I (AD 1440-69), and the trend culminated under Moctezuma II (1502-20) with the widespread substitution of members of the nobility of lineage for officials whose rank was based on service alone.

Nevertheless, the Aztec situation is one where distant warfare and conquest operated in addition to a highly developed tribute and market economy linking a number of previously independent states. Warfare was not the dominant means of inter-state political relations. The same can be said of the Quiché during the Late Postclassic (Carmack 1981).

A concrete consequence of warfare is that in a community suffering repeated attacks, there should be evidence of burning. For example, when Pedro de Alvarado attempted to conquer the Quiché capital, he entered the stronghold of Utatlán only to discover that it was a trap (Díaz del Castillo 1912:277):

> Some Indians from Quezaltenango warned Pedro de Alvarado that that very night it was intended to burn them all in the town if they remained there and that many squadrons of warriors had been stationed in the barrancas so that as soon as they saw the houses were burning they should join the people of Utatlán and attack them [the Spaniards] some from one side and some from the other and that with the fire and the smoke they would be helpless and would be burned alive.

The practice of burning houses must have been a common aspect of native warfare; for example, one conqueror actually had to prevent his allies from burning the Chiapanec capital at Chiapa de Corzo. Díaz (1912:302) describes Luis Marín's threats, as well as his allies' actual attempts, to burn the town:

> And he [Luis Marín] sent to tell them to come promptly to make peace and he would pardon them for what was past, but if they did not come, we would go and look for them and make worse war on them than before, and would burn their city. Owing to those hectoring words they came at once and even brought a present of gold and excused themselves for having made war and gave their fealty to His Majesty, and prayed Luis Marín not to allow our allies to burn any houses, for before entering Chiapa they had already burned many houses in a small pueblo situated a short distance before reaching the river, and Luis Marín gave them his promise and he kept it, and ordered our Mexican allies and those we had brought from Quechula not to do any harm or damage.

This practice of burning communities during periods of warfare was also practiced by Zapotec armies. Redmond (1983:27) cites the Dominican Friar Francisco de Burgoa (1674) in discussing their techniques of conquest: "In some instances they proceeded to subjugate communities '*a fuego y sangre*' by setting them on fire and by massacring any inhabitants who resisted." These examples indicate that if such tactics were being practiced in Prehispanic times, it should be possible to find the remains of burned houses. Of course, burned houses alone would not confirm that warfare was the cause of burning since accidental burnings (e.g., kitchen fires, lightning, etc.) could also have occurred. Landa (in Tozzer 1941:40-41) describes the effects of a hurricane in the Yucatán in 1464:

> This wind overthrew all the large trees causing a great destruction of every kind of game; and it destroyed also all the tall houses which, since they were covered with straw and contained fire on account of the cold, were set on fire; and they burned up a large part of the people.

Still, precisely this sort of danger could have been avoided by spacing houses more widely. Overriding considerations such as defense would have made it necessary to live in dense clusters that increased the danger of fire from both military and natural causes.

Before continuing with the next category of material culture I will briefly mention, once again, the example of stylistic change in houses from the Middle Virginia area during the 1760s (Glassie 1975). Soon after the introduction of Georgian-styled houses, there followed a prolonged conflict with England, eventually leading to a decrease in trade between the two nations. By that time the Georgian style was already well known as a symbol of high status and marked the owner as someone who had strong connections with the centers of national and international power. Continued building of the Georgian style houses in the early 1800s required an amalgamation of traditional local styles in order to make it acceptable (Glassie 1975:91-95). Builders developed their own elite architectural traditions rather than continue to emulate those of a foreign enemy power against whom the new republic was rebelling.

Household Artifacts

Increasing warfare will decrease the accessibility of imported products. This is because warring neighbors create unfavorable conditions of exchange with one another and because warfare decreases the reliability and safety of exchange routes. In addition, the emulation of exotic goods used by and available from neighboring enemies will decline.

Spencer (1982) has argued that some societies may engage in conquest to meet their internal needs for nonlocal materials and items used as prestige markers. In addition to this, however, warfare may serve as a replacement for, or supplement to, exchange of prestige materials, thereby decreasing the need for nonlocal exotic goods. Alternatively, the acquisition of nonlocal prestige items may be used as an excuse or justification for war on another group. In other words, warfare, in general, provides a domain for the maintenance of social and political differentiation.

At the household level there will be two consequences of this. First, the frequency of imported goods will decline as warfare increases. Second, the differences in the distribution of these goods between elite and non-elite households will decrease. This is primarily because performance in warfare should become more important than the acquisition of imported prestige goods in the display of status.

I expect two other changes in household material culture. First, there should be a decline in evidence for specialized production as warfare increases (conversely, as exchange increases, evidence for specialized production should increase). For example, if a community was able to exchange cotton cloth for obsidian, evidence for cotton spinning and weaving implements will increase along with an increase in obsidian. If this pattern were interrupted by warfare on a regular or increasing basis, the production of cloth for exchange would decline, resulting in a noticeable decrease in weaving and spinning implements. Even if exchange were redirected somewhere else, these items would decline in frequency.

Second, the actual items used in warfare will increase as it becomes more frequent. The items most likely to preserve archaeologically are projectile points and other stone implements of war. Arrow and dart points used in warfare would be present both at the site of any engagement as well as in the community where weapons would be manufactured, maintained, and stored. If a community was the site of a military engagement, then even more points will make their way into the archaeological record. Therefore, changes in the quantities of projectile points in household deposits should be generally related to changes in the frequency or intensity of warfare.

One additional expected effect of warfare is that it should increase the stylistic homogeneity of locally produced artifacts between elite and non-elite households (cf. Hodder 1979:451-452 for a parallel situation). Increased interregional conflict would force the elite to see themselves as more dependent upon the local non-elite than other nonlocal elite. If interregional divisions among warring elite become larger than intracommunity class divisions then this would be symbolized along several dimensions of material culture. I expect increasing *differences* between political regions and increasing *similarity* between social strata within a single polity. This should apply to a wide range of material symbols and would be especially true of the sorts of items that would be used by both classes in intracommunity and intercommunity relations: clothes, personal ornamentation, serving vessels, ritual or ceremonial items, and weaponry.

Examples

The effect of warfare on trade is given in many examples which show that not only would direct exchanges between states diminish, but long distance trade by merchants would also decline. Díaz (1912:293) discussed how the Chiapanecs disrupted trade:

> All the people in this neighborhood stood in great fear of the Chiapanecs for certainly at that time they were the greatest warriors that I had seen in all New Spain, although that includes Tlascalans, Mexicans, Zapotecs and Mijes, and this I say because the Mexicans had never been able to master them. At that time the province was thickly peopled and the natives of it were

> extremely warlike and waged war on their neighbors the people of Zinacantan and all the pueblos of the Quilena language, also against those called the Zoques and continually robbed and took prisoners in other small pueblos where they were able to seize booty, and with those whom they killed they made sacrifices and glutted themselves.

> In addition to this on the roads to Tehuantepec they had many warriors stationed at bad passes to rob the Indian merchants who traded between one province and the other, and because of the fear of them trade between one province and another was sometimes stopped.

Ethnographic examples of increasing stylistic similarity in artifacts between elite and non-elite with the increasing importance of warfare are scarce, but Hodder (1979:451-452) gives an archaeological example of this general process for Neolithic societies. Nevertheless, the argument remains the same as for house features (above): when interregional conflict increases, sumptuary rules are likely to decline so that the elite would not be as socially distinct from the non-elite. The emphasis would turn to social distinctions based on gradations along a similar scale rather than completely different scales. In other words, with increasing warfare the elite will have access to more of a given artifact class, but not exclusive access to it. In this way, gradations of differentiation between social strata will replace abrupt breaks.

Subsistence Goods

Warfare should have no direct effect on the distribution of subsistence remains in households, either plant or animal; however, indirectly one could argue that plant and animal foods could take the place of nonlocal prestige items as status markers when warfare increases. The elite would, no doubt, always have consumed more food of higher quality than the non-elite, probably given to them in the form of tribute. It is possible that increased consumption of high quality foods such as deer and dog meat during phases of increased warfare could serve to emphasize the social distinctiveness of the elite while not at the same time making them completely different from their own lower-status fellow community members. This would be akin to the elite having houses in the same style as commoners but simply made larger or from more costly materials. Based on this assumption, any differences between elite and non-elite in types of food consumed will decrease, while in elite households quantities of foods considered more prestigious will increase.

Settlement Pattern

Warfare will have the strongest affect upon a regional settlement system. This is especially true for settlements housing the elite elements of society. First, civic-ceremonial settlements will be located at defensible sites, or measures will be taken to improve a community's defensibility. Second, rural, non-elites will shift closer to defensive locations, if not actually within the confines of a larger defensible settlement (Webster 1977:353).

There is ample evidence throughout much of Mesoamerica for this settlement shift during the Postclassic period. In the Quiché area, settlements were increasingly located in defensive locations on hills, on spurs overlooking ravines, and on bends in rivers. Miles (1965:278) sums up the pattern nicely in saying that the Late Postclassic period in highland Guatemala

> saw sweeping change in the location of town sites. The midhighland valley and slope sites with poor defense qualities were largely abandoned, and new centers on defensible heights or spur plateaus were constructed. In a few cases old sites, well placed for security, were rebuilt with new architectural features that accompanied the general revision in living conditions.

In neighboring regions to the west, she says there was less change between the Early and Late Postclassic period settlement patterns, presumably because in these areas settlements had already been built with defense in mind. Therefore, in situations where warfare has been a major dimension of inter-polity relations for a long time, continued warfare may not lead to more changes in the settlement pattern. But, as one would expect, settlements previously adjusted to non-warring interactions will later assume a defensive posture as conflict increases.

Within a fortified or defensible community, the density of structures will increase as warfare increases. This would be especially true if the community were under threat of attack and not simply engaged in faraway raiding or conquest. One consequence of this increasing density is that topographic considerations may override other considerations in house group or civic-ceremonial layout, as Johnson (n.d.) has shown for Topoxte in the Peten. The constraints of having to locate a settlement on a hilltop, ridge, or behind a wall may make it impossible to replicate a settlement pattern dictated by pre-warfare ideological considerations.

I would expect, then, that as warfare increases in intensity (e.g., the threat of direct attack) the settlement will become increasingly densely packed and that, in turn, standardized layout, building orientation, or spacing will break down.

Another consequence of warfare is that it would have different effects on community settlement pattern, depending upon its intensity. Here, I will look at several levels of warfare on the community level: (1) victim of sporadic raids, (2) participant in major battles outside the community, (3) victim of regular raids or under threat of conquest. In the case of sporadic raids, there will be little change in the community's settlement pattern. Likewise, if the community engaged only in distant battles then the settlement pattern should remain unaffected. If, however, regular raids victimized the community then I expect it to shift to a defensive posture. First, the inhabitants would locate in a defensible area; second, they would aggregate within the area; and third, they would construct fortifications. The threat of conquest might lead to complete disbandment of the community, especially in the case where the conquering group is much larger and more powerful. Later, I will discuss the effects of conquest in more detail.

Examples

Herrera (Tozzer 1941:217) mentioned the effects of raids and persistent warfare and conquest on the settlement pattern in Tutulxiu province, Yucatán:

> They found them then living together in pueblos in very civilized fashion ... In the middle of the places they had the pueblos and near them the houses of the lords and priests and important people, and further away those of the common people. And the public wells were in the plazas. This dwelling thus together was on account of the wars because of which they ran the risk of being captured, sold and sacrificed. But with the wars of the Spaniards they were scattered.

Defensive aggregations of settlements are a good indication of the relatively constant nature of warfare. This kind of pattern also suggests that each side was evenly matched. Fortified settlements, which prove effective as defenses against small, irregularly supplied armies, prove to be traps when confronting larger, more efficient armies. Such was the case, for example, when the Inca besieged the fortress site of Cerro Baul in the Moquegua valley of southern Peru (Moseley et al. 1982:4).

The Mam ruler, Caibil Balam, found himself in the same position during Gonzalo de Alvarado's assault on his capital, Zaculeu (Woodbury 1953:13-19). The long siege was difficult for the Spaniards and their Mexican and Tlaxcalan allies, but they were able to wait out the Mam who were eventually reduced to "eating the hides of their shields" (Woodbury 1953:19).

When warfare, rather than complete conquest, was frequent over a long period of time, such as in the highlands of Chiapas during the Early Classic period, settlements were located in highly defensible locations (Adams 1961). By the Late Classic period, most sites with both civic-ceremonial structures and residential zones were located on hilltops that, if not walled, were ringed with steep terraces. For example, Cerro Ecatepec and Moxviquil (Adams 1961; Culbert 1965) are two sites to which access can only be gained by a steep climb from the valley bottom. Chamula, conquered by Captain Luis Marín in April of 1523, was also fortified. Díaz (1912:306) described the site of Chamula as a "steep hill and fortification" above the plain, where horses could not maneuver. It was protected by ditches on two sides, and the whole was barricaded (Díaz del Castillo 1912:305-306). It may have been the civic-ceremonial center where the people from surrounding communities retreated during times of war, since Díaz (1912:306) mentions a small deserted pueblo nearby where the attackers obtained wood and boards for their engines of siege.

In the northern Yucatán peninsula increasing inter-polity conflict through the Late Postclassic period led to the fortification of a number of regional capitals such as Mayapán. There, a huge wall surrounded the entire community, including within it the whole range of social classes. Webster (1980:843) contrasts this community pattern with earlier centers where the walled zone included only elite households and the civic-ceremonial structures.

Civic-ceremonial Structures

Warfare would have had a similar effect on changing architectural styles of civic-ceremonial structures as it would have had on changing elite houses. The style of public structures may be changed to make them different from those of an enemy. Changing the orientation and layout of buildings are two possible types of change, but even more likely would be rebuilding in more traditional styles. Also, buildings related to new lineages or other groups increasingly involved in warfare could be promoted in importance and could replace other previous buildings as centers of ceremonial activity. The main force at work here would be the decrease in emulation of nonlocal styles and, instead, the elaboration of local styles. The long-term process would be one of differentiation from enemies and emulation of allies. In a regional matrix of small competing polities I would expect the emergence of a large number of stylistic variants of civic-ceremonial architecture.

One physical impact of warfare that may show up archaeologically is evidence for the destruction of temples. This military tactic was a common one throughout Mesoamerica (Palerm 1956:131). Palerm (1956:134), citing Diego Durán, gives the example of the Aztec conquest of Chiapa de Corzo where the temple and all of its inhabitants were captured and burned. As Adams (1966:148-149) has pointed out, one Aztec hieroglyphic symbol for conquest of a community was "the representation of a destroyed or burning temple." This is to be expected if civic-ceremonial structures symbolized a community's relations with other communities, with the gods, and the relations between elite and commoners. All of these relationships would be changed if the community suffered defeat during warfare. If the community was conquered, the imposition of a new political order would have been simpler for the conquerors if the key symbols of the old order were destroyed (Redmond 1983:22).

ELITE COLONIZATION

Household Features

The colonization of an area by outside elites should have distinctive effects upon many types of household features. The most notable change would be the construction of new elite houses in styles that were previously unknown within the community. This would take the form of a break with earlier elite styles, and the change would be drastic compared with the changes expected if local elite were simply emulating nonlocal styles.

The differences between elite and non-elite houses would become more pronounced than earlier. The commoners might eventually begin to emulate the new elite, but this would be a gradual process and one most probably subject to sumptuary laws. In the archaeological record there should be evidence for continuity in styles for non-elite households while, at the same time, there should be evidence for a great deal of discontinuity for elite households.

The colonizing elite would find it to their advantage to maintain close links, including exchange relations, with their homeland. So, in addition to building initial structures in their foreign styles and using materials of those they were accustomed to, they would continue to emulate styles in their homeland, at least until a greater degree of independence was established. Rapoport (1969:109), in addressing this situation, has said that in choosing the actual materials of construction:

> Certain materials may be related to those used in a previous habitat prior to migration, and thus represent archaic survivals. We have already seen the tenacity with which migrants cling to old dwelling forms in new areas, and this also applies to materials. A good example of such practices is California, where the Spanish in the northern counties use adobe, the Russians use logs, and the Americans build with frame construction; little stone is used by any of them in spite of its availability.

The nature of changes following the colonization process would depend upon the relative importance of warfare and exchange and the links these created between the community and its neighbors. Even so, the initial changes at the moment of elite colonization would be distinct from any other type of interregional interaction. They would be faster and restricted to elite households.

Another expected effect of elite colonization is that both visible household features (walls, roofs, house shapes) as well as more hidden features (hearths, altars, caches) would be different for elite and non-elite (Donley 1982). For example, the structure and characteristics of indoor storage facilities in immigrant elite households could differ from those in houses of the local non-elite. Details of construction might differ between regions, and the more different the non-visible features between the elite and the non-elite, the more likely the elite came from outside the local traditions of house-building.

Examples

The Quiché region is one where this process of elite conquest and colonization shaped the history of particular communities. The original inhabitants of the area were Quiché speakers, called the *Wuk amak'* whose territory was invaded by warlords from the Gulf Coast area. These warlords later became the Quiché rulers and nobility. According to Carmack (1981:44), upon their arrival they set up their own centers in isolated and defensible mountain locations. This type of colonization will be discussed in the next section. From these initial communities, however, the elite ventured out into the *Wuk amak'* communities, eventually conquering them and intermarrying with local Quiché-speaking women. The locals fought valiantly against the conquerors to begin with but eventually were dominated by the newcomers. In Carmack's (1981:123) analysis of the native sources he concludes that "many peoples submitted peacefully to the Quiché warriors, offering to be wife givers and tribute-paying vassals (*ikan*)." The warlords retained their symbols of high status, including house styles (Carmack 1981:48, 51). Later, as the Quiché conquered surrounding areas they sent nobles out into tributary provinces to administer them. Presumably, they took Quiché house styles with them. One reason that I expect this is that among the Quiché the noble lineages were actually referred to as *Nim ja*, or "big houses" (Carmack 1981:160, 164). Although big houses (actually long council buildings) apparently came to be used primarily for administrative purposes and stood for the lineage as a whole, they were closely associated with palaces. Quiché palaces were much more residential in function and eventually were more important in administrative functions than the big houses (Carmack 1918:193):

> The residential quarters (*cochoch*) of the rulers of Utatlán, especially of the *ajpop*, became so elaborate that they overshadowed the public component (big house) of a lineage building complex.

Carmack (1981:294) speculates that the palaces at Utatlán were designed and their "construction directed by the ruling lords." If this were the case then palaces of lesser nobles in outlying communities taken over by Quiché elite were probably also distinct, especially since houses were such an important symbol of high status (Carmack 1981:48).

Household Artifacts

With an abrupt, nonlocal elite takeover of a community there should be a pronounced increase in the differences between artifacts found in elite and non-elite households. Elite households can be expected to have a number of nonlocal artifacts that would stand as symbols of their higher social standing and of their unique relationships with elites in other communities. The immigrant elite can be expected to bring some number of these nonlocal items with them, but they would also maintain exchange relationships with the higher-ranking communities from which they came, ensuring continued access to prestige items.

Two different types of elite colonization should each have different consequences. The first type of colonization is by invitation to the nonlocal elite to take control of the highest status positions in the society. The second is a forcible conquest by foreign elites. If the first took place, there might be more syncretism between the local and immigrant elite. If the second took place there would be a greater discontinuity between pre-and post-conquest elite stylistic traditions.

After the colonization of a community by foreign elites there could be some continuity in the use of local symbols of prestige. In fact, the new elite might appropriate local symbols in addition to their own in order to ensure their superordinate position with respect to possible internal sources of competition. This would be increasingly likely with succeeding generations of the immigrant nobility. Finally, there might come to be more similarity between the symbols of the new elite and the symbols of the local elite, after generations of emulating some distant higher-ranking community.

It should be possible to distinguish between both of these types of elite colonization and the case of gradual emulation by locals. The main distinguishing characteristic would be that which I mentioned for household architecture and features: during elite conquest there would be an abrupt replacement of prestige symbols in elite households only. Presumably, the new elite would replace or demote the old local rulers, as well as their symbolic baggage.

Examples

An example of elite colonization and its impact on portable material culture again comes from the Quiché area. The conquering warlords apparently had exclusive access to a range of symbols (some of which would enter the archaeological record). Carmack (1981:47-48) describes the breadth of the social differentiation between the conquering warlords and their subjects:

> Their descent lines had to be kept pure, a condition that they believed made them superior to other peoples and thus gave them the right to rule. As befitting rulers, they were to live higher than and separate from other peoples. Special foods, clothes, ornaments, utensils, language, and elaborate residences would symbolize their high status.

As Fox (1978) has demonstrated, this ethnohistoric pattern has left highly visible and distinctive settlement distributions and civic-ceremonial architecture throughout the Quiché area. Less extreme cases should also be visible, even with a minimum of separation between the old elite and the interlopers.

Subsistence Goods

The immigrant nobility can be expected to have access to exotic, imported foods since sumptuary laws for foods did exist throughout Mesoamerica. We have already looked at the expansion in use of imported foods during a period of increased exchange. If the local elite group is actually replaced by foreign elites, then there might be a dramatic increase in the degree to which exotic foods are used as status markers, and certainly there could be additional foods or replacement foods added to the list. Furthermore, there may be new ways of preparing and storing foods used among the new nobility. All these foods, and evidence for their means of preparation and storage, could preserve archaeologically and provide information about rapid shifts in food consumption and/or preparation among the elite. My expectation is that there would not be a correspondingly rapid change among the non-

elite; rather, they would gradually emulate the new elite (if permitted to).

Examples

The Quiché nobility claimed special foods as a symbol of their high status (Carmack 1981:48). They associated many exotic prestige items with the east, the most sacred direction, and among these were tropical fruits such as the *zapote* (Carmack 1981:82).

With elite colonization, there may also be shifts in food preparation technology that accompany the introduction of new foods or even the introduction of new food preparation techniques.

Settlement Pattern

Regional and community settlement patterns are likely to be the most revealing source of information about the process of elite colonization. One reason for this is that on the regional level the settlement pattern is affected by economic, political, and religious considerations. The takeover of a state by elite from outside could be expected to have repercussions in all these systems. After colonization, a polity's capital might be completely abandoned in favor of a smaller community that previously was only a secondary or tertiary center. The new political order would have different considerations in determining settlement function and location.

One implication of an elite immigration is that the new rulers and nobles would come with previously established relations with outside areas. New military and exchange alliances might decrease the need for defensive location of settlements, especially if the elite represented a colonial extension or outpost of a larger state. The new ruling stratum might think it preferable to relocate settlements where they could not be used as fortresses by a rebellious local population.

I expect several observable changes in the internal layout of settlements. One such change would be the construction of a new elite residential area isolated from the rest of the community. If the old elite already had a discrete residential location, within a walled zone or on a hilltop, then this might be taken over by the new elite. It is here that they would build new residences or rebuild old residences in the style of their own building traditions.

Another expected change is the reorganization of the commoner wards of the settlement. If additional, local commoners were aggregated within the bounds of the settlement, then the pattern of the community might change to meet the prescribed form of the conquering elite. Yet, there should be little, if any, change in their household-level patterning. The non-elite would maintain traditional styles in rebuilding their houses. Therefore, with a new immigrant elite, the entire settlement's layout might change, but there should be a clearly recognizable local tradition among the commoners. Minimally, I expect the elite residential core to become different after colonization.

In the case of elite colonization, the layout of the ceremonial center, which in all cases is organized and administered by the elite, would undergo modification. I would expect new ceremonial traditions requiring changes to be made in the design of the civic-ceremonial center. Here again, the pattern of change would not differ markedly from the process of elite emulation encouraged by alliances and exchange relations. Nonetheless, the speed and abruptness of the change would be much greater if brought about by an influx of conquering elite than if by a local elite emulating foreign styles.

One reason for expecting these changes to take place after elite colonization is the incoming elite's need to display their social distance from the local non-elite. Because elite residences and ceremonial buildings and their layouts are symbols of status and prestige, these buildings would have to be correctly constructed in order to convey the necessary meanings. In fact, the ability of the new elite to rearrange and modify the old order on the scale of the entire community would be a powerful display of their strength and dominant position. Furthermore, the exaction of tribute and services necessary to accomplish this would impress upon the entire community and its dependencies the power of the new elite.

Examples

When the Quiché elite were able to consolidate control over the central highlands of Guatemala, some old centers were abandoned, and the elite built new centers in locations that were best suited to the needs of the new political order. Because the Quiché was essentially a conquest state, new towns were located in defensible locations, but the commoners' hamlets were small and scattered widely about the countryside.

The nearer the conquered communities were to the Quiché heartland the greater the degree of change was made to the community's settlement layout (Fox 1978). More distant communities on the edge of the Quiché domain underwent less modification. Some, like Zaculeu, the Mam capital, remained on the same site and retained the same ceremonial structures and orientation after conquest by the Quiché in the 1400s. In this case, the Mam elite remained in control of their own community and only had to pay tribute to the Quiché. Instead of being conquered by the Quiché, the Mam were simply brought into a position of subordination. But at the site of Chutixtiox, north of the Central Quiché, there is clear evidence that the community was brought under Quiché domination in the early 1400s (Fox 1978:69). Fox (1978:76) suggests that the site might have been Kumatz, reported in early chronicles to have been "burned and subjugated by the Central Quiché in the early decades of the fifteenth century." He further notes:

> The similarities and discrepancies of this pattern to that of the Central Quiche may correlate with Late-phase and Early-phase ceramic complexes, respectively, at Chutixtiox. The similarities, in other words, may be a central Quiche-influenced veneer over an earlier non-Central Quiche pattern (Fox 1978:75).

This is a good example of a conquering elite taking over and modifying a ceremonial center. It is even more striking since contemporary centers such as Chutinamit, located only 4 km downstream, have ceramic evidence of Late Postclassic occupation and relations with the Central Quiché, but underwent little or no modification of the ceremonial center. Fox

(1978:80) sums it up by saying that "settlement patterning at Chutinamit is apparently independent of Central Quiche influence." Ultimately, then, this community would have had a much lower status, probably housing the majority of the pre-Quiché conquest local elite who would have been subordinate to the elite in Chutixtiox.

Civic-ceremonial Structures

The same logic underlying changes in the elite households and the community-level settlement pattern can be invoked to predict changes in the civic-ceremonial structures of a site. A new elite from outside the local tradition would be expected to build a new or refurbish the existing civic-ceremonial center of a community since the symbolism of the public religious and administrative structures stands for the elite who, in turn, represent the community as a whole. If a nonlocal elite took over a center, I would expect a rapid modification if not complete destruction of the old structures and rebuilding in their own styles.

If, however, a community was conquered, but the local elite were allowed to maintain control, there may have been little or no immediate modification of the ceremonial structures. Modifications would be more gradual, as under conditions of exchange; in this case, exchange would probably involve the giving of tribute as a symbol of submission to the non-resident conquerors.

Examples

That existing civic-ceremonial structures were likely to be modified by a colonizing elite is expected since these structures symbolize the community and the elite's control over it. This is well illustrated by the Quiché view of their sacred towns. Carmack (1981:182) says that the Quiché lords "thought mainly in terms of buildings rather than the lands on which they were constructed." The buildings were manifestations of the Lords' link with their Toltec ancestors and housed the sacred symbols of the nobility's close relationship with the gods. The sacred activities and rituals that took

place in the Quiché capital of Utatlán revolved around the various monumental constructions which were both enormous and ornate compared to all other buildings. As Carmack (1981:183) puts it, "To the Quichés these activities made Utatlán and its companion towns 'marvelous,' 'beloved,' and 'magical': they transformed the towns into sacred shrines." Perhaps even more important was the specific layout and the symbolic implication of a building's shape, style, height, orientation, size, and position within the ceremonial complex. All of these variables were part of an organized ideology and communicated specific ideological information. If an elite found itself in control of a provincial center without the necessary monumental architecture they could hardly "make do." Part of the process of *being elite* would be based upon the physical act of constructing and maintaining the appropriate ceremonial center with all the requisite structures and their individual characteristics. It would be difficult for a newly conquering, nonlocal elite to convince the locals of their high status if they did not behave as nobles and rulers.

COLONIZATION BY WHOLE COMMUNITIES

Household Features

Colonization of a region by states forming whole new communities in an area that was either sparsely populated or completely abandoned would have the most visible impact on the archaeological record of any of the processes discussed so far. Two different possibilities can be considered. First, a colony, consisting of almost the complete range of social groups and classes as found in the homeland, can begin a completely new community on a previously unoccupied location. Second, a colony can replace or completely dominate the local population, which then becomes a lower stratum, and build anew a community based on patterns typical of the homeland. In both cases almost the entire range of material culture would be in the style of nonlocal traditions, including both elite and non-elite segments of the community.

All house features for both nobility and commoners would be very different from anything that had existed in the region before. The archaeological remains of such a phenomenon should be visible for almost any category of house feature. Features likely to communicate social information to other members of the community and members of other communities, and features relatively free of such information, should both be different from earlier local traditions and be similar to those of the parent state.

An exception to this would arise in the use of construction materials. Houses and features may be made out of the same materials as the local populace used previously, especially if the environment restricted types of materials available (Rapoport 1969:109). Notably, even in this case, there should be details of house design and workmanship indicative of a nonlocal building tradition.

Examples

In almost all cases of colonization, communities replicate house styles common to the homeland (Rapaport 1969:109-110). The Quiché region, once again, provides some good archaeological examples. Postclassic Quiché colonies built houses in the same style as those in vogue nearer the center of the state. For example, houses in colonies in the Chixoy River Valley were built in several different styles, but all were much the same as at other Quiché sites: Pueblo Viejo Chixoy (Hill 1980:124) and Cauinal (Fauvet Berthelot 1981:63ff).

Household Artifacts

Household tools and other artifacts will be distinctly different in a new colony from those used previously by a local population. Furthermore, these differences will exist for both noble and commoner segments of the society. If the colonizers brought with them new technologies, systems of production, or specializations then the changes would be expected to be even more pronounced.

In the case of bud-off colonies, beginning in previously uninhabited areas, the entire assemblage will be nonlocal. In the case of colonies invading already occupied areas and either displacing or absorbing local populations, there might be some merging of technological and stylistic traditions. The degree of amalgamation will be correlated with the extent of assimilation or absorption of the local population. The similarity between the local and nonlocal patterns should decrease as one looks at higher status segments of the community.

A distinction must be made between bud-off communities within a state's territory and those that push beyond the outer frontier of its domain. The former case may not involve encounters with different ethnic groups or political units. In the second case, the likelihood of encountering existing local populations would be much greater. This has implications for the settlement pattern configuration, the incorporation of locals as subservient ethnic social segments, and the subsequent processes of inter-polity relations.

Examples

When the Quiché warlords first entered the highlands of Guatemala they formed their own discrete colonies and claim to have been relatively isolated from the local *Wuk Amak'* Quiché, at least in the initial stages. Carmack (1981:51) presents two possibilities for ceramic variability of the Quiché, although there is little actual evidence. They apparently had only a few of the Gulf Coast ceramic types such as Fine Orange ware. This, he notes (citing Fox 175:77), could be explained by the Quiché warlords taking local wives who presumably would have made pottery (or have pottery made) following local traditions. Carmack's own studies of the chronicles suggest, however, the possibility that the warlords brought their wives with them. They would have made nonlocal styles of ceramics. We would expect that, through time, as the warlords conquered increasingly larger numbers of locals and brought them into their tribute and production system, their colonies would include more elements and styles of local technology.

Subsistence Goods

A new colony would naturally be constrained by the same environmental limitations affecting previous inhabitants, but it might also have some additional food crops, or preferences, that were not previously known in the area. With colonization, the chances of new types of subsistence remains showing up in the archaeological record are much greater than for any of the other processes under consideration. Both elite and non-elite households should have evidence for this.

Differences between elite and non-elite households would exist, but these would not necessarily be the same differences that existed in the "pre-colonization," local communities.

Examples

An example of this comes from the Quiché. The historical chronicles name the kinds of revered foods that were associated with the invading warriors' Gulf Coast home land and given as tribute to the rulers of Tulan (Chichén Itzá) (Recinos and Goetz 1953:48). These included cacao, zapote, and *pataxte* (Carmack 1981:44-46). If the Quiché warlords maintained relations with the coast then they might have been able to obtain these goods by trade or as tribute:

> They will pay tribute to you in the form of shields, bows, quetzal feathers, and lime, as well as jade, metals, green and blue feathers; and they will give you writings, scrolls, calendars, and cacao. The enemy peoples will pay these to you in tribute, and they will be yours (*Annals of the Cakchiquels*; trans. R.M. Carmack 1981:48).

The example of cacao leads me to suspect that additional nonlocal, high-status plant and animal goods would be used, at least by the elite in the new colonies.

Settlement Patterns

Colonization strongly affects both regional and community settlement patterns. Furthermore, the settlement configuration is determined by the nature of the colony and the conditions it faces. A colony that settles in a contested area would necessarily have to take defensive precautions, whereas one occupying a neutral or abandoned area could afford not to protect itself. A distinction between these two possibilities can allow the definition of a state's territory. Colonies that penetrate beyond established frontiers into areas occupied by other states would soon be subjugated by those states if they could not defend themselves. Colonies that occupied sparsely inhabited areas within their own state's territory would have little need for defensive considerations, especially if the colony was just a secondary or tertiary center. Therefore, identifying whether or not a colony was defensible can provide evidence of state expansion.

Examples

Fox (1978:8) has used ethnohistoric and archaeological information to distinguish between sites that were taken over by Quiché administrators and ones that became completely new Quiché colonies:

> It should be possible to correlate various forms of Quiche political domination known from ethnohistory—enclaves of aristocratic administrators, large Quiche colonies, and tributary relationships in material goods or military service—with various kinds of Quiche influence evident in the settlement record. Thus, complete Quiche settlement patterns in other ethnic regions may indicate Quiche colonies, whereas single Quiche plazas in non-Quiche civic centers are theorized to correspond to enclaves of Quiche administrators.

Perhaps the clearest evidence of this is in the seven initial Quiché settlements occupied by the Quiché warlords upon entering the highlands of Guatemala around AD 1250. These settlements are known as the Chujuyub group and were occupied for about 100 years, until 1350 when the Quiché shifted their capital to the Quiché Basin some 10 km farther south. The significant aspect of these early settlements is the small Early-phase Chujuyub civic centers manifest architectural features that first occur in Mexico, including, apparently, the Tabasco Gulf Coast. The Mexican features discernible among the poorly preserved Chujuyub remains are the I-shaped ball court; the *talud-tablero* balustrades on temples; long structures; rectilinear plazas; and cone-shaped tenons for temple reliefs. (Fox 1978:66)

The style of layout for these centers is generally more similar to the Gulf Coast patterns than those already in use in the highlands. Furthermore, they were ideally suited for defense; all were located on the tops of steep hills or ridges (Carmack 1981:65; Fox 1978:66). These earliest settlements were small and probably represented little more than a colonial foothold in the area. That they were not elite colonies or administrative centers to begin with is illustrated by Carmack's (1981:60) description of an attack by the locals on the Quiché warlords.

> The native peoples were both willing and able to engage the encroaching warlords in warfare. One confederation of native groups planned and carried out an attack on the main fortified settlement (Jakawitz) of the Quiché forefathers. Another group defended its territory from the top of a prominent mountain (Mukbalsib).

Originally, the Quiché colonies must have been relatively self-sufficient. Judging by their claimed mandate to go forth and exact tribute, they must have tried to acquire dependencies as soon as possible. After approximately 100 years of warring and welding together a state, they were ready to shift their capital down to the Quiché plains.

Civic-ceremonial Structures

Changes in the civic-ceremonial structures of a community which began as a colony would be similar to the changes in one which had been colonized by nonlocal elites. Fox (1978:8), as mentioned above, hypothesized that in the former case there should be rebuilding of the earlier ceremonial complex, and in the latter

case there should only be small modifications of the local center with, perhaps, the addition of a new plaza complex to house the outside administrative enclave. I think an even more reliable indication of complete colonization would be the removal of a community to a previously unoccupied location and the adherence to distinctly nonlocal styles of architecture and forms of construction. One definite indicator of complete colonization would be the building of nonlocal ceremonial structures in non-elite wards and lower-order communities. This would indicate that the non-elite segments of the society, as well as the elite, came from a nonlocal tradition. And, of course, the rapidity with which these changes appear in the archaeological record would correlate with the extent of colonization.

Another indicator of a colony from outside the region would be the use of nonlocal materials and construction techniques. This would be especially useful if evidence could be found for a shift to local building techniques a short period after the initial colonization.

Examples

When the original Quiché forefathers settled in the Chujuyub area and built several communities, including Jakawitz (Chitinamit), they used some very unusual construction techniques. In addition to the Gulf Coast style layout and buildings used in their ceremonial structures, they used fired bricks for building material but did not plaster their buildings with stucco. As Fox (1978:67) puts it:

> Indeed, the heavy use of bricks at Chitinamit seems anomalous with such abundant rock outcrops on its slopes. Bricks are rare in Late-phase Quiche construction and quite unusual throughout Mesoamerica. They are, however, a major construction material on the Tabasco Gulf Coast and the adjacent alluvial plain, where building stone is scarce. ... This is the precise region that Carmack (1968) argues, from ethnohistoric and linguistic data, to be the Quiche homeland.

Even if the original Quiché colonists were not familiar with techniques of stone masonry or plaster-making, local artisans among their newly subjugated vassals should have been. One explanation for the lack of early Quiché stone and plaster working is that they had no subjects and, in fact, the animosity between the Quiché and the local population prevented learning about local construction techniques.

DISCUSSION

All of the above examples can only suggest the kinds of changes likely to take place in the archaeologically observable record as one or another of the four specific processes under study becomes dominant for a time. Other processes that I have not considered here, or even combinations of the four, could influence change in the material record in new ways. Let me briefly look at the interplay between exchange and warfare.

There is little question that almost all complex societies engage in both warfare and exchange and that both go on at the same time. There is no need to expect that warfare diminishes as exchange increases or vice versa. Instead, it may taper off for a time and become *relatively* less important in the internal political dynamics of the community.

Pryor (1977:121-122) found little empirical evidence that increasing warfare leads to a decrease in external trade or that increasing trade leads to a decrease in warfare. In fact, he was monitoring market variables, and they probably did not comprise the most important exchange mechanism in the Maya area during the Postclassic period.

The question still remains: why would warfare or exchange become more or less important through time? The answer lies in the study of two levels of sociopolitical organization. The first is the intracommunity level, and the second is the intercommunity level. One faction within a polity might be cut off from access to nonlocal exchange relations but may still be able to increase its status through military success. A political unit surrounded by other contentious polities may have to expand its military apparatus in order to avoid conquest by a stronger neighbor. Such

a political environment creates opportunities for rivalries within a society and allows them to be played out in new ways. Internal rivalries also change the external political environment. Alliances by one or another faction with some outside group might transform previously favorable but shifting political relationships into treacherous ones.

Notwithstanding this constant interplay between exchange and warfare, it is clear from the foregoing discussion that, over the long run, if one or the other is more important, then it will have directly observable effects upon the material culture and settlement patterns of a community. Furthermore, the nature of the founding of a secondary state, whether it be colonization by elites or by complete communities, will have quite different impacts upon archaeologically observable patterns.

The relationship between these four processes has not been specified, although there are some basic trends. Trade relations may give way to warfare in the majority of cases, mainly because of the difficulty of ensuring favorable trade over the long run. In Mesoamerica the rationale for warfare is given time and again as a way of obtaining tribute, slaves, or as retaliation against the interruption of trade. These, in turn, spark cycles of conquest and colonization—usually aimed at controlling resources in neighboring regions.

These general expectations for change in the archaeological record can be used to monitor a particular secondary state's evolutionary history and determine the changing impact of these specific processes. The next chapter will describe the region chosen for study and will outline its prehistory. It will also briefly introduce the Postclassic Maya archaeological site of Canajasté, where I collected the kinds of data discussed above in order to monitor the relative impact of each of the four processes under consideration.

ENDNOTES

1 In 1995, Olivier de Montmollin published
a more comprehensive set of models describing
the expansion of Maya polities into upper
Grijalva region during the Late-Terminal Classic
period. These likely apply to the Postclassic
period as well and incorporate parts of the
four models that I describe in this chapter. His
seven models are: 1. Elite interaction, 2. Elite
emulation, 3. Elite invitation, 4. Elite conquest,
5. Elite leap-frog, 6. Steamroller expansion, and
7. Commoner migration (1995:33-36).

CHAPTER 5

ENVIRONMENT AND ARCHAEOLOGY OF THE UPPER GRIJALVA REGION

ENVIRONMENT

Looking out upon the huge expanse of the Grijalva River Valley, one is immediately struck by the seemingly endless tiers of mountains rising in the distance. These mountains ring the east end of the upper Grijalva River Basin. Dozens of rivers and streams flow from the mountain flanks and eventually converge, one after the other, to form the first part of the Grijalva River. The Grijalva runs northwest through the center of Chiapas before finally descending to the Gulf Coast lowlands and on to the Atlantic Ocean. All of the streams that discharge from the mountains to form the Grijalva, taken together, can be called the upper tributaries (Lee 1975). For the residents of this region, the stream valleys provide the link to places high in the mountains and to the oceans beyond (Navarrete 1978a).

The valley bottomlands sit at about 700 m above sea level and rise slowly to the piedmont that extends up to about 1200 m. From this point the climb quickly steepens and the traveler's pace slows until broad upland plateaus or mountain passes are reached (Lovell 1980). To the north is the Central Plateau or Central Highlands that roughly parallels the Grijalva Valley (Müllerried 1957). They range in elevation from 1400-1600 m above sea level, with some higher peaks near San Cristobal de Las Casas reaching up to 2800 m. In spite of the high mountains, access to the northern lowlands by way of the Central Plateau can easily be gained by heading north past the Montebello Lakes and down to the Usumacinta River's drainage system (Agrinier 1983).

Eastward in Guatemala, one faces a much steeper climb. The Cuchumatan massif rises up to heights of 2500 m only 40 km from the Chiapas border (McBryde 1947). The Cuchumatan Mountains and the highland plateaus south and east of them form the Western Highland zone of Guatemala (Borhegyi 1965; McBryde 1947; West 1964). One of the largest rivers originating in this zone is the Selegua River that drains the Huehuetenango Basin in Guatemala before heading down the mountain into the Grijalva Basin. To the south and southwest runs the Sierra Madre, a strip of extremely steep mountains flanking the Pacific Coastal plain (Waibel 1946). This range is 50-60 km wide, with peaks over 3000 m above sea level. There are few passes through the mountains to the coast, but those that do exist follow the larger streams that form the Grijalva's tributaries (Navarrete 1978b; Woolrich and Manuel 1948). The southeastern portion of this range merges into the volcanic mountains that form the Guatemala Highlands (Corzo 1946; Müllerried 1957). Many of the active volcanic peaks throughout the region continue to spew gas and rock and, periodically, blanket wide regions with volcanic ash.

West and northwest, the Grijalva River flows through a wide basin that forms the Central Depression of Chiapas (García Soto 1969; Peña 1951). This is one of the most productive agricultural areas of southern Chiapas, however, a large portion of the Central Depression has now been dammed for the production of hydroelectric power. Prehistoric commerce between the upper Grijalva region and the rest of western Chiapas would have relied on canoe transport up and down the river (Lee 1980a), as well as numerous overland routes that later came to form the Camino Real (Lee 1980b; Navarrete 1978b).

Rainfall

The high mountains create a rain shadow effect that makes the entire upper Grijalva region quite dry even during the rainy season, much more so than most of the rest of tropical southeastern Mesoamerica (Vivó 1964). Mean annual precipitation ranges between 800 and 1200 mm (Helbig 1964:37-45). This is only one half to one quarter of the 2000-4000 mm of rainfall in the Pacific Coastal zone near Tapachula (Helbig 1964). The mean number of days per year that receive rainfall lies between 100 and 125 (Echegaray Bablot 1957; Helbig 1964). Rains always begin by April and continue to a peak in midsummer, eventually tapering off completely by late November. The five rainless months are indeed dry: ground water disappears and most trees, shrubs and other plants drop their leaves.

Vegetation

Because of the comparatively arid nature of the Grijalva Depression, the general descriptions for vegetation zones in Mexico do not give the necessary detail for understanding the specific conditions of the upper Grijalva region (e.g., Beard 1944; Goldman 1951; Gómez-Pompa 1965; Leopold 1950; Wagner 1964). Fortunately, as Voorhies (n.d.) points out, some detailed studies have been conducted that allow a more precise characterization of the area's vegetation.

The vegetation is quite variable throughout the valley but can be generally characterized as Tropical Deciduous Forest (Breedlove 1973; Miranda 1952, 1975:84); however, in the southern part of the region, between the San Miguel and San Gregorio Rivers, conditions are even more arid, and the vegetation formation is referred to as Short Tree Savanna (Miranda 1975:95-98; Voorhies n.d.:4). The Short Tree Savanna is characterized by short, gnarled trees, comprised mostly of acacias but including a number of other hardy specimens.

The Tropical Deciduous Forest is more diverse with 30 to 50 assorted species of trees forming two stories (Breedlove 1973:159). It has recently been cleared over most of the valley for farming and cattle ranching; but where it remains it is almost impenetrable. Where rivers or streams traverse areas covered by this type of forest, they are lined with a completely different riparian vegetation. It is usually denser than

the deciduous forest and contains evergreen trees that grow to much greater heights than the surrounding vegetation.

Fauna

The Grijalva Depression is home to almost the entire range of mammals, birds and reptiles found in Mesoamerica (Álvarez del Toro 1952, 1971, 1972, 1977; Flannery 1969; Leopold 1959). There are few large mammals in the region today, but, in the past, white-tailed and brocket deer, tapir, coyote, fox, mountain lion, jaguar, and collared peccary were common (Álvarez del Toro 1977; Álvarez del Toro et al. 1984). Small mammals, such as rabbit, armadillo, opossum, agouti, porcupine, skunk, raccoon, and small wild cats are still prevalent. The rivers have plentiful small fish and other reptiles, as well as snails, molluscs, and crabs. Land reptiles, including iguanas and other lizards, and a wide range of snakes, are to be found (Álvarez del Toro 1972; Chávez. 1969).

The Immediate Environs of Canajasté

The archaeological site of Canajasté is located on the Lagartero River (15° 55' 49.13" N; 91° 49' 16.44" W) about 15 km upstream from (i.e., north of) its confluence with the San Gregorio River, one of the largest of the Grijalva's tributaries. The Lagartero is lined with dense riparian vegetation mainly consisting of huge sabino and ceiba trees. Back from the river margin, in places where it has not been cleared for milpa, is an even denser deciduous forest. Cleared areas left fallow after only a short period of use quickly revert to forest. If not regularly burned, most of the small shrubby trees, which have deep tuberiferous root systems, soon sprout exuberant growth at the end of the long dry season.

The combination of short tree forests and riparian formations encompasses almost the entire environmental variability in the region. There are no lakes, and it is at least a day's walk east before one gets to the zone of evergreen oak-pine forest that ascends the Cuchumatan Mountains. Ancient Canajasteños, situated near the headwaters of one of the largest rivers in the area, would have been able to make ready use of both riverine and forest resources.

The agricultural land surrounding the site today consists of both irrigated fields and milpa patches. Everywhere except on the valley bottom the terrain is extremely rocky. The whole area around Canajasté is covered with outcrops of hard limestone. This rocky terrain, as well as the irrigated bottomlands, is worked right up to the international border by *ejidatarios* from the *colonia* of Las Delicias located 8 km away. Present day farmers from Las Delicias irrigate the whole Camcum-Canajasté Valley bottom with one main canal and several feeder canals. The water comes from the Camcum spring which is dammed and fed by way of a small concrete and stone canal that runs several hundred meters along the valley edge. Another canal takes water from the Canajasté spring to more fields in the valley bottom, and these are shared by the Las Delicieños and ejidatarios from another colonia located farther to the north. The springs allow irrigation of sugar cane and bananas as well as some crops of maize. All of these crops are grown for local consumption.

The land across the international border is worked by farmers and ranchers from the Guatemalan towns of La Unión, Ojo de Agua, and Chacaj, in much the same way and for the same purposes as their Mexican neighbors.

Where the Camcum River enters the Lagartero, it has built up a 3-4 m high travertine cliff, and the lime-charged waters cascade off its edge. Farmers siphon off the water for irrigating neighboring maize fields by using troughs of dug-out logs propped up on spindly poles.

Many of my workmen, all of whom came from Las Delicias and who have worked their entire lives on this land, occasionally brought their shotguns and rifles to work in the hopes that they might spot rabbits or collared peccary along the way. They said that deer used to be plentiful, too, but that nowadays they were rarely seen. Some animals in the area, however, have not been hunted to near extinction and are still readily caught. Freshwater snails (*Pachychilus* sp. and *Pomacea* sp.) live in great numbers in the slow-moving streams throughout the region,

and the Lagartero, Camcum, and Canajasté Rivers are no exception. Today local residents harvest them with great enthusiasm. Even more pleasure is generated by hunting crabs and frogs in the swampy margins of the river. This is night work. I accompanied my workmen on a crabbing expedition one evening and, with the aid of flashlights, they hand-scooped the small crabs off the stream bottom. When they spotted frogs they were quick to smash them with the flat sides of their machetes and pop them into the bag. No more than an hour after beginning, each man had a little pot on the boil, stuffed to capacity with crabs, frogs, snails, and a few onions for flavoring.

PREVIOUS ARCHAEOLOGICAL WORK IN THE UPPER GRIJALVA REGION AND NEIGHBORING ZONES

Pre-1900

Before the twentieth century very few of the many intrepid Mesoamerican explorers and archaeologists found their way into the upper Grijalva region, on either side of the Mexico-Guatemala border. In 1840 John Lloyd Stephens passed through the zone on his famous trip but did not describe any of the archaeological sites (Ekholm and Martínez 1983:256). Eduard Seler (1901) visited the area in 1895-96 and later described some of the larger sites. He mainly visited the Late Classic sites of Chinkultic in Mexico and Chaculá and Quen Santo just across the border in Guatemala.

1900-1970

From 1900 to the early 1970s very little archaeological exploration was conducted in the region (Marquina 1939; Piña Chan 1967). In 1925 Frans Blom and Oliver La Farge (1926-27) passed through the zone while searching for "lost tribes and temples." Some of the temples they happened across included sites previously described by Seler. They restricted their efforts primarily to the larger Classic Period sites, such as Hun Chavin, Tenam Puente, and Chinkultic near Comitán on the Central

Plateau, overlooking the Grijalva Valley. They also visited the large center of Tenam Rosario, another Late Classic site, down in the valley itself. Blom returned in 1928 and discovered a series of caves near Rancho La Cieneguilla only a few kilometers from the border (Blom 1983; Blom and Duby 1955-57; Piña Chan 1967). In these caves he found a number of cremation burials consisting of burned human remains in tall-necked jars decorated in a style similar to ones from highland Guatemala (Blom 1954). Some of the jars contained fragments of textiles along with other offerings (Blom 1954; Blom and Duby 1955-57; Wauchope 1942). Oliver La Farge and Douglas Byers (1931) visited the adjacent region in Guatemala in 1927. They got as close as Nentón; their studies of several sites between Nentón and Huehuetenango provide the only published archaeological information from that region.

The next addition to our knowledge of the upper Grijalva region was made by Gareth Lowe during his survey of the zone that began in 1955. Lowe (1959) discovered approximately 20 sites in the region upriver from the confluence of the San Miguel and San Gregorio Rivers. The sites he recorded range from the Late Preclassic through the Early Colonial periods. His work has provided the basis for several more projects carried out by members of the New World Archaeological Foundation (NWAF).

1970-1985

Archaeological research in the upper Grijalva region between 1973 and 1985 was carried out exclusively by the NWAF. Under the impetus and direction of Thomas A. Lee, Jr., a reconnaissance of the municipalities of La Trinitaria, Comalapa, and Chicomuselo located 300 new sites and revisited all of the previously discovered sites (Bryant, Clark et al. 2005; Lee 1975, 1981; Lee et al. n.d.). Lee's initial reconnaissance provided the basis for a ten-year project studying the prehistory, early Colonial history, linguistics, and ethnoarchaeology of the region (Lee 1981).

Álvarez Asomoza (1982) surveyed the neighboring Las Margaritas region, to the north, and while he discovered a number of Preclassic and Classic period sites, he recorded only one major Postclassic site.

THE UPPER GRIJALVA MAYA PROJECT

Regional Survey

Lee's survey concentrated on the zone between the piedmont of the Central Plateau on the north, the Mexico-Guatemala border on the east, the San Miguel River on the south, and the confluence of the San Miguel and San Gregorio on the west. This constitutes an area of some 1500 km². Since access to this area was and remains difficult, and since much of the zone is covered with either Short Tree Savanna or Tropical Deciduous Forest, his reconnaissance concentrated on rivers, the margins of roads, and cultivated fields near towns. With the help of local farmers and ranchers, Lee's survey in 1973 and 1974 located approximately 200 new sites. Most of them were sketched and located on aerial photos, and a sample surface collection of sherds and other artifacts was made (Lee 1975; Lee et al. n.d.).

In conjunction with Lee's 1974 survey, James White (1976) conducted a similar survey in the municipalities of Chicomuselo and Comalapa, concentrating on the south side of the San Miguel River. He recorded another 60 or more sites, thereby adding a great deal to our understanding of that previously little known area.

In 1979 Sonia Rivero T. surveyed in more detail the northern part of Lee's zone, test-excavating a sample of Classic period sites and mapping some previously unmapped sites (Rivero Torres 1987, 1990).

The first truly systematic survey in the region was conducted in 1983 by Olivier de Montmollin in the Santa Inés-El Rosario Valleys, La Trinitaria (De Montmollin 1989b). He recorded 177 new sites in a 52 km² area, bringing the total for the whole upper Grijalva region to approximately 500 sites.[1]

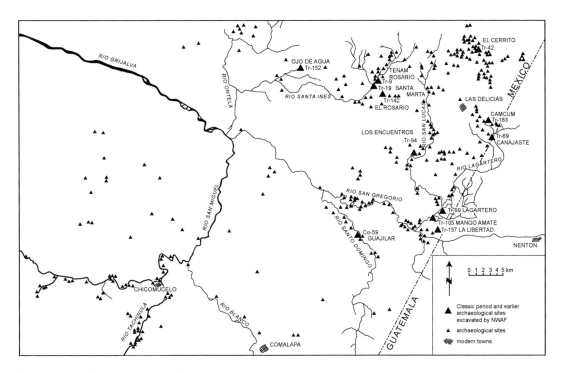

Figure 5.1. Sites in the upper Grijalva study region.

One of the salient features of the data recovered during the initial reconnaissance, and subsequently confirmed by De Montmollin's work, is that by far the majority of the nearly 500 sites date to the Late or Terminal Classic period—i.e., the Mix ceramic phase AD 650-900 (Clark, Lee, et al. 2005). Of special concern to this study is the fact that relatively few of these—only 26 as of 1985—had evidence to suggest a Postclassic occupation.

Excavations

The reconnaissance was combined with a program of excavation aimed at sampling at least one site from each major period of occupation. Excavations were carried out as more or less independent projects, with each researcher responsible for his/her own choice of site and plan of excavation. Generally, though, the archaeologists recovered comparable information from each site, and the whole provides a fairly clear view of the major cultural

developments in the area. These I will attempt to summarize in the following section.

CHRONOLOGY

The basic chronological outline for the area is based on ceramic cross-ties with other areas, primarily the central Grijalva Basin and neighboring highland Guatemala. Some radiocarbon dates have also been recovered, but few of the major excavations have yet been reported in detail, therefore, the dating is still tentative. All Classic period and earlier sites mentioned are located in Figure 5.1, and Figure 5.2 charts the chronology of the late phases (post-AD 650).

The assigned ages for the cultural-historical periods in the upper Grijalva region are somewhat confusing, since over the decades different researchers have used various cutoff points for each period. Here, I use the chronology presented in the most recent publication which provides a detailed ceramic

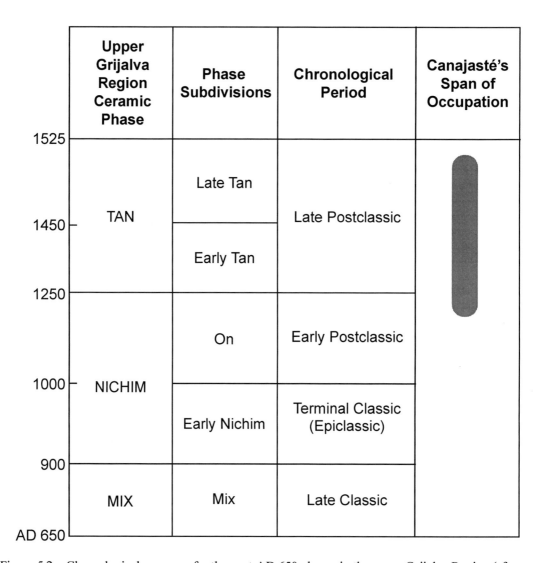

Upper Grijalva Region Ceramic Phase	Phase Subdivisions	Chronological Period	Canajasté's Span of Occupation
1525			
TAN	Late Tan	Late Postclassic	
1450			
	Early Tan		
1250			
NICHIM	On	Early Postclassic	
1000			
	Early Nichim	Terminal Classic (Epiclassic)	
900			
MIX	Mix	Late Classic	
AD 650			

Figure 5.2.   Chronological sequence for the post-AD 650 phases in the upper Grijalva Region (after Clark, Lee, et al. 2005:7 and De Montmollin 1995:22).

typology for all phases in the region (Bryant, Clark et al. 2005). The one exception, however, (as shown in Figure 5.2) is the Terminal Classic (sometimes called the Epiclassic). This phase was omitted from the new ceramic sequence because it is ceramically very difficult to distinguish from the subsequent Early Postclassic "Nichim" phase (Bryant, Lee, et al. 2005:549). Olivier de Montmollin (1995:22), however, called the Terminal Classic period the "Nichim" phase (which he dated from AD

850-1000) and referred to the Early Postclassic as the "On" phase (AD 1000-1250). I have adjusted his timing of the Nichim phase to a starting date of AD 900 to correspond with Clark, Lee, and Bryant's (2005) chronology and call it early Nichim. I have retained the On phase to designate the Early Postclassic and use this as a label for the late half of Clark, Lee, et al.'s (2005) Nichim phase. I also subdivide the Tan phase into an Early and Late Tan, with an estimated time division about AD 1450. To make matters even more confusing, in the chapters that follow, when I refer to Canajasté's Early Postclassic occupation I am specifically talking about the later part of the On or early Tan subphases, and its Late Postclassic occupation is most likely a late Tan subphase. In other words, there is essentially no Early Nichim at Canajasté, and probably very little On phase, except perhaps its final decades. To make this clear, Figure 5.2 shows Canajasté's range of occupation relative to the upper Grijalva region's general chronological sequence.

Archaic Period (pre-1900 BC)

Only one site had any evidence of an Archaic occupation. Camcum Rockshelter (Tr-183), located in a cliff overlooking the spring from which the Camcum River emerges had some lithic tools that Lee thinks may be Archaic (Lee and Clark 1980, 1988). The deposits in the shelter, and down its slope, were mainly freshwater snail shells harvested from the streams in the Camcum-Canajasté Valley. The usage of the rockshelter as a temporary refuge appears to have remained unchanged throughout the whole prehistoric sequence; near the surface Late Postclassic period artifacts are interspersed in the shell midden (Lee and Clark 1980, 1988).

Early and Middle Preclassic Periods (1900–300 BC)

Unlike the Archaic period, there is a great deal more evidence of Early and Middle Preclassic periods. Further downstream, towards the Angostura Canyon, Lowe (1959:11, Fig.3; see also Lowe 2007) reports seven sites with Early Preclassic ceramics and figurine fragments. Upstream from the San Miguel-San Gregorio confluence there are four sites with evidence of an Early Preclassic occupation (Clark, Lee, et al. 2005). At most of these sites there are only a few Preclassic sherds, and these are identified by their similarities to the much better known ceramic sequence from the Soconusco region on the Pacific Coast (Clark and Cheetham 2005; Lee 1980c). Other sites in the study region may

also have earlier Preclassic remains, but more work needs to be done to find the evidence.

Middle Preclassic sites, too, are rare in the region (compared with the later Classic period), but two sites with large assemblages of ceramics dating to this period have been well-excavated: La Libertad (Tr-157) and Santa Marta Rosario (Tr-19) (Bathgate 1980; Miller, n.d.b). Over 100,000 Middle Preclassic sherds have been recovered from these two sites alone, providing a clear picture of the range of ceramics present in the region at the time (Miller et al. 2005).

La Libertad grew to become the regional center of a large chiefdom centered in the territory between the Lagartero and Dolores Rivers (Clark 1988; Clark and Lee 1984; Miller n.d.a, n.d.b; Miller et al. 2005). The site is located near the Lagartero River only a few hundred meters from the Guatemalan border. Clark and Lee (1984) have argued that the site was an important node in an obsidian exchange network and had strong links with major centers in highland Guatemala where most of the obsidian originated. In later periods, other sites located on the Lagartero River, also with close exchange links with highland Guatemala, developed into some of the largest regional centers. This particular zone is ideal for controlling exchange because it is close to the Guatemala highlands, yet canoe traffic can navigate the Grijalva River as far down stream as Chiapa de Corzo (Lee 1980a). It is also the point at which foot trails heading up the steep river valleys in Guatemala must begin (Navarrete 1978a): the Rincón Tigre (Selegua) and Dolores and Nentón Rivers all provide access to the highland basin of Huehuetenango.

Another site with Middle Preclassic architecture is Guajilar (Co-59) on the Santo Domingo River (Lee 1978a). Although the site remains largely unknown, Guajilar at this time was smaller than La Libertad and may have been a dependency of it (Clark and Lee 1984).

There are many other Late Preclassic sites in the region, but instead of naming them all, I will only mention an important fact about their distribution. Most of the sites are located in open terrain, usually along the banks of the major rivers. The locations of some of the largest sites in the study area during this time period are replicated in succeeding periods. I will return to this matter in Chapter 10. It is thought that these sites were occupied by early Zoque peoples and that they represent the easternmost distribution of this cultural tradition along the Grijalva Valley. During the next period we begin to see the beginning of the end of the centuries-long Zoque occupation of the region.

Late Preclassic period (300–100 BC)

The Late Preclassic is poorly represented in the upper Grijalva region. One of the few known is the site of Potrero Mango (Tr-172), excavated by Lee in 1980 (Lee 1980c; Clark, Lee, et al. 2005). According to Bryant and Clark (2005a), the once thriving Middle Preclassic centers of La Libertad and Santa Marta Rosario were abandoned by about 300 B.C. and the remnants of the population moved to the nearby site of Potrero Mango. Clark, Lee, et al. (2005) point out that this was likely the time of the first penetration of Lowland Maya peoples into the upper Grijalva region, and this may account for some of the disruption and abandonment of Middle Preclassic sites.

Protoclassic Period (100 BC–AD 300)

During the Protoclassic period the upper Grijalva region became home to Maya peoples occupying the zone for the first time (Bryant and Clark 2005b). Small colonies were initially founded towards the end of the Late Preclassic period or early in the Protoclassic period, such as El Cerrito (Tr-42), a site excavated by Clark in 1980 (Clark and Lowe n.d.). Clark found Chicanel style ceramics, which date to the Late Preclassic/Protoclassic period in the southern Maya Lowlands, along with some other indications of early Maya cultural practices such as a particular style of cranial deformation (Bryant and Clark 1983).

Bryant and Clark (1983:225-226) postulate that El Cerrito and a number of other similar sites near it may represent a Maya penetration into a hostile area, since all these sites are located on defensible hilltops. There are the alternate possibilities that they were only elite colonists or even local elite adopting nonlocal styles. Excavation of some of the other sites that span this Protoclassic transition to Maya culture is necessary in order to determine the process whereby the upper Grijalva region became "Mayanized."

Mango Amate (Tr-105) is a late Protoclassic site (AD 100–300) located near the (by then) abandoned Late Preclassic site of La Libertad. It was excavated by Paillés (n.d.; Paillés and Avila 1987), who found evidence of domestic structures and other remains that link it to the general Maya sphere. This and other contemporary sites will shed more light on the question of the pre-Maya to Maya transition in the area.

Early and Middle Classic (AD 300–650)

Early Classic (AD 300-500) and Middle Classic (AD 500-650) occupation in the zone appears to have been slight, but most likely the evidence is buried beneath the large, later centers. Early Classic ceramics are best represented at the site of Ojo de Agua (Tr-152) (Bryant 2005, 2008; Bryant and Lowe 1980; Ceja Tenorio n.d.) and Lagartero (Tr-99) (Ekholm 1979a).

Late Classic (AD 650–850) and Terminal Classic (AD 850–1000)

By the Late Classic period (Mix phase, AD 650–850), the number of sites increased dramatically. During the latter part of the Mix phase—generally referred to as the Terminal Classic period (and which may have extended across the boundary of the Late Classic/Early Postclassic transition, from about AD 800–1000), there was an even larger increase in the number of sites in the region. Several large sites spanning these periods have been excavated: Lagartero (Tr-99) (Ekholm 1979a, 1979b; Ekholm and Martínez 1983), Tenam Rosario (Tr-9) (Agrinier 1983, n.d.), Ojo de Agua (Tr-152) (Bryant 2008; Bryant and Lowe 1980; Ceja

Tenorio n.d.), and Guajilar (Co-59) (Lee 1978a; Bryant and Clark n.d.)[2]

Two of the sites that developed into huge centers in the upper Grijalva region are Lagartero and Tenam Rosario. Lagartero is a sprawling center that covers 9 km² of riverine peninsulas in the Lagartero River (Ekholm and Martínez 1983). Originally discovered by members of the NWAF in 1973, parts of it were later excavated by Ekholm and Gurr in 1975 and 1976 (Ekholm 1979b; Gurr-Matheny 1987). The main civic-ceremonial constructions at the site date to the Late Classic Period (AD 650-800); however, the occupation began earlier and continued with some interruptions into the Late Postclassic period (Ekholm n.d.a). Ekholm and Martínez (1983) speculate that canoes must have been used for transportation within the site and, it is quite likely that access could be had, with minor portages, to all points downriver. One of the key aspects of the site is that it is only accessible by water and, therefore, highly defensible, unlike the earlier site of La Libertad just to the south. If warfare became an important process during the Classic period, then sites like Lagartero, in a strategic location with respect to communication routes and highly defensible, must have been more successful than their neighbors. Many of the artifacts recovered from the site, such as obsidian cores and blades, came from highland Guatemala and demonstrate the continued importance of interregional exchange between the upper Grijalva region and Guatemala (Clark 1988; Clark and Lee 1984).

Lagartero's preeminence might, like La Libertad before it, have derived from its key location at the upper end of the Grijalva Valley—not far from the small valleys that wind their way down from the Cuchumatan Mountains (Ekholm, pers. comm.). The shift of the regional center upriver from La Libertad to the site of Lagartero probably means that, for a Classic period community to be successful in trade, it also had to be able to defend itself against warring competitors.

Agrinier's (1983, n.d.) work at Tenam Rosario has helped to show what the Terminal Classic (AD 850-1000) social and political organization was like. Most sites that were occupied during the Late Classic were also occupied during the Terminal Classic. But, in addition, dozens of new sites were founded throughout the study area. Tenam Rosario seems to have been one of these (Agrinier n.d.:242). Agrinier argues that it was begun as a colony from the upper Usumacinta River zone, primarily because it had a series of small sculptures in similar styles to ones from Yaxchilán and Piedras Negras (Agrinier n.d.:245). Furthermore, these sculptures, as well as some other characteristics such as architecture, were more similar to those at Usumacinta sites than they were to nearer sites such as Tenam Puente or Bonampak.

Excavations at the Tenam Rosario hilltop ceremonial center, as well as in the huge residential site of El Rosario (Tr-142) at the base of the hill, should provide enough evidence to sort out more precisely the nature of the colonization process. One thing is clear from De Montmollin's settlement studies of the Santa Inés-El Rosario Valley: Tenam Rosario was at the apex of a polity with at least 161 separate sites, all within a 6-km radius of it, and probably in some way supporting it (De Montmollin 1989a). The elite controlling the center, and some of the secondary or tertiary centers, may have come to the area from outside; nevertheless, some portion of the population, if not the bulk of it, is undoubtedly of local origin. And, of course, the question arises: could Tenam Rosario have been built by local elites who formed a close exchange relationship with more distant centers such as Yaxchilán? The defensive nature of the civic-ceremonial center on the hilltop, roughly 100 m above the valley floor, may be secondary to the symbolic nature of the position so high and visible to all surrounding communities (J. Marcus 1983b). This is partly borne out by the relative lack of defensibility of almost all the other communities in the survey, although many of them, too, are on hillsides above the valley floor (De Montmollin 1989b).

What might these large Classic period communities have had to offer distant states in the highlands of Guatemala? One of the key resources might have been cotton (J. Marcus 1983a:476). Craft specialists at Lagartero made elaborate polychrome pottery and figurines (Ekholm 1979a, 1979b), thousands of which were thrown into a ceremonial dump in the main plaza. The figurines are particularly notable for their degree of detail, including elaborately molded impressions of woven cloth tunics on both male and female images (Ekholm 1979a). When Spaniards first entered the area it was then renowned for its "growing, processing and weaving of cotton cloth" (Lee 1980a:417, 1980b:21). Even today cotton production continues in the Santa Inés-El Rosario Valley and has caused the mechanical destruction of part of the residential site of El Rosario (Tr-142).

Postclassic period (AD 1000-1525)

When the Classic Maya polities began to disintegrate, during the period from about AD 850–1050 (Culbert 1973), the upper Grijalva region was not spared. Most Terminal Classic sites such as Tenam Rosario were abandoned completely, never to be reoccupied. The area was not completely abandoned, however, and some sites show evidence of an Early Postclassic reoccupation (Nichim ceramic phase, AD 900-1250). Some idea of the magnitude of the upheaval is obtained by looking at the numbers of sites that have evidence of Early Postclassic occupation compared with those occupied during the Late/Terminal Classic. Of the 400 or so sites found in the municipality of La Trinitaria, including those from De Montmollin's surveys, perhaps 20 have unequivocal evidence of Postclassic occupation. And of these, only four or five have a Postclassic occupation as their major component (see Chapter 10). In contrast, preliminary analyses indicate that Late/Terminal Classic sites comprise about 90 percent of the total (Lee et al. n.d.).

No sites appear to have had a solely Early Postclassic component. Most common is the occurrence of Early Postclassic artifacts in caches or burial offerings in Late Preclassic or Classic period mounds and plazas. This means that the entire area was either depopulated during this period or it had populations greatly dispersed over the whole region and not integrated into a hierarchical network of communities. Future work may reveal that Early Postclassic occupations are buried beneath Late Postclassic structures and can only be found by intensive surface collection or excavations.

The inescapable conclusion is that the region must have been relatively open for internal growth and/or colonization during the first century or two after the Terminal Classic abandonment. Whether or not growth could occur would depend upon both the internal social, economic, and political dynamics, and the kinds of and potential for interactions with neighboring regions. If earlier periods of growth were spurred on by the need to produce for exportation then the condition of the external markets would greatly affect the overall ability of the society to maintain growth.

The timing of political and economic growth in the upper Grijalva region is important because it allows a determination of the nature of interregional interactions and their potential for stimulating local growth. The first major period of growth took place during the Late Preclassic period, and the closest links were with Chiapa de Corzo, one of the most important early centers in Mesoamerica (Lowe and Agrinier 1960). The next major period corresponded to the growth of Kaminaljuyú, and other large centers nearby, during the Early Classic period. Finally, during the Postclassic period, growth did not take place until Zaculeu, the Mam capital, and Utatlán, the Quiché capital became integrated into a dominant highland Guatemalan power. One of the central questions of this study is: how did the rise of these centers affect the political development of Postclassic polities in the upper Grijalva region?

The main sites with evidence of Early Postclassic occupation (Figure 5.3) are: El Limón (Tr-13); Canajasté (Tr-69); Los Encuentros (Tr-94); Lagartero (Tr-99); Aguazarca (Tr-227); La Mesa (Tr-376 [RV140]); Guajilar (Co-59); and the unnamed site of Co-54. All of these sites, as well as other smaller ones, will be dealt with in more detail in Chapter 10. I will, however, briefly introduce them here so that the descriptions of Canajasté in the following chapters can be seen in a regional context.

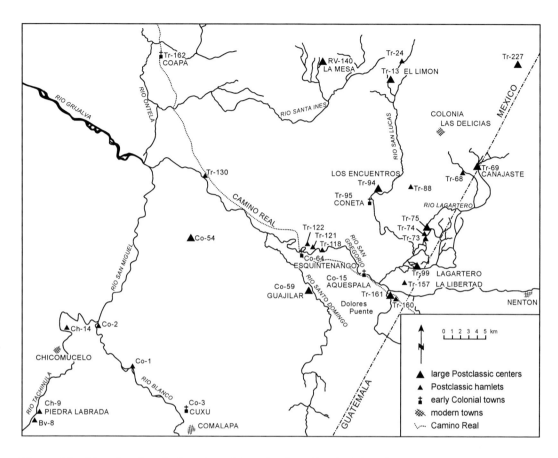

Figure 5.3. Map showing the location of Postclassic and Colonial Period sites.

El Limón appears to have been constructed and occupied entirely during the Postclassic period. It is located near the headwaters of the San Lucas River about 12 km upstream from Los Encuentros. The site sits on a low ridge overlooking the valley but is not highly defensible. It may have an Early Postclassic component below the Late Postclassic (Tan phase AD 1250-1525) structures, but as yet no excavation has been carried out.

At Los Encuentros, on the San Lucas River, Lee and Bryant (n.d.a) excavated parts of several structures in the site's center and found a substantial Late Classic occupation, one responsible for most of the mound construction at the site. In the deposits were some sherds of Early Postclassic age, primarily Tohil Plumbate (Lee 1978b; Shephard 1948). There were also

some figurines and spindle whorls made from Fine Orange paste that probably came from the Gulf Coast Lowlands (Becquelin and Baudez 1979-82; Berlin 1956; Lee and Bryant n.d.a;). Still, most of the Postclassic construction at the site appears to be a Late Postclassic veneer over the Classic mounds or the construction of long low mounds in the Postclassic style. There was some refurbishing of the main plaza with the addition of a long low mound flanking it on one side.

Lagartero had surface evidence of a large Late Postclassic occupation, including numerous house mounds that have now been destroyed by agricultural activity. Late ceramic vessels and offerings were placed on several of the large mounds, and many of these rolled down the sides causing sherds to become scattered over the main plaza zone and to become intermingled with the earlier deposits (Ekholm pers. comm.). But the Early Postclassic occupation seems to be restricted only to the beginning of that period, with several burials in the main plaza containing plumbate vessels and other ceramics in Early Postclassic styles. However, there was no construction dating to this period.

Aguazarca was discovered by Ronald Lowe in 1980 (Clark and Lowe n.d.) but, so far, little is known about it other than that it has a small residential zone surrounding some civic-ceremonial structures on a fortified ridge.

La Mesa was discovered by De Montmollin in 1983 (he assigned it the additional number: RV140). De Montmollin (pers. comm.) thinks it is mainly Early Postclassic, and, if so, it would be one of the largest Early Postclassic sites in the entire study region.

Little is known about Co-54 except that it was a large Classic center with scatters of Early and Late Postclassic ceramics on the surface. Some of the Early Postclassic sherds were Tohil Plumbate.

At Guajilar, Lee's excavations uncovered some Late Classic house platforms that had been rebuilt during the Early Postclassic (Nichim phase AD 900-1250) (Bryant and Clark n.d.; Lee 1978a). Notably, there was not much evidence of Postclassic rebuilding of the mounds or construction of new ceremonial mounds. The Late Postclassic occupation seems to have been restricted to the intrusion of "water jar" cremation burials in the main Preclassic and Classic period mounds.

All of the sites, with either Late Postclassic (Tan phase AD 1250-1525) or both Late and Early Postclassic (Nichim phase AD 900-1250) occupational evidence, are relatively small and have little civic-ceremonial architecture that can be attributed to those periods. The basic dichotomy is between sites that re-use older centers versus those that are completely new occupations. One hypothesis that explains this is that the people who re-used older sites were, in fact, descendants of the earlier communities and represent a long-time local population. Re-using the older buildings and putting burials in the older mounds would act as a validation of

ancestral genealogies and link the residents to the region. In contrast, communities founded in new locations by immigrants, and which were not physically associated with older centers, probably would have little to gain by claiming descent from or association with local ancestors. Instead, they would probably emphasize that their social status derives from nonlocal elite lineages, perhaps in the neighboring regions from whence they came. Canajasté falls into the category of Postclassic settlements founded in a completely new location.

I will not describe the Late Postclassic sites and their relations in this section since they are treated fully in Chapter 10. However, I should mention that there were a total of 26 sites with definite or probable Late Postclassic occupations. When the analysis of the reconnaissance data is completed I am sure that this total will increase somewhat. Most of these are represented only by small scatters of Postclassic ceramics on the surface of larger sites occupied during the Preclassic or Classic periods. The next section will briefly discuss the Early Colonial settlements in the upper Grijalva region.

Early Colonial Period (AD 1525-1800)

Lee's work on the Coxoh-Tzeltal Early Colonial period archaeology and ethnohistory provides another comparative base for this study (Lee 1979a, 1979b, 1980a, 1980b; Lee and Markman 1977, 1979). Soon after the Conquest, the Spaniards gathered the population into several communities along the *Camino Real*, or royal highway linking the *capitanía* of Guatemala in Guatemala City with Ciudad Real (San Cristobal de Las Casas) in the highlands of Chiapas. According to Lee and Markman (1977:58):

> Three of the most important villages, Aquespala, Escuintenango, and Coapa, were located on the Camino Real that ran between San Cristobal de las Casas and Guatemala City, seat of the Capitanía de Guatemala which also included the modern Mexican state of Chiapas. Escuintenango and Coapa were both over night stopping

points on this route. Coneta and Cuxu, the other Coxoh villages, were located well away from the Camino Real.

These towns as well as several others throughout Chiapas were founded as *pueblos de indios* for the express purpose of congregating Indians in more manageable communities—both in terms of conversion to Catholicism and taxation. Figure 5.3 shows the location of these *reducciones*, as such towns were called throughout much of New Spain. Lee (1980b:21) says that none of the Coxoh-Tzeltal towns were founded on Postclassic period communities since:

> The Spanish priests were, of course, interested in moving the native population away from old locales, in order to remove it from the sight of the architectural remains of the pre-Columbian religion. Another reason, not often considered in this regard, is that to try and restructure a community on the site of an already existing one would obviously be hampered by the native land tenure system and individual interests already acquired, recognized and functioning. Since it can be demonstrated, that in the pre-Columbian era the native leaders tended to live as near their community center as the Spanish did in theirs, the re-use of a native community center site could have put into conflict the very elements the Spanish needed as collaborators in order to control the population without the constant presence of their standing army which was already stretched too thin.

In addition to these reasons, the Spanish priests may have been confronted with drastically reduced population levels within the first 20 years after conquest (Gerhard 1979; MacLeod 1973; Wasserstrom 1983a, 1983b). In the upper Grijalva region the populations were already small and relatively dispersed to begin with (Lee 1980b:21), so any further decline resulting from epidemics may have forced many natives to abandon their communities. Late Postclassic centers in the upper Grijalva region could well have been reduced to small villages even before the Spaniards began to congregate the remnants

of the pre-Conquest population into Early Colonial reducciones.

The two Early Colonial communities nearest to Canajasté were Coneta and Aquespala. Both of them were probably founded in the early 1500s not long after the initial Spanish contact in 1528 (Lee 1980b:23). Although the exact date of abandonment is not known, both may have been empty by the early or mid-1700s (Lee 1980b; Lee and Markman 1977:60). Coneta was located only 2 km from the Postclassic center of Los Encuentros, and much of the population may have originally come from that community. Lee (1980b:21) found a minimum of 87 houses at the site and estimates that it was one of the smaller Colonial towns. Aquespala is badly preserved but is thought to be smaller than Coapa, another of the Colonial sites investigated by Lee, which has an estimated 325 domestic residences (Lee 1980b:21). Aquespala is located 7 km downstream from the Postclassic center of Lagartero and is 18.5 km from Canajasté.

Unfortunately, no documents have yet been found that suggest where the people who made up these Spanish Colonial pueblos de indios came from, so it is impossible at this point to tell if any of them, and presumably this would mean the closest one, Coneta, received residents from Canajasté. One way of determining this would be to compare the house styles at the Colonial sites with those at the Late Postclassic sites to see if any strong similarities existed. Postclassic sites with residences most similar to those at a given Colonial site would be the most likely candidates for identification as the source communities of the Colonial population. To date, not enough is yet known about the range of Postclassic house styles in the upper Grijalva region to do this.

THE CANAJASTÉ PROJECT

During the summer of 1980, at Thomas Lee's invitation, I began an analysis of the settlement data from his 1973-74 reconnaissance as part of a report on the project's findings (Lee et al. n.d.). Most of the site maps were sketched in on the survey forms, and I was using these to describe the sites. When I reached Tr-69 (Canajasté's site number in the Trinitaria designation scheme) there was no sketch map. As it turned out, earlier that year, while excavating at the Camcum rockshelter, only 2 km northwest of Canajasté, Lee was able to have the NWAF's topographer at the time (Kristi S. Butterwick) complete a detailed contour map of the site. When I saw the pencil draft version of the map it was immediately clear that the site was completely different from the dozens of Late/Terminal Classic sites that I had already described for the report. From the map I could see that a loop in the river served as a moat for the community by enclosing all but one side of the village center. Across the only vulnerable neck of land the villagers had erected a stone wall. The remains of dozens of house terraces and platforms were jammed within the walled zone and made up a densely packed settlement. Upstream, on both sides of the river, the rest of the villagers built their houses (Figure 5.4). But most striking, compared with the bulk of the settlements in the region, was that there was not a single pyramidal mound over two meters high in the ceremonial center. Instead, all the civic-ceremonial structures were long low buildings. Even small Terminal Classic communities of a few dozen houses had at least one large, square-shaped pyramid mound. The ceremonial structures at Canajasté looked more like the kinds of structures used for elaborate house platforms during earlier periods, while tall pyramids were completely lacking.

Judging by the site plan, which looked like the Postclassic settlements described in archaeological reports in the western highlands of Guatemala (Borhegyi 1956; Fox 1978; La Farge and Byers 1931; Shook 1952; Smith 1955; Wauchope 1970), I was convinced that the site was Postclassic. The sample of artifacts collected from the site during the initial reconnaissance, and then later during the mapping project, was brought out of storage and re-examined. With the help of Thomas Lee and Douglas Bryant, who had excavated at the other Postclassic site of Los Encuentros, we determined that the sample of sherds was Late Postclassic in age.

Based on this evidence we organized a weekend trip to the site during the *canicula*, a short break in the summer rainy season, in July of 1980. I wanted to excavate some small test pits in the residential area to determine the depth of the deposits and to see how well they corresponded to the surface collections. In addition, I hoped to make more extensive surface collections in both the zones inside and outside the wall. Three 1 by 1 m test pits were excavated within the walled zone and surface samples of artifacts were collected from all parts of the site. I noted then that several structures in the main plaza were very badly looted, as Lee had observed during his first visit to the site in 1973.

The Surface Remains and 1980 Test Excavations

Initial test excavations and surface collections were aimed at increasing the sample of artifacts from the site and finding out whether there were any earlier components. Parts of the site had been recently tilled by hand for milpa planting and so we were able to collect many ceramics and stone tools. The ceramics were all similar to Late Postclassic ceramics from neighboring sites that had been tested earlier during the NWAF's excavations. They included forms that were diagnostic of the Late period, such as tall-necked water jars with strap handle lugs and red-and-black polychrome geometric designs (Lowe 1959; Navarrete 1962; Wauchope 1970), hemispherical bowls with the same polychrome decoration on the interior, plainware jar fragments poorly fired and containing both fine- and coarse-ground calcite temper, flat ceramic griddles, and both large- and small-holed colanders. There were no ceramics that suggested any occupation earlier than the Postclassic period and nothing to indicate even an Early Postclassic occupation.

One of the main discoveries from the testpit excavations was that the deposits were, at most, only about 30 cm deep. This, combined with the strictly Late Postclassic ceramics, led me to expect a very short occupation of perhaps no more than 250 years. After completing the

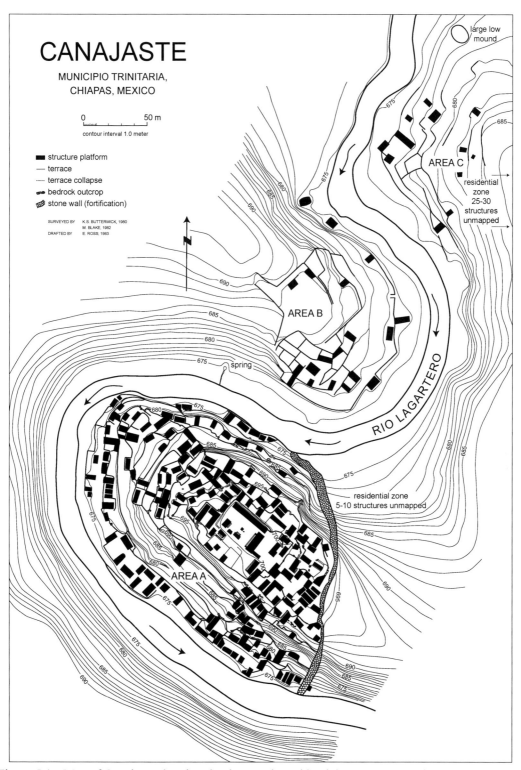

Figure 5.4. Map of Canajasté showing the three main residential areas: A, B, and C.

large-scale excavations it turned out that this
expectation was wrong and that there was
a substantial Early Postclassic occupation
buried beneath the Late Postclassic structures.
Nevertheless, the surface itself represented the
latter part of the community's occupation and
based on the initial testing I thought that, at
Canajasté, I had found the archaeological record
of a relatively short-lived Postclassic town. It
soon became clear, though, that it was nothing
of the sort, and instead, the site was a record of
continuous change over the community's four-
century long history.

The surface collections from the site yielded
124 pieces of obsidian, primarily blade sections
and primarily from the San Martín Jilotepeque
source in Guatemala. John Clark (n.d.) analyzed
the test collections and found that: (1) almost
twice as much obsidian came from San Martín
Jilotepeque as from El Chayal, (2) that the
density of obsidian in the test pits (no./m^3) was
significantly higher than from almost all other
sites in the upper Grijalva region and, (3) that
there were numerous projectile points in the
sample, again, more than found in other sites of
similar time period.

Combined with this, the initial collections
yielded other items that could only have
come to the site from well outside the region:
porous basalt from highland areas to the east,
other types of obsidian from Central Mexico,
serpentine or greenstone from the rivers that
drain the highlands, and marine shell from
the Pacific or Gulf Coasts. These items, and
the possibility of finding many more different
imports, suggested that the site would be a
good candidate for investigating the process of
interregional exchange.

The large number of projectile points
found on the surface suggested that there was
a likelihood that warfare was important in the
site's history. This of course contributed to the
impression already formed by the community's
location on a gooseneck in the river with the
only accessible approach blocked by a stone
wall 230 m long and 2.5 m high. The walled
zone enclosed an area of three hectares within
which were packed at least 200 houses. This
density of 66 houses per hectare is many times

that of any other site studied so far in the entire
upper Grijalva survey region. It also indirectly
suggests that warfare was a major part of
the interregional processes into which the
community was drawn.

The mapped house remains that covered
the surface of the site were generally in good
condition. But they were also much less
substantial than house remains from some
earlier sites. The vast majority consisted of
only one or two courses of unworked limestone
cobbles outlining a rectangle, with the length
approximately twice the width, much like
Postclassic houses reported in other parts of
the Maya area (Chase 1981; Fauvet 1973, 1981;
Heighway 1973; Hill 1982; Ichon 1975). Few
were visibly raised on platforms and those
that were elevated were, at most, 30 cm above
their terrace. There had been little modern
disturbance to the residential part of the site, and
that which had taken place resulted from natural
erosion or hand tilling. There has been little
or no stone robbing for modern constructions
primarily because there is no large settlement
nearby. Therefore, with the site cleared of
vegetation, the layout of the community must be
much as it was shortly after abandonment and
collapse of the buildings.

Because of the relative lack of disturbance,
it was easy to discern differences among the
structures from their surface remains alone.
The houses were either isolated or in small patio
groups (called "house groups" throughout this
study), ranging from two to four houses each.
Three things were apparent from my initial
reconnaissance of the site: (1) the largest houses
were also the ones with the most worked stone
in their platform retaining walls; (2) the largest
houses were in the largest house groups; and (3)
they were located nearest the ceremonial center
within the walled zone.

Based on these characteristics: size of
houses, number of houses in house group, height
of platform, amount of worked stone in platform,
and proximity to the main plaza, I found only
three groups of houses that might have belonged
to the highest-ranking elite households in the
community. These are House Group 2 (with
Structures 21, 22, and 23), House Group 26

(with Structures 36, 37, 38, and 39) and House Group 27 (with Structures 15, 16, and 17). All are immediately adjacent to the ceremonial center and would have had more access to this zone than any other households.

All other house groups within the walled zone, although smaller and less well constructed than the so-called elite groups, are not very different from them. There is less diversity and differentiation among house groups in this community, presumably the most important in the region, than there was within tertiary Terminal Classic sites such as El Rosario (Tr-142) and Los Cimientos.

Even though there was not the same degree of differentiation in house labor investment at Canajasté as at other sites during earlier periods, that which was visible was fairly obvious. The largest house in House Group 2, the group closest to the main plaza, was 15 m long and 5 m wide, one third again the length of most other houses at the site. Furthermore, its platform was raised about 50 cm above the house group patio and was faced with worked stone which may have been plastered over. This was enough evidence to suggest that there was some social differentiation within the community. But, in addition to this, there is also the inside wall/outside wall division. Another 100 or so houses are located outside the wall across the river in Areas B and C. Not all of these structures have been mapped in the same detail as within the walled zone, but those that have been mapped indicate generally the same range of styles and sizes as the majority of houses inside the wall. Only one structure approaches the size of Structure 22 in House Group 2, and that is a 14 m long house in Area C; however, it is associated with two other relatively small houses in its group, and its platform consists of only two courses of unworked cobbles.

Based on the surface remains of house groups alone, the site appeared to have enough social differentiation (1) to make an elite/non-elite distinction and (2) to test for the differential effects of the various processes on these two classes through time. In addition, the ceremonial center was preserved enough to map it accurately and to compare the plans with centers at other neighboring sites. Furthermore, because many of the structures were looted, it would be possible to peer into the looters' pits and look for evidence of earlier structures or structural rebuilding.

Structure 9 was the most remarkable of the ceremonial structures but also the most disturbed (Figures 5.5 and 5.6). It had masonry walls that were replastered and repainted as many as nine times. Still evident on the scattered plaster fragments in the looters' heaps were blue, green, red, yellow, and black paint, obviously remnants of a mural. The presence of a small temple at the site with such elaborate painting and such obvious ceremonial importance suggests that there must also have been local nobility. All available ethnohistoric evidence for the Maya area clearly states that the priests who ran the temples were members of the nobility. Only nobles and their priests could have supported such an endeavor at Canajasté, and only they could have directed the ceremonial activities indicated by such a structure. Therefore, the ceremonial complex with the Structure 9 temple provides additional evidence for social stratification at the site.

A comparison between Canajasté and other upper Grijalva region sites will be made in later sections. Nevertheless, at this point it is worth mentioning that there do seem to be more differences than similarities between Canajasté and other Postclassic sites such as Los Encuentros, Lagartero, and El Limón.

Selection of Canajasté for Excavation

Canajasté was chosen for a large-scale excavation project in order to study the specific processes of change in a secondary state. It was chosen for the following reasons. First, the preliminary mapping, surface collections, and test excavations at the site showed that it was one of the largest and most complex centers during the Late Postclassic period and, thus, likely to have been the center of a small state participating in the processes under consideration here. Second, there was also evidence that the site was actually involved in both interregional exchange and warfare.

Figure 5.5.   Structure 9 before excavation. This building had been severely looted a few years before we arrived at the site. The walls had been knocked down and all that remained was a pile of rubble.

Third, preliminary tests suggested that the site was built anew during the Postclassic, with no earlier occupation, and, therefore, it represented either a relocation of local populations or a migration of colonizing peoples into the area. Fourth, some of the differences between Canajasté and other sites already investigated in the study area, such as construction of civic-ceremonial architecture and layout of community center, suggested that the site may have been a colony from neighboring Guatemala. Apart from these four reasons, Canajasté was also clearly one of the most important Postclassic centers in the upper Grijalva region and any additional information that could be collected would be useful for understanding the Postclassic prehistory of southeastern Mexico and western Guatemala.

The next chapter will discuss the excavation strategy and describe the changes in domestic architecture that will be used to evaluate the relative importance of the four processes in the site's history.

ENDNOTES

1   In subsequent years De Montmollin has continued to survey more zones within the upper Grijalva region and has been able to add detailed information about several hundred more sites (De Montmollin 1995).

2   See Clark, Lee, et al. (2005) for a recent summary of the archaeological projects, the time periods, and ceramic phases in the upper Grijalva region.

Figure 5.6. Close-up of wall sections of Structure 9. These toppled wall sections still retain a stucco layer surface over well-prepared masonry.

CHAPTER 6

THE HOUSE GROUP EXCAVATIONS

EXCAVATION STRATEGY

I chose an excavation strategy that facilitated the recovery of as much evidence as possible for change in the houses through their life spans. I needed to know the sequence of architectural and artifact changes in each house in order to compare these changes from house to house. The goal of comparing trajectories of changes in houses, rather than reconstructions of individual houses, dictated the excavation strategy. I had originally planned to excavate a large sample, somewhere between one-quarter and one-half, of each house and thereby collect all the requisite information about their feature and artifact changes. But, after excavating two houses in their entirety, I became convinced that a great deal of evidence for individual house floors would have been missed. In some cases a small sample of the house would have led to a misinterpretation of the pattern of household evolution. This, in turn, would have made it difficult to infer the processes under study. For example, had I simply excavated a small portion of some houses they would have looked like single constructions with few modifications. In the case of Structure 2, I would have missed the entire first four phases of house construction and would have misidentified the deposits and sequences of constructions. In fact, Structure 2 went through one of the most complex series of constructions and destructions of all the excavated houses.

Therefore, each house was completely excavated. This strategy slowed excavation considerably, but the information recovered from each structure was extremely detailed.[1] In the end I was able to excavate seven houses belonging to three separate house groups. The modifications to each house group are as important to understanding the evolution of the household as are the modifications to

any individual house; hence, I decided to excavate as many houses in each group as possible. In fact, the sequence of additions to a house group could be even more important for understanding household changes than the sequence of modifications to a single house. Thus, the general strategy was to excavate entire house groups rather than sample one structure from each group. This also helped to avoid the problem of functional differentiation among the structures; for example, a kitchen in one group was not compared to a living structure in another.

SAMPLE SELECTION

The sample of house groups selected for study was chosen as follows. There were three main residential areas at the site (Areas A, B, and C; Figure 5.4), and within each area was a large number of houses, most of which fell into house groups (also called patio groups) ranging up to three houses per group. I had hoped to excavate at least one house group from each area and, if possible, two. Neither aim was accomplished. Instead, I excavated three house groups from Area A (Figure 6.1). These three house groups comprise the entire sample of excavated house platforms and, unfortunately, the two other residential areas remain unsampled. The house groups that I did excavate were selected judgmentally. The main criterion used was one of relative "eliteness." In order to search for evidence of the specific processes, I needed a sample of elite houses to compare with a sample of non-elite houses. Since there was no certain way of picking houses that may have belonged to each of these social strata, I had to choose house groups from each pole of the spectrum. By choosing a house group that appeared, on the surface, to be the largest and most elaborate at the site, I was sure to include

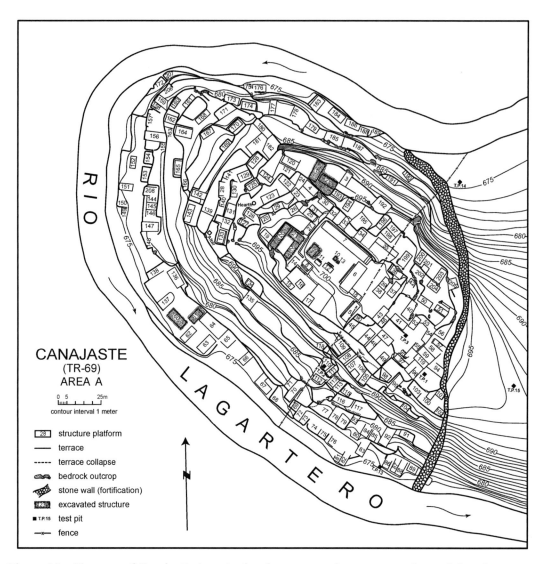

Figure 6.1.   Plan map of Canajasté, Area A, showing excavated structures and test pit locations.

the remains of at least one elite household. And, by choosing a house group that appeared to be as unelaborated as possible, compared with the supposed elite group, I was likely to include the remains of a non-elite household. In terms of this distinction, I excavated one elite group (House Group 2) consisting of Structures 21, 22 and 23, and two non-elite house groups. One of these, House Group 1, was comprised of Structures 1, 2, and possibly 3, while the other, House Group 25, was comprised of Structures 60 and 61.

House Group 2, located near the ceremonial center, was the largest elite residence at the site and chosen specifically for that reason (Figure 6.2). House Group 1 was chosen because it was the best preserved of the simple groups of house platforms visible during the initial stages of site clearing. Later in the fieldwork, when the site was more thoroughly cleared, we observed that there were many more house groups similar to Group 1. House Group 25 was chosen for excavation after we had completed excavation of the other two groups. In House

Figure 6.2. House Group 2 prior to excavation. Structure 22 is in left foreground,
Structure 21 in upper right, and patio area in center-right of photo (facing NE).

Group 2, I discovered the first clear evidence
for an Early Postclassic occupation of the site.
Structure 22 in that group appeared to have
been continuously occupied since the initial
founding of the community, sometime late in
the Early Postclassic period. House Group 1, on
the other hand, had little evidence of this early
occupation.

It was essential, therefore, to determine
whether any other house groups had been
occupied or constructed during the Early
Postclassic. I especially wanted to know if any
non-elite house groups in Area A had an early
occupation, so I chose another house group in
a different part of Area A. This house group
(House Group 25) appeared to have been built
upon a small terrace and had the potential of
covering earlier houses or midden deposits.
It did, in fact, have more Early Postclassic
deposits contemporaneous with the earliest
one in the elite House Group 2. I was therefore

able to increase the sample of Early Postclassic
deposits but only at the price of not being able
to afford the time to excavate in any other of
the residential areas. However, in terms of my
overall understanding of the site's development,
the trade-off was worth it.

Dating the House Groups

Based on the analysis of ceramics and
comparisons with other excavated sites in
the region, it was immediately clear that the
excavated houses dated to the Postclassic
period (Navarrete 1962, 1966; Wauchope
1970). As discussed in Chapter 7, the only
ceramics recovered that appeared to predate
the Postclassic period consisted of a few highly
eroded Classic period sherds, most of which
were found in construction fill. Even so, I
thought it would be useful to obtain some carbon
14 dates from each house group. Appendix A

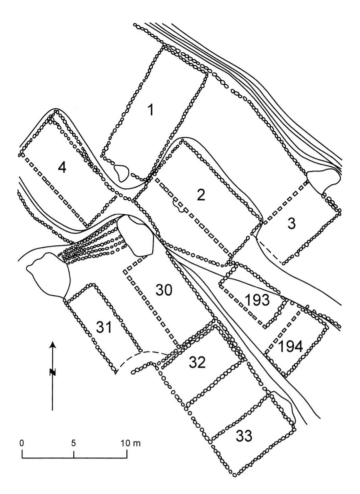

Figure 6.3.   Plan map of House Group 1 showing location of the main structures in the group (1, 2, and possibly 3) as well as some of the neighboring house remains from other unexcavated groups.

presents a more detailed analysis of the five radiocarbon samples submitted for analysis. All five samples fell between AD 1150 and AD 1635 (calibrated), in other words, the late end of the Early Postclassic period to the end of the Late Postclassic period, and into the Early Colonial period (although there is no evidence of occupation post-1525).

SUMMARY OF HOUSE GROUP EXCAVATIONS

This section will briefly introduce the reader to the main characteristics of each of the

house groups. The next section will describe, in much more detail, the trajectories of changes through which each house in each group passed.

House Group 1 (Non-elite)

This group is located on the north side of Area A. It consists of two and possibly three separate structures that formed a U-shape around a small patio (Figure 6.3). The group sits on a terrace that is about 12 m wide and follows the contour of the hillside midway between the river and the ceremonial center. The open side of the patio drops off steeply to the next terrace

Figure 6.4. House Group 1. View of Structure 2 in the foreground showing one of its fully excavated floors. At the top of the photo (facing NW) is Structure 1 (with screen and backdirt piles on top of it). To the left is a small patio area between Structure 2 and the terrace that rises up to the adjacent house group. The photo is taken from Structure 3.

4 m below. Upslope is a series of house terraces and on either side are more house groups.

In this house group only two structures were completely excavated, Structures 1 and 2, although Structure 3 probably was associated with the patio (Figure 6.4). Structure 3 was smaller than the other two structures and one end had eroded off towards the house group on the terrace below. Like most house groups in this part of the site, some of the structures have their long axis parallel to the terrace while others are perpendicular to it. Both Structures 1 and 3 are perpendicular to the terrace, reaching from the terrace riser below to the riser above. They thereby effectively cut off all access along the length of the terrace. To obtain access to the house group one would have had to either climb down though the house group above or

climb up through the house group below or go through the structures themselves. This limited access to the house group is characteristic of the site. It is a style of house group layout that appears to be associated with the latter half of the site's occupation and may be related to either an increased need to restrict traffic flow in such a crowded settlement or with a defensive settlement configuration.

Structure 1

This 11 m by 4 m house, whose long axis bisects the terrace, cuts off all traffic along the terrace from the west. The house was well defined and visible on the surface as a raised mound of earth about 40 cm high and outlined by a retaining wall of unworked cobbles about two to three courses high. All the artifacts

Figure 6.5. Structure 2, stone steps leading from house patio to Floor 1.

recovered appear to be Late Postclassic, probably the later half.

Structure 2

When the site was first cleared, this structure was only visible as a small terrace sitting about 1.5 m above the main terrace on which stood the whole house group (Figure 6.4). The small terrace measured 12 m by 7 m. There were no indications of house foundations on the surface, but as we excavated, it became clear that there were foundations for an earlier house that had been buried beneath slope-wash. Below this partly buried house foundation were four and possibly five superimposed, earth floors. After the last one had been destroyed, the terrace was expanded and a long rectangular house platform was built, partially covering the earlier house deposits. This new house was the same style as Structure 1. It was a long, narrow platform of earth construction fill retained

with one to two courses of squared-stone slabs. Structure 2 had very few features besides the retaining walls and floors. One set of stone steps led from the house down to an enclosed private patio between the house and the back terrace riser (Figure 6.5). From that patio another set of three stone steps led down to Structure 1.

The artifacts collected provide evidence of a long Late Postclassic occupation; however, upon closer analysis of the ceramic collections, the lowest floor (Floor 4) proved to have a high frequency of Early Postclassic ceramics, perhaps making it contemporaneous with Structure 22 in House Group 2.

House Group 2 (Elite)

This house group consisted of three house structures, all of which were excavated (Figure 6.6). The group is located immediately adjacent to the ceremonial center and is the largest and

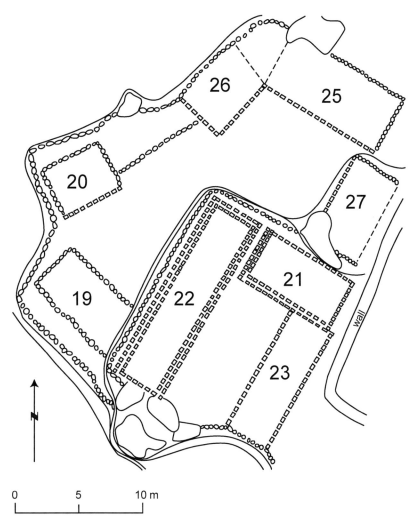

Figure 6.6. Plan map of House Group 2 showing the location of the house platforms (Structures 21, 22, and 23) and several unexcavated houses nearby.

most elaborate at the site. It functioned as a set of domestic structures from its inception and might have belonged to the ruling group (the highest ranking lineage).

The three structures in this group are arranged around a small U-shaped patio. They are tightly clustered and, in fact, two of the structures actually share a wall. The open side of the patio drops off to a small terrace about 1 m below. The house group sits on a large terrace at one of the highest points of the site, just below the level of the ceremonial center.

Structure 21

This house was a low rectangular platform clearly visible on the surface, as were all the houses in the group. It measured 10 m by 4.5 m and was about 30 cm high. It became clear only after the complete excavation of neighboring Structure 22 that this house was built after Structure 22 had been occupied for a long time. Whereas Structure 22 had been built during the Early Postclassic period, Structure 21 was added to the group during the beginning of the Late Postclassic period.

Figure 6.7. Structure 22, showing full length of the house with Floor 1
removed and exposing construction fill beneath (facing NE).

Structure 22

This house was the largest at the site and
certainly the most impressive in the house
group. It was begun during the Early Postclassic
period and predated the other two structures in
the group. It is the earliest house excavated and
may well be one of the earliest at the site.

The initial structure was a 10 m by 5 m
rectangular platform. The side facing upslope
towards the house group's patio was only
30 cm high while the downslope side of the
platform formed a 2 m high terrace. During
the initial occupation of the house, refuse
was tossed off the end of the platform and
accumulated at the base of the house platform.
These refuse deposits were capped and sealed
in by extensions of the house's length and
replasterings of its floor. The house platform
was extended in length and width during the
Late Postclassic until it totaled 15 m long by 5 m

wide (Figure 6.7). The artifacts recovered in the
midden layers show that the occupants had ready
access to exchange items as early as the Early
Postclassic period, and this continued into the
Late Postclassic (see Chapter 7). This house had
the most evidence for continuous reconstruction
and renovation, and it had the largest proportion
of nonlocal artifacts. If it was not the ruler's
residence then it must have belonged to high-
ranking nobles.

Structure 23

This was the smallest structure in the house
group, measuring 8 m by 4 m. It was also the
last to have been built and, in fact, the builders
tacked it onto Structure 21 so that one end of
it shared a wall with that house. The form of
construction was the same as the others: it had
a stone slab retaining wall of only two to three
courses, reaching a height of about 20 cm, with

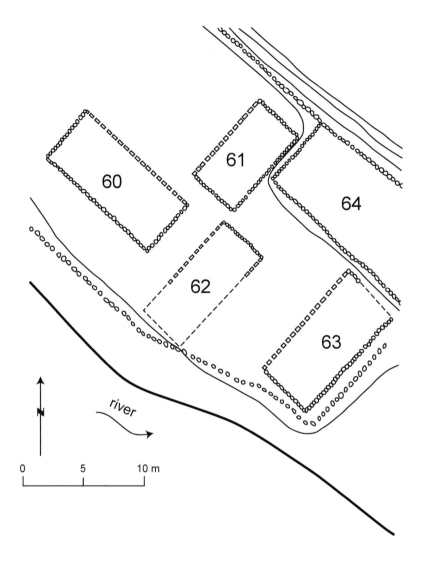

Figure 6.8.   Plan map of House Group 25 showing the location of the main house platforms (Structures 60 and 61). Several other house platforms in neighboring groups are also shown.

cobble construction fill. Most of the artifacts dated to the Late Postclassic period.

House Group 25 (Non-elite)

As already mentioned, this house group was excavated to increase the sample of Early Postclassic deposits. There were no indications on the surface that this had an early component, but the platforms were large enough and on

terraces so that they could have been built upon earlier deposits.

The group was located on the south side of Area A but almost as far away from the ceremonial center as possible. It sat 12 m from the river's edge. The group consisted of two visible structures that formed an L-shaped configuration around a large patio (Figure 6.8). Both structures rested on small terraces raised no more than 50 cm on their downslope sides. Because the group was situated at the base of the

Figure 6.9. Structure 60, showing the layer of construction fill underlying Floor 1 and the large boulder and stone slab used as retaining wall (facing N).

steep hill leading up to the ceremonial center, portions of the structures nearest to the slope were covered with eroded slope-wash from above. This increased the chances that earlier deposits had been sealed beneath the visible structures.

Structure 60

This structure was an 11 m by 4.5 m house with foundations consisting of stone cobbles and slabs. The long axis of the house was parallel to the river. The side nearest the river was formed by a 60 cm high retaining wall constructed of two to three courses of large cobbles and boulders (Figure 6.9). The side facing away from the river fronted the patio and was formed by only one course of well-trimmed slabs.

Within the platform were found at least two successive floors. Below them were an earlier retaining wall and an earlier house

below the structure. The earlier structure was only partially covered by Structure 60; the rest of it extended beneath the unexcavated patio. An Early Postclassic midden associated with this structure was excavated. The main part of Structure 60 was Late Postclassic.

Structure 61

This structure was a 10 m by 4.5 m house built on a small terrace-platform, only 50 cm high on its downslope side. It, too, was Late Postclassic but, unlike Structure 60, had no underlying Early Postclassic deposits. The platform retaining wall was made of a combination of stone slabs and cobbles (Figure 6.10). It had been expanded to widen the building at least once. And, at one stage, a staircase was added on to the side facing the patio. Both this structure and Structure 60 had the best prepared retaining walls facing

Figure 6.10. Structure 61, showing the construction fill under Floor 5 (facing NE). In spite of the large roots that have disturbed part of the floor the architectural features were mostly intact.

the patio, while the sides facing away were constructed of much rougher stones. This was a pattern common throughout the site.

Summary

The excavations of the houses produced a total of 45 separate depositional units, including 27 house floors or parts thereof, 18 middens, earth and ash lenses, and six infant burials. The tables in Appendix B list the excavated deposits for each structure with their unit designations, deposit types and descriptions, excavation lot numbers making up the unit, the total volume of the excavation, and the percentage of each deposit screened. It also presents a time period designation for each. Table 6.1 summarizes this information by time period (Early/Late Postclassic), social stratum (Elite/Non-elite), and

structure and deposit (Floor, Midden, etc.). All disturbed deposits such as slope wash, terrace collapse, and construction fill were omitted from analysis in this study.

TRAJECTORIES OF HOUSEHOLD DEVELOPMENT

This section presents the detailed evidence for change in each of the three house groups. Each underwent a series of changes, both in terms of features and artifacts. Before evaluating the evolution of each household it is first necessary to look at the changes that each individual structure went through. Many of these changes are quite small in nature, such as adding on to the length of a house, re-plastering a floor, placing a burial into the floor, creating a refuse midden off one end of the structure,

Table 6.1. Excavated house structures and deposits used in the analysis: excavation unit numbers, excavation lots per unit, and total excavated volumes (m³)

House	Deposit	Unit	Lots	Volume (m³)
Late Non-Elite				
STR-1	FLR-1	4	3,4,5,6,7,15,16	5.17
	FLR-2		21,23,24,25,26,27	5.31
STR-2	FLR-1	5	3,4,5,6,8,29,33	2.29
	PFL-1		21,22,23,24,31,32	6.41
	FLR-2		45,46,47,48	4.62
	FLR-3		50,51	2.01
	MID-1		14	.11
	MID-2		15	.18
	MID-3		16	.26
	MID-4		25,26	1.83
	MID-5		27	.16
	MID-6		28	.24
	MID-7		30	.42
STR-60	FLR-1	10	1,2,3,4,5,6	8.45
	FLR-2		15,16,17	1.48
	MID-1		18,19,20,21,22,23	4.56
STR-61	FLR-1	11	3,4	2.52
	FLR-2		7,8,9	1.51
	FLR-3		1,2,10,11,12	2.99
	FLR-4		13,14,15	1.03
	FLR-5		17,18,19,20,21	4.12
Sub-totals				55.67
Early Non-Elite				
STR-2	FLR-4	5	52,53	.72
STR-60	MID-2&3	10	24,25,27,28	1.38
	MID-4		26	1.95
Sub-totals				4.05
Late Elite				
STR-21	FLR-1	8	1,2,3	2.03
	FLR-2		7,8,9	1.62
	FLR-3		12,13	1.41
	FLR-4		14,16	.96
	FLR-5		17,18,19	.80

House	Deposit	Unit	Lots	Volume (m³)
STR-22	FLR-1	7	1,2,3,4,5	10.26
	FLR-2		7,8,9	2.40
	FLR-3		11,12	1.93
STR-23	FLR-1	9	1,2,3,4	2.39
	FLR-2		9,11,12,13	2.85
	FLR-3		14,15,16	2.10
Sub-totals				28.75

Early Elite

STR-22	FLR-4	7	13,14	1.87
	FLR-5/AL-1		6,15,16,17,19,23	2.71
	EL-1		22	.82
	EL-2		25	1.17
	MID-1		20,26	1.24
	MID-2		24	.23
	MID-3		27	.24
	MID-4		29	1.76
	AL-2		30,33	.46
	MID-5		32,34	1.18
Sub-totals				11.68

Summary Sub-Totals

Non-elite	59.72
Elite	40.43
Late Period	84.42
Early Period	15.73

and so on. Taken together, however, these minor changes represent the evolutionary history of the house group.

In the sections that follow I describe the structures within each group in order of construction, beginning with the earliest floors and then continuing to the latest ones. The deposits were numbered sequentially as they were uncovered so that in all cases Floor 1 is the most recent, or stratigraphically uppermost, floor in a house. Chapter 7 presents the artifacts associated with each major architectural change and examines the changing technology and exchange relations in which the households participated.

House Group 1 (Non-elite)

This group of two and possibly three houses went through the following sequence of construction (Figure 6.3). First, a small single terrace was built on the main terrace. Structure 2, in its earliest form, was built directly on the terrace. It must have been a simple structure with an earthen floor and no stone wall base. It went through a series of burnings and rebuildings until, finally, a much larger house was built on the terrace. The terrace itself may have been expanded at this time, but there was no direct evidence for this. At about the same time or perhaps slightly later, Structure 1 was

Table 6.2. Estimated dimensions, length-width ratio, and floor area (m²) for all excavated houses.

House	Floor	Period	Length (m)	Width (m)	Length/ width ratio	Area (m²)
Non-Elite						
STR-1	FLR-1	Late	11.5	5.0	2.3	57.5
	FLR-2	Late	11.5	5.0	2.3	57.5
STR-2	FLR-1	Late	10.4	4.2	2.5	43.7
	FLR-2	Late	7.5	5.5	1.4	41.3
	FLR-3	Late	7.0	4.0	1.8	28.0
	FLR-4	Early	5.0	4.0	1.3	20.0
STR-60	FLR-1	Late	12.0	4.8	2.5	57.6
	FLR-2	Late	12.0	4.8	2.5	57.6
STR-61	FLR-1	Late	8.8	4.4	2.0	38.7
	FLR-2	Late	8.8	4.4	2.0	38.7
	FLR-3	Late	8.8	4.4	2.0	38.7
	FLR-4	Late	8.8	5.2	1.7	45.8
	FLR-5	Late	8.8	4.4	2.0	38.7
Elite						
STR-21	FLR-1	Late	7.8	3.8	2.1	29.6
	FLR-2	Late	8.4	4.4	1.9	37.0
	FLR-3	Late	7.5	4.4	1.7	33.0
	FLR-4	Late	8.2	4.4	1.9	36.1
	FLR-5	Late	8.2	4.4	1.9	36.1
STR-22	FLR-1	Late	15.3	3.8	4.0	58.1
	FLR-2	Late	15.5	4.8	3.2	74.4
	FLR-3	Late	15.5	5.0	3.1	77.5
	FLR-4	Early	15.7	5.0	3.1	78.5
	FLR-5	Early	16.7	5.0	3.3	83.5
	RWA-5	Early	13.9	5.0	2.8	69.5
	RWA-3	Early	11.2	5.0	2.2	56.0
STR-23	FLR-1	Late	10.2	4.4	2.3	47.5
	FLR-2	Late	10.2	4.4	2.3	47.5
	FLR-3	Late	10.2	4.4	2.3	47.5

built. The large terrace on which it sits and on which the whole house group sits may also have been expanded at this time. Both Structure 1 and the latest version of Structure 2 are different from the earlier houses. They are long rectangular structures on low platforms, rather than square buildings closer to the ground. Structure 3 is in the same style as these later structures and so may be contemporaneous, although it is impossible to be certain without excavation.

Structure 2

Since the earliest constructions of Structure 2 were simply earthen floors with no platforms or retaining walls, I do not have as clear an idea of it as I do for the later structures. The first phase of construction was the building of a small terrace approximately 6 m wide and 7 m long. The back edge of the terrace was formed by an irregular bedrock outcrop, while the front edge was a cobble and boulder retaining wall about 1.5 m high. It was filled with earth and cobbles and devoid of artifacts. The first house floor was little more than compacted terrace fill with the bedrock protruding through in many places. If this house had stone retaining walls they could have been removed for later constructions. The floor remnants extend to the back of the terrace, and one wall may have abutted the upslope riser. The floor fronting the terrace edge was not well enough preserved to determine whether the house extended to the edge of the terrace or sat back from it. Likewise, both ends of the house are not well preserved; they suffered from erosion and from later terrace maintenance.

Judging by the shape of the initial terrace, I estimate that the house was about 4 m by 5 m and almost square in shape, with no platform (Table 6.2 presents the dimensions and floor areas for all the excavated houses). The floor (Floor 4) (Figure 6.11) is located directly on top of the construction fill layer with large outcrops of bedrock protruding through it. If the house was built over these bedrock outcrops, then the floor must have been extremely irregular. It seems that this first floor was short-lived; either it was destroyed by the house burning down, or it was replaced by the next floor which was

raised up somewhat higher above the earlier floor. There was a crushed bowl and a crushed olla on the floor. Near one of the burned floor patches was a concentration of charcoal that may have been part of the house superstructure.

The next stage of floor construction was almost identical to the earlier one (Figure 6.12). I estimate the house to have been the same size and shape as the previous one. The floor itself was made of a hard-packed earth that was similar to the one below it: it was a yellowish color and contained a high density of small pebbles. In some areas of the floor, a burned clay surface was well preserved. In others, there were patches, up to a meter in diameter, of unburned, white clay. These small burned patches of Floor 3 were 4 to 5 cm thick and had apparently covered the entire structure to the bedrock outcrops. Overlying these patches of burned floor, as well as in areas where it was not burned, were large chunks of burned wall daub with well-defined cane impressions (Figure 6.13). I infer that this second construction burned to the ground.

There were not as many artifacts on this surface as one would expect from a burned house, but the debris was likely cleared off and used as a fill, perhaps to raise the next house construction even higher above the bedrock outcrops. While the ceramics associated with Floor 4 were primarily Early Postclassic, the ceramics from Floor 3 were more closely related to the Late Postclassic period.

The next phase of house construction was much the same as the previous one, only larger. Its estimated extent was 7.5 m by 5.5 m. Floor 2 was built on top of parts of the collapsed wall material from the previous house (Figure 6.14). Excavations of Floor 2 recovered this burned material as parts of Floor 3 were exposed. In some areas of the house, Floor 2 directly overlaid a rough construction-fill layer. Lying on top of Floor 2 were large pieces of burned wall daub. This structure apparently suffered the same fate as the one below it; it burned to the ground, baking patches of clay floor and preserving pieces of wall material. In some respects, Floor 2 and its walls were different from the previous house. The floor was clay, but

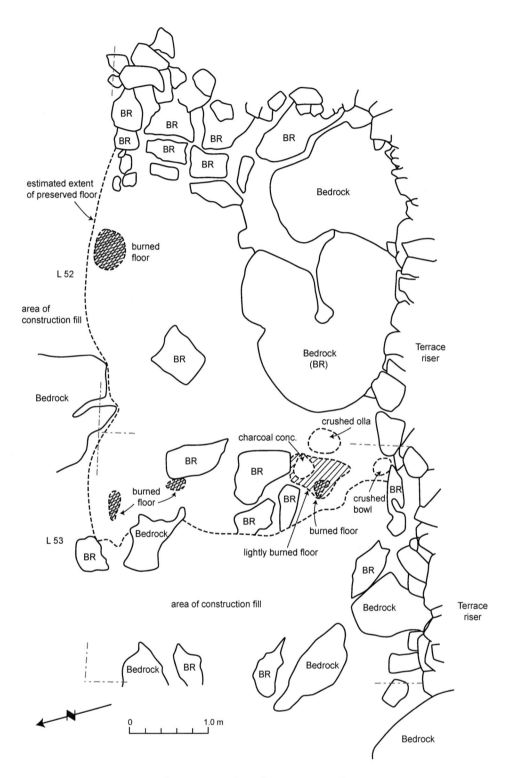

Figure 6.11. Plan of Structure 2, Floor 4.

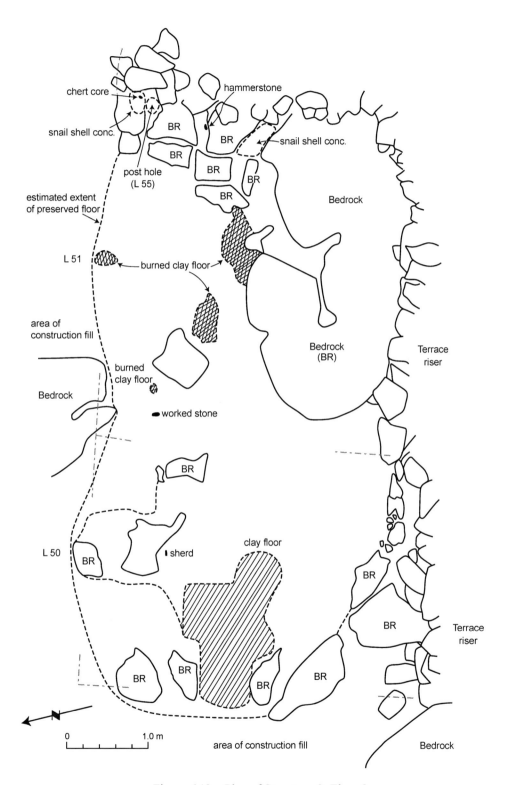

Figure 6.12. Plan of Structure 2, Floor 3.

Figure 6.13.   Structure 2, large fragment (28 cm x 8 cm) of burned wall daub with cane impressions, resting on Floor 2.

a much thinner layer—only 2 to 3 cm thick. The cane impressions in the daub also show that the earlier house used pencil-thin cane in the walls, while the later house walls used cane that was twice as thick. When the house burned down, only patches of the floor were burned and thus well preserved. In most areas the floor was just a hard-packed, level surface that could be traced out between burned patches.

There were large numbers of artifacts in the Floor 2 material, and these are, for the most part, Late Postclassic types.

In excavating Floor 2, I found a patch of a more recent unburned clay floor above it. It was either a later house floor or, a well-prepared part of the patio which covered all of these earlier floor deposits. After the structure associated with Floor 2 had burned down, the whole construction pattern of this house group was changed to that seen for House Group 2—the elite group near the ceremonial center.

The entire house terrace was expanded prior to the construction of the new structure. The terrace was partially cleared off because all traces of the earlier house floors were missing. A stone slab retaining wall was laid down on top of and bisected Floor 2. This wall split the terrace in two along its length. Then, construction fill was brought in to raise the house platform about 30 cm high. This layer of construction fill had to have been brought in from some spot off-site because it consisted of earth mixed with a crumbly white lime rock that is not part of the site's substratum. This new house platform sat on the front edge of the terrace and was 10.5 m long by 4.5 m wide. Part of the terrace, which had been the location of earlier house floors, now became a patio between the new house platform and the riser at the back of the terrace.

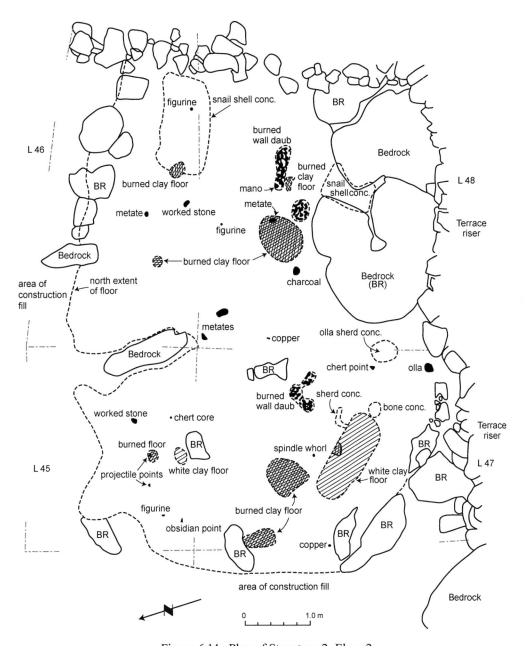

Figure 6.14. Plan of Structure 2, Floor 2.

Access from the house to this small, semi-enclosed patio was not entirely private, since there was a step of three stone slabs leading down from it to the back side of Structure 1.

There were no indications of the type of wall material used for this most recent phase of construction. The floor was only hard-packed earth and, since it had been exposed, was not well preserved. It was unburned. After this house was abandoned the terrace was never reoccupied.

Sometime during occupation of the house, an infant burial was placed beneath the floor and dug into the lime rubble construction fill.

Figure 6.15.   Infant burial in Structure 2 (5/44). Golondrina Unslipped: Calcite Temper Variety jar with fillet banding on shoulder. Jar was covered with a Golondrina Unslipped: Golondrina Variety comal.

It was a relatively simple burial. The dead infant was placed in a large, calcite-tempered olla that had previously been broken. Its base was missing, and the base of a different olla was placed inside it to seal the bottom. The mouth of the olla was loosely sealed with a broken *comal* which, in turn, had a metate fragment placed on top of it. The large comal sherd was placed upside-down over the olla (Figure 6.15; see also Chapter 8,). On its cooking surface were spots, as though drops of some substance, perhaps copal incense or blood, had been burned and left carbonized stains on it before being buried. There were no other inclusions in the burial vessel.

The house floor had few artifacts on or in it. The patio, on the other hand, had a high density of artifacts.

During the occupation of this phase of the house several middens were formed (Figure 6.16). Along the edge of the semi-enclosed patio, just at the base of the terrace riser leading to the houses upslope, the residents accumulated dense concentrations of refuse. One of these, Midden 7, formed on top of the patio and had been capped by a collapse of the terrace riser. Another was a stratified sequence of three midden layers, Middens 6, 5, and 4, with the top layer, Midden 4, capped by terrace collapse. These midden layers were quite restricted in area, but they did have a wide range of artifacts in them. The terrace collapse that had slumped down over the top of these layers, covering the middens as well as the patio, contained a high density of artifacts, many of them Early Postclassic. This means that there must be an earlier house structure or midden directly upslope.

At the base of the terrace supporting Structure 2, directly on top of the house group's main patio, was another small midden,

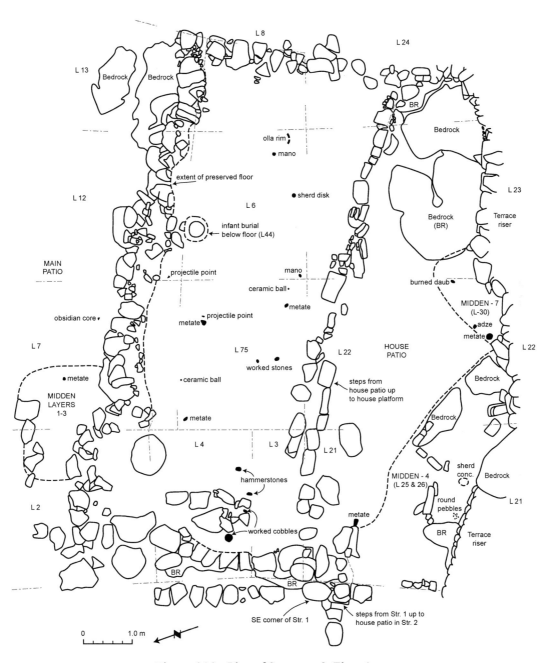

Figure 6.16.   Plan of Structure 2, Floor 1.

consisting of three layers, Midden 3, 2, and 1. The Midden 1 layer was covered by material that had collapsed down from the Structure 2 terrace. There were numerous artifacts of many types in this midden and most derived from the occupants of Structure 2 during its last phase of occupation.

Structure 1

This structure was a late addition to the house group and corresponds to the latest construction phase of Structure 2. At some time prior to the first phase of house construction, the main terrace was built up. Test excavations probed down into the terrace construction fill underlying the house and found that earth and boulders containing very few artifacts had been hauled in to raise the terrace above the tops of the irregular bedrock outcrops. It was on this level terrace that the residents of House Group 1 erected the second main structure. This house was built in the same style as the majority of visible structures on the site's surface and was nearly identical to the most recent version of Structure 2.

Structure 1 was a low building, at first only a few centimeters above the level of the house group's patio, but during later construction, it was raised (Figure 6.17). The floor (Floor 2) was a hard-packed, earthen layer about 5 cm thick that had been covered with a thin (1-2 cm) layer of white lime-clay. The lime-clay layer was preserved in only two areas, one at each end of the house. These patches of floor ranged from 40 cm to 120 cm in diameter, and none of them had been burned. Floor 2 was outlined by a retaining wall that consisted of one to two courses of cobbles and small boulders, none of which had been worked. In the southeast corner, and midway along the east wall, bedrock outcrops had been incorporated into the wall. There was a narrow passageway about 1 m wide between the south end of the house and the terrace riser leading up to the terrace behind the house. This passage way terminated at a set of stone steps, three stones wide, leading up to the inner patio of Structure 2. This layout, combined with the stylistic similarity between the two houses, confirms the impression that Structure 1 was built during the latest occupation of Structure 2. Also, since there was no earlier house below Structure 1 it may well have been an addition to the household group.

In House Structure 1, Floor 2, many artifacts were distributed over the floor, most of which were broken and discarded fragments. There were not, however, enough to indicate any particular activity areas. There are larger features, though, that do suggest activities. A hearth was located near the northwest corner

of Floor 2. It was simply a burned patch of floor 60 to 80 cm in diameter. The hearth was about 8 to 10 cm thick and burned to an orange color, from top to bottom—although it was not fired to a brick hard consistency. This suggests long periods of low heat rather than a short-term intense heat that might be expected from walls and roof burning down (Denis 1982). In Structure 2 the patches of burned floor were much thinner and harder than this hearth.

During the occupation associated with Floor 2, two infants were buried in the northwest corner of the house beneath the floor (see Chapter 8). One of them (L18) was placed (without a container) directly below the floor surface. The other (L28) was contained in an undecorated coarse-ware jar of the kind used for most domestic cooking purposes. It was placed in a small pit, a few centimeters deep, and covered with earth. This burial was similar to the one in Structure 2 (L44).

The only clues to house-wall construction consisted of one dubious posthole in the southeast corner of the house (L17).

In digging through Floor 1 down to the top of Floor 2, I encountered approximately 10 cm of earth deposits that were relatively rich in most classes of small artifacts. This material could have been collapsed wall daub from the Floor 2 structure that was simply leveled and tamped down to form Floor 1. There were no burned wall daub chunks, such as we found in the early floors of neighboring Structure 2, another indication that the earliest phase of the structure simply collapsed and did not burn down. If it were a wattle-and-daub wall, then that would account for the build-up of the next floor several centimeters before the next house was built. If it was only a cane-walled house, then the next floor must have been built up by bringing in a quantity of earth fill from outside the area of the immediate house group. At any rate, the next structure built increased the height of the platform by 5 to 10 cm and included the addition of a course or two of cobbles to the retaining wall. The overall dimensions remained 11.5 m by 5 m covering a total of 57.5 m².

The re-flooring of Structure 1 served to raise the platform, but it did not change the

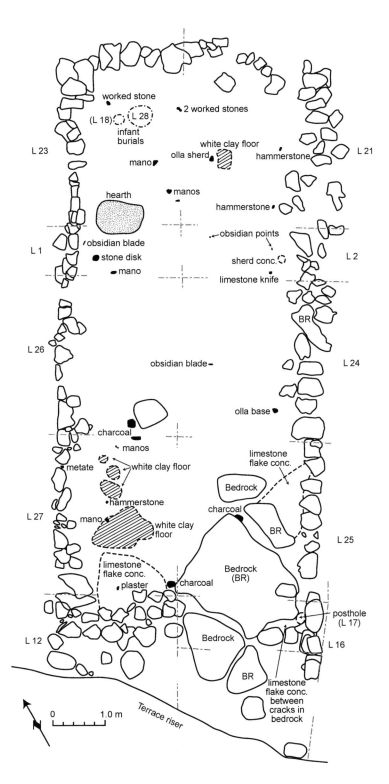

Figure 6.17.   Plan of Structure 1, Floor 2.

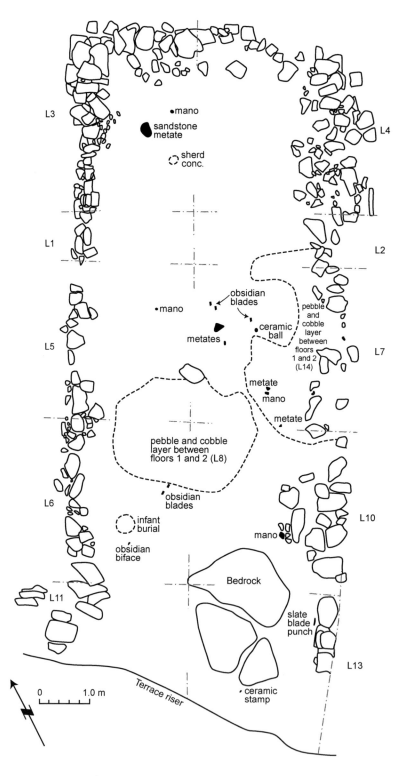

Figure 6.18. Plan of Structure 1, Floor 1.

Figure 6.19.   Infant burial in Structure 1 (4/9). Golondrina
Unslipped: Calcite Temper Variety jar with rim missing.

style or basic layout (Figure 6.18). There was no evidence that the floor had been covered with white lime-clay or any other material. Instead, only hard-packed earth was encountered. One aspect of the house's reconstruction that I do not fully understand took place apparently just prior to laying down the floor. In the central part of the structure a shallow pit about 2 m in diameter and 15 cm to 30 cm deep was dug. In this area all the cobbles and pebbles were collected and placed in a single layer over Floor 2, forming a rectangular concentration or bed of stones 10 cm thick (L8). A more irregularly shaped concentration was formed to the east of the shallow pit along the retaining wall (L14).

The pit itself was only noted by its yellow, sandy earth and lack of rocks or artifacts. It appears that the builders dug into the center of the structure, penetrated the terrace construction fill below Floor 2, picked out all the rocks and large artifacts, and then placed these in the two rock concentrations. No such features were encountered in any of the other houses.

At some point during the occupation of this house, an infant was buried beneath the floor in the broken base of a used, plain water jar. The burial partially penetrated a well-preserved patch of Floor 2 (Figure 6.19).

There were no structural features such as postholes to indicate the nature of house

construction. Nonetheless, the thickness of the
floor deposit suggests that it, in part, may have
been made up of collapsed wall daub. Since
the floor was not burned, nor were there any
burned chunks of wall daub, I cannot be certain
that the walls were made of wattle-and-daub.
It is, therefore, likely that the walls collapsed
slowly and that any remnants of floor or wall
daub were, being near the surface, destroyed by
subsequent root action. Otherwise, the house
could have been a simple cane-walled structure,
much like the final phase of Structure 2's wall
material.

House Group 2 (Elite)

The three houses excavated in this group
have the longest and most complex history of
those studied at Canajasté (Figure 6.6). The
group started as a single house during the Early
Postclassic period and then expanded to two
and subsequently three structures during the
Late Postclassic. The house with evidence for
the earliest occupation, Structure 22, is also the
largest and most elaborate house, not only in the
house group but in the entire site. Structures 21
and 23 were also substantial buildings, but each
was several meters shorter than the final version
of Structure 22.

The first building phase on the terrace
must have been located towards the south end
of Structure 22. It sat atop a large bedrock
outcrop that later served as the base of all
subsequent construction phases. None of these
early floors remain so I do not know exactly
what the earliest structure looked like. However,
part of its north retaining wall was preserved,
and it was therefore possible to estimate its
location. This first house underwent a series
of expansions in length throughout the Early
Postclassic and achieved its maximum length
by the end of that period. Structure 21 was
added to the group at some point during the
Late Postclassic period, covering some midden
material deposited by the residents of Structure
22. Structure 22 was re-floored and increased in
height three times during the Late Postclassic.
Structure 21 underwent at least five re-flooring
episodes and each of these may have been part

of a more complete rebuilding. After Structure
21 had been occupied for some time a new house
was added to the group—Structure 23. This
house was built directly on the patio with little
initial modification to it. Then it was raised by
two re-floorings and the addition of a layer of
construction fill and a stone retaining wall.

I will first describe the construction
sequence for the initial house in the group,
Structure 22, then continue with Structure 21
and finally Structure 23.

Structure 22

As already mentioned, this house belonged
to one of the highest elite members of the
community. The data for the earliest phases
of house construction are fragmentary, but
there is enough information to indicate that the
style of construction was different in the Early
Postclassic compared with the later period.
A large sample of stratified midden deposits
associated with the house was excavated.
These midden deposits were trapped below the
northward additions to the house's length as the
residents expanded their dwelling. Figure 6.20
shows the north-south profile of the structure
and the relationships among the various deposits
and features. Figure 6.21 illustrates the phases
of growth that Structure 22 underwent. Phase
1 was the initial construction phase where the
northern extent of the house was formed by
Retaining Wall 3. The wall was a well-made
stone construction that footed onto a bedrock
outcrop (Figure 6.22). Only 1.2 m of its height
remained preserved—it might have been higher
at one time, then leveled for a more recent floor.
This original structure is only represented by
the north end, the west side, and the east side
retaining walls. No preserved floor that could
have been attributed to this first structure was
discovered.

During the occupation of this phase of the
house, at least five midden and ash layers were
formed to the north of the structure. These
deposits began with Midden 5, which overlaid
bedrock and sterile deposits (Figure 6.20a). The
midden began at the foot of the retaining wall
and extended north for at least 4 m and possibly
5 m. On top of this a layer of white, ashy midden

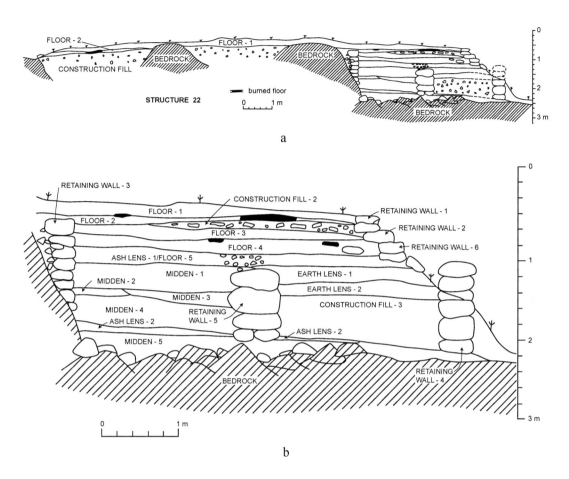

Figure 6.20. North-south profile of Structure 22: a) Whole structure; b) Expanded profile of north end of structure.

accumulated (Ash Lens 2; Figure 6.20b). It extended north approximately 3.5 m from the foot of the retaining wall. Middens 4, 3, 2, 1, and the Ash Lens-1/Floor 5 deposit succeeded the Ash Lens-2 deposit until 1.2 m of deposits had built up (see Figures 6.23-6.28). These middens contained a wide variety of artifacts, animal bones, and charred plant remains.

The next phase of construction (phase 2) extended the length of the house by 2.7 m (Figure 6.27). Retaining Wall 5 cut through the midden deposits down to bedrock. It was laid parallel to Retaining Wall 3 and the retaining wall on the western side of the structure was also extended to form a new corner. No new retaining wall extension was needed on the

eastern side because the floor would have been level with the existing ground surface (near where Structure 21 was eventually built). The end result of this extension was to form a split-level house, with the new extension's floor at least 40 cm below the level of the main house floor (assuming that level to be indicated by the top of Retaining Wall 3). There were no steps leading up from the new floor to the old, main house floor, but access could have been gained by way of the patio or perhaps a wooden step or stone which was later removed.

I suspect the motivation for the extension of the house and construction of Retaining Wall 5 was at least two-fold. First, the residents may have been increasing in number or status within

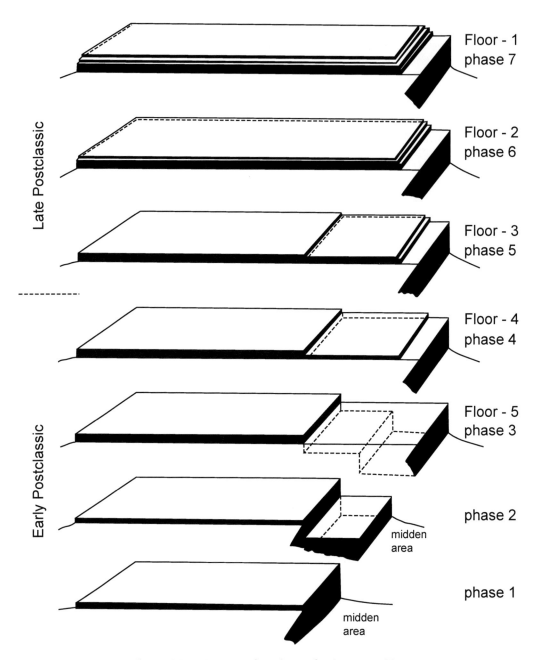

Figure 6.21.   Construction phases for Structure 22.

the community and signaled that change by investing labor in house construction. Second, if the density of housing was increasing in the community, it may have become appropriate or necessary to limit the disposal of trash in areas near the house. This may have been compounded by the construction of a neighboring house group (Structures 25, 26, and 27) just to the northeast of House Group 2 (Figure 6.6). The new house group may have claimed as their own patio the very zone where the residents of Structure 22 were dumping their

Figure 6.22.   Structure 22, Retaining Wall 3 forming the end of the structure platform (facing SW).

trash. This interpretation is backed up somewhat by the lack of new midden deposits forming at the base of Retaining Wall 5, contrasting with what happened previously at the base of Retaining Wall 3.

The top of Ash Lens 1/Floor 5 appears to have formed the floor of this extension (Figures 6.20b, 6.28). It was not well prepared and, in fact, may not have been used for very long. I have estimated the size of the first structure (construction phase 1) by placing its southern end at the same location as during the most recent construction phase. There was no preserved evidence of house floors or other Early Postclassic middens to the south of Retaining Wall 3. The house may have extended to the second large bedrock outcrop or it may have extended to the third large outcrop (Figure 6.20a). The one piece of evidence, however, that leads me to think that the initial structure

extended all the way south is that there are no old corners or breaks in the retaining wall along the west side of the house to the south of Retaining Wall 3. Both the corners formed by the juncture of Retaining Wall 3 with the west retaining wall and Retaining Wall 5 with the northward extension of the west retaining wall were clearly visible. This is because the type and size of stone used in the retaining walls changed with each extension and because the new walls were simply abutted to the old ones rather than bonded. South of Retaining Wall 3 there was only a continuous bond wall, at least as far as the second large bedrock outcrop. South of that outcrop the retaining-wall stones had begun to slip off the rock and tumble downslope—obscuring any clear impression of presence or absence of more recently abutted walls. Test probes into the construction fill south of the large bedrock outcrops (Figure 6.20a)

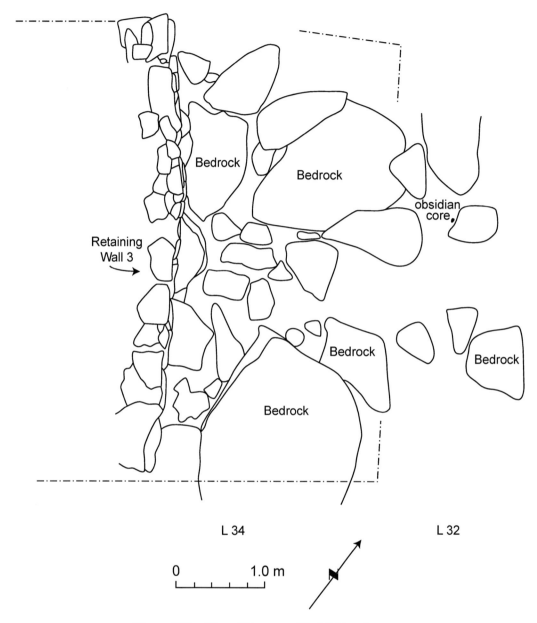

Figure 6.23.   Plan of Structure 22, Midden 5.

failed to reveal any buried end walls. It is most probable, then, that the house floor for phase 1 of construction reached between the bedrock outcrops and attained a maximum length of 11.2 m. At this early stage the house was 5 m wide, indicating a total estimated area of 56 m². The phase 2 extension out to Retaining Wall

5 increased the length of the house to 13.9 m resulting in new area of 69.5 m².

The next extension (phase 3) lengthened the house by 2.8 m. This new extension was made by laying six courses of boulders more or less parallel to Retaining Wall 5, and as in the previous extension, lengthening the north

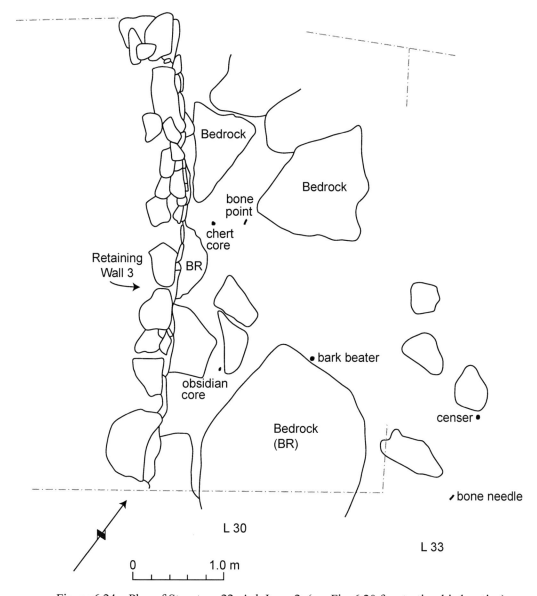

Figure 6.24.   Plan of Structure 22, Ash Lens 2. (see Fig. 6.20 for stratigrahic location)

end of the western side. Retaining Wall 4 appears to have been built up to the level of Retaining Wall 5 (Figures 6.20b, 6.28). The space between the two retaining walls was filled with a construction fill of earth, cobbles and boulders, and artifacts. This construction fill layer (Construction Fill Layer 3) (Figure 6.20b) was then capped with two earth lenses that may also have been used to raise the floor to match the height of the top of the new retaining wall.

These two earth lenses may also have been temporary floors at a lower level than those associated with Retaining Wall 5, thus forming another level in the already split-level house. However, when Earth Lens 1 was added to make the floor level with the top of Midden 1 there would have been one continuous floor from Retaining Wall 3 to the edge of Retaining Wall 4. The total floor area for the house would then have been 83.5 m², with a length of 16.7 m and

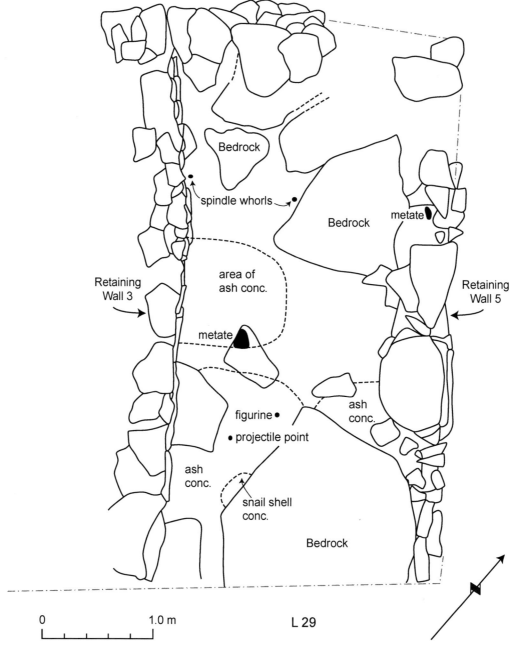

Figure 6.25. Plan of Structure 22, Midden 4. (see Fig. 6.20 for stratigrahic location)

the same width as before (5 m). This was the maximum extent of the house: all subsequent modifications reduced the total floor area. At this stage, Structure 22 was slightly more than

four times the size of Structure 2 (Floor 4) in House Group 1.

Another phase of construction took place when Floor 5/Ash Lens-1 was laid down from

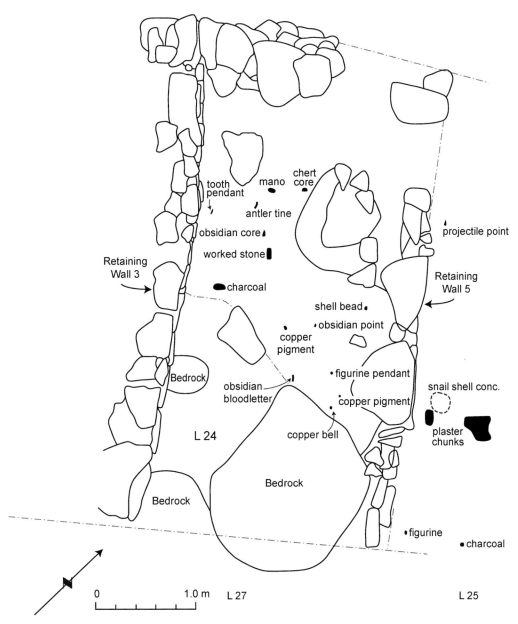

Figure 6.26.   Plan of Structure 22, Middens 2, 3, and Earth Lens 2. (see Fig. 6.20 for stratigrahic location)

Retaining Wall 3 to Retaining Wall 4 thus covering the earlier midden and earth layers. These layers were extremely rich in all types of refuse. Once deposited, they were leveled and tamped down into a hard floor. Closer to the base of Retaining Wall 3, the deposits were more ashy. I would explain the differences in the Floor 5/Ash Lens 1 deposit the following

way. Retaining Wall 4 was built after the ashy part of the Floor 5 deposit had already been laid down. This ashy lens was simply the top of the refuse heap and a continuation of the deposits directly below it at the base of Retaining Wall 3. Prior to the construction of Retaining Wall 5 and Retaining Wall 4 the deposit would have fanned out, forming a steep sloping mound to the north

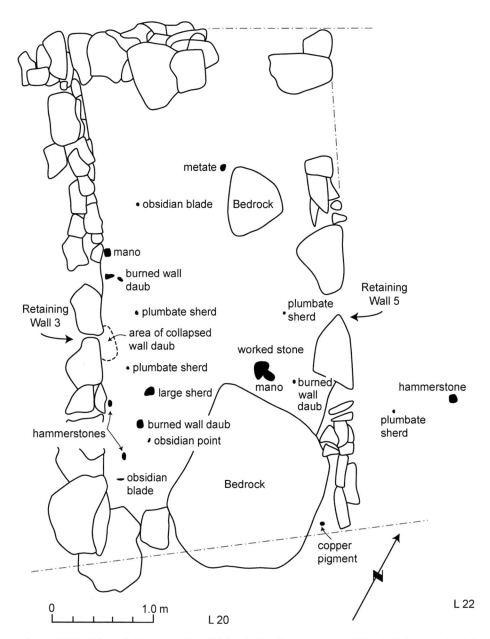

Figure 6.27.   Plan of Structure 22, Midden 1, Earth Lens 1. (see Fig. 6.20 for stratigrahic location)

of the structure. The construction fill layer (Construction Fill Layer 3) and the earth lenses (Earth Lens 1 and 2) represented an attempt to build the base for Floor 5. The top of the refuse mound was probably pushed out and leveled out to the edge of Retaining Wall 4. Figure 6.21 shows the sequence of three construction phases

that led to the completion of Floor 5. During phase 1 the midden layers accumulated up to the level of Ash Lens 1, the top of which later became the surface of Floor 5. During phase 2 the midden layers were bisected and a formal house extension was built using the underlying middens as a floor base. Later, during phase 3 of

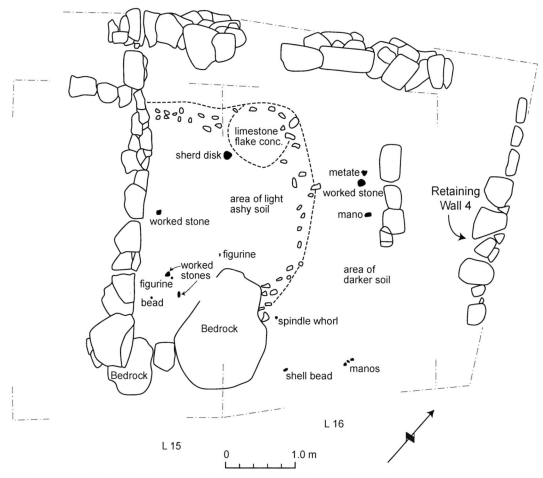

Figure 6.28. Plan of Structure 22, Floor 5, Ash Lens 1. (see Fig. 6.20 for stratigrahic location)

construction, the house was extended again and construction fill was brought in to raise the floor. This new floor was probably no higher than the original top of the midden layer.

The next phase of construction (phase 4) consisted of an addition of a new layer of floor material (Floor 4; Figure 6.29). This new floor capped the Floor 5/Ash Lens 1 layer. Its north end was reduced by the addition of a new two-course, stone retaining wall (Retaining Wall 6) embedded into Floor 5 (Figure 6.29). The new retaining wall shortened the length of Structure 22 by one meter. The house's new total length was now only 15.7 m, reducing the floor area to 78.5 m². This floor ranged between 10 cm and 20 cm thick. After this base material had been laid down, the floor was capped with a layer of

hard, light-colored clay. Only two patches of this floor remained preserved.

Floor 4 was the last construction, at least the last one with any preserved traces to have been made during the Early Postclassic period. It may have been transitional between the Early and Late Postclassic periods. Nonetheless, it provides a good example of the continuity between the two periods. It is stratigraphically between the early and late deposits, and, in terms of artifact styles, the materials collected from the Floor 4 deposit are also similar to what went before and what came later. It is difficult to determine what part of this is simply the result of early materials mixing in from the Floor 5/Ash Lens 1 deposit below; however, because Floor 5 was relatively hard packed and differed

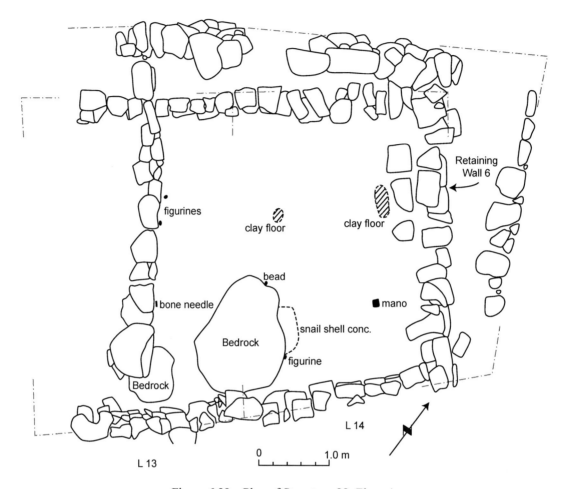

Figure 6.29. Plan of Structure 22, Floor 4

distinctly from Floor 4 in its color, texture, and density of artifacts, I am assuming they are separate assemblages.

During excavation Floor 4 appeared to have been an independent and clearly distinguishable deposit. At first, I thought it might have been the initial Late Postclassic occupation of the house, but later, after studying the ceramics and other artifacts, it became clear that this was an Early Postclassic construction. What is most interesting, though, is that Floor 4 (construction phase 4) reverses several trends set during the previous Early Postclassic construction phases. First, there was a contraction of the house's length. Second, it was done by building a retaining wall along the end which was only two

courses high—much like the style used in all the later houses on the site. Third, there was a greater than expected frequency of some types of ceramics characteristic of the Late Postclassic period. All this provides the impression that there was a period of accelerated change in house and artifact styles during the occupation of the structure and that this is what would traditionally be characterized as the arbitrary "break" between two archaeological phases. It may well not have been a break at all and represented, instead, evidence for much more complex shifts in both intracommunity and intercommunity relationships.

Floor 3 represents the first Late Postclassic occupation of the house (Figures 6.30-6.31).

Figure 6.30.   Structure 22, white clay-plaster Floor 3 remnant.

The basic layout of the house was the same as before; in fact, Floor 3 was a re-flooring of the extension only (phase 5). I found no evidence of this floor in the entire south end of the house. Over most of the house's area the residents made use of the same retaining walls and floor as before. They did, though, shorten the north end once again. This was done by laying another course on top of Retaining Wall 6 which, eventually, formed the base of Retaining Wall 2. This only shortened the structure by 20 cm. The modification brought the top of the northern retaining wall almost up to the level of Retaining Wall 3. It was also the same height as the top of the long retaining wall that formed the whole west side of the house.

The floor had been capped with a layer of hard, light-colored clay, mixed with lime, to form a crumbly plaster. The floor material was well preserved over much of the surface area, both from burning and from being covered after abandonment by a layer of construction fill. This

is surprising since the capping material was only 1 cm to 2 cm thick. The burned patches provide the first indication of the house's possible burning. Structure 21 also had several floors that suffered burning during the Late Postclassic, suggesting that the whole house group had been destroyed by fire.

Floor 2 (phase 6) is the first to reach from one end of the house to the other without a formal split-level (Figure 6.32). The floor did, however, remain sunken about 10 cm below the level of the floor in the rest of the house. The walls were shortened on all sides, indicating the first complete rebuilding of the house. This would probably have been necessary if, as I suspect, the previous construction burned to the ground. The north end of the house, above Floor 3, was raised with a thin layer of construction fill (Construction Fill Layer 2). This put Floor 2 closer to the level of the south end of the house floor. It would have been during this construction phase that the remnants of

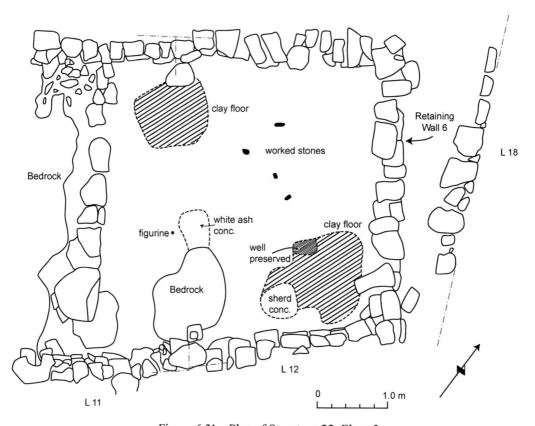

Figure 6.31.   Plan of Structure 22, Floor 3.

earlier floors in the south end of the house were removed.

One of the most impressive aspects of this new house is the new retaining wall that was built along the entire length of both sides of the house (Figure 6.32). This new retaining wall was two to four courses high along the west side of the house and as many as six courses high along the east side which faced the patio. Towards the southern end of the house the retaining wall was badly preserved. This retaining wall was set back about a meter from the main house terrace retaining wall (Retaining Wall 3) along the west side; however, along the east side the retaining wall appears never to have changed position. The side that faces the patio was the most carefully prepared. The many courses of well-trimmed stone slabs are all laid with their flattest end or side neatly aligned with surrounding stones while the inner edges are irregular and

project into the construction fill. This retaining wall, which would have formed the visible house platform or the base on which the house stood, could well have been plastered, even though no plaster now remains.

The dimensions of the house during this phase of construction were 15.5 m long by 4.8 m wide, for a total floor area of 74.4 m². In both the north and south ends of the house there remained several preserved patches of floor. This floor material was a hard-packed clay with a good deal of lime mixed in to whiten it. This cap of floor material was up to 4 cm thick in some spots, and none of the patches was burned. On the floor, as well as in its matrix, there were few artifacts, with the exception of the south end of the house. Figure 6.32 shows the localized distributions of artifacts recovered in the south end, as well as the general lack of artifacts over most of the floor surface. No features besides the

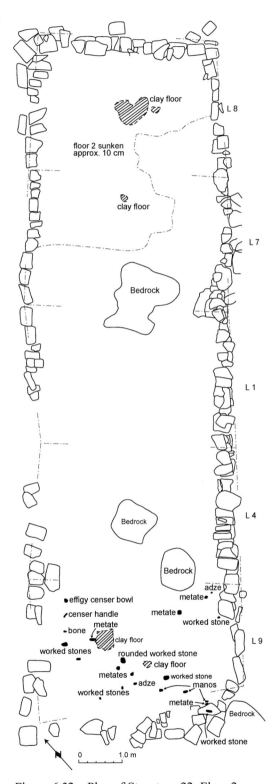

Figure 6.32.   Plan of Structure 22, Floor 2.

retaining walls and the floor were found. Three large outcrops of bedrock were exposed and must have been part of the floor.

Finally, the house was rebuilt one last time—the seventh and last discernible construction phase (Figure 6.33). This phase involved the addition of another floor layer (Floor 1) that completely covered the previous floor. It also included the construction of a new retaining wall surrounding the new floor. This new retaining wall consisted of a single course of stone slabs laid on top of Floor 2 and set in from Retaining Wall 2 along both sides of the structure (Figure 6.7). This retaining wall was visible on the surface when excavations of the house were begun. Most of the stones in the wall were only half covered by the earth matrix that was labeled Floor 1. The construction of this new retaining wall reduced the dimensions of the house to 15.3 m long by 3.8 m wide. The new floor area totaled 58.1 m². The house's total area by construction phase 7 was only two square meters larger than the estimated floor area for construction phase 1, but a full 25 m² less than the peak size for construction phase 3. As with the floor below it, Floor 1 had no features in it. There were also few artifacts recovered in situ on, or in, the floor.

The most salient aspect of the sequence of changes that this structure underwent during its long occupation is the ever increasing ratio of length to width. Even though Structure 22 decreased in total floor area during every reconstruction after construction phase 3, the residents were reluctant to give up length and, instead, narrowed the house. This insured that Structure 22 remained the longest dwelling at the site and the longest structure outside of the ceremonial plaza. Thus, despite the fact that Structure 22/Floor 1 had roughly the same total floor area as Structure 1/Floor 1 in House Group 1, Structure 22 was almost 50 percent longer and would certainly have appeared to be a much larger house. Even more important, in terms of status display, is that Structure 22 looked much more like the ceremonial structures that it flanked than any of the other houses.

Structure 21

This house went through a long sequence of rebuildings, but they were not nearly as complex as the ones encountered in Structure 22. Structure 21 was built during the Late Postclassic and did not exist during the Floor 4, or earlier, occupation of Structure 22. Structure 21 was added to the house group as Structure 22 was diminishing in size.

The first phase of construction involved leveling the terrace area, especially in the zone near Structure 22. The retaining wall, which forms the boundary of the house group on its north side, was extended east towards a bedrock outcrop. The area between the retaining wall and the patio was filled with cobbles, boulders, and earth, above a layer of artifact refuse that could have been part of Structure 22's Early Postclassic midden. The construction fill layers contained quantities of burned wall daub, charcoal, and earth that might have originally come from clearing off debris from Structure 22 in order to prepare it for the construction of Floor 2, as well as to prepare a base for the first floor of Structure 21. When this leveling stage was completed the builders tamped down earth on top of the fill to make a floor. The floor for this earliest phase is not well preserved. Only one patch of Floor 6 was recovered, just enough to indicate that there may have been an earlier structure but not enough to allow an estimation of the structure's size. It is also possible that this patch of Floor 6 was actually an early hearth used prior to the laying of Floor 5.

Floor 5 was well preserved over most of the house, having large remnants of both burned and unburned patches (Figure 6.34). The burned areas were found at both ends of the house while the central section had none. The floor had been made of a thin layer of hard-packed clay with a high lime content and, at one time, it must have completely capped the construction fill base. The only exceptions to this would have been those areas where the bedrock protruded through the floor. Scattered around the floor were chunks of burned wall daub, baked a brownish orange color from intense heat. Many had impressions of the cane wall preserved on

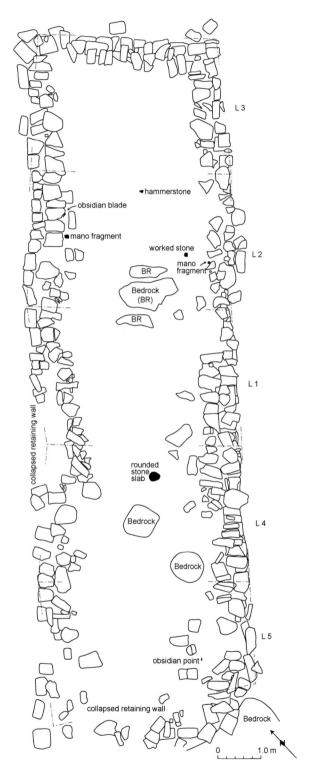

Figure 6.33.   Plan of Structure 22, Floor 1.

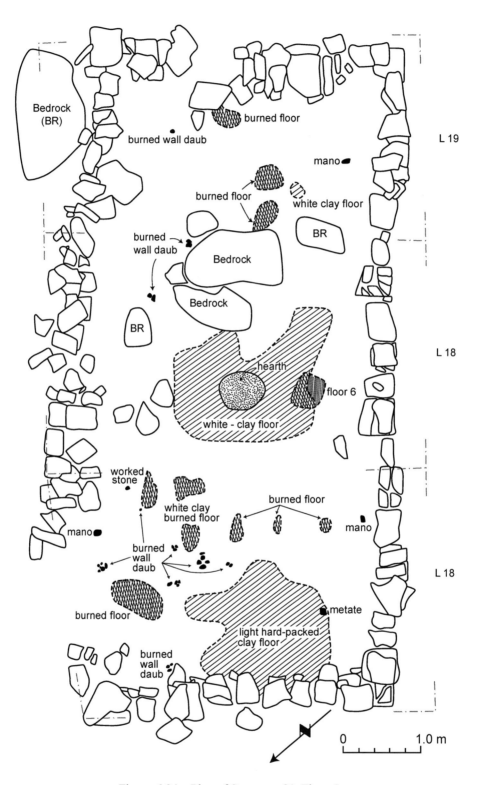

Figure 6.34.   Plan of Structure 21, Floor 5.

their inner sides. In the center of the house was a circular hearth, consisting of burned orange soil and white ash about 5 cm thick. It sat directly on top of a large area of white clay floor which was unburned, even under the hearth. The hearth was almost identical to the one found in Structure 1. There were few artifacts scattered about the floor deposit, suggesting that most of the debris was cleared away before the next floor was laid down. The retaining wall that outlined the floor area was built on the original construction fill layer and, as will be seen, was constantly raised during the life of the house. The house's dimensions during this phase were 8.2 m long by 4.4 m wide, for a floor area of 36.1 m².

After the bulk of the debris from the collapsed house had been cleared away the remainder was leveled to form the next floor (Floor 4). This floor was a 5 cm thick layer of earth with a very thin layer of light-colored clay (1 to 2 cm thick) capping it. Like its predecessor, it provides evidence that the new house was destroyed by fire. In several areas of the floor there is none of the clay cap remaining. Nonetheless, in others there are patches ranging from 40 cm to 1.2 m in length—some burned and others unburned (Figure 6.35). Towards the west end of the house there were several chunks of burned wall daub. Some ground stone tools and other artifacts were encountered in the floor deposit. Also, a hearth was found in exactly the same location as the one associated with Floor 5. Overall, this house seems to have been almost identical to the one below it, suggesting that it was rebuilt by the same people. Even the dimensions of the house remained unchanged.

After the destruction of the house by fire for the second time, people returned to rebuild it. They followed essentially the same design as before, but this time they shortened the east end of the structure by almost a meter (Figure 6.36). The rest of the retaining walls remained unchanged except for the addition of another course of stone slabs to heighten them. The new length was 7.5 m, which diminished the floor area by approximately 3 m² to a size of 33 m². Large areas of floor had been well preserved; in fact, Floor 3 had the best preserved floor

of all the 26 or so floors excavated at the site. Figure 6.37 shows the large areas of white clay floor, some of which were almost two meters in length, along with the SE retaining wall that shortened the house. The rest of the floor was presumably covered with the same material, but it either eroded away during the life of the house or was broken up and dispersed after abandonment. The material that made up the floor capping was only 2 to 3 cm thick while the bulk of the floor matrix consisting of earth was about 5 cm thick. In the central floor area was a burned patch of clay floor that might have been either a hearth or an accidentally burned patch of floor. If the burning were accidental, then it, along with the other burned patch and the chunks of burned wall daub, indicate that this house structure also burned to the ground. This would have been the third time that the building burned. In this case, however, little of the well-preserved floor was burned, and the patches that were burned were located roughly in the same area as previous hearths. The burned wall daub was located only in the area where daub was recovered in the previous construction phase (Floor 4). It might have been churned up by recent tree roots. This combined evidence suggests that the structure associated with Floor 3 did not meet its end in a blaze.

Regardless of what happened to the structure associated with Floor 3, it was certainly replaced with a new building. Not only was the floor replaced, but the house was lengthened back to its original size. Figure 6.38 shows the layout of the new structure and the location of preserved patches of floor. This Floor (Floor 2) was a 5 cm thick layer of compacted earth that had been capped with a layer of light clay about 2 to 3 cm in thickness. This layer of clay was preserved in some areas by burning and also by the deposits that later covered it. The floor extended over the top of the retaining wall that formed the southeast end of the previous structure, abutting a new retaining wall laid down on the surface of the floor below. This new retaining wall was made of large stone slabs and flat boulders, generally larger than the stones used in other walls in the house. It expanded the length of the house to 8.4 m, slightly longer than

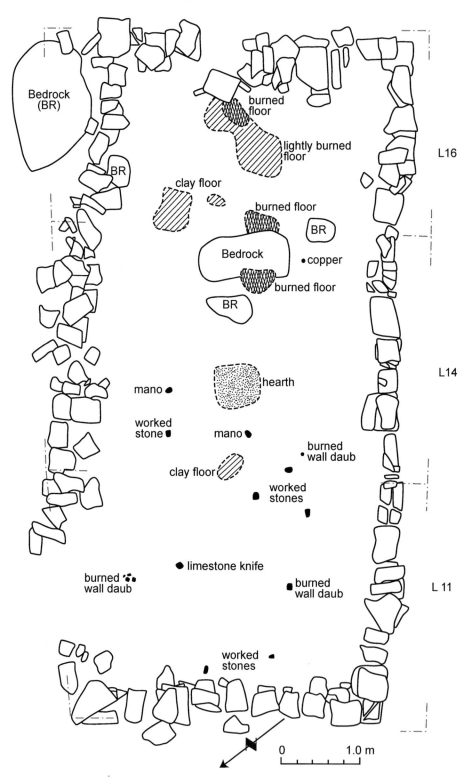

Figure 6.35.   Plan of Structure 21, Floor 4.

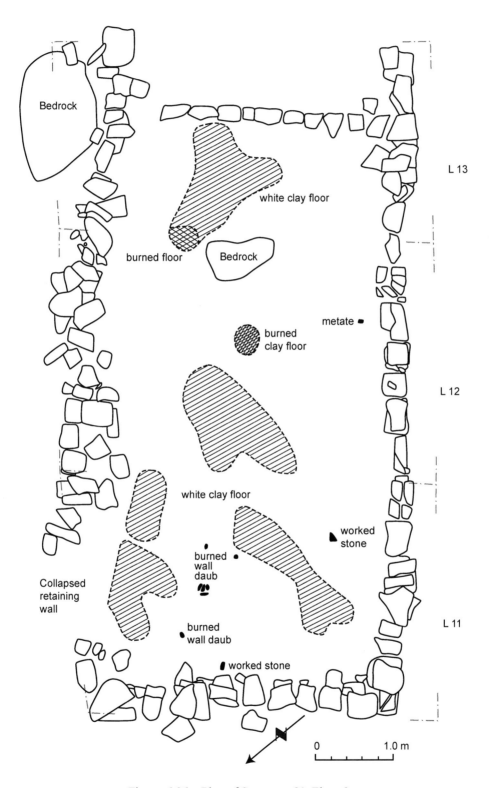

Figure 6.36. Plan of Structure 21, Floor 3.

Figure 6.37.   Structure 21, Floor 3 exposed, showing an earlier buried
retaining wall forming the SE end of the house (facing NW).

the first phase of construction and providing a
new floor area of 37 m².

As with the previous structure, there is
little evidence that the building burned down,
even though some patches of burned floor were
discovered. These burned areas were small—no
more than 20 cm in diameter. There were no
fragments of burned wall daub recovered. If the
structure did burn down, then either the walls
were made of light cane with no daub covering,
or the debris was swept away. The burned
floor patches may have been caused from heat
generated by a hearth, however, the pattern of
burning is more like that found on the floors of
structures that definitely did burn down. Few
artifacts and no other features were discovered
in the floor deposits.

After the abandonment of this phase of the
structure, residents returned to rebuild once
again. This time they raised the new floor by

first putting down a layer of construction fill
over Floor 2 and then laying a cap of earth
for the floor base. The construction fill layer
was 10 cm thick and consisted of earth mixed
with a very high density of small cobbles and
pebbles. In the northwest end of the structure
the builders used thin flagstones for fill instead
of pebbles. The compacted earth floor laid on
top of the construction fill layer was about 10
cm to 15 cm thick, raising the level of the new
platform approximately 25 cm above Floor
2 and about 50 cm above the house group's
patio. Even so, the floor level was still below
the surface level of neighboring Structure 22.
There was no evidence of a clay floor covering
as in previous floors, but, since this floor
would have been exposed after the house's
abandonment, a thin capping would not have
preserved.

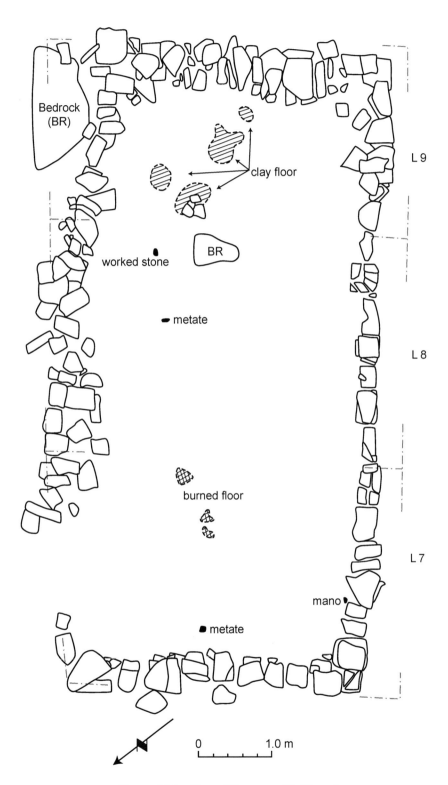

Figure 6.38.   Plan of Structure 21, Floor 2.

In addition to raising the floor, a new inner retaining wall was laid. This wall was virtually identical to the last retaining wall built over the surface of Structure 22; it was a single course of stone slabs set in from and parallel to the main platform wall. In this case the retaining wall sat directly on top of the new floor (Floor 1). Figure 6.39 shows this addition to the structure as well as the distribution of artifacts throughout the Floor 1 deposit. The net effect of this new retaining wall was to reduce the total size of the structure. The length and width decreased to 7.8 m and 3.8 m respectively, yielding 29.6 m^2 of floor space. There was no evidence that this last structure burned down. In fact, none of the excavated houses showed evidence of burning during their last occupation.

Structure 23

This structure was first built during the Late Postclassic, sometime after Structure 21. By comparison with Structures 21 and 22, this house was rather hastily made and with less effort or care. It was tacked onto Structure 21, using that building's southeast wall as its own. Three floors were discovered, but it is not certain that these were all house floors. The first two may have been patio floors used by the residents of the house group as out-of-doors activity areas prior to the construction of Structure 23. The last floor was definitely associated with a house and was constructed along the lines of the other house structures at the site.

The first phase of occupation or use of this area would, in any case, have been as a patio, probably much like the area below Structure 21 would have been used before the series of buildings was built on that location. The surface was originally an area of bedrock outcrops with earth fill and refuse accumulated in the dips and crevices between the rocks (Figure 6.40). Sometime during the Late Postclassic the residents leveled the area to use as a patio (almost no Early Postclassic artifacts were found). The surface was covered with a very thin layer of plaster only 1 cm to 2 cm thick. Only a few remnants of this plaster floor were recovered, but one of the patches of plaster

found in situ had been painted red, suggesting that the house group's patio may have been quite elaborate. Unfortunately, none of the patio areas away from the houses were tested to determine if there existed more such plastered and painted patio. It remains possible, therefore, that this initial plastered patio surface was, after all, a house floor (Floor 3; Figure 6.41). If so, then the house did not have retaining walls, or they were removed later on, and its exact area is unknown. I assume that the area was actually used as a house and that the first structure on this spot was perhaps peripheral and, perhaps, made use of an existing patio floor. Later, this floor was re-coated with a layer of white lime-clay, only a few small patches of which were preserved. This layer was much more similar to the material used as flooring in most of the houses, rather than plaster or stucco like the floor below. Also, it was not painted. This second floor (Floor 2; Figure 6.42) was, most likely, a house floor, mainly because the material used—a white lime-clay—would not have survived a rainy season if exposed to the open air.[2] The preserved areas were dried and cracked like most of the house floors and, therefore, had probably been covered by a roof. The floor's size for each phase of construction is estimated at 10.8 m long by 4.4 m wide, giving a total floor area of 47.5 m^2. The floor plans show the many bedrock outcrops projecting through the floor, just as in most of the other structures described so far.

The last phase of construction provides the most solid evidence of a structure (Figure 6.43). A 20 cm layer of construction fill was laid over top of Floor 2 and held in place by a two-course high retaining wall of stone slabs and cobbles. The construction fill contained numerous artifacts but consisted mainly of earth, cobbles, pebbles, chunks of plaster from large collapsed buildings, and many fragments of grinding stone tools. The uneven surface of construction fill was capped with an earth floor about 5 cm to 10 cm thick. The retaining wall, as already mentioned, was not as well built as the earlier stages of construction of the two neighboring houses in the group. Furthermore, the builders simply appended this house onto the

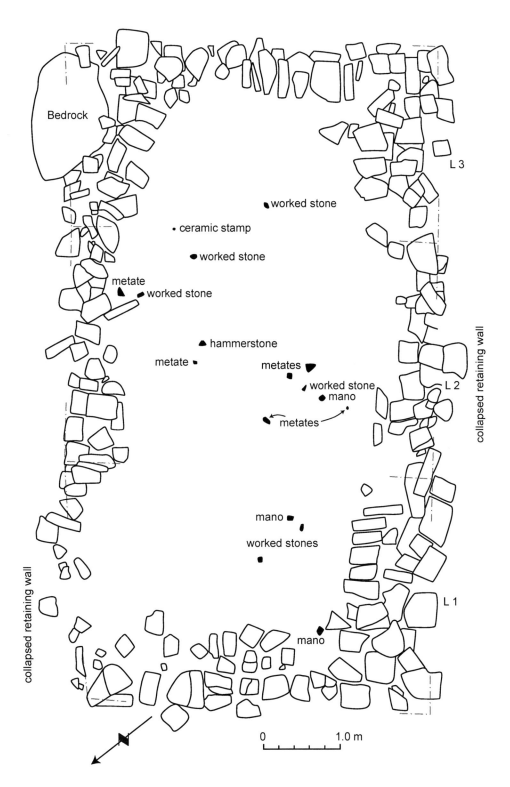

Figure 6.39. Plan of Structure 21, Floor 1.

Figure 6.40.   Structure 23, showing bedrock underlying the construction fill that was used to raise the floor up to the level of the wall stones (facing S).

end of Structure 21. It was probably built around the same time as Floor 2 of Structures 21 and 22 and occupied until they were abandoned. As with the other two structures in the house group, there is no evidence that the floor of this last phase of construction was plastered or covered with a specially prepared lime-clay mixture. The overall dimensions for the house during this last phase of construction were the same as the previous estimates: 10.2 m by 4.4 m, providing 47.5 m² of floor space.

No one structure in the house group was much larger than the excavated houses from other groups or from houses observed on the surface of the site. But the combined floor area for House Group 2, assuming that all the structures were occupied at the same time during their last construction phase, totaled 135.2 m². It had 33 percent more floor space

in its three structures than House Group 1 had in its two structures (totalling 101.2 m²). If Structure 3 was part of House Group 1, then the group's total floor area would have equaled that of House Group 2. This demonstrates that floor area alone cannot be used to distinguish the relative status of households. Instead, it is the other characteristics of the structures in House Group 2 that make it stand out from House Group 1 and the other unexcavated house groups at the site. Its proximity to the ceremonial center, its higher platforms, the well-laid masonry of the platforms, the extreme length of Structure 22, and the consistent use of lime-clay or plaster for the house floors and patio, combine to emphasize the high status of the household and to distinguish it from other households. This distinction holds up when House Group 25 is compared to House Group 2.

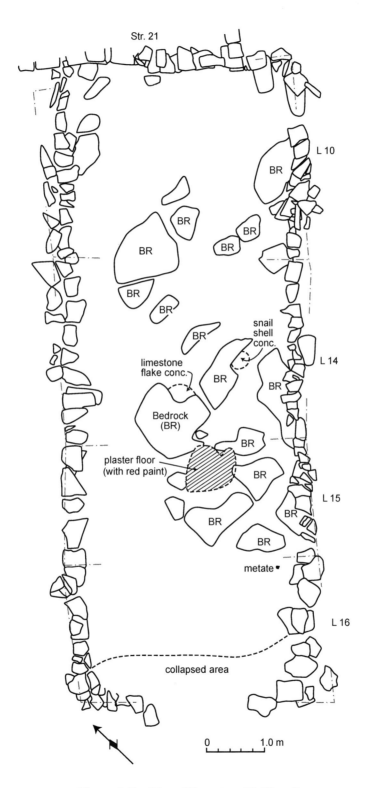

Figure 6.41. Plan of Structure 23, Floor 3.

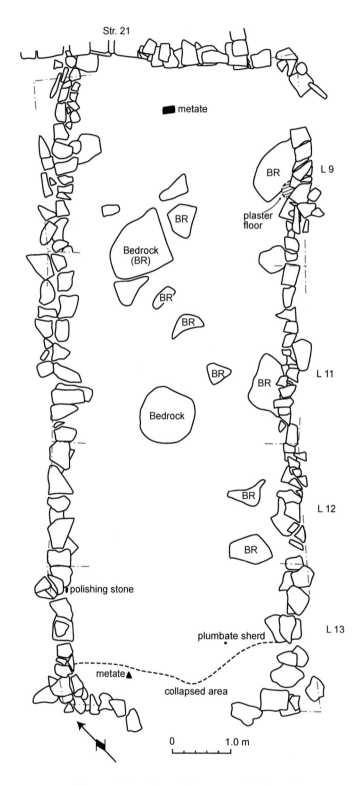

Figure 6.42.   Plan of Structure 23, Floor 2.

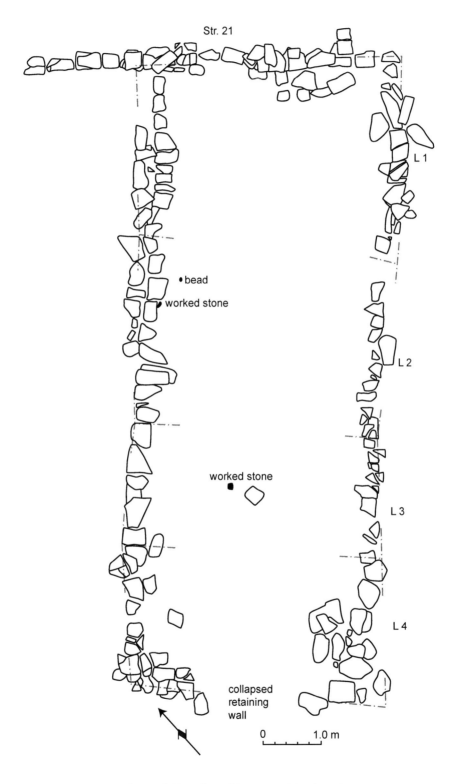

Figure 6.43. Plan of Structure 23, Floor 1.

House Group 25

This group consisted of two houses, Structures 60 and 61, located on a relatively broad natural terrace just above the river (Figure 6.8). The two most recent house platforms were visible on the surface and were obviously part of the same group. After the site was cleared for mapping I noticed that groups of houses could be distinguished in some cases by the quality of construction of their retaining walls. When two or sometimes three structures flanked a common patio the platforms' retaining walls that faced onto the patio were often made of neatly squared and carefully laid stone slabs. The retaining walls on the sides of the platform that faced away from the patio were made of a mix of rounded cobbles, boulders, and slabs, often irregularly and unevenly laid. The emphasis on careful construction and elaboration of only the inward-facing side of the house has some implications for relations among households that I will discuss later. But a more practical benefit of the pattern is that it allowed me to detect groupings of structures that were probably occupied by a single household. In the case of Structures 60 and 61, it was clear they shared a patio which was more or less cut off from the rest of the community. Usually the only time a house group's patio opened outward was when it was cut off by a substantial terrace drop, thereby restricting access to the group. This was the case for both House Groups 1 and 2 during the Late Postclassic. House Group 25 represents the other option. The open sides of the patio either faced another structure or a steep terrace riser.

The sequence of construction in this house group is not as clearly understood as I would wish, primarily because I did not have time to completely excavate an Early Postclassic structure that underlay the patio. Nevertheless, I did find part of its retaining wall and associated middens and so can make some partial comparisons with the structures that replaced it in the house group and with other house groups. It appears that there was a house structure located in the area that later became the patio. This house had a small porch facing the river. Refuse was discarded beyond the porch. Later,

during the Late Postclassic, the large platform for Structure 60 was built over the refuse deposits, porch area, and retaining wall of the earlier structure, much the same as Structure 2 replaced the earlier constructions under it. At some point during the occupation of Structure 60, neighboring Structure 61 was added to the house group. I discovered two Late Postclassic floors in Structure 60 and five in Structure 61. There were no other structures associated with the group. Since the earliest evidence for occupation of the locale was discovered under Structure 60, I will begin with its description.

Structure 60

Not enough of the Early Postclassic structure underlying the house group was recovered to say much more than that it existed; however, it faced the river, judging both by the location of a possible corridor or porch between the south wall of the structure and the river, and by the similar location of a midden area. This initial structure was built on flat, unterraced ground, with one course of cobbles forming the base of the walls. Figure 6.44 shows two long retaining walls, the location of the unexcavated structure floor, and the midden areas. The retaining wall on the right (northeast) is the one that belonged to the early structure. Refuse material was thrown downslope towards the river and accumulated as several midden layers. Later, residents of the house built another retaining wall that partially covered the midden and ran more or less parallel to the early house wall. This second retaining wall was about two courses high and retained a layer of construction fill that provided a level surface between the house and the river (Floor 2). It is possible that this wall was more than just a porch or patio retaining wall outside the house. It could have been an extension to the previous house's width, or it could have been the southwest side of a house formed by the other retaining wall. If this were the case, the house was only 3.4 m wide and over 9 m long—a structure far narrower for its length than any other house on the site. There was evidence that the floor did not quite reach as far as the retaining wall and, furthermore, it was poorly preserved in most places. These two lines

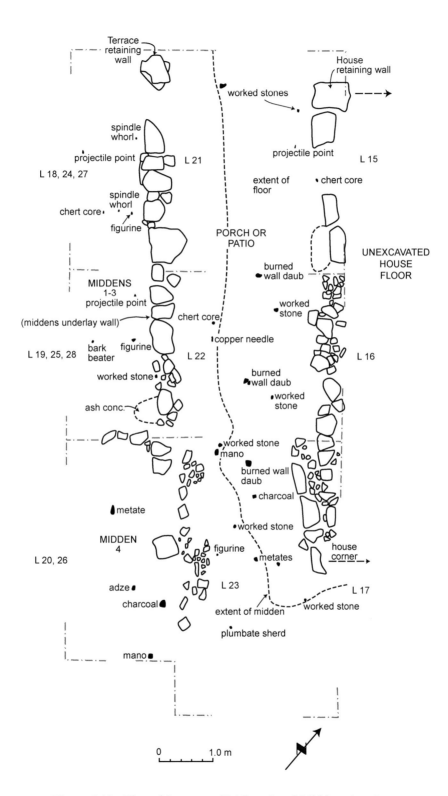

Figure 6.44.   Plan of Structure 60, Floor 2 and Middens 1 to 4.

of evidence combine to support the proposition that the area between the two walls was a porch or patio.

In several areas of the porch were chunks of burned wall daub that must have come from a house destroyed by fire. The fact that none of the floor area was burned suggests that perhaps this material was from some other area and brought in as fill or that the Early Postclassic house burned down. This may have marked the transition between the Early and Late Postclassic periods.

Following this construction, the whole layout of the house group changed, and the structure itself was rebuilt. Figure 6.45 shows the plan of the new building built over the remains of the first phases of construction. Part of the earlier retaining wall was used as a base for the new building. In addition, a line of finely squared stone slabs was placed along the length of the structure on the side facing the patio. The main aspect of the construction is that a new retaining wall was built to act as a terrace on the downslope side facing the river, completely replacing the previous one. This terrace formed the southwest side of the structure. It sat on top of the earlier midden layers and was between four and six courses high. It held the platform construction fill that extended the width of the house and provided a new level floor. The material used for fill was the same as that used in the most recent construction of Structure 2. It was a earth and pebble mix with large lumps of crumbly, white limestone and very few artifacts, definitely brought to the house group from some off-site location (Figure 6.9). The fill completely covered the previously added terrace retaining wall. The ends of the house were formed by one to two courses of boulders and cobbles that served as retaining walls and, in combination with the side retaining walls, held in the earth floor material.

The floor was a hard-packed earth up to 15 cm thick over the whole platform. There was only one small patch of preserved floor remaining that had a white clay surface, and this was in the southeast end of the structure. There was no other evidence of extensive floor preparation such as in several of the structures

in House Group 2; however, in the floor layer were found chunks of burned daub, indicating that the house may have had wattle-and-daub walls. But since the floor layer was so thick and badly disturbed, it was not possible to determine whether these burned daub chunks were just part of the floor fill carried in from some other part of the site or whether they were from an in situ burning. There were no burned floor patches to confirm this latter possibility. Therefore, I think it most likely that the structure associated with Floor 2 did not burn. Instead, the structure probably collapsed more slowly, and most of the floor surface was eroded away or, being near the surface, destroyed by roots.

The overall dimensions of the floor as outlined by the retaining wall were 12 m by 4.8 m, for a total of 57.6 m^2. In the central area was a stone platform sitting on the floor and consisting of one course of stone slabs. It was rectangular, 1.4 m by .8 m, and only about 15 cm high. There were no signs of ash or charcoal indicating that it could have been a hearth, nor were there any artifacts to suggest a different function. It was the only structure with such a feature, although Structure 1 had a larger, more irregular rock concentration on its surface.

The residents placed an infant burial in the center of the structure, penetrating the floor and cutting into the buried retaining wall. The infant skeleton (L14, Figure 6.46) sat in a fillet-banded, plainware jar capped with a broken comal. As with the burial in Structure 2, the comal had several dots or drips of some burned substance on the surface.

There was not a large number of artifacts on the floor surface, but those that were recovered indicated the structure to have been Late Postclassic in age. The relatively thick floor layer suggests the possibility that there was more than one re-flooring of the house during the Late Postclassic and that, because floor preservation was so poor, no distinguishing characteristics remained between the possible floor layers. This was the only structure where the earth floor was so thick and where I was unable to distinguish more than one layer in 15 to 20 cm of deposit. It is quite possible that the residents here simply used earth as construction fill to raise the floor

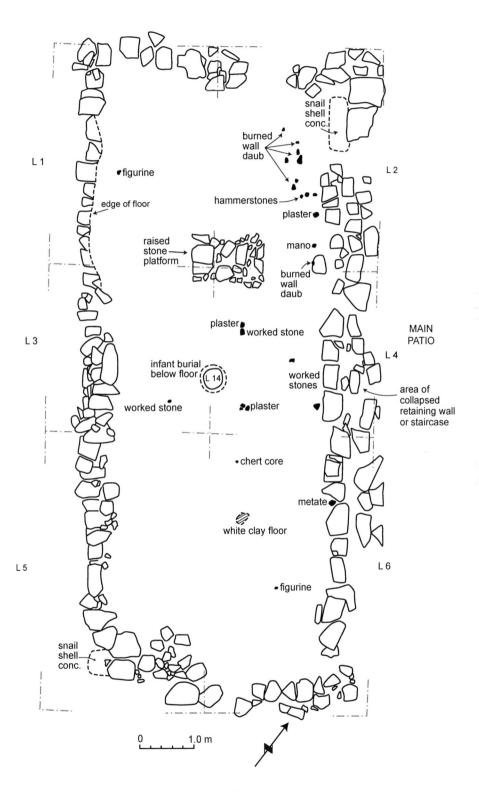

Figure 6.45. Plan of Structure 60, Floor 1.

Figure 6.46.   Infant burial in Structure 60 (10/14). Golondrina Unslipped: Calcite Temper Variety
jar with fillet banding on shoulder (visible on right side of vessel). This jar was also covered with
fragments from two Golondrina Unslipped: Calcite Temper Variety comales.

level instead of using a fill containing rubble, as
was done by other households.

Structure 61

No evidence was found for an Early
Postclassic occupation of this structure. It was
first built during the Late Postclassic period
and then rebuilt four more times after being
destroyed. The first structure was a house built
partly on the hard-packed, sterile substrate and
partly on a terrace extension. Figures 6.47 and
6.10 show this floor (Floor 5) and its retaining
walls. The southeast side of the house was
not parallel to the northwest side; instead, it
narrowed towards the north end where it abutted
a bedrock outcrop. The floor was prepared with
hard-packed earth; no plaster or other flooring
material was found. There were some burned
wall daub fragments but no other evidence

that the structure had burned down. A large
metate fragment and numerous small ones were
scattered about the floor, but there were no
features. The overall dimensions were 8.8 m by
4.4 m with a floor area of 38.7 m^2.

The next stage of construction included
two major modifications. The residents added
a staircase facing the patio, and they laid a clay
floor over the previous earth floor (Figure 6.48).
The staircase was built by depositing a layer of
construction fill along the entire length of the
house outside the retaining wall and then setting
in two rows of stone slab steps. The staircase fill
was the same white, crumbly limestone material
used to build up Structure 60's platform. The
top step of the staircase was level with the top of
the floor but not covered by the new clay layer.
It may have effectively widened the house by
80 to 90 cm. The new dimensions would have

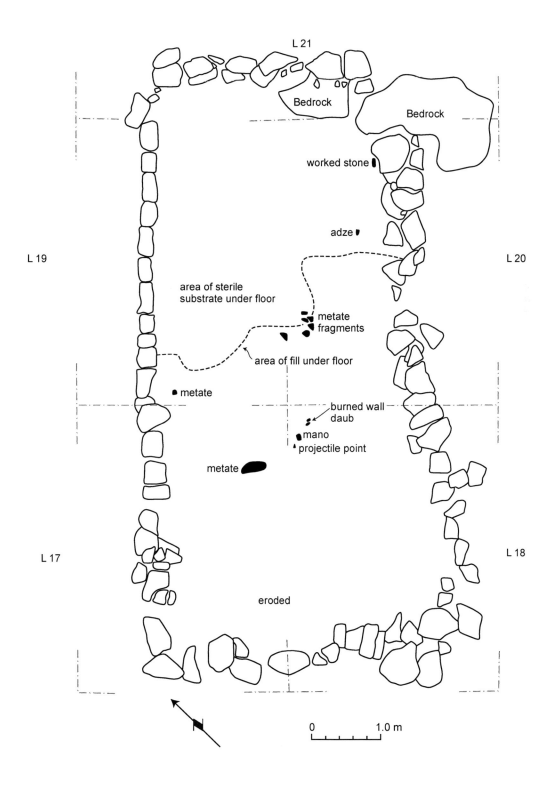

Figure 6.47.   Plan of Structure 61, Floor 5.

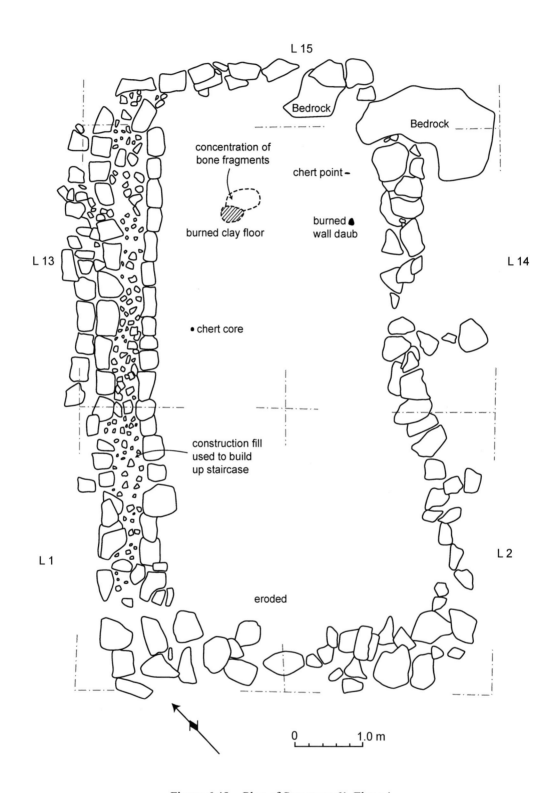

Figure 6.48.   Plan of Structure 61, Floor 4.

been 8.8 m long by 5.2 m wide, with a floor area of 45.8 m². There was one patch of burned clay floor in the north end of the house and nearby a chunk of burned wall daub. No more indications of a conflagration were discovered, but other remains may have been swept off of the platform before the next phase of construction began.

This next phase of construction consisted primarily of an earth re-flooring of the house. The floor was capped with a thin layer of clay. One patch of it remained preserved after burning. It is near the location of the patch on Floor 4 below. This consistency in location indicates that the burned floor area was a hearth (Figure 6.49). Also, there were no other burned patches on the floor nor were there any burned chunks of wall daub.

During this construction phase another course of large stone slabs was added to the northwest side's retaining wall at the top of the staircase. This would have reduced the house to its former size, if indeed the top of the staircase during the previous phase was part of the floor. In the north end of the house, buried beneath Floor 3 and penetrating into Floor 4, was a partial infant skeleton (L16). It was badly preserved: only part of the cranium remained, and this had been covered over by several pebbles, small cobbles, and a metate fragment. This was similar, in its lack of preparation, to a burial in Structure 1.

The residents re-floored the house (Floor 2), once more raising it a few centimeters. This time the floor came up to the level of the stone slabs placed at the top of the stairway during the last construction phase. The dimensions of the structure remained the same during this refurbishing since there were no modifications to the retaining walls (Figure 6.50). The floor itself was replastered with a white lime-clay which only preserved in the northern end of the structure. Because the northern end of the structure was upslope, and was covered by earth eroding down the hillside from above, the floor materials in this end of the house stood a much greater chance of being preserved. No patches of floor were preserved in the southern end of the house. Near the northeast retaining wall were recovered several large chunks of burned wall

daub that may have been pushed up against the wall after an earlier structure had burned down. They were not associated with this particular floor as there were no other indications of burning. There were very few artifacts and no features on the floor of the structure during this phase of construction.

The final phase of construction was a simple re-flooring (Figure 6.51). Floor 1 was constructed by laying down a thick layer of earth over the previous layers. I found no evidence of any more elaborate floor covering material. It is not known whether the walls were also rebuilt during this phase. Several artifacts were distributed over the floor area, but there were no features such as hearths.

DISCUSSION

The main aspects of the changes in house styles with respect to the processual model under consideration are: (1) the differences between the houses at the site and at neighboring sites in the region; (2) the differences between elite and non-elite; and (3) the way those differences changed during the community's occupation.

In terms of the aspect of change, there is too little known about the house architecture at contemporary sites in the region to make worthwhile comparisons. Nonetheless, something is known about the Terminal Classic period in the upper Grijalva region (Agrinier n.d.; Bryant and Clark n.d.; De Montmollin 1989b; Rivero Torres 1987), and I can say that the Early Postclassic houses at Canajasté are not very similar. Terminal Classic houses were quite variable, but for the most part they were squarer and more substantial than the Postclassic houses. They often had a finer crushed construction fill that helped to raise their platforms higher. Often, too, their floor areas were greater. Several houses at Los Cimientos had square inner platforms and possible room divisions (Rivero Torres 1987). For now, the differences that do exist between Terminal Classic house styles in the study region and the Postclassic house styles at Canajasté suggest that the latter were built in a nonlocal tradition.

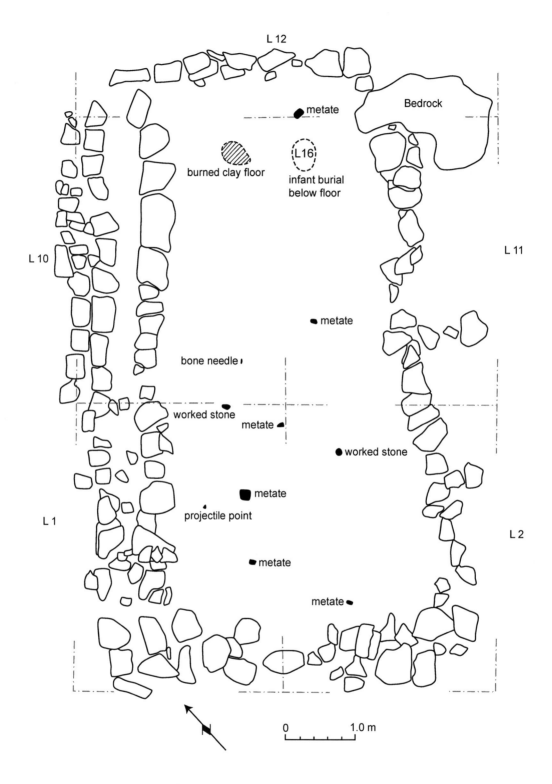

Figure 6.49.   Plan of Structure 61, Floor 3.

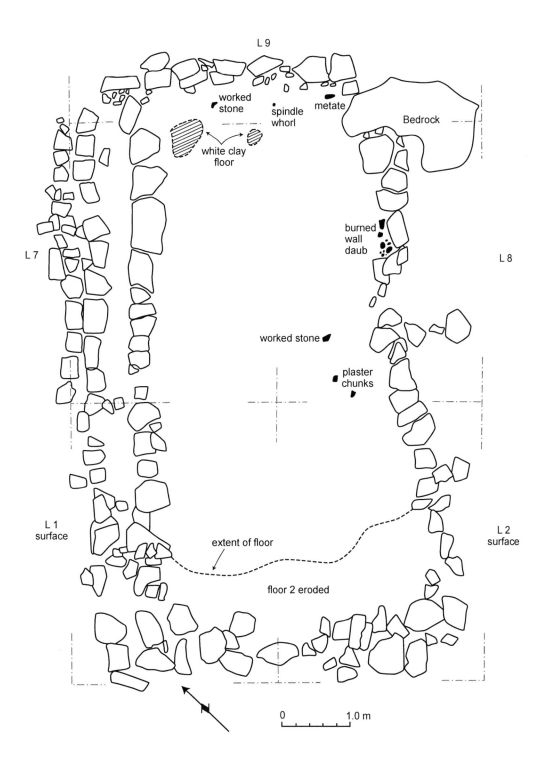

L 9

worked stone

spindle whorl

metate

Bedrock

white clay floor

L 7

burned wall daub

L 8

worked stone

plaster chunks

L 1 surface

extent of floor

floor 2 eroded

L 2 surface

N

0   1.0 m

Figure 6.50. Plan of Structure 61, Floor 2.

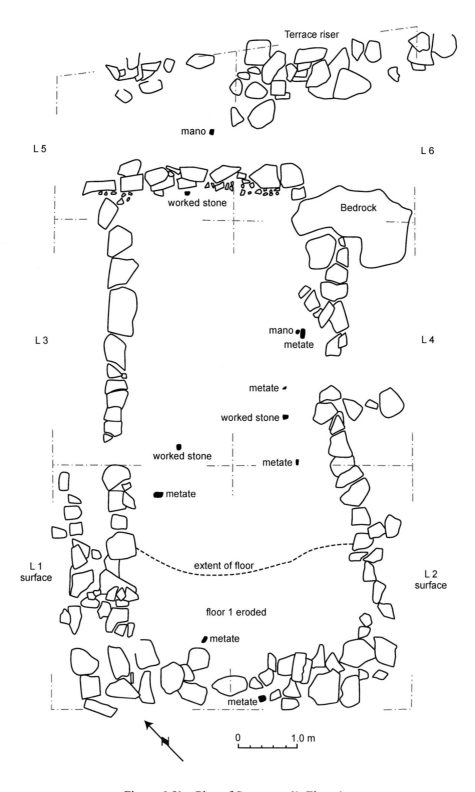

Figure 6.51.   Plan of Structure 61, Floor 1.

Based on the evidence for a founding of the site in a previously unoccupied location, the first Canajasteños came into the region from somewhere other than the upper Grijalva. Unfortunately, there are no house excavations from the immediately neighboring sites in Guatemala to determine if they brought their house styles from there.

I will now examine the second and third areas of comparison: differences between the elite and non-elite houses in the Early and Late Postclassic. Here it will be possible to make some more definite statements. The most important pattern is that in the Early Postclassic there was a great deal of difference between elite and non-elite house styles. Furthermore, the elite in Structure 22 built and rebuilt their houses several times adding on to their length and re-flooring them, while the non-elite in Structure 2 apparently did not. Non-elite houses remained low to the ground, had earth floors, and were squarer. Towards the end of the Early Postclassic the elite emphasized the length of their house, at the expense of width, and maintained a distinct style, setting themselves off from the non-elite.

At the beginning of the Late Postclassic the elite in House Group 2 added on new structures to their compound instead of simply making their initial house larger. The non-elite continued to build their houses in the same style as earlier and, thus, the difference between the two classes remained. It was during the first part of the Late Postclassic that the houses—both elite and non-elite—show evidence of repeated burnings. Whether the burnings were accidental or by warfare, the occupants returned to rebuild their houses in the same styles as before, with the elite (in Structure 21) and non-elite (in Structure 2) maintaining the same distinctive differences. Finally, in the latter part of the Late Postclassic period, the non-elite began to build their houses after the style of the elite. They also began to add new structures to their compounds, forming patio house groups much as the elite had. This change shows that the non-elite were beginning to invest more in house constructions and that they were being allowed to emulate the elite. The elite, meanwhile, were elaborating their traditional style and staying ahead of

the non-elite in terms of the size of individual structures, rather than by changing the style of their structures.

This is the trend predicted if warfare becomes a more dominant mode of inter-polity relations for a state. What is most striking is that by the end of the Late Postclassic most houses at the site were built in the same style that the elite had used from the outset of the Early Postclassic occupation.

It appears that community-wide house styles were being emphasized and that these styles were an elaboration of, what was by then, a local tradition. The evidence of house burnings and the increasing stylistic similarity of houses are most likely the result of increasing warfare. As we will see in Chapter 8, changes in over a dozen classes of artifacts and subsistence remains show that interregional exchange decreased at the end of the Early Postclassic period as warfare was increasing. At this point, I can summarize the pattern as one of intruding colonists, probably from neighboring highland Guatemala, who initially emphasized interregional trade (during the Early Postclassic) and then became increasingly involved in warfare as time went on.

ENDNOTES

1 Supplemental information collected as part of the Canajasté Archaeological Project, including feature and artifact photographs, drawings, data, tables, and field notes are available online at **cIRcle**, the permanent digital research repository at the University of British Columbia Library. The Canajasté research archive is located under the UBC Laboratory of Archaeology collection: https://circle.ubc.ca/handle/2429/321.

2 Both Figures 6.41 and 6.42 which show these floors are somewhat misleading because they also show a retaining wall. This retaining wall was not present when these floors were used and is only included to suggest the likely limits of the structures associated with Floors 2 and 3.

CHAPTER 7

THE HOUSEHOLD ARTIFACTS

Changes in the intensity of exchange and warfare and the colonization of an area by elites or by entire communities will have different effects on the portable material culture and items of subsistence used by individual household members. The question posed here is: how are changes in the artifacts from household deposits related to the social changes that took place during the household's life-span?

Monitoring the changes in artifacts and subsistence remains from house floor to house floor and then comparing these changes among houses is, in many ways, more difficult than monitoring variation in architecture. This partly because the assumptions required are less reliable. For example, the artifacts that enter into house deposits, patios, and middens are not necessarily associated with the occupants and builders of the house. Conversely, many of the tools and artifacts used in the building might have been discarded elsewhere. Excavated household debris may not always be representative of the total range of goods in use during a house's occupancy. In temporary hunting and gathering campsites there is a close correspondence between the tools used in a shelter and the tools discarded in and near it (Yellen 1977). In sedentary communities, refuse must be constantly cleared from heavily used living spaces (Hayden and Cannon 1983).[1] As a result, we cannot expect a one-to-one correspondence between the artifacts in an archaeological house and the activities that took place in it. Even in a living household the material culture at a single point in time may not accurately "reflect" the activities that take place in the house, let alone the social or political status of the household members (Hayden and Cannon 1984; Wilk 1984). Small artifacts and fragments generated year after year by the householders, however, will be lost within the

house, trapped in dirt floors and eventually become part of the archaeological record. These small artifacts, recovered in situ, are a direct result of past household activities. Their study, while perhaps not as representative of ongoing activities as the artifacts and debris left behind in a hunter-gatherer campsite, can tell us a great deal about the activities that took place in the house.

Unfortunately, few ethnoarchaeological studies have tried to gather information about the effect of household changes on the debris left behind.[2] Admittedly, studying change is extremely difficult since it requires many years of careful observation and recording the effects of a household's changing social interactions on its consumption and discard patterns. Only such a study would provide the kinds of information necessary to answer the question of how refuse can be used to study change.

Lacking such a study, there still remain some assumptions that can be made. One such assumption is that changes in frequencies or types of archaeological artifacts will be caused by changes in the household's consumption and disposal activities. These activities are, in turn, related to social and political processes that affect the community as a whole, and it is their change that I am interested in monitoring (Douglas and Isherwood 1980). Since a number of artifacts will be influenced by the same processes in the same way, it should be possible to separate random variation from processual variation.

Even more important than this assumption, reliable or not, is the way comparisons are made. By avoiding the goal of synchronic reconstruction of the entire community, it is possible to look for trajectories of change in individual households. Individual sequences or trajectories of household change can then be compared across many households during the span of a community's occupation. This requires knowledge of changes in artifacts and subsistence remains from layer to layer, floor to floor, in each house or group of houses used by a household. This is the same procedure used for the analysis of changing household features in the previous chapter. That step necessarily came first because the house features are the minimal units of analysis for the artifact assemblages. They define the trajectories of artifact change.

In looking for changes in artifacts from floor to floor or midden layer to midden layer, I will be stating, for example, that House X underwent several re-floorings. Associated with each is a group of artifacts, some part of which represents a portion of the artifacts discarded or lost by the residents during the occupation of the floor. If from floor to floor there is a steady increase in the frequency, proportion, or density of some class of artifact, say imported spindle whorls, then it is the increase in spinning activities and the increase in importation that is of interest in understanding the changing processes. This trajectory can then be compared to other households where there may be different sequences of changes in the quantity and types of spindle whorls.

At this point I should restate that I am not looking so much for evidence that one household or group of households were spinners and others were not, nor that both the elite and non-elite households used and discarded tools for spinning cotton. Instead, I am trying to determine whether, for example, in households with evidence for spinning, its importance increased, remained the same, or decreased through time. Furthermore, I am interested in whether or not the tools used were imported, and if the frequency of imported tools changed. Finally, I want to know if the kinds of changes that took place differed between the elite and the non-elite households in the community.

One assumption necessary for this analysis is that the artifacts recovered actually originated from household members. As mentioned earlier, it is certain that some portion of the debris generated by household residents will be discarded away from the house or patio.

This in itself is worthy of consideration in understanding household and community organization (Binford 1981). Dump and discard locations, if their role in the social and economic organization is properly studied (e.g., Wright et al. 1980), and not viewed as sources of distortion of the "real" picture, can be some of the best sources of processual information. Nonetheless, there is another problem that is more difficult to deal with: the introduction of items into house deposits as part of the construction materials.

In Mesoamerica, as elsewhere in the world, house floors, walls, platform fill, and in some cases even roofs, are often made of earth (or adobe). When the earth is taken from locations outside the community or even deep pits within, it is likely to be sterile. However, when it is scraped off the surface from locations within a community, it can contain either contemporary or earlier refuse. If, for example, builders re-floor a house with earth taken from such a location, the floor matrix may contain quantities of artifacts that had nothing to do with the activities associated with the residents of that particular floor. Similar inclusions can also be introduced in wattle-and-daub walls (Figure 7.1). When the walls and floor are made of the same earth and when that is taken from locations relatively near the house, then it may be impossible to distinguish collapsed wall daub from the floor material, or either of these from the surrounding patio area.

This is not a problem in situations where the floor material consists of layers of fine sand or clay that has obviously come from a sterile location (Flannery 1976:16) and when preserved chunks of the walls show no signs of containing intrusive earlier materials. But throughout Mesoamerica, and certainly in the villages visited during the Coxoh Ethnoarchaeological Project, the primary floor material consisted of nothing more than a tamped level surface, either no different from, or even made from, the soil surrounding the house (Blake and Blake 1988). Villagers constructed wattle-and-daub walls in similar fashion.

In the Tzeltal community of Aguacatenango, where the Coxoh Project spent three months during 1979 studying households,

Figure 7.1. Man in Aguacatenango, Chiapas, preparing mud to daub on a newly built house wall.

I conducted a brief study of the contents of daub walls. Appendix C describes the community conditions and house construction techniques that may lead to artifacts being incorporated in walls. Two conclusions derive from these observations and apply to the analyses that follow. First, the numbers of most items contained in the walls is quite high (Figure 7.2). If combined with estimates of the contents of floors of similar thickness, then one could have a sizeable sample of artifacts from a house excavation that had nothing to do with the activities taking place within the house. Figure 7.3 shows a collapsed house structure in

Aguacatenango where the daub has fallen off the wattle walls (which are still standing), showing the considerable amount of wall material that can cover a house floor. Second, the size of such inclusions is often very small, less than 3 cm, and this is precisely the size of items that would be expected to get lost and work their way into earth floors, in spite of regular sweeping. Such items included in the floors could outnumber primary refuse left behind by the residents, depending upon the length of the house's occupation.

Because of this, it might be "safer" to study middens associated with houses and not run

Figure 7.2.   Geoff and Joanna Spurling counting artifacts in
wattle-and-daub wall in Aguacatenango, 1979 (see Appendix C).

the risk of misinterpreting household activities based on extraneous floor and wall inclusions; however, there are several precautions that can be taken to minimize the risk and allow one to be confident that the artifacts in the house were indeed left there by the occupants. First, it should be possible to analyze the earth used for the floor to determine whether it comes from sterile deposits outside the community. If so, artifacts in the floor probably resulted from the household's activities and not from previous ones. Second, if there are any preserved chunks of wall daub they can be examined to see whether there are significant inclusions. If there

are, then one should consider the possibility that extraneous artifacts had been accidentally included. Third, if it can be established that there is some limited mixing, then the separate floors from one house could be examined to see if the earth used to make the floors comes from the same source area. If it does, one could assume that the degree of mixing is constant from floor to floor.

One of the advantages of looking at change in types and numbers of artifacts is that constant mixing would not affect the direction or degree of change. In contrast, "reconstruction" of the household's activities for purposes of

Figure 7.3. Mud walls of a wattle-and-daub house collapsed
on top of the house floor in Aguacatenango.

comparison with other households would be
hindered. Fortunately, the kind of processual
analysis used in this study does not rely on a
prior social or economic reconstruction before
evaluating the changes that took place. Finally,
the interpretations based on changing artifacts
are only one facet of the pattern of change to be
studied. For the interpretations to hold they must
coincide with the trajectories of change revealed
by the house features, settlement patterns, and
civic-ceremonial structures.

ARTIFACT RECOVERY TECHNIQUES

At Canajaste, the artifacts were recovered
by screening all of the house deposits using 5
mm mesh screens. Excavation proceeded slowly
in order to expose the deposits stratigraphically
and find all remnants of earlier floor and wall
constructions and earlier midden layers. In the

process, the locations of all artifacts found in
situ were plotted on floor plans. Notably, the
majority of items were small and so had to await
discovery during screening. In general, there
were few large artifacts such as ceramic vessels,
manos or *metates*, or obsidian cores on the
house or patio floors. Large artifacts were more
common in construction fill brought in to build
up a house floor or terrace. Artifacts recovered
in the house floor deposits were much smaller,
usually in the 1 cm to 3 cm range, and were
usually broken. There were no concentrations of
items that might have been caused by localized
and recurrent activity areas. Most items
represent the long-term accumulation of small
artifacts during daily activities.

The assemblages of artifacts used in
the analysis that follows depend upon their
association with particular features, as described
in the last chapter. Floors were identified during

excavation, and as soon as one was found it was exposed over the entire house surface. At that point the floor was excavated in manageable lots, 2-3 m on a side, down to the beginning of a new layer. Thus, all the artifacts associated with a particular floor were actually *in* it. Most floors were only 5 cm thick, made primarily of packed earth, and so any given floor could have trapped some small artifacts during its life span. Any artifacts immediately above the floor were included with whatever deposit overlaid it. For example, if a layer of construction fill was laid down over the top of a floor in order to elevate a new floor level, then the artifacts above the floor were included in the layer of construction fill. No artifacts associated with construction fill deposits are included in the following analyses because it is impossible to be sure where they came from or whether they were even used by the household. Likewise, all terrace collapse material and slope-wash deposits are excluded. The only deposits that are used for the comparisons described in the following sections are house floors, patio floors, and middens associated with the floors or patios.

IMPORTED GOODS

A distinction between locally produced and imported artifacts must be made in order to investigate the changing importance of the interregional processes under study (Table 7.1).[*] In general, I expect the elite to have had more imported items than the non-elite, regardless of the processes underlying the community's founding or its continued interaction with its neighbors. But, as outlined in Chapter 4, the differences between elite and non-elite should change, through time, in predictable ways as the relative importance of each specific process changes. To sum up the expectations: increasing exchange should allow the elite to have increasing amounts of imported items, and increasing warfare should restrict the elite's importation of goods. Colonization by foreign elites should rapidly increase the differences

---

* All tables cited in Chapter 7 appear immediately at the end of the chapter text.

between elites' and non-elites' access to imported items. If the whole community, both elites and non-elites, began as a colony then both groups should have high frequencies of nonlocal items at the outset. Subsequent differentiation between elite and non-elite would then depend upon exchange and warfare with local populations and with their own homeland. These expectations should hold for both ritual and utilitarian goods.

Unfortunately, it is difficult to distinguish between the importation of nonlocal items and the local emulation of nonlocal styles. If people imported nonlocal materials, such as clays, obsidians, or basalts and then manufactured their own tools after foreign fashions, it would be even more difficult to distinguish between these two possibilities.

This last case should not be discounted but there are several reasons why it is unlikely. In preindustrial societies it is more efficient to transport finished items than raw materials. Part of the reason for this is that waste materials are produced during the manufacturing process. It would cost less to transport finished items and thereby avoid transporting potential manufacturing waste. For example, in producing pottery, some pots always crack during drying and firing, and clay is, therefore, lost. In the example of metate production, a great deal of raw material must be chipped away and discarded (Hayden and Nelson 1981). In both cases it would be preferable to transport finished or nearly finished items in order to reduce transportation costs. Both the exporter and the importer would benefit, especially when there is no easy means of bulk transportation available.

Even more important is the labor investment in finished items making their exchange value greater than for raw materials. By exporting finished or nearly finished items, the exporters can trade both their materials and their labor. Nevertheless, larger and more powerful polities should prefer to import raw materials and to invest their labor in the production of finished items. The larger the polity the more likely it could import raw materials and export finished products. Conversely, the smaller the polity the less likely it would import unworked raw materials or unfinished items.

Both the ethnohistoric documents and the archaeological record indicate that communities the upper Grijalva region were less developed politically and had smaller populations than most of their neighbors in highland Guatemala, such as the Mam, Quiché, and Cakchiquel. During the Late Postclassic period these groups controlled the obsidian and basalt sources and provided many of the imports brought into the upper Grijalva region. Both obsidian and basalt tools were imported in finished or nearly finished form. At Canajasté, there is very little obsidian or basalt manufacturing debris.

The same is true for all other items, including ceramics. There are ceramic similarities between the upper Grijalva region and the western highlands of Guatemala. People in the upper Grijalva region either imported ceramics from their Guatemalan neighbors, or they used local materials and emulated the styles in these other regions. It is likely that they imported clays and tempers from Guatemala and also emulated Guatemalan ceramic styles.

Hill (1980:42) observes that in the Quiché area of Baja Verapaz, and indeed throughout much of Guatemala where Maya peoples still manufacture ceramics, most communities do not sell or trade their raw materials (Reina and Hill 1978). These materials, clays and tempers, are conceived of as part of the community and not to be sold or traded. Only finished ceramics are traded. In highland Chiapas, modern potters also use local sources for clay and temper. This is true for communities that produce ceramics for export as well as for those that produce ceramics for local consumption (Deal 1998).

Therefore, in the analysis of the Canajasté artifacts, I assume that items made of nonlocal materials were imported in a finished or nearly finished form. Items made locally, of local materials, were made either in the local style or were attempts to copy foreign styles. The obsidian analysis, for example, shows that most of it was imported as prepared cores and none as unworked blocks. Blades were then made at the site and used either without modification or, with

a minimum of labor were made into scrapers, knives, drills, and projectile points.

In the sections that follow I evaluate the changes that took place in eight categories of artifacts (Figures 7.4a-c). I will present the patterns of change in ceramics, obsidian, obsidian projectile points, spinning, weaving and sewing tools, grinding stones, marine shell ornaments, metal artifacts, and obsidian bloodletters (Table 7.2). All of the analyses are carried out in the same format: I look for sequential changes in each house and then compare the changes in elite houses to those in non-elite houses. This makes it possible to determine if the elites and non-elites were becoming more similar or more different through time. I begin with the ceramic analysis because ceramics are also used to distinguish between the Early and Late Postclassic period. I also rely on ceramic frequencies for several ratios of artifact density.

CERAMICS

Ceramics are ideal for monitoring the changing importance of exchange, warfare, and colonization at Canajasté because they are sensitive to both internal and external mechanisms of interaction. The following expectations derive from the discussion presented in Chapter 4. If people from within the upper Grijalva region founded Canajasté, then their ceramic styles should be similar to styles used in surrounding communities. If Canajasté was founded by colonists from outside the upper Grijalva region, then their ceramic styles should be different from local patterns. If Canajasté was colonized by nonlocal elites then only the elites would have nonlocal ceramic styles. Subsequently, warfare and exchange would cause new changes in the degree of ceramic differentiation between the elite and non-elite. With increasing exchange, ceramic style differences between the elite and non-elite would increase. With increasing warfare, the ceramic styles of elite and non-elite would become more similar.

The transition from Early to Late Postclassic marks a rapid change in most

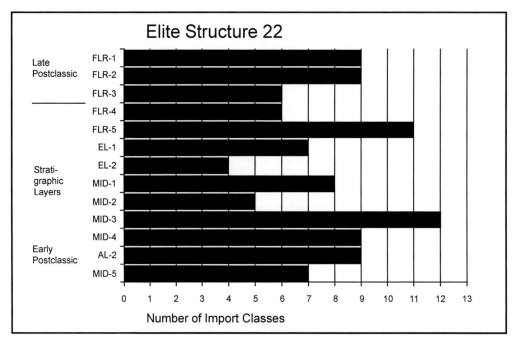

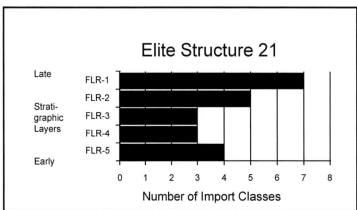

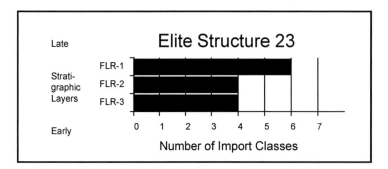

Figure 7.4a.   Graphs of the numbers of import classes present in each deposit of House Group 2, Structures 21, 22, and 23 (from Table 7.2). Y-axis is the stratigraphic sequence of deposits within a structure.

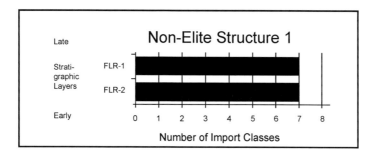

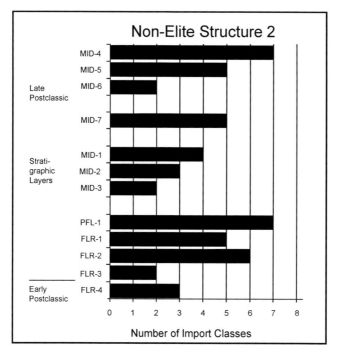

Figure 7.4b. Graphs of the numbers of import classes present in each deposit of House Group 1, Structures 1 and 2 (from Table 7.2).

ceramic types.[3] This shift in ceramics was used to date the house floor and midden deposits to the Early or Late Postclassic period. Spindle whorls and figurines also changed after the Early Postclassic period and so were also used for dating the house deposits.

Why did this stylistic change take place at Canajasté? Which of the mechanisms under study was predominantly responsible for the change? Before trying to answer these questions it is necessary to take a closer look at the Early Postclassic ceramics from the various excavated house groups.

There were more ceramic styles in the Early Postclassic period than in the Late Postclassic. In order to compare the two periods, I have grouped the vessels into three broad functional classes. These are (1) cooking, (2) serving, and (3) storing (or transporting) vessels. Ceramics were also classified into stylistic types based on shape (i.e., forms such as jars, bowls and dishes, *comales*, and colanders) and decoration (i.e., slipped/unslipped, painted, incised). Within each group there were some types that occurred mainly in the Early deposits, some that occurred in both the Early and Late deposits, and some

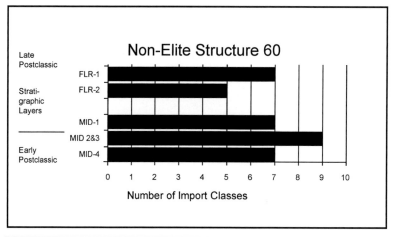

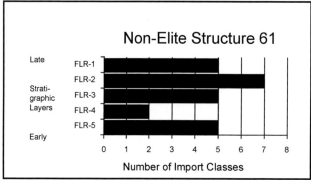

Figure 7.4c. Graphs of the numbers of import classes present in each deposit of House Group 25, Structures 60 and 61 (from Table 7.2).

that occurred mainly in the Late deposits. When these temporal subgroups were formed there were nine groups of vessel types which I have labeled Groups 1 to 9 (defined below). These analytical groupings make it possible to observe both functional and stylistic ceramic change over the community's life span. Appendix D discusses all of the ceramic types in each of these groups.

Ceramic Comparisons with Neighboring Regions

Little is known about Early Postclassic ceramics in the upper Grijalva region, making it difficult to compare them with the ceramics from Canajasté. This is because there are so

few known Early Postclassic sites in the upper Grijalva region—and of these, fewer still have been excavated. Some of the large sites with Early Postclassic occupations have few if any of the types that are common both at Canajasté and at sites farther to the east in Guatemala. Near Canajasté, the sites of Los Encuentros, Guajilar, Tenam Rosario, and Lagartero have very few of the ceramic types that are most distinctive of the Early Postclassic deposits at Canajasté: Choom Red-on-unslipped, Cacomixtle Red-and-black, Chupaflor Red-and-black, and Tol Polychrome: Wide-band Variety (Bryant, Lee, and Blake 2005:522). Only Los Encuentros and Guajilar have Gavilan Red (Figure 7.5) and Tohil Plumbate, two other types common at Canajasté. Meanwhile, all four of these sites with Early

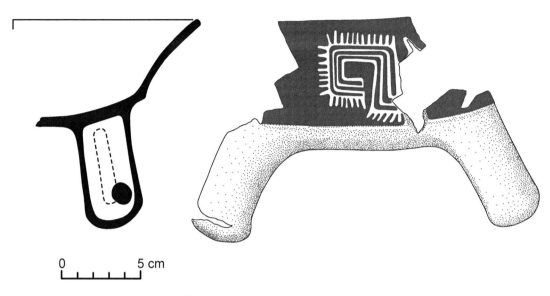

0   5 cm

Figure 7.5. Late Postclassic Gavilan Red: Fortress Variety tripod dish (B-101). This particular specimen is painted with a dull red paint on buff interior and exterior. It is the only one with a resist design.

Postclassic deposits (besides Canajasté) were major Late Classic centers and share many of the same Late Classic ceramic types (Blake et al. 2005:418-420).

    The distinctive Early Postclassic ceramics from Canajasté are more similar to types found in the western highlands of Guatemala (Wauchope 1970) than to those from the upper Grijalva region. The most common Early Postclassic hemispherical bowl type from Canajasté is Tol Polychrome: Wide-band Variety, an early variant of the dull-paint, polychrome style that Wauchope (1970:110, Fig. 62d-f) describes for highland Guatemala. These bowls have black and red geometric and naturalistic, animal designs painted on a tan slip and appear to be a precursor to the same dull-paint, hemispherical bowls (Tol Polychrome: Tol Variety) that became widely distributed throughout western Guatemala and the upper Grijalva region during the Late Postclassic period. The Early Postclassic variant is slightly larger, has broader lines, and has more naturalistic bird motifs than do the later variants (Figure 7.6). The later variant with predominantly geometric motifs has much

thinner lines (Figure 7.7). Early bowls of this type have one broad black band on the interior just below a thicker, red rim band. The later type has two narrow black bands below the red rim band. The similarities between these two bowl types include forms, size, paste, surface finish, color, and design layout. The later style is undoubtedly an outgrowth of the earlier one.

    There are few other decorated bowl types that evolved in situ. A distinct break exists between most Early and Late styles (see Table 7.4 for all counts and percentages for all decorated bowls). Several decorated bowl types simply do not carry into the Late Postclassic period. Figure 7.8 illustrates some of the interior- and exterior-decorated bowls restricted to the Early Postclassic period.

    Figure 7.9 charts the shifts in percentages of the nine subgroups of ceramics from elite to non-elite deposits and from Early to Late deposits. The chart is based on the tallies of rim sherds only and includes all of the unmixed floor and midden deposits (Table 7.6). The nine subgroups were determined by separating the types that occurred most commonly in the Early deposits from those commonly found in both

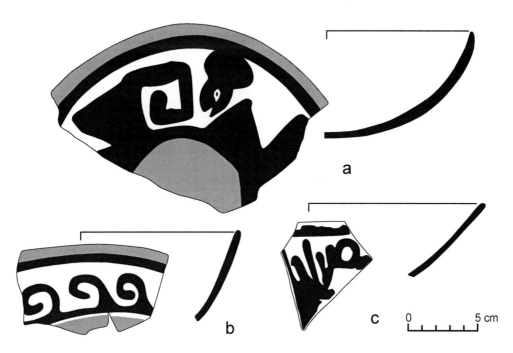

Figure 7.6. Early Postclassic Tol Polychrome: Wide Band Variety bowls (B-40): a) geometric motif; b) hook motif; c) bird motif.

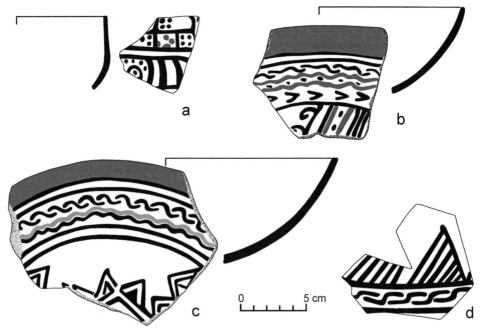

Figure 7.7. Late Postclassic Tol Polychrome: a) Tol exterior decorated bowl (B-67); b) and c) Tol interior decorated bowls (B-42); d) Tol water jar (neck sherd) (J- 13)

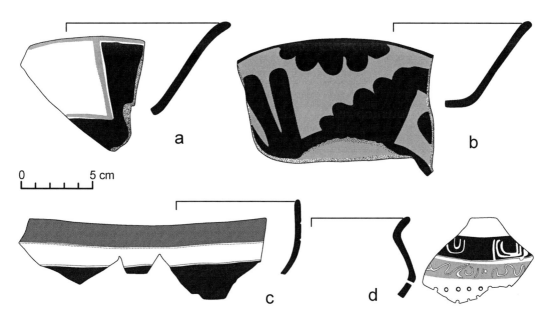

Figure 7.8. Early Postclassic bowls and colander: a) Tol Polychrome: Wide Band Variety (B- 40); b) Cacomixtle Red-and-black: Cacomixtle Variety (B-46); c) Chupaflor Red-and-black: Incised Variety (B-22); d) Chupaflor Red-and-black: Incised Variety small-holed colander (C-20).

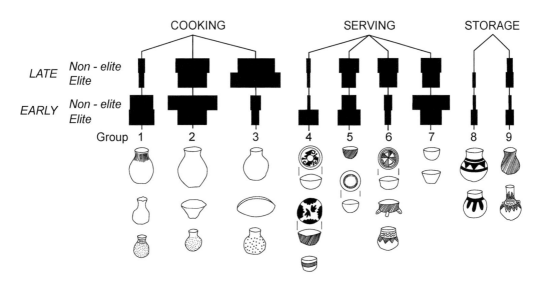

Figure 7.9. Chart of the changes in percentages of ceramic types (rim sherds only) from Early to Late Postclassic, between elite and non- elite house groups. Within each of the three main categories of vessels, cooking, serving, and storage, the groups are arranged from early types to late types as one moves from left to right.

Early and Late deposits, and those common in only the Late deposits.

Figure 7.9 allows a visual comparison of the overall relative density of each ceramic subgroup in each of the four types of aggregate deposits (Late elite and non-elite, and Early elite and non-elite). Since the densities are standardized to a percentage of total density, the type of deposit (floor or midden) does not influence the variation. The overall relative density of cooking, serving, and storing vessels remained about the same in both periods, but the variation between elite and non-elite changed considerably.

Changes in Cooking Vessels

Group 1 cooking vessels consists of Golondrina Unslipped: Calcite-temper Variety jars (brushed neck sub-variant) (C-7), Saraquato Unslipped: Saraquato Variety jars (C-4), and Chupaflor Red-and-black: Incised Variety decorated colanders (C-20). Group 1 vessels were relatively more abundant in the Early deposits than in the Late deposits (Table 7.3), but there was little difference in their relative abundance between elite and non-elite households.

Group 2 cooking vessels occurred in the same relative density in both Early and Late deposits. They include Golondrina Unslipped: Calcite-temper Variety jars (C-1), Golondrina Unslipped: Red Rim Variety small-holed colanders (C-65), and Saraquato Unslipped: Saraquato Variety coarse rough bowls (heavily burned) (C-36) (Table 7.3). They were more common in non-elite households in both the Early and Late periods.

Group 3 ceramics were abundant in the Late period households and included: Golondrina Unslipped: Golondrina Variety jars (C-2), Golondrina Unslipped: Calcite-temper Variety comales, both plain rim (C-14) and fillet rim (C-61), and Golondrina Unslipped: Calcite-temper Variety large-holed colanders (C-63) (Table 7.3). Although vessels in this group were used by both the elite and non-elite, they were even more common in elite households.

Changes in cooking vessel usage have important implications for the interregional mechanisms impinging upon the community. Cooking vessels were, for the most part, made locally. Their private use compared with the public use of serving or storage and transport vessels, means that cooking pots would be the last to change and the least likely to have been traded or copied. In contrast to changes in serving vessels, most stylistic changes in cooking vessels would result from a change in the actual populations using them. Furthermore, functional changes in cooking vessels would indicate the introduction of new or different ways of preparing and consuming food.

The extent to which new food preparation techniques were introduced is an indication of the extent to which large scale social change took place. Figure 7.9 shows that both stylistic change and functional change occurred during the transition from Early to Late Postclassic. Cooking jars with brushed necks all but died out. Finer tempered jars (which could also have been undecorated storage jars) became more common. But most importantly, a whole new food preparation complex was introduced: the production of tortillas. The new ceramics used to make tortillas include colanders for straining the boiled corn and griddles or comales for cooking the flat corn cakes. Both large-holed colanders and comales are part of a technological complex used in making tortillas, one that is still common today throughout the Maya area and much of Mesoamerica.

Tortillas were not made at Canajasté until the end of the Early Postclassic period. Judging by the rapid introduction of comales and large-holed colanders, and their stronger association with Late elite households, they were probably introduced as a higher status technology by the elite (Marcus 1982:248; Thompson 1930).

In the Early Postclassic period, Group 3 vessel types were rare, but slightly more common in non-elite house deposits than in elite deposits. By the Late Postclassic, Group 3 vessels were most common in elite households. This suggests that either a nonlocal elite colonized the site in the Late Postclassic, and introduced a new corn preparation technology, or that the existing local elite rapidly adopted this technology in emulation of a foreign elite. Changes in food preparation and consumption, especially changes involving corn, the mainstay of the Maya diet, were probably not taken lightly. These changes are a part of the Late Postclassic Maya elite's emulation of Central Mexican customs, including the tortilla-making tradition. Tortilla-making technology dates to much earlier times in Central Mexico and Oaxaca (Caso and Bernal 1965:879, 894). Rands and Smith (1965:109) say that the use of comales was much more common in highland Guatemala than in the Maya Lowlands, and, therefore, their use may have spread to the upper Grijalva region from highland Guatemala.

Changes in Serving Vessels

I have already mentioned the stylistic changes in dull-paint, polychrome bowls. Other stylistic changes also occurred. Group 4 is comprised of several decorated bowl and dish types and is the one group that nearly disappeared during the Late Postclassic. Included are six types: Chupaflor Red-and-black: Incised Variety incised exterior bowls (B-22) (Figure 7.8c), Chupaflor Red-and-black: Chupaflor Variety dishes and bowls (B-24), Cacomixtle Red-and-black: Incised Variety incised exterior bowls (B-26), Chupaflor Red-and-black: Gouged-incised Variety bowls (B-28), Tol Polychrome: Wide Band Variety dishes and bowls (B-40) (Figure 7.6a-c), and Cacomixtle Red-and-black: Cacomixtle Variety dishes and bowls (B-46) (Figure 7.8a-b).

Group 5 bowls include Coneta Red: Alan Variety (B-31), Possible Tol Polychrome: Tol Variety (B-44) (both Early and Late variants), and Choom Red-on-unslipped: Choom Variety dishes and bowls (B-48). This group of bowls is found almost as commonly in the late deposits as in the early deposits. They are more simply decorated than the Group 4 bowl types and are likely candidates for local manufactures.

Group 6 bowls are also found in both Early and Late Postclassic deposits—but are much more common in Late deposits. They include interior painted Tol Polychrome: Tol Variety

(B-42) (Figure 7.7a-c), Gavilan Red: Gavilan Variety and Fortress Variety tripod dishes (B-38 and B-101) (Figure 7.8), Tol Polychrome: Tol Variety barrel-shaped exterior decorated bowls (B-67) (Figure 7.7a) and likely Tol Polychrome: Tol Variety bowls with heavily eroded surfaces (B-33).

Group 7 bowls consist of two undecorated types: Golondrina Unslipped: Golondrina Variety dishes and bowls (B-30) and Golondrina Unslipped: Golondrina Variety tripod dishes (B-32). This group was equally common in the Early and Late Postclassic periods. Both types share the same range of shapes, from incurved to straight, outflaring sides.

The changes in these bowls from Early to Late period and between elite and non-elite are similar to changes in the cooking vessels. In Early Postclassic deposits, decorated bowls were much more common in elite houses than in non-elite houses, and the non-elite had higher densities of undecorated bowls (Figure 7.9). If these decorated bowls were imports, then the elite clearly had greater access to imported goods. The disappearance, by the end of the Early Postclassic, of all bowl types that could have been imports, corroborated evidence presented earlier for decreasing exchange. Only the types with the least amount of decoration persisted into the Late Postclassic period. Figure 7.9 shows that differences between the elite and non-elite in the percentages of bowl groups 4, 5, and 7 were much greater during the Early Postclassic than in the succeeding period. By the Late Postclassic non-elites had only slightly higher percentages of bowls than elites.

This pattern suggests that elite access to imported and decorated bowls diminished and that bowls ceased to be used by the elite as symbols of higher status. It also indicates that activities using decorated bowls, such as feasting, declined in frequency. Late Postclassic elite and non-elite bowl styles became more similar, a pattern predicted if warfare increased in importance. The variation in bowl styles is most consistent with a process of decreasing exchange during the Early Postclassic and increasing warfare during the Late Postclassic. There is no evidence for colonization by nonlocal elites after the initial founding of the community.

Changes in Storage Vessels

Figure 7.9 shows that decorated vessels whose function was either storing or transporting materials were always relatively scarce (see Table 7.5 for all counts and percentages of plain bowls and storage jars). Group 8 vessels included three types of decorated jars, all of which were quite rare: Chupaflor Red-and-black: Incised Variety jars (J-16); Cacomixtle Red-and-black: Cacomixtle Variety jars (J-12 and J-70); and Xela Polychrome: Xela Variety jars (J-68). Golondrina Unslipped: Golondrina Variety jars (C-2) in Group 3 could also have been used for storage; however, it has been included with the cooking vessels because its lack of decoration suggests use in private contexts, and cooking activities cannot be ruled out.

Group 8 jars were stylistically similar to many bowl types in Group 4. They, too, were confined almost exclusively to Early Postclassic deposits and may have been imports. Their higher frequencies in elite house deposits suggest that they were status markers.

Group 9 jars occurred in both Early and Late deposits and included the following types: Choom Red-on-unslipped: Choom Variety jars (J-8), Xela Polychrome: Xela Variety strap handle jars (J-18) and Coneta Red: Alan Variety strap handle jars (J-19) (Figure 7.7d). As with the other ceramic categories, there is more differentiation between the elite and non-elite in the Early Postclassic than in the Late Postclassic.

Within-period Changes in Bowls and Dishes

The previous discussion outlined the broad changes between Early and Late Postclassic and between elite and non-elite households. It showed that there were some significant changes in trade and warfare (as indicated by ceramic variation), two mechanisms affecting social relations between the elite and non-elite during the Postclassic. I will now try to be more specific about the effects of trade and warfare by examining changes in the consumption of bowls and dishes within each household. Figure 7.9 shows that the elite used more serving vessels during the Early period and, then, in the Late period, both classes used nearly equal amounts.

The differences in bowl use between elite and non-elite households should be greater if Canajasté began as a small colony of elite foreigners dominating and reorganizing a local population than if it began as a complete colony. If, after Canajasté's founding, the differences between elite and non-elite became more pronounced, then trade would have been the dominant mechanism of interregional interaction. If the differences between elite and non-elite decreased, then trade diminished as warfare increased in importance.

Were there significant changes in the differentiation between the elite and non-elite in their use of decorated bowls? In order to answer this question, I calculated a ratio of decorated to undecorated rim sherds (see Table 7.5 for counts and ratios of total number to volume excavated for all functional groups). Table 7.7 (subtotals) shows that in the Early Postclassic the ratio of decorated to undecorated bowls was 4.3 times greater in the elite than in the non-elite houses. By the Late Postclassic period, the ratio dropped in elite houses from 2.7 to 2.1, but it increased in the non-elite households to the same level as the elite.

Figure 7.10a-c graphs these changing ratios for each house's stratigraphic sequence. The graphs show that the ratio of decorated to undecorated bowls was low in the Early non-elite deposits compared with the succeeding period. In Structure 60, for example, there was an increase in the ratio during the Late period. In the Early Postclassic elite Structure 22 sequence, there was an increase in the ratio up to a high of 6.5, but it generally remained stable throughout. The ratio always remained higher in the elite household than in non-elite households. Decorated bowls continued as status indicators to the end of the Early Postclassic period.

A comparison of the decorated bowl ratio in the elite house group with the non-elite house groups, suggests that the community began with an elite class that maintained and increased its

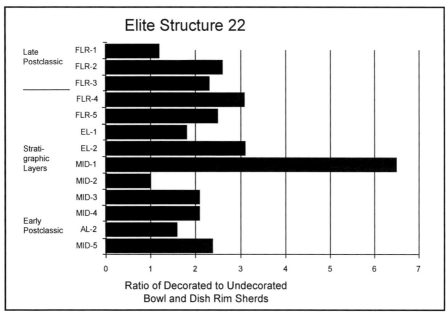

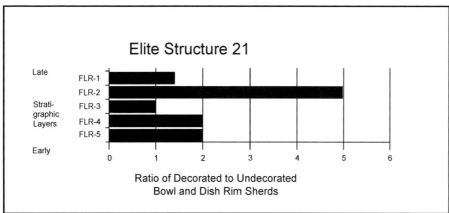

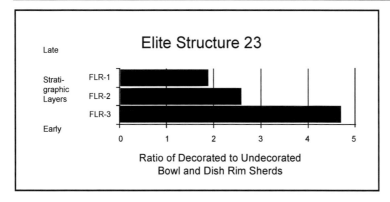

Figure 7.10a. Changing ratios of decorated to undecorated bowl rim sherds for House Group 2, Structures 21, 22, and 23 (from Table 7.7).

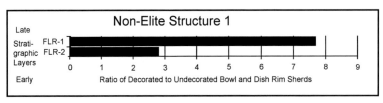

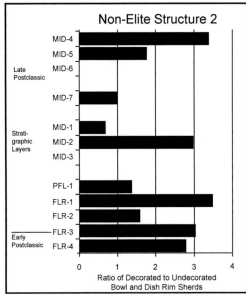

Figure 7.10b.   Changing ratios of decorated to undecorated bowl rim sherds
for House Group 1, Structures 1 and 2 (from Table 7.7).

differentiation from the non-elites by controlling the exchange and consumption of goods such as serving vessels. Subsequently, elite access to, and use of, decorated bowls declined. Their consumption patterns became more like the non-elite. For example, by the Late Postclassic there was a decrease in the decorated bowl ratio in elite Structure 22 while in both non-elite households the ratio increased. Therefore, decorated bowls were no longer used to indicate status differences between the two classes.

In the non-elite households that continued to be occupied into the Late Postclassic (Structures 2 and 60), there was an increase in the decorated bowl ratio. In the elite household, on the other hand, there was a decrease in the ratio. Subsequently, the decorated bowl ratio dropped in all of the houses. In the nine Late Postclassic sequences, only two showed an increase: the Structure 2, Midden 6 to 4 sequence where the

ratio rose from 0 to 2.8, and the Structure 1 sequence where it rose from 2.8 to 7.7. All three of the Late Postclassic elite sequences in House Group 2 showed a drop in the ratio during the last part of the period.

The similarity between elites and non-elites in the changes of the decorated bowl ratio suggests that either more low-ranking households acquired these symbols of status, or they were no longer used as status markers. This is the outcome predicted if warfare dominated intercommunity relations and the elite had much to gain by emphasizing community solidarity and down-playing the stylistic and symbolic differences between themselves and the commoners. One possible explanation is that the non-elite were now allowed access to previously restricted symbols of status in return for military service.

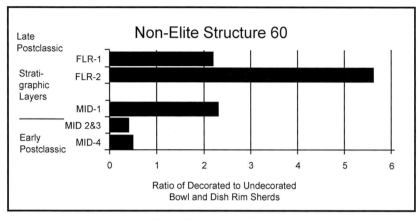

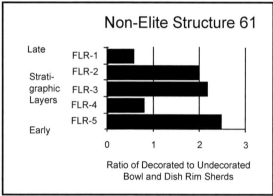

Figure 7.10c.   Changing ratios of decorated to undecorated bowl rim sherds for House Group 25, Structures 60 and 61 (from Table 7.7).

The Late Postclassic decrease in decorated bowls signifies that activities requiring their use declined. The density of plain bowls generally decreased during the Late Postclassic (Figure 7.9), however, they did increase in percentage in some houses. Decorated bowls were not replaced by plain bowls in all houses. This pattern lends support to the hypothesis that social functions requiring bowls declined. The trend may also be related to the previously mentioned change in cooking technology—the increased use of comales and large-holed colanders. If more maize was consumed in the form of tortillas, then perhaps less was consumed as *pozole*, thereby reducing the number of small serving vessels needed (see the section on grinding stones).

OBSIDIAN ANALYSIS

Obsidian was brought to Canajasté from distant sources in Mexico and Guatemala and, therefore, can tell us much about interregional trade. And because trade can be interrupted by conflict, the movements of obsidian can also tell us indirectly about warfare. This section will examine variation in: (1) obsidian sources, (2) frequencies, (3) use-wear, and (4) manufacturing stages.

Obsidian Sources

Table 7.8 presents the number of pieces of each source type in each deposit. The obsidian source identifications were made by John Clark using techniques outlined in Clark and

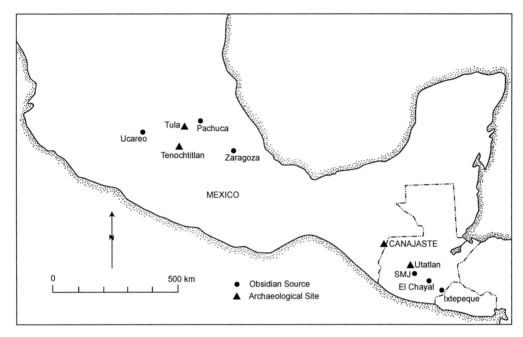

Figure 7.11.   Map of the obsidian source locations mentioned in the text.

Lee (1984:241-43) and Clark (1988). Briefly, all the pieces were sorted visually into several groups (or subtypes) based on color, surface texture, inclusions such as particles or bubbles, and translucency. The main groups were San Martín Jilotepeque (SMJ, 7 subtypes), El Chayal (7 subtypes), Ixtepeque (3 subtypes), black Mexican (2 subtypes), and Pachuca. Samples of one or two pieces for each type and subtype were analyzed by Fred W. Nelson of Brigham Young University using X-ray fluorescence spectrometry (Appendix E).

Most of the subtypes proved to come from the sources that were visually determined by Clark, but a few were re-assigned to new groups after X-ray fluorescence analysis. Within the category of black Mexican obsidian, three sources were represented: Ucareo, Zaragoza, and one unknown source. There were relatively few of these Mexican types. Since they are all from the most distant sources and represent only 1.6 percent of the total sample they have been lumped together for purposes of this analysis. The obsidian source locations are shown in Figure 7.11.

If Canajasté began as a colony from highland Guatemala, maintaining throughout its history strong exchange links with communities in that area, Guatemalan obsidian types should dominate the collection. But there should be shifts in the frequency of different types as political and economic relations with neighboring polities change. I anticipate some changes in the relative importance of the three main Guatemalan types because they were all within different political territories. Any change in the relations among the various polities in highland Guatemala could have had an impact on the quantities of different obsidian types that were traded into Canajasté.

Within-community variation in the consumption of each type of obsidian could depend on the processes by which the obsidian entered the site. For example, if the mix of sources was about the same for all houses, then obsidian probably came into the site through a single, centralized agency. If the mix of obsidian sources was distributed differently from house to house, there was likely a more haphazard procurement strategy. In that case, each household may have had its own trading links with outside suppliers (Pires-Ferreira 1975; Winter and Pires-Ferreira 1976:306).

Guatemalan versus Central Mexican Obsidian

Referring to Table 7.8, it is clear that the Canajasteños imported more obsidian from highland Guatemala than any other source. Obsidian from the three Central Mexican sources of Zaragoza, Ucareo, and Pachuca amounted to less than four percent of the total, in both the Early and Late Postclassic and in the elite and non-elite houses. The obsidian data suggest that Canajasté's main economic ties were with other polities in Guatemala, rather than with polities to the west.

Clark's (n.d.) analysis of obsidian from other Postclassic sites in the upper Grijalva region shows basically the same pattern as at Canajasté. There is one exception, however. The Early Postclassic site of La Mesa in the El Rosario-Santa Inés Valley had more Mexican than Guatemalan obsidian. Sixty-eight percent of the obsidian was from the Mexican sources of Ucareo, Zaragoza, Pachuca, and (possibly) Zacualtipán. Only 32 % of the obsidian came from Guatemala (De Montmollin and Clark, pers. comm. 1984).

Sites such as La Mesa in the western part of the study area may have traded more vigorously, via the Grijalva Valley, with polities to the west of Chiapas—polities that linked into Central Mexican trading networks. Other communities to the west of Canajasté also consumed larger quantities of Mexican obsidian: Guajilar (14%), Tenam Puente (30%) (Clark, pers. comm. 1984). Sites in the eastern upper Grijalva region consumed much smaller quantities of Mexican obsidian: Los Encuentros (2%) and Dolores (9%). A recent study of obsidian from the ballcourt at Classic period Lagartero shows that 16 of 20 samples come from El Chayal, three from Ixtepeque, and only one from Zinapecuaro-Ucareo in Michoacan (Rivero Torres et al. 2008).

Canajasté may have been one of a series of polities in the upper Grijalva region which formed the western frontier of highland Guatemalan trading partners. Further to the

west, polities traded more with their own western neighbors. If Canajasté was founded as a bud-off colony from the western highlands of Guatemala, then it would have maintained strong trade relations with its parent community. The obsidian distribution data suggest that to the west of Canajasté there was a disruption of trading networks. Communities in this western zone, although consuming Guatemalan obsidian, also consumed a good deal of Central Mexican obsidian.

Inter-house Variation in Obsidian Sources

The next step is to examine the changing proportions of different Guatemalan obsidian types present in Canajasté's house deposits. The two main obsidian types were San Martín Jilotepeque and El Chayal, comprising 68.2 % and 26.6 %, respectively, of the total excavated collection. Table 7.8 shows that obsidian from the other Guatemalan source, Ixtepeque, was never very common. In fact, there were only 97 pieces (2.8%) from this source in excavated deposits.

The ratio of San Martín to El Chayal obsidian in each house deposit shows how their relative importance changed. I have combined adjacent floor and midden layers in order to even out variation due to small sample sizes. The main trend (Tables 7.8 and 7.9) is that San Martín obsidian declined and El Chayal increased from the Early to Late Postclassic. This happened in both elite and non-elite households. In all but one case, the highest ratio of San Martín to El Chayal occurred in Early Postclassic house floors and middens, or it occurred in the early part of the Late Postclassic. The exception was Structure 61 where the ratio of San Martín to El Chayal increased in the Late Postclassic.

In both Structures 22 and 60, the ratio changed during the Early Postclassic period. The Structure 22 sequence began with 7.2 times as much San Martín as El Chayal. It then dropped by the middle of the sequence and finally rose once more by the end of the Early Postclassic. In Structure 60 the ratio of San Martín to El Chayal also rose towards the end of the period. And in Structure 2 the ratio in Floor 4 was 2.0—almost as high as in any other deposit in that house. The pattern for the Early Postclassic was one of an initial peak in the ratio of San Martín to El Chayal. Later, access to San Martín obsidian declined, only to rise once more towards the end of the period.

At the onset of the Late Postclassic period there was a decline in the San Martín/El Chayal ratio only in elite house Structure 22. In one of the two non-elite houses there was a slight decline and, in the other, an increase in the ratio. In two out of three houses the ratio of San Martín to El Chayal obsidian stayed constant or increased in the Late Postclassic. It was not until after this that the San Martín to El Chayal ratio dropped. When it did, it dropped in all houses except Structure 61.

Interpretation of the Obsidian Source Patterns

If the San Martín to El Chayal obsidian ratio (i.e., the "mix" of obsidian imported) was determined outside the site, then the changing proportions from each source would not necessarily indicate anything about the relations between Canajasté and its immediate neighbors. It would tell us more about the relations among the groups that controlled the obsidian sources. If, however, each source of obsidian was independently obtained, that is, San Martín from one neighbor and El Chayal from another, then the shift in the ratio reveals something quite different. It suggests that Canajasté's own political relations with its neighboring trading partners changed. The previous analysis allows us to distinguish between these two alternatives.

First, the consistent pattern of change in each house indicates that there was a centralized distribution system and individual households did not independently acquire obsidian. Second, it suggests that the community as a whole obtained its obsidian from an intermediary where the proportions of each type of obsidian were already determined. Since San Martín obsidian was the primary type during both periods, it was the one source that declined most during the Late Postclassic. This supports the suggestion made in the last section that

political relations within highland Guatemala shifted at the beginning of the Late Postclassic period. One possible cause of this is that conflict between the Quiché and the Cakchiquel, who controlled the San Martín Jilotepeque source, reduced the amount of obsidian being traded from that source. In turn, conflict between the Quiché and the Mam (Recinos et al. 1950:221) may have reduced the overall amount of obsidian being traded into central Chiapas. Also, increased demand by these expanding states may have reduced the available supply to more distant areas like Canajasté. These last two possibilities would not explain the increasing proportion of El Chayal obsidian. El Chayal obsidian came from within Pokom territory to the southeast of the Quiché region. They may have been able to continue to export obsidian westward through Quiché territory since their relations were better with the Quiché than with the Cakchiquel (Miles 1957).

In order for obsidian to reach Canajasté, it must have traveled through Quiché territory, through Mam territory, and finally, through Jacaltec or Chuj territory. Communities at any point along the way could have choked off the supplies, either by increased demand of their own or by warfare disrupting exchange relations. The Late Postclassic decline in obsidian at Canajasté could have been caused by conflicting relations among any combination of groups along the routes from the sources. It also could have been caused by conflict between Canajasté and its own neighbors. As discussed below, most of the other artifact evidence suggests the latter possibility. The decline in obsidian available to each household may also have resulted from community growth while the supply remained constant. But the changing ratio of San Martín to El Chayal obsidian was probably of the Quiché's or Cakchiquel's doing.

In conclusion, it appears that once during the Early Postclassic, and once again during the Late Postclassic, there was a shift in distant relations among the groups that controlled the obsidian sources and traded in the obsidian products that eventually made their way to Canajasté.

Canajasté's Obsidian Importation

Changes in the amount of obsidian that was brought into the site point directly to changing patterns of exchange. In the last section it was shown that, during the Late Postclassic period, the community's access to San Martín Jilotepeque obsidian decreased relative to El Chayal obsidian. But what of the overall quantity that was imported? Do the shifts in sources correlate with an increase or a decrease in obsidian from each source?

In order to answer these questions the raw obsidian counts must first be transformed to ratios of some other "variable." The two I will use here are counts per cubic meter of excavated deposit and the ratio of obsidian to rim sherds. The first measure gives a density that makes the houses comparable with one another and factors out variation based on differing lengths of occupation or sizes of deposit. Nonetheless, since middens could have higher obsidian densities than floors, there are problems with this measure—especially since most of the Early Postclassic deposits are middens and most of the Late Postclassic deposits are floors. The second measure circumvents this problem by comparing the quantity of obsidian in a deposit to the quantity of rim sherds. This should make broader comparisons possible by factoring out the function of the deposit (i.e., midden or living floor).

There were 3423 pieces of obsidian from the 159.5 m^3 of screened excavated deposits.[4] This gives an overall density of 21.5 pieces of obsidian per m^3. For the unmixed house deposits only, the density is 26.6 pieces per m^3. The average weight of the obsidian is estimated at 1.12 g per piece (using a sample of 619 pieces, which included all the manufacturing stages, such as core fragments, blades, etc., for one source). The weight density (g/m^3), therefore, is almost identical to the count density (no./m^3), and it is the count density that I use in the subsequent analysis.

The obsidian density at Canajasté was many times higher than observed at the neighboring Postclassic sites in the study area (Clark n.d.,

pers. comm. 1984). Canajasté's high obsidian density is similar to that found in primary centers or centers near obsidian sources (Clark 1981). Because Canajasté is 150 km away from a major obsidian source, and yet still has such large quantities, it must have been an important distribution and consumption center within its region.

Even though Canajasté had a large quantity of obsidian compared with most other neighboring sites, the absolute amount was not huge. In fact, a series of simple calculations estimates show that one person could easily have brought in each year's supply for the whole community. I estimate that only 900 g of obsidian per year was consumed at the site; roughly 2.6 g (2-3 pieces) per house per year. If only half the houses were occupied then the rate of consumption was about 5.2 g per year.

One implication of this estimate is that if the supply remained constant over the site's history, then as the community grew, the per house consumption rate would have dropped. This would cause the incidence of tool re-use (and, thus, use-wear) to increase. As I shall demonstrate, in the use-wear section below, there is good evidence for this trend.

Household Variation in Obsidian Frequency

Table 7.10 presents the obsidian counts for all deposits. Looking first at the totals of obsidian density and obsidian to rim sherd ratio for each social class in each time period, we see significant variation. The Early Postclassic elite had access to more obsidian than the Early non-elite and more than either class had in the Late Postclassic. The broad trend was that during the Early period the elite consumed more obsidian than the non-elite. By the Late Postclassic both classes consumed about as much obsidian as the Early non-elite. The community's decreased access to obsidian occurred mainly at the expense of the elite households, but the non-elite's level of consumption also dropped.

The Structure 22 sequence indicates that obsidian density declined markedly, with the main decline occurring by about the middle of the sequence. The obsidian to rim sherd ratio for Structure 22 (Table 7.10) showed the same decline until the middle of the sequence (from Midden 3 to Midden 2). From that point on, the ratio remained constant until the very last floor, when it almost doubled (but remained scarcer than during the Early Postclassic).

In several of the Late Postclassic houses the obsidian to rim sherd ratio increased—in opposite fashion to the density measure. In five of the Late Postclassic sequences there was a decrease or only a minor increase in the obsidian to rim sherd ratio, and in all of them (except Structures 2 and 23) there was a decrease in the obsidian density. In summary, obsidian consumption began to decline during the Early Postclassic, a trend which continued into the Late Postclassic.

Obsidian Use-Wear

In this section I will examine some of the implications of the decline in obsidian trade for understanding Canajasté's relations with its neighbors. If the conclusion of the previous section is correct and obsidian consumption did indeed diminish, I would expect there to have been an increasingly heavy use and re-use of obsidian tools. The first hypothesis I test below is: as the importance and ease of interregional trade increased, more nonlocal commodities, such as obsidian, became available at Canajasté. The more obsidian there was, the more rapidly did new pieces replace used ones, and obsidian use-wear was light. The reverse should also hold: when obsidian was less plentiful, it was used more and, thus, would show heavier use-wear.

The second hypothesis I test is that the elite at Canajasté had more obsidian and discarded it more rapidly than the non-elite. Therefore, obsidian in elite households should have less use-wear than that in non-elite households. If the obsidian trade declined, and both classes had less of it, then obsidian use-wear should increase in both elite and non-elite households.

Before discussing the patterns, I will describe the methods used for determining obsidian use-wear. Each cutting edge on each piece of obsidian (they were predominantly

blades and so most had two edges) was classified into the following use-wear categories:[5]

(1) Little or no use.
(2) Cutting soft: cutting soft materials and not much use.
(3) Cutting medium: moderate use on hard materials or heavy use on soft materials.
(4) Cutting hard: heavy use on hard materials.
(5) Scraping soft: scraping soft materials, little use.
(6) Scraping medium: moderate use on hard materials or heavy use on soft materials.
(7) Scraping hard: heavy use on hard materials.
(8) Whittling: carving wood—very heavy use.

For the purposes of this study I needed an index of heavy use and, therefore, reduced these categories to two: heavily-used pieces and lightly-used pieces. I summed categories 3, 4, 6, 7, and 8 for a count of heavily-used edges, and summed categories 1, 2, and 5 for a count of unused or lightly-used edges. The use-wear ratio is the count of heavily-used edges divided by the count of lightly-used edges (i.e., the "wastage rate," Clark [1988]). The higher the ratio, the greater the relative proportion of heavily-used obsidian.

In order to test the hypotheses I grouped the data differently than in the previous analyses in this chapter. The house sequences used here are summarized in Table 7.11.

In Structures 1 and 2 in House Group 1, there are four instances of increasing use-wear during the Late Postclassic, but it remained lower than in the single Early Postclassic Floor 4. Structure 2 began with a high use-wear ratio in Early Postclassic Floor 4. It then dropped in Late Postclassic Floors 3 and 2 (combined) only to rise again in Floor 1 and Patio Floor 1 (combined). The two midden sequences in Structure 2 also show slight increases in the use-wear ratio during the Late Postclassic. Like Structure 2, Structure 1 also had an increase in the use-wear ratio during the Late Postclassic.

The trends are clearer in House Group 25 where Structure 60 has a larger sample of Early Postclassic deposits. The use-wear ratio was low in Midden 4 and then increased in the subsequent Midden 2 and 3 deposits. The use-wear ratio rose in the succeeding Late Postclassic deposits (combined Midden 1 and Floor 2) and then decreased in Floor 1. Note, however, the use-wear ratio remained higher in both these Late deposits than in the previous Early deposits. In Structure 61 there was a large increase in the obsidian use-wear ratio. The combined Floor 5, 4 and 3 deposits have a ratio of 1.09 while the succeeding Floor 1 and 2 deposits have a ratio of 2.03, the second highest of all the excavated deposits.

Structures 21, 22 and 23 in elite House Group 2 show an even more striking pattern. The Early Postclassic midden deposits in Structure 22 show the lowest overall obsidian use-wear ratios with a trajectory of gradually increasing use-wear throughout the sequence. By the Late Postclassic period in Structure 22, obsidian use was even heavier than at the end of the previous period. The Floor 3 and 2 deposits show a ratio of almost 2:1. The other two Late Postclassic structures in the house group also show an increase in obsidian use-wear through the Late Postclassic.

The two Early Postclassic sequences and eight of the ten Late Postclassic sequences show an increase in the use-wear ratio. In two of the three house groups there is a higher level of use-wear in the Late Postclassic than in the Early Postclassic. The only exception is Floor 4 in Structure 2 where the use-wear ratio dropped from extremely high to moderately high.

For the community as a whole I conclude that the flow of obsidian began to drop during the Early Postclassic and continued to drop towards the end of the period. This pattern suggests that the elite gradually began to lose control over obsidian exchange. Earlier, they had more obsidian to expend than the non-elite. Over time, obsidian became scarcer and they, too, were forced to use and reuse their available obsidian until it showed signs of heavier use-wear. In the Late Postclassic period the use-wear ratio continued to rise for both the elite and non-

elite so that by the end of the period there was little or no difference between the two classes in their access to and use of obsidian.

Obsidian Technology

This section attempts to answer two main questions about changes in the organization of obsidian trade and production at Canajasté: (1) in what form did the obsidian enter the site; and (2) did the elite control access to obsidian?

If obsidian trade was more important during the Early Postclassic than the Late Postclassic, as other analyses have already suggested, then a wider range of both finished and unfinished obsidian products, including cores, should have entered the site during the Early period. With the decline of the obsidian trade the frequency of items, such as cores, should be reduced.

Another expectation is that if the elite controlled the obsidian trade, they should have consumed and discarded the widest range of obsidian products and manufacturing debris. The non-elite, in contrast, should have consumed finished blades. If, however, the elite did not control obsidian trade or production, then both classes would have consumed the same types of obsidian products. Based on the results of other analyses presented so far, I expect there to have been greater differences in obsidian consumption between elite and non-elite households in the Early Postclassic than in the Late Postclassic. I also expect that if obsidian exchange declined during the Late Postclassic period, there would have been a general decline in manufacturing by-products. Not only would all households have less obsidian, but most of it would have been finished blades.

A description of the classification scheme used and its rationale are presented in Clark (1988) and Clark and Lee (1984). I have modified it slightly by combining several reduction categories into two broader groups (Table 7.12): (1) manufacturing by-products and other miscellaneous obsidian items; and (2) blades, including first-series and prismatic blades. A ratio between these two classes is presented in Table 7.13. It is calculated by dividing the count for manufacturing by-products, and related material, by the count for blades. The higher the ratio, the higher the proportion of manufacturing debris in the sample; the lower the ratio, the greater the proportion of blades in the sample.

There was little variation in the ratio among the various house deposits. Blades were uniformly more common than manufacturing by-products, except in one deposit where they were the same. For all deposits combined, the ratio was 0.21, that is, almost five blades for each piece of obsidian manufacturing debris. Looking just at the early deposits, the ratio is 0.22 and 0.24 for the non-elite and the elite respectively. In the late deposits the ratio was 0.19 and 0.17 for the non-elite and elite respectively. The general trend, then, was one of decreasing manufacturing debris, either produced at or imported into the site. The early elite had, along with their larger quantity of obsidian, the largest amount of manufacturing debris. They also had the most core fragments and other types of debris produced by on-site manufacturing of blades. Even so, at no time did manufacturing by-products account for a significantly large proportion of the obsidian sample. I conclude that more manufacturing did take place in the Early Postclassic elite household and less in the non-elite households.

Looking at the Structure 22 sequence in Table 7.13, the most clear-cut pattern is the gradual decline in manufacturing debris in the first three midden layers. Early in the Early Postclassic sequence the proportion of manufacturing debris rose and subsequently was maintained at fairly high levels. It only gradually dwindled to initial levels by the end of the Late Postclassic. The major peaks in the manufacturing by-product/blade ratio stopped before the end of the Early Postclassic when interregional trade began to decline and warfare was on the rise. This trend corresponds to a decrease in the elite's access to obsidian cores, at which point they had no greater amount of manufacturing by-products than any of the non-elite households. This pattern confirms that trade decreased by the end of the Early Postclassic. Whatever control the elite had over obsidian trade and implement manufacturing in

the Early Postclassic period, they apparently lost in the Late Postclassic.

OBSIDIAN PROJECTILE POINTS

The relationship between warfare and exchange can be explored in a general way by comparing changing projectile point frequencies with changing obsidian frequencies (blades and other non-projectile point obsidian artifacts) (Figure 7.12). With increased warfare there should be more projectile points. But, if warfare restricted trade, then less obsidian would be imported and, therefore, less obsidian would be deposited at the site in general. With increased exchange there should be more obsidian and fewer projectile points. Here, I will use the obsidian data from Table 7.10 in the preceding obsidian analysis. There are two ways of making obsidian artifact frequencies comparable to projectile point frequencies. One is to standardize the frequency of obsidian to the number of rim sherds in the deposit in the same way as done for arrow points. Another is to calculate the obsidian density as a ratio of total number of obsidian artifacts per cubic meter of excavated deposit. Looking first at Structure 22, where we have the longest continuous sequence of occupation, both ratios are plotted in Figure 7.13. The broken line shows the obsidian to rim sherd ratio and the gray line the ratio of obsidian to volume of excavated deposit. To make the obsidian to rim sherd ratio visually comparable with the arrow point to rim sherd ratio I have multiplied it by ten. The gray line shows that obsidian density was highest in the Early deposits and then dropped rapidly. It then leveled off in the last Early Postclassic layer (Floor 4) and, finally, maintained its lowest level for all three Late Postclassic floors.

The obsidian to rim sherd ratio was highest in the first four layers. Then beginning with Midden 2, there was an abrupt drop that was maintained through the Early Postclassic deposits and into the Late Postclassic. There was an increase in the obsidian to rim sherd ratio in the final floor.

The relationship between the two sets of artifacts—obsidian on the one hand and arrow

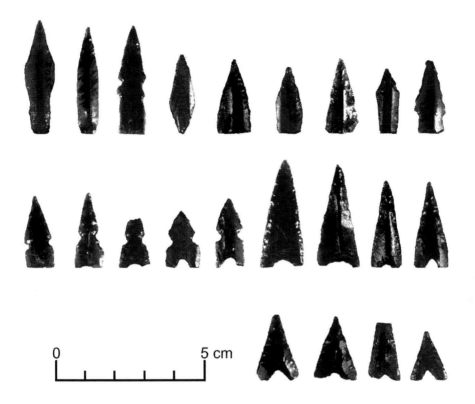

Figure 7.12. Various styles of obsidian projectile points recovered from the excavations and surface collections at Canajasté.

Elite Structure 22

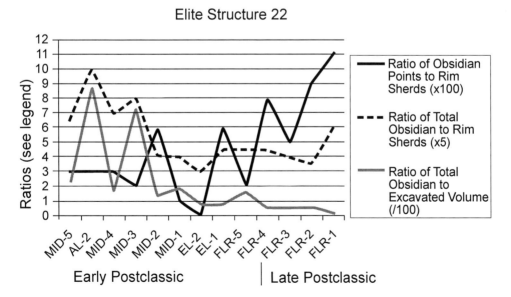

Figure 7.13. Structure 22, ratio of projectile points to rim sherds, and to obsidian. Obsidian density is also plotted.

points on the other—is clearly an inverse one.
When obsidian importation was at its peak
relatively, few projectile points made their way
into the deposits. Later, corresponding with the
drop in obsidian density at the site, there was an
increase in projectile points. The ratio of points
to rim sherds fluctuated rather widely over the
remaining sequence of Early Postclassic layers
and then jumped to its highest point as obsidian
density dropped to its lowest level.

During the Late Postclassic the obsidian
density remained low, although the ratio of
obsidian to rim sherds increased. In other words,
there is evidence that the obsidian trade picked
up somewhat. The last Late Postclassic floor
(Floor 1) had a higher obsidian to rim sherd ratio
than 60 percent of the Early Postclassic deposits,
even though it had the lowest density of obsidian
overall. Before examining the trajectories of
the other excavated houses I will summarize
the interpretations that can be made about the
processes of trade and warfare based on the
analysis of Structure 22.

Judging by these data and bearing in mind
that I have no evidence for the length of time
each layer represents, there appears to be a
differential effect of warfare on trade and vice
versa. That is, when trade declined there was
an almost immediate indication of increasing
warfare. With evidence for prolonged, low levels
of trade there were fluctuations in the frequency
of arrow points, but there was a gradual
increasing trend. Finally, trade re-emerged to a
certain extent after a major social change (the
Late Postclassic transition), despite the evidence
for continued warfare. This suggests that if
military, social, and political institutions develop
during periods of decreased trade, they may
not be so quick to break down after long-term,
stable military alliances allow trade to begin to
flourish once again.

One useful way of looking at the data
is plotting the proportion of obsidian arrow
points to the total amount of obsidian. This
allows one to see what proportion of the total
obsidian resource people were willing to devote
to projectile points—an approximation of the
prehistoric Canajasteños' defense budget. When
plotted in Figure 7.14a (Structure 22) it is clear

that an increasingly large proportion of the
incoming obsidian was devoted to projectile
points. The median for the Early Postclassic
layers is .2 while that for the Late Postclassic
layers is .9, four and one-half times larger. In a
sense, arrow points became more "expensive"
but were manufactured, nevertheless.

Turning to the other excavated houses in
the sample, there is a degree of confirmation
of the patterns already observed in Structure
22. Figure 7.14a-c plots the ratio of obsidian
arrow points to obsidian for all the structures.
The X-axis presents the number of arrow points
divided by the number of pieces of obsidian,
and the Y-axis shows the temporal sequence of
layers in each house, progressing through time
from bottom to top. The immediate impression
one gets is that there is little patterning.
However, the median values for all Late deposits
(median=.10; range=0 to .37) and for all Early
deposits (median=.3; range=0 to .13) show that
greater proportions of obsidian were being
devoted to projectile points in the Late deposits
than in the Early deposits. This could have come
about either through an increase in the numbers
of projectile points or a decrease in the amount
of obsidian. Actually, both things happened,
and it is difficult to separate the effect of one
from the other. The easiest way of doing so is to
calculate a ratio of projectile points to rim sherds
for the overall deposits.

Table 7.14 presents these calculations and
shows that the proportion of projectile points
to rim sherds doubled in the Late Postclassic
deposits. Calculating the ratio by rim sherd
weight, instead of counts, would reveal an
even more dramatic increase because Early
deposits are mostly middens and the sherds
are on the average much larger. But even with
a conservative rim-count estimate there is an
increase in projectile points. One interesting
observation is that, since Early deposits are
middens, the artifact density (number per m³ of
deposit) is extremely high. Even so, the density
of projectile points is only slightly higher in the
Early Postclassic deposits: 2.4 per m³ compared
with the 1.9 per m³ in the Late Postclassic
deposits.

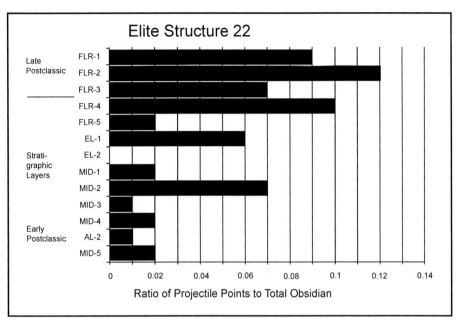

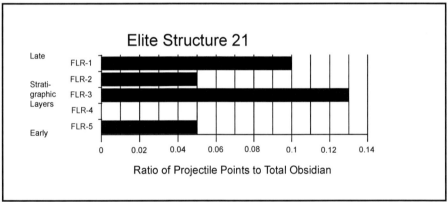

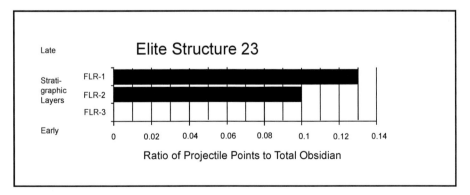

Figure 7.14a.   Ratios of projectile points to obsidian in all elite structures: House Group 2, Structures 21, 22, and 23 (from Table 7.14).

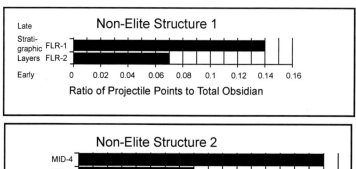

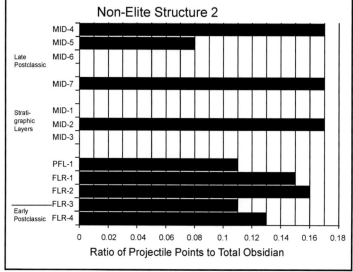

Figure 7.14b.   Ratios of projectile points to obsidian in all non-elite structures: House Group 1, Structures 1 and 2 (from Table 7.14).

Returning to Figure 7.14b-c, it can be seen that the floor deposits in Structures 1, 2, 60, and 61 all had densities equal to or higher than the Late Postclassic median of .10. This is similar to the pattern in Structure 22. Structures 21 and 23, however, had deposits with no projectile points. The most relevant aspect of the patterning in these data is that, in the floor deposits of most structures, there was an increase in the arrow point to obsidian ratio. The only exceptions are Structure 2, where there was a decrease (but never below the median), and Structure 60, where the ratio dropped from .10 to .8—still many times above the Early Postclassic median.

Looking at the midden deposits, there was an increase in the Structure 2, Midden 6 to 4 sequence but a dramatic fluctuation from 0.0 to 0.17 and back to 0.0 in the Midden 3 to 1 sequence. In Structure 60 there was a strong

increase in the Early Postclassic middens and then a drop in the Late midden. Nonetheless, the drop was still only to 0.8—well above the overall Early Postclassic median.

In a previous section I stated that trade, based on the frequency of import classes present, was on the rise during the Late Postclassic, although it remained below the Early Postclassic levels. If projectile points are indeed an indication of the importance of warfare, then it seems, too, that warfare was also on the rise. This means that although warfare increased as trade decreased, it did not then decrease again as trade later increased. This could be an indication of a restructuring of the society and the successful incorporation of warfare into the political operation of Canajasté's relations with other communities (Webb 1974, 1975; Webster 1975). This pattern fits with Pryor's (1977:121)

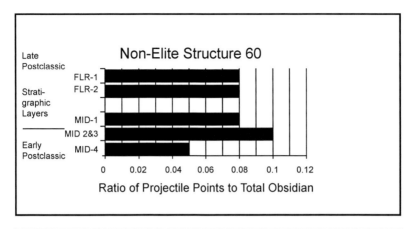

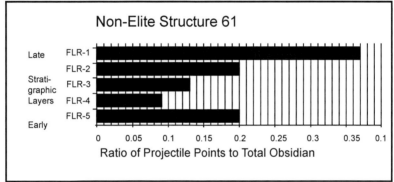

Figure 7.14c. Ratios of projectile points to obsidian in all non-elite structures: House Group 25, Structures 60 and 61 (from Table 7.14).

findings that warfare does not always reduce the frequency of trade, especially market exchange.

One change that would lead to the observed patterns is that the Early Postclassic/Late Postclassic transition was brought on by increased warfare with neighboring communities. Warfare increased after, and possibly in *response* to, a decrease in trade. The community was drawn into ever-increasing military endeavors and maintained itself by using warfare as its prime form of inter-polity relations. Eventually, military success may lead to the growth of the community, and resources continued to be expended on warfare—but farther afield. This is corroborated by the decrease in house floor and wall-burning episodes and the expansion of the community outside the walled zone. I will return to this last point later. Notably, the maintenance of high numbers of projectile points suggests that, once

in place, military activities were not easily or quickly disbanded. In fact, they continued to thrive in spite of evidence for decreased direct threat of attack on the community.

Projectile Point Styles: Elite/Non-Elite Differences

The large sample of obsidian projectile points affords the opportunity of using them to monitor other variables in addition to changing quantities of the weaponry of warfare. Obsidian arrow points made from prismatic blades were the most numerous stone tools found at Canajasté: a total of 292 was recovered from the seven houses, test excavations, and surface collections (Figure 7.12). For the house deposits alone there is an average of 38 points per house. Table 7.15 shows the break-down of point

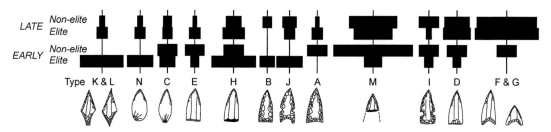

Figure 7.15.   Chart of changes in the percentages of projectile point types from the Early to Late Postclassic, between elite and non-elite house groups. The styles are ordered from left to right in relation to their relative age (beginning with Early Postclassic on the left).

styles for the 194 points found in unmixed or undisturbed deposits.

I have, for the purposes of comparison, sorted out 14 styles or types of points using fine-scale, nonmetric attributes. These types are visually very homogeneous within each group, in part, because of the relatively large sample available (Figure 7.15).

Based on the relative proportions of each type within Early, Late, mixed and surface samples I was able to make a preliminary estimation of the chronological placement of different styles. Some styles are more frequent in Early deposits, some are common to both Early and Late deposits, and some are dominant in the Late deposits. For the purpose of the analysis, I have grouped type K with L, and type F with G, since they are stylistically very similar.

Figure 7.15 shows a seriation of these points and presents the differences between elite and non-elite deposits for each period. It is based on the data in Table 7.15. One assumption used here is that the points were deposited at a rate commensurate with their frequency of use and, thus, their importance in warfare. Also, I assume the majority were deposited by the people who lived at the site. If the town was raided repeatedly, however, I would expect raider's points as well. These might be distinguished as different styles of points made on different types of obsidian.

No types were restricted to only Early or Late deposits. In fact, there was a great deal of continuity in styles through time. Five types

were predominantly Early, five were both Early and Late, and only two types were more common in the Late deposits.

The most intriguing pattern is that in the Early houses there were significant differences between point styles used by the elite and those used by the non-elite. Of the types that occurred most frequently in the Early deposits (K & L, N, C, and E), both K & L and N were restricted to elite households. Their relative frequency declined in the Late Postclassic, but the elite continued to have more than the non-elite. Type C was an exception in that it was equally common in the elite and non-elite households in both periods. Type E, on the other hand, was more common in Early non-elite households, then, later, it became more common in elite households. There are a number of types that were relatively common in both periods: H, B, J, A, M (broken tips), and I. These are ordered on the chart from left to right as they shift from an association with Early deposits to an association with Late deposits. These types show similar patterns of changing frequency in elite and non-elite deposits. In the Early deposits there was a great deal of differentiation between the elite house group and non-elite house groups. During the Late period there was much less differentiation than earlier. Furthermore, the association of a projectile point type with elite or non-elite does not carry through the periods. Of the five types (excluding tips) only two remained more common in either elite or non-elite houses. For example, type H points were more common in elite houses during the Early

Postclassic and remained more common among the elite during the following period, although the degree of difference diminished. Finally, for the two types that became more common in the Late Postclassic period, types D and F & G, there is exactly the same kind of shift. Type D was predominantly a non-elite style in the Early Postclassic and became more common among the elite. For types F & G, both the elite and non-elite had many times the relative number of these points during the Late period than they did during the Early period.

In all cases, the similarity between elite and non-elite increased from Early to Late. Furthermore, the Early non-elite seem to have had more of the later period styles than the elite did. This may result from an erroneous placement of some of the non-elite house deposits in the Early period. Ceramically, however, there is not much reason to doubt the chronological placement of the house deposits. The main pattern—one of increasing similarity between the two social classes through time—also was noted in the ceramics. Previously, in developing the expectations for changes in material culture, I predicted that stylistic differentiation between elite and non-elite should decrease as warfare increases in importance. In the last section it was shown that the overall shifts in projectile point frequencies tended to support the interpretation that warfare began to increase during the end of the Early Postclassic and continued throughout the Late Postclassic. The stylistic changes and status associations of these same projectile points confirm the hypothesis of increased warfare. The argument, recapitulated, is that stylistic emulation of elites by commoners would tend to increase in the face of a community-wide threat of military encounter.

Changing Late Postclassic Point Styles

I have looked at broad changes from the Early to Late Postclassic for all the styles and have found that increasing stylistic similarity between elite and non-elite is consistent with the other evidence for increasing warfare. But, I have not examined the finer-scale changes

within periods. One problem is that the sample sizes for individual projectile point styles are so small that it is difficult to observe trajectories of change within each household. Nonetheless, it is worthwhile attempting to see how the processes of trade and warfare differentially affected the elite and non-elite.

One trend, which was observed by looking at all projectile points combined, was that during the Late Postclassic the density of projectile points continued to increase. Even so, there was evidence (in numbers of classes of imports) that trade fell to its lowest levels near the end of the Early Postclassic, remained low during the initial stages of the Late period, and then began to increase in importance once more (see Figure 7.4a-c).

This pattern can be examined by looking at the Late period projectile point styles. I expect that we can determine whether trade or warfare was more important in external political relations by determining whether elite/non-elite differentiation was continuing to decrease or beginning, once again, to increase during the Late Postclassic. I have already noted that both warfare and trade were increasing, even though trade probably lagged behind warfare. The question is: were the elite, who supposedly controlled military activity, also beginning to promote more trade to supplement their sources of income?

In terms of changing projectile point styles, I would expect that if warfare was dominant there should have been an increase in proportions of Late point styles for both elite and non-elite. The differences between them should not increase. In other words, the similarity observed in Figure 7.15, (especially Late period styles D and F & G), for the elite and non-elite, should continue to increase if warfare retains its importance. On the other hand, if warfare indeed sparked growth in community size and complexity, and increased stability towards the end of the period, trade might have become a more dominant form of inter-polity relations. The elite could begin to distance themselves from commoners once again by elaborating exclusive styles on a number of artifacts and features, including projectile points.

Grouping point styles D and F & G together, since they behave in a similar way in Figure 7.15, I calculated their proportion of the total number of arrow points in each deposit. Table 7.16 presents these data for all the Late Postclassic deposits. Where possible, I have included the most recent Early Postclassic deposit to show how the pattern extends across the Early-Late transition. In five of eight depositional sequences there was an increase in these styles during the Late Postclassic, in two there was no change and only in one did these styles decrease.

To make the change even more visible I have grouped the Late deposits for each house or midden into an early half and a late half. All the late halves were not necessarily contemporary with each other. For example, I think that both Floors 1 and 2 in Structure 1 were contemporary with Floor 1 and Patio Floor 1 in Structure 2. Not only were the house styles similar, but the proportions of point styles were nearly identical. Furthermore the proportions of these styles were similar to the latest floors of Structure 22, 23, 60, and 61. The latest layers in Structure 2 (the Midden 6 to 4 sequence) differed only in that they had an even higher proportion of these point styles. Table 7.16 shows that the earliest half of the deposits contained lower proportions of the point styles. They were even rarer in two elite houses, Structures 22 and 23.

The basic pattern that emerges both on the fine-scale floor-to-floor trajectory and on the slightly coarser, early half/late half trajectory is that the points that became the most common in the Late Postclassic were not introduced until the Late Postclassic was already underway, and then they became almost equally popular among both the non-elite and elite. Still, the elite house group had one house where the Late points were never in use (Structure 21) and another where they declined (Structure 23). Structure 21 had the fewest points of any house, and, therefore, it is not surprising there were none of these Late styles present. And, Structure 23 showed a decrease in the styles but to a level still higher than in all but one depositional sequence (Structure 2, midden). This demonstrates that there was little in the way of increasing

differentiation of point styles between the elite and non-elite *during* the Late Postclassic period. Furthermore, it strongly supports the interpretation made earlier that warfare was on the rise and continued as a dominant mode of inter-polity relations through the Late Postclassic.

SPINNING, WEAVING, AND SEWING TOOLS

Spinning, weaving, and sewing tools are useful indicators of both exchange and craft production—for the community as a whole as well as for particular classes within the society. If the elite controlled or sponsored the manufacture of cotton cloth then they should have had more spinning, weaving, and sewing tools than the non-elite. If any of these tools were imported, the elite would certainly be expected to have more of them. Increases in warfare that result in, or from, disruptions and unpredictability in interregional trade networks, might cause a decline in specialized production, a homogenization of production across the social classes, and a drop in the imported tools of production. As production becomes more dependent on local consumption, then the rate of production should drop, causing a decline in the use of specialized tools such as those used for manufacturing cotton cloth.

Spindle Whorls

Previous analyses in this chapter have indicated that interregional exchange decreased towards the end of the Early Postclassic and warfare increased. Here, I will look at the distribution of spindle whorls from the excavated house deposits to determine how well they fit the pattern.

There are three main categories of spindle whorls from Canajasté: (1) an elaborate, mold-made type that was traded into the site during the Early Postclassic period (Figure 7.16a-b, d-e); (2) a handmade, coarser type—with either no designs or only simple geometric designs—that was associated with Late Postclassic deposits (Figure 7.16f) and (3) a wooden whorl that had

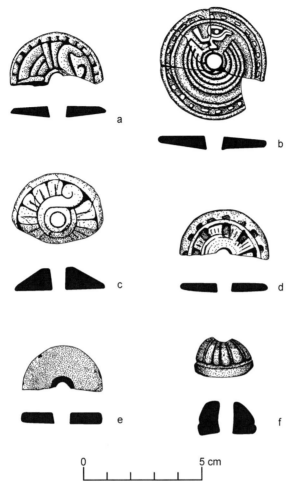

Figure 7.16. Types of spindle whorls recovered from the house excavations at Canajasté. Early Postclassic types: a-b, c (wood), d-e; Late Postclassic type: f.

been charred and deposited in a mixed midden or construction fill deposit (Figure 7.16c). This last type was similar in design to the Early Postclassic ceramic whorls.

The mold-made whorls are similar to ones found in Postclassic sites all over southern Mesoamerica. At the site of Toniná, some 100 km north of Canajasté, archaeologists recovered a particularly large sample of these whorls (Becquelin and Baudez 1979-82:fig.234). Closer to home, they have been found in several of the cremation burial caves in the zone surrounding Canajasté and at many of the excavated sites in the upper Grijalva region.

Twenty spindle whorls were found at Canajasté, all of them fragments and presumably discarded or lost in the houses or their associated middens. Several fragments were rejoined after being recovered from different deposits and some, from different houses, were made from the same mold. There are too few specimens to trace subtle changes in frequency during each period, therefore, I will begin by examining the Early-Late Postclassic differences.

Of the 20 spindle whorls, 18 were associated with Early Postclassic deposits. Four of these were in Early Postclassic construction fill. Considering that more Late houses than Early houses were excavated, the Early Postclassic households made greater use of ceramic spindle whorls than did their Late Postclassic counterparts. Of the 18 spindle whorls associated with these early deposits, 13 were mold-made and imported from outside the region. Only two spindle whorls were found in Late Postclassic contexts.

The drop in ceramic spindle whorls at the end of the Early Postclassic period suggests that either spinning cotton declined in importance or that people shifted to non-preservable, wooden whorls. No Late Postclassic wooden whorls were found, however, and the only wooden whorl was associated with Early deposits (Figure 7.16c). Since it was carved in a shape and with a design closely resembling the early style ceramic whorls it was probably Early Postclassic.

Spinning cloth must have declined markedly at the end of the Early Postclassic period at Canajasté. As an alternative to local manufacture, Late Postclassic people could have imported, or taken as tribute, ready-made cloth from outlying communities in the region.

Another aspect of the decline in frequency of spinning tools, and one that helps in understanding the processes involved, is the change in differences between elite and non-elite use of whorls. Table 7.17 shows the distribution of whorls between the elite and non-elite in both periods. During the Early Postclassic the elite household used almost all the spindle whorls—15 of the total 20 recovered. By the Late Postclassic there were no spindle whorls discarded in any of the three elite houses in House Group 2; however, two found their way into Late, non-elite houses. In all of the Late deposits only two spindle whorls were found. None was even found in the mixed Late deposits (deposits, though mixed, which might have been more closely associated with Late floors). The absolute number of spindle whorls is low in the Late deposits, but even standardizing the count to a ratio of whorls to total rim sherds or to volume of excavated deposits the values are still low.

The spindle whorl counts for Early elite and Early non-elite are 15 and 3 respectively, but since the volume of earth excavated in

Early non-elite deposits was low, the absolute counts do not mean much. Calculating ratios of whorls to rim sherds or to excavated volume produces quite a different picture. The ratio of spindle whorls to rim sherds (Table 7.17) shows that the combined elite deposits (Structure 22) had 15.7 whorls/1000 rim sherds whereas the combined non-elite deposits (from Structures 2 and 60) totalled 13.8/1000 rim sherds. Relative to ceramics, there was not much difference between the Early elite and non-elite in the number of spindle whorls. In contrast, the ratio of whorls to excavated volume gives a different trend. In the Early elite deposits there were a total of 12.8 whorls per 10 m^3 whereas for the Early non-elite there were only 7.4 whorls per 10 m^3. Taken together, these two types of ratios mean that the elite were using and discarding more, but not significantly more whorls than the non-elite.

The hypothesis that cotton spinning and weaving for external exchange would decrease in times of increasing warfare is borne out by the decrease in the use of spindle whorls from the Early to Late Postclassic. The similar distribution of spindle whorls between elite and non-elite suggests that the elite were not alone in producing spun cotton but that both classes were involved. Still, both ratios suggest that the elite used slightly more spindle whorls than the non-elite. Since spinning and weaving are very time-consuming processes, it is likely that all members of the community would have had to be included in the activity in order to produce enough cloth for local use, as well as exchange. The slightly greater frequency of spindle whorls in elite households hints that they may have been the primary importers as well as the main users of spindle whorls.

Cotton cloth was probably one of the items made by Early Postclassic Canajasteños to exchange for whorls and other imported goods. Since most of the imported whorls were found in the elite household, they must have controlled their importation and distribution. But the elite also used them to spin cotton in their own households, as the discard of broken whorls in their midden and floor deposits demonstrates. Spinning took place in the non-elite household in the same way, if not with the same intensity. One possible explanation for non-elite cotton spinning is that commoners spun thread to exchange with the elite households for imports or to give to them as tribute. The elite, in turn, might have exchanged the spun cotton or woven cloth to other communities for nonlocal items. They also might have given it as tribute to other, higher-status elites in neighboring states in Guatemala.

I think the most convincing evidence that cotton cloth spun during the Early Postclassic at Canajasté was meant for exchange or tribute is that spinning became much less important when warfare increased. If spinning was for local consumption then there should have been no decrease in its intensity during the Late Postclassic.

At the time of the Spanish Conquest, in various Mesoamerican societies, spinning and weaving was considered one of the only proper crafts for female members of elite households (Díaz del Castillo 1912). Furthermore, as among the Quiche, only nobles were allowed to wear cotton clothes while the commoners were expected to wear clothes made from coarser fibres such as maguey (Carmack 1981:149; Estrada 1955:73; cf. Tozzer 1941:89). On the basis of the present data, it is impossible to determine if there was such a restriction at Canajasté. I can only say that during the Early Postclassic both nobles and commoners were using spindle whorls and, thus, spinning cotton. What was done with the finished cotton cloth can only be assessed by looking at tools involved in the next stage of production—weaving and sewing. The following section looks at their distribution in more detail.

Bone Weaving and Sewing Tools

Another way of examining the changes in the production of cloth goods for exchange is to look at the bone tools used in weaving and sewing the spun cotton. If the elite were in control of cloth production then they may be expected to weave and sew more than non-elite households. But they may also be expected to encourage the non-elite to invest their labor in

production and then demand a portion of the finished goods as tribute.

As with spindle whorls there were more weaving and sewing tools in the Early period than in the Late period (Table 7.18). This indicates, once again, that weaving decreased in importance in the Late Postclassic. In the early deposits there were four times the number of weaving and sewing tools per 10 m³, and there were twice as many tools per 1000 rim sherds as in the late deposits. Using both methods of standardizing the quantities of weaving and sewing tools it is clear that they were more frequent during the Early Postclassic than later.

Monitoring the differentiation between the elite and non-elite is more complex, but it corresponds well with what was found in the spindle whorl analysis (Table 7.18). During the Early Postclassic the elite houses had nearly three times more weaving and sewing implements than the non-elite houses. But during the Late Postclassic period, weaving and sewing tools were two to four times more common in non-elite houses than in elite houses. The non-elite households retained about the same quantity of weaving and sewing tools from the Early to Late Postclassic while the quantity declined among the elite. This leads me to hypothesize that the non-elite maintained the same level of production and that this level was not dependent upon the volume of external exchange. The elite household, on the other hand, reduced its production of cotton cloth. They may have initially invested labor in surplus weaving for the purposes of long-distance exchange and, when the exchange network broke down, their need to manufacture sewn and woven products decreased. This strongly supports the hypothesis that the elite engaged in, and controlled, the craft for exchange purposes, and the non-elite were engaged in production for domestic consumption which did not change with decreasing exchange.

When all spinning, weaving, and sewing tools are combined, both ratios (tools per 1000 rim sherds and tools per 10 m³ of excavated volume) show trends *within* each period (Table 7.18). The trends are not clear-cut, but the data show that, during the Early period, the Structure

22 sequence underwent a rapid early growth and would have peaked when interregional exchange was most vigorous. Following this, there was a steady drop in the number of spinning, sewing, and weaving implements deposited in the Structure 22 middens. However, towards the end of the Early period there was, once again, an increase in the frequency of these items, ending in another precipitous decline by the beginning of the Late Postclassic. In the two non-elite, early deposits, where the temporal sequence is not as complete as in Structure 22, and where the deposits probably date to the late end of the Early period, there were relatively large numbers of these tools, but later they declined in relative frequency. The overall trend for the Early deposits is that the elite household maintained high levels of these tools throughout its history. The non-elite households began with a relatively high frequency of spinning, weaving, and sewing tools. One household showed a decline towards the beginning of the Late Postclassic while the other maintained the same rate of consumption of these tools.

During the Late Postclassic the elite household had a different trend in almost every house. In Structure 22 there was an increase in spinning and sewing tools—but never up to the levels that were in use during the Early Postclassic. In Structure 21 there were never any of these tools in use, and none made their way into any of the five Late Postclassic floors. In Structure 23 there was an initial increase in the number of tools (from Floor 3 to Floor 2) and then a decrease down to about the same levels as in Structure 22. In the non-elite structures there was also a decline through each sequence. Three of the four houses showed substantial drops in the number of spinning and weaving tools, and in only one was there a minor increase. In the Structure 2 middens there were no spinning, weaving, or sewing tools at all, even though the tools were present in the contemporaneous floors and patio. In Structure 60, by contrast, these tools were found only in the middens but not in the floors.

Summarizing these shifts in the tools of cloth production, I can say that they were more important Early and became less so in

the Late Postclassic. Furthermore, the decline continued throughout the Late Postclassic; both the elite and non-elite made less cloth. Assuming the community members continued to wear cotton clothing, I think this trend has important implications for the relative position of the community in its regional hierarchy. One is that Canajasté became able to exact tribute in finished products from its neighbors. This is exactly what would be expected if warfare rather than exchange became the more important means of intercommunity interaction. It would also ensure that everyone had a vested interest in maintaining the military structure since there would be few other ways to obtain items that community members needed.

GRINDING STONES

Basalt Manos and Metates

Two types of material were used for manos and metates: metamorphosed sandstone and vesicular basalt (Figure 7.17). This section will deal with the porous basalt grinding stones since they were imports from Guatemala, and the next section will examine locally-made sandstone manos and metates.

No basalt manos or metates were recovered whole from any of the excavations or surface collections. Since excavations concentrated on house floors and only a few small middens this finding is not surprising. These tools, being both large and relatively "valuable," are not likely to have been lost in houses or middens. All of the metates were fragmentary, and most showed use-wear. Judging from the shape of the fragments, the metates were generally rectangular in outline and had three feet (Figure 7.17a-b). Mano fragments were the long, two-handed type called *brazos* (Figure 7.17e-f).

No porous basalt occurs locally, but it is known to come from areas in the Cuchumatan Mountains and the northern flank of the Sierra Madre in Guatemala. Some large boulders may be carried down the steep river valleys that eventually join with the Grijalva, but even these sources are many kilometers from Canajasté. The basalt manos and metates that came into

Figure 7.17. Metates and manos from house excavations at Canajasté. Vesicular basalt metates: a, b; sandstone metates: c, d; vesicular basalt manos: e, f.

Canajasté must have been imported. Therefore, changes in their quantity and distribution are likely to reveal something about interregional exchange patterns.

This argument relies on the assumption that there was no technological shift in the activities requiring the use of manos and metates. Increasing or decreasing frequencies of grinding stone fragments may be related to shifts in the way maize was ground and, ultimately, consumed. Earlier I mentioned that, during the Late Postclassic, large-holed colanders and comales for preparing maize and cooking tortillas increased. Since maize must be well ground in order to make tortillas that are both smooth and hold together properly, it is possible that the need for manos and metates would increase along with the new food preparation technology. Conversely, if, in the Early Postclassic, maize was consumed primarily in the form of pozole (a porridge), or *tamales* (leaf-wrapped and steamed balls of maize dough), I expect there to have been more frequent use of ceramic or gourd bowls in that period. Figure 7.10 shows that, proportionately, both decorated and plain bowls were more common in the Early period.

There are, therefore, two conflicting expectations. On the one hand, declining interregional trade should lead to a decrease in imported basalt manos and metates. On the other hand, the apparent increase in tortilla preparation would lead to a greater use of and need for grinding stones. People could have used either locally made metates or imports. If trade declined, the people at Canajasté should have increased their use of local grinding stones, and if trade was maintained or increased, they should have consumed more imported basalt manos and metates. Finally, an increase, during the Late Postclassic, of both imported and local manos and metates would be conclusive evidence of changing food preparation practices rather than increasing overall trade.

These expectations can be evaluated by looking at the evidence for the changing frequencies of porous basalt grinding stones in Table 7.19. The table shows two major trends in the consumption of these tools. First, their use almost doubled from the Early to Late Postclassic. Second, the differentiation between elite and non-elite also increased from the Early to Late period. Both the ratio of the basalt grinding stone weight to excavated volume and the ratio of grinding stone count to rim sherds increased through time. The summary totals in Table 7.19 show this pattern most clearly.

Unfortunately, there were many deposits that lacked fragments of manos or metates. In fact, the total in the house deposits was only 92. It is difficult, therefore, to monitor the within-period trends. Since the sample sizes are so small and since one prehistoric house cleaning episode could easily destroy the observable trend, I will limit the analysis to "large-scale" comparisons. I measured the changes in basalt grinding stone frequency in two ways. One was to divide the combined weight (gm) of the various pieces in each deposit by the volume excavated (m^3). The other was to divide the count of grinding stone fragments in a given deposit by the rim sherd count (then multiply the result by 100 to make the figures more readily comparable). Both indices showed essentially the same pattern.

The ratios increased in most of the Late Postclassic houses. The only exception was Structure 61 (Table 7.19), which maintained the highest levels of these tools, suggesting that basalt grinding stone importation was on the rise during the Postclassic.

All other imported artifacts showed the opposite pattern. The most likely explanation is that the community simply did not make the same use of this technology during the Early Postclassic. Another possibility is that these items were imported from much closer regions than many of the artifacts discussed, such as obsidian, marine shell, and metal. They may have been obtainable within the state's immediate political network through local exchange. Also, since they are more or less utilitarian tools and not ritual objects they may have been subject to different processes of exchange. Still another possibility is that they were imported from a zone in western Guatemala, a zone with which people in the upper Grijalva region maintained trade relations, despite the general decline in trade with everyone else.

It is not surprising that at least one imported item increased in frequency during the Late Postclassic. Nonetheless, it is worthwhile to emphasize that this was the only import related to food preparation and may relate to a technological shift as much as a change in trade relations. The change in trade relations may have been towards an increasing emphasis on local exchange and a de-emphasis of long distance exchange of exotic elite goods. The technological shift in food preparation may have been a process of emulation of neighboring elites that was partly based on those very trade relations. The above pattern leads to the possibility that narrow, much more localized trade relations were maintained during the Late Postclassic while warfare continued as the dominant strategy of inter-polity relations.

Local Sandstone Manos and Metates

Most manos and metates made of local obdurate sandstone are not elaborately worked; in fact, only one side of the metate is usually flattened, and the other is left in its natural state (Figure 7.17d). Only one sandstone metate in the sample had been pecked to form feet (Figure 7.17c). After a long period of use, a metate grinding surface becomes very smooth and shiny and has to be pecked to re-roughen it for effective use. The manos are also simple and require little shaping.

Table 7.20 shows the summary weights and counts, densities, and ratios to rim sherds for the combined deposits. As expected, local grinding stones also increased from the Early to the Late Postclassic. In terms of the total weight to volume ratio the increase was about 50 percent. In terms of the count to rim sherd ratio the increase was three fold. The Early non-elite had no fragments of local grinding stone. This could be a problem of sample size. The Early elite, on the other hand, had four fragments. During the following period there was little difference between the two classes, with the elite having only slightly more than the non-elite. The key trend—increasing use of local grinding stones in combination with the increasing use of imported basalt grinding stones—confirms that there was a shift in the community's maize preparation practices rather than an overall increase in trade.

The Early to Late Postclassic shift in food preparation technology for both the elite and non-elite is the kind of change expected if the site was completely taken over by people from outside the locale. However, since at Canajasté it was more a quantitative than a qualitative change (the technology did exist in Early Postclassic deposits), a process of emulation of non- local styles, or elaboration of existing local styles, is a more plausible explanation for the shift. The former interpretation accords well with increasing exchange and the latter is more likely with increasing warfare.

MARINE SHELL ORNAMENTS

Several types of shell artifact were recovered, all of them from species of shell common to the Pacific Coast, some 150 km from the site. Some artifacts may also have come from the Gulf of Mexico or Caribbean Sea, both 300 km from Canajasté. All of the shell artifacts appear to have been objects of personal adornment, such as bracelets, beads, and pendants. Furthermore, they were imported in their finished form; none of them are only partially worked, and there was no shell manufacturing debris recovered.

The following analysis combines all of the following types of shell artifacts recovered in the house floor and midden deposits:[6] *Glycymeris gigantea* bracelets, *Oliva spicata* tinkler beads and a pendant, *Agaronia propatula* tinkler bead, *Prunum apicinum* beads, and *Olivella* sp. beads (Figure 7.18). There were several other small beads, discs, pendants, and a possible whistle mouthpiece made from unidentifiable shells. Shell artifacts that were found in the construction fill and disturbed deposits were not used in the analysis. These include at least two other species: *Anadara grandis* and *Venticoloria isocardia*.

Altogether, 51 pieces of shell artifacts were recovered from the house deposits; their distribution is presented in Table 7.21. The extremely small numbers in any one deposit as well as the large number of deposits with no occurrences hinders a fine-grained analysis of change from floor to floor or from midden layer to midden layer. There are some clear patterns evident, however, between the Early and Late periods.

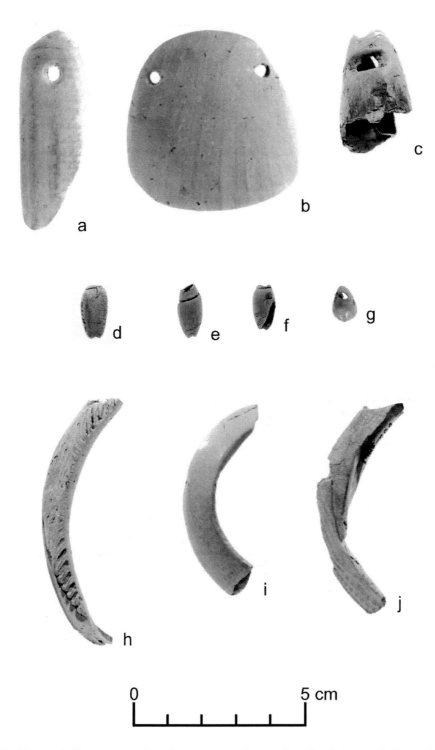

Figure 7.18. Marine shell ornaments from house excavations at Canajasté. Large shell pendants: a, b; Oliva spicata pendant: c; Agaronia propatula beads; d-f; Punum apicinum bead: g; Glycymeris gigantea bracelets: h-j.

Structure 22 shows that there was an almost continuous increase in imported marine shell ornaments from Midden 5 to Midden 2. This increase was 16-fold in terms of pieces per m^3 of excavated deposit and 11-fold in terms of the ratio of shell to rim sherds. Next there was a decline in both ratios: no shell was recovered in Earth Lens 2. The final Early Postclassic layers displayed a small increase once again. The Early Postclassic deposits in Structure 60 (which were probably late in the sequence) showed an increase of density (number per m^3) and a slight decrease in the number to rim sherd ratio. Structure 2, Floor 4, lacked marine shell. The Early Postclassic pattern, overall, showed a significant growth in marine shell deposition; this peaked midway through the sequence. The elite had many more times the amount of shell than the non-elite. By the end of the period, however, there was not much difference between the amounts deposited in the elite and non-elite households: both consumed about as much as the initial early elite had. The combined densities and ratio to rim sherds for the Early Postclassic (Table 7.21) show that the elite had either slightly more than (per m^3) or slightly less than (ratio to rim sherds) the non-elite.

The Late Postclassic sequences in all the various houses contained considerably less shell than did those of the Early Postclassic. But, apart from the fact that they had less, there was an interesting shift during the period. Most of the houses, both elite and non-elite, show an increase in shell, followed by a decrease. The only exceptions were one non-elite house (Structure 2) and one elite house (Structure 22), where there was an increase in one measure and a decrease in the other, and Structure 23, where there was an increase in both. Furthermore, almost all the initial Late Postclassic house floors had no marine shell. The Late Postclassic began with a highly reduced import of marine shell compared with the Early period, but it did increase slightly towards the end of the period only to drop once again.

Calculations for the combined deposits (Table 7.21; summary totals) show that the Late Postclassic period had about one-fifth the

density (per m^3) and one-half the ratio of shell to rim sherds that the Early Postclassic had. The elite, for both periods combined, had almost twice as much shell as the non-elite had.

The implications of these changes for the shifting roles of exchange and warfare in Canajasté's history are as follows. The elite enjoyed a slightly greater access to shell during both periods—especially during times of active shell trade. When it decreased (i.e., from Early to Late Postclassic), the differences between the two classes diminished slightly—although the differences were never very significant. The most important pattern is that the trade in marine shell ornaments peaked just before the end of the Early Postclassic and then declined. This pattern parallels the changes in obsidian importation, even though the two classes of items probably came from different areas. On the basis of this evidence, one could argue that trade in most nonlocal goods, from various different regions, was declining towards the end of the Early Postclassic. This is my expectation if warfare increased over large areas, interrupting trade relations with Guatemala, the Pacific Coast, Central Mexico, and the Gulf Coast.

The fact that marine shell ornaments decreased in importance, even though they were probably used almost exclusively in personal ornamentation, suggests an even greater increase in similarity (or, at least, a decrease in differentiation) between elite and non-elite than I would have expected. Perhaps more locally available objects were used as ornamentation in place of imported shell. Unfortunately, no other class of artifacts was found that could be used to test this conjecture, and, in all likelihood, most personal ornaments would have been perishable, such as feathers, skins, tattoos, hair styles, and clothes.

In summary, trade in shell ornaments decreased through time as did the elite's preferred access to it. The elite became more like the non-elite as this trade decreased, just as would be expected under conditions of increasing warfare.

METAL ARTIFACTS

As with several other classes of imported artifacts, very few pieces of metal were recovered in the excavations. Since none of the excavations uncovered ceremonial caches, offerings, or adult burials, it is not surprising that there were few "luxury exotics" such as metal.

There were only two types of metal present: copper and gold. The copper artifacts included a needle, ring, bells, bell clapper, wire-work ornament, bi-point, rolled spear point, lumps, and pigment-ore lumps (Figure 7.19a-f). The gold artifact was a small scroll-shaped portion of leafwork over a wood or carbon core (Figure 7.19g).

Most of the items were badly broken or bent, and many were recovered from mixed and disturbed deposits. Only 17 metal artifacts were found in undisturbed deposits; these are tallied in Table 7.22. Again, this number is too small to assess trends or variation that could shed light on within-period shifts in exchange. But looking at the broader changes, the elite had greater quantities of metal (with respect to both volume excavated and ratio to rim sherds than the non-elite). Also, metal artifacts were more common in the Early period than in the Late period. The volume index shows that both the early elite and non-elite had more than their counterparts in the Late period and that within each period the elite had more than the non-elite. In fact, the early elite house contained over three times the amount of metal artifacts that the non-elite houses had.

When we compare this pattern with the ratio to rim sherds, the same basic pattern emerges, with the exception that the late elite had slightly more metal artifacts than any other group, especially the non-elite.

Summing up these trends, the amount of metal artifacts declined from the Early to the Late Postclassic. In spite of this decreased supply, the elite maintained control over, or access to, metal items, and they used and discarded more than the non-elite. This was essentially the same pattern noted for marine shell ornaments.

OBSIDIAN BLOODLETTERS

Bloodletters are one class of artifact that could potentially reveal a great deal about elite/ non-elite differences. Bloodletters are especially useful since, in addition to being used for ritual purposes, they are also imports. The implements recovered that are hypothesized to have been bloodletters are distal portions of blades that have very fine, even, unifacial retouch on both sides near the tip. This retouch gives them a sharp, lanceolate shape. Bloodletters were used for ritual purposes in auto-sacrifice ceremonies. I would expect that in circumstances where the elite were more involved in and responsible for sacrifice rituals, as compared with of the non-elite, there should be more of these artifacts in elite households. And if the degree of differentiation between elite and non-elite were to decrease, both groups should tend towards similar rates of use of these implements.

Table 7.23 presents the distributional data for the 16 bloodletters. Four of them were recovered in mixed deposits and were excluded from the analysis. The 12 remaining bloodletters were distributed primarily in the early elite house deposits, but some were also found in the late deposits. The main patterning is as follows. Bloodletters were much more common in the Early Postclassic than in the Late Postclassic. During the Early Postclassic period they were found only in the elite household; none were found in the non-elite household. During the Late Postclassic, obsidian bloodletters were found in almost equal quantities in the elite and commoner house deposits.

I am not certain why there was a decline in their use, but it does imply a shift away from household-based, elite ritual. This decreasing use of bloodletters suggests that, as the elite decreased their use of these ritual implements, their use by non-elite actually increased. The outcome was one of decreased differentiation between the two classes—precisely the pattern observed in most of the other types of material culture discussed so far.

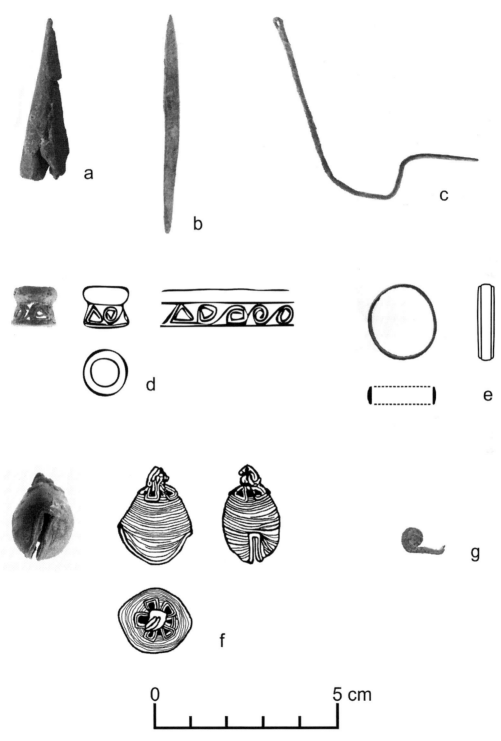

Figure 7.19. Metal artifacts from house excavations at Canajasté. Copper artifacts: a. spear point; b. bipoint; c. needle; d. wire-work ornament; e. ring; f. bell; Gold artifact: g. ornament.

DISCUSSION

I have examined a number of different classes of artifacts, each of which may be linked into an evaluation of the relative influence of the specific inter-polity political relations affecting the history of Canajasté. Each type of artifact, considered separately, is not as convincing as the whole group of artifacts or when combined with the other lines of evidence such as domestic architecture. Here I will summarize the discussion thus far with reference to the household artifacts. There are two dimensions of temporal change: (1) quantitative, and (2) stylistic variation between the elite and non-elite.

The community began in the Early Postclassic with a relatively wide rift between the elite and non-elite. Compared with the early non-elite, the elite had more types of ceramics and larger quantities of most types, particularly decorated bowls that may have been imported. They also obtained more obsidian, including manufacturing by-products, indicating their greater control over obsidian trade. The early elite had roughly the same quantity of obsidian projectile points as the non-elite had, but the elite used different styles of points. With several other imported artifacts the elite also had more than the non-elite: spindle whorls, basalt grinding stones (ratio to m^3 of deposit), marine shell ornaments, copper artifacts of various kinds, one gold artifact, and obsidian bloodletters.

During the initial occupation of Canajasté, there were no complete disjunctions between the two classes as there was with house styles. This suggests that the site began as a whole colony that came from outside the region. The differences between the two classes were not as distinct as would be expected had there been only an influx of foreign elite. Although there is not much comparative material available, it appears that there were differences in house styles, ceramics, and degree of access to imports, such as obsidian, between Early Postclassic Canajasté and its neighbors. The most likely explanation is that the community was founded as a complete colony from somewhere outside the immediate region.

I also think that both warfare and exchange were important to the new polity's interregional interactions. As a new colony, Canajasté may have met with resistance from other local towns, and there may have been a constant threat of low-level warfare. Even so, it is clear that a large number of exchange relations were also maintained during the Early Postclassic and that the elite controlled trade.

Towards the end of the Early Postclassic, exchange began to decline in importance for the community. Almost all imports declined in frequency: ceramics, obsidian, spindle whorls, metal artifacts, and marine shell. The only import to increase was basalt grinding stones, and this might be correlated with a shift in maize preparation technology. Throughout the Late Postclassic, exchange was carried out but at a much lower level than earlier. The goods that the Canajasteños did receive, such as obsidian, were more heavily used. They reduced their production of goods such as cotton cloth which could have been exchanged.

In addition to this decline in exchange, was a de-emphasis on the material symbols of stratification. The non-elite began to emulate house styles and artifacts that, previously, only the elite used. Also, there was a decline in the differences in artifact quantities between the two classes. During the Late Postclassic both the elite and non-elite used increasingly similar quantities, types, and styles of ceramics, obsidian, obsidian projectile points, weaving and sewing tools, *manos* and metates, and marine shell ornaments. Copper artifacts were the only import that the elite continued to control.

This trajectory of increasing stylistic similarity in the symbols which had earlier been distinctive of social stratification is exactly the trend expected under conditions of increasing warfare and decreasing exchange. Additional evidence for increasing Late Postclassic warfare was provided by higher frequencies of burned house walls and floors, and larger numbers of obsidian projectile points.

In spite of the gradual shift from exchange to warfare as the dominant mode of intercommunity relations, Canajasté seems to have thrived. There may have been subtle remnants of elite/non-elite differentiation: only the non-elite buried their deceased infants below house floors. Elite infants were presumably cremated, as were adults, and placed in caves in the surrounding valley.

In conclusion, the trajectory of changes in household artifact distributions forms a pattern that corresponds closely to the changes in household architecture and features. The kinds of changes noted between elite and non-elite households support the following interpretation of the state's history. Canajasté began as a complete colony (perhaps incorporating some locals into its non-elite population) and maintained rather distinct elite/non-elite differentiation, primarily through control of sumptuary goods imported from outside the region. Towards the Late Postclassic period, warfare increased, and, consequently, exchange decreased in importance. There was also a de-emphasis of the material symbols that had previously distinguished the elite from the non-elite. Despite this trend, the elite continued to flourish, probably because they controlled warfare. In fact, the community, as a whole, expanded throughout the period. Towards the end of the occupation, symbols of elite's status may have been emerging once more (for example, in the differential mortuary treatment of infant burials, as discussed in the next chapter).

ENDNOTES

1   As part of a study of this question and others relating to the relationship between household material culture and social and economic variables, Brian Hayden undertook an ethnoarchaeological study of three contemporary Maya communities. I was able to participate on his project for three months in each of three consecutive years, from 1977 to 1979. Many of the assumptions I use in

the analysis that follows derive from my own observations made during this research and from those of Brian Hayden and other project members (Blake 1984a, 1988; Blake and Blake 1988; Deal 1982, 1998; Hayden and Cannon 1982, 1983, 1984; Hayden and Nelson 1981; Nelson 1981).

2   For an excellent example of a successful attempt to do this, see Moore and Gasco (1990).

3   The ceramics of the upper Río Grijalva region have now been published in detail, and the main types are described for all the excavated sites, including Canajasté and its neighbors (Bryant, Clark, and Cheetham 2005). The ceramic type descriptions in this work derive from analyses of the excavated collections and replace many unpublished reports, theses, and dissertations—including the doctoral dissertation on which this volume is based (Blake 1985). For the Postclassic ceramic typology, see Bryant, Lee, and Cheetham (2005). Appendix D contains a concordance of the types and groups used in the present report with the Type-Variety descriptions presented in the newly published ceramic typology.

4   This does not include an additional 400 artifacts such as projectile points, transversely retouched blades, scrapers, and bloodletters, which comprise only 10 percent of the sample.

5   John Clark studied all the obsidian from Canajasté, identifying sources, use-wear, and technological types; therefore, his use-wear classifications are directly comparable with other collections that he has studied in Chiapas. The classification methods are fully discussed in Clark (1988).

6   All of the identifications were made with the help of Barbara Voorhies. I also consulted Keen (1971).

Table 7.1. Major categories of imports and their probable region of origin.

Category		Subcategory	Region of Origin
Obsidian	1.	San Martín Jilotepeque	Guatemala
	2.	El Chayal	Guatemala
	3.	Ixtepeque	Guatemala
	4.	Zaragosa and Ucareo	Central Mexico
	5.	Pachuca	Central Mexico
Basalt	1.	Metates	Guatemala
	2.	Manos	Guatemala
Metal	1.	Copper bells, ornaments, ring, needle, bi-point, lumps	Central America
	2.	Gold ornament	Central America
Marine Shell	1.	*Glycymeris* bracelets and pendant	Pacific Coast
	2.	*Oliva* tinkler beads and pendant	Pacific Coast
	3.	*Prunum* beads	Pacific Coast
	4.	*Olivella* beads	Pacific Coast
	5.	Miscellaneous disc, pendants, and beads	Pacific?
Ceramic Artifacts)	1.	Plumbate sherds	Pacific Coast
	2.	Mold-made spindle whorls	Gulf Coast
	3.	Finely made figurines	Gulf Coast

Table 7.2. Distribution of all imports.

House	Deposit	Obsidian: Sources	Basalt: Manos Metates	Metal: Copper Gold	Marine Shell: Types	Ceramics: Plumbate Figurines Whorls	Total
Late Non-elite							
STR-1	FLR-1	4	2	0	1	0	7
	FLR-2	4	1	0	2	0	7
STR-2	FLR-1	4	0	0	1	0	5
	PFL-1	5	1	0	1	0	7
	FLR-2	4	1	0	1	0	6
	FLR-3	2	0	0	0	0	2
	MID-1	3	1	0	0	0	4
	MID-2	2	1	0	0	0	3
	MID-3	2	0	0	0	0	2
	MID-4	4	2	0	1	0	7
	MID-5	2	1	0	1	1	5
	MID-6	2	0	0	0	0	2
	MID-7	4	1	0	0	0	5
STR-60	FLR-1	5	1	0	0	1	7
	FLR-2	3	0	1	1	0	5
	MID-1	4	0	1	1	1	7
STR-61	FLR-1	3	1	0	1	0	5
	FLR-2	4	0	0	2	1	7
	FLR-3	4	1	0	0	0	5
	FLR-4	2	0	0	0	0	2
	FLR-5	4	1	0	0	0	5
Median							5
Range							2-7
Early Non-elite							
STR-2	FLR-4	3	0	0	0	0	3
STR-60	MID-2&3	4	0	1	2	2	9
	MID-4	3	2	0	2	0	7
Median							7
Range							3-9
Late Elite							
STR-21	FLR-1	3	2	0	2	0	7
	FLR-2	3	0	0	1	1	5
	FLR-3	2	0	1	0	0	3
	FLR-4	2	0	1	0	0	3

Table 7.2. Continued.

House	Deposit	Obsidian: Sources	Basalt: Manos Metates	Metal: Copper Gold	Marine Shell: Types	Ceramics: Plumbate Figurines Whorls	Total
	FLR-5	2	1	1	0	0	4
STR-22	FLR-1	5	2	1	1	0	9
	FLR-2	5	2	0	2	0	9
	FLR-3	5	1	0	0	0	6
STR-23	FLR-1	4	0	1	1	0	6
	FLR-2	3	1	0	0	0	4
	FLR-3	3	1	0	0	0	4
Median							5
Range							3-9
Early Elite							
STR-22	FLR-4	3	0	0	1	2	6
	FLR-5	5	2	0	3	1	11
	EL-1	4	0	2	1	0	7
	EL-2	4	0	0	0	0	4
	MID-1	4	2	0	1	1	8
	MID-2	3	0	0	2	0	5
	MID-3	5	1	1	3	2	12
	MID-4	5	1	0	1	2	9
	AL-2	5	1	0	2	1	9
	MID-5	4	0	0	1	2	7
Median							7.5
Range							4-12

Table 7.3. Counts and percentages (in parentheses) for all cooking vessel rim sherds.

House	Deposit	Total Rim Sherds	Fine Temper Jar C-2	Plain Comal C-14	Fillet Rim Comal C-61	Large-holed Colander C-63	Coarse Temper Jar C-1	Small-holed Colander C-65	Coarse Rough Bowl C-36	Brushed-neck Olla C-7	Coarse Rough Jar C-4	Decorated Colander C-20
Late Non-Elite												
STR-1	FLR-1	159	15 (9.4)	39 (24.5)	1 (.6)	0	29 (18.2)	2 (1.3)	3 (1.9)	1 (.6)	2 (1.3)	0
	FLR-2	51	1 (2.0)	5 (9.8)	0	0	10 (19.6)	0	8 (15.7)	3 (5.9)	0	0
STR-2	FLR-1	158	9 (5.7)	36 (22.8)	0	1 (.6)	46 (29.1)	1 (.6)	1 (.6)	1 (.6)	1 (.6)	0
	PFL-1	495	39 (7.9)	90 (18.2)	4 (.8)	0	99 (20.0)	4 (.8)	13 (2.6)	1 (.2)	11 (2.2)	0
	FLR-2	128	9 (7.0)	3 (2.3)	1 (.8)	0	13 (10.2)	0	7 (5.5)	5 (3.9)	4 (3.1)	0
	FLR-3	30	6 (20.0)	0	0	0	4 (13.3)	0	5 (16.7)	0	0	0
	MID-1	18	2 (11.1)	6 (33.3)	1 (5.6)	0	2 (11.1)	0	0	0	1 (5.6)	0
	MID-2	18	1 (5.6)	5 (27.8)	0	1 (5.6)	6 (33.3)	0	0	0	0	0
	MID-3	0	0	0	0	0	0	0	0	0	0	0
	MID-4	133	10 (7.5)	32 (24.0)	2 (1.5)	0	30 (22.6)	0	2 (1.5)	0	4 (3.0)	0
	MID-5	50	3 (6.0)	5 (10.0)	0	0	8 (16.0)	0	3 (6.0)	0	2 (4.0)	0
	MID-6	14	2 (14.3)	0	0	0	4 (28.6)	0	0	0	1 (7.1)	0
	MID-7	96	12 (12.5)	29 (30.2)	1 (1.0)	0	13 (13.5)	0	2 (2.1)	1 (1.0)	2 (2.1)	0
STR-60	FLR-1	252	20 (7.9)	58 (23.0)	1 (.4)	0	38 (15.1)	0	6 (2.4)	4 (1.6)	6 (2.4)	0
	FLR-2	105	7 (6.7)	3 (2.9)	1 (.9)	0	12 (11.4)	1 (.9)	15 (14.3)	2 (1.9)	3 (2.9)	0
	MID-1	355	32 (8.9)	22 (6.1)	1 (.3)	0	34 (9.5)	0	60 (16.7)	15 (4.2)	21 (5.9)	0
STR-61	FLR-1	19	2 (10.5)	4 (21.0)	0	0	5 (26.3)	0	0	0	0	0
	FLR-2	19	3 (15.8)	2 (10.5)	0	0	2 (10.5)	0	2 (10.5)	0	0	0

Table 7.3. Continued.

House	Deposit	Total Rim Sherds	Fine Temper Jar C-2	Plain Comal C-14	Fillet Rim Comal C-61	Large-holed Colander C-63	Coarse Temper Jar C-1	Small-holed Colander C-65	Coarse Rough Bowl C-36	Brushed-neck Olla C-7	Coarse Rough Jar C-4	Decorated Colander C-20
	FLR-3	88	18 (20.5)	18 (20.5)	0	0	13 (14.8)	0	3 (3.4)	2 (2.3)	2 (2.3)	0
	FLR-4	10	0	0	0	0	1 (10.0)	0	1 (10.0)	0	0	0
	FLR-5	44	2 (4.6)	1 (2.3)	0	0	3 (6.8)	0	7 (15.9)	3 (6.8)	1 (2.3)	0

Late Elite

House	Deposit	Total Rim Sherds	Fine Temper Jar C-2	Plain Comal C-14	Fillet Rim Comal C-61	Large-holed Colander C-63	Coarse Temper Jar C-1	Small-holed Colander C-65	Coarse Rough Bowl C-36	Brushed-neck Olla C-7	Coarse Rough Jar C-4	Decorated Colander C-20
STR-21	FLR-1	42	4 (9.5)	9 (21.4)	1 (2.4)	0	3 (7.1)	0	0	0	2 (4.8)	0
	FLR-2	35	4 (11.4)	18 (51.4)	0	0	2 (5.7)	0	1 (2.9)	0	0	0
	FLR-3	12	1 (8.3)	9 (75.0)	0	0	0	0	1 (8.3)	0	0	0
	FLR-4	10	3 (30.0)	0	0	0	0	0	3 (30.0)	1 (10.0)	0	0
	FLR-5	9	0	2 (22.2)	0	0	0	1 (11.1)	2 (22.2)	1 (11.1)	0	0
STR-22	FLR-1	94	5 (5.3)	9 (9.8)	0	0	37 (39.4)	0	3 (3.2)	4 (4.3)	0	0
	FLR-2	95	4 (4.2)	13 (13.7)	0	0	31 (32.6)	2 (2.1)	2 (2.1)	2 (2.1)	1 (1.1)	0
	FLR-3	58	8 (13.8)	6 (10.3)	0	0	8 (13.8)	0	3 (5.2)	2 (3.5)	2 (3.5)	0
STR-23	FLR-1	167	15 (8.9)	51 (30.5)	2 (1.2)	0	24 (14.4)	0	0	1 (.6)	2 (1.2)	0
	FLR-2	53	3 (5.7)	7 (13.2)	0	0	7 (13.2)	0	0	1 (1.9)	1 (1.9)	0
	FLR-3	72	43 (59.7)	5 (6.9)	0	0	5 (6.9)	0	1 (1.4)	1 (1.4)	0	0

Early Non-Elite

House	Deposit	Total Rim Sherds	Fine Temper Jar C-2	Plain Comal C-14	Fillet Rim Comal C-61	Large-holed Colander C-63	Coarse Temper Jar C-1	Small-holed Colander C-65	Coarse Rough Bowl C-36	Brushed-neck Olla C-7	Coarse Rough Jar C-4	Decorated Colander C-20
STR-60	MID-2&3	129	7 (5.4)	2 (1.6)	0	0	20 (15.5)	0	25 (19.4)	16 (12.4)	8 (6.2)	0
	MID-4	60	3 (5.0)	1 (1.7)	0	0	12 (20.0)	0	10 (16.7)	4 (6.7)	5 (8.3)	0
STR-2	FLR-4	34	2 (5.9)	0	0	0	4 (11.8)	0	3 (8.8)	2 (5.9)	0	0

Table 7.3. Continued.

House	Deposit	Total Rim Sherds	Fine Temper Jar C-2	Plain Comal C-14	Fillet Rim Comal C-61	Large-holed Colander C-63	Coarse Temper Jar C-1	Small-holed Colander C-65	Coarse Rough Bowl C-36	Brushed-neck Olla C-7	Coarse Rough Jar C-4	Decorated Colander C-20
Early Elite												
STR-22	FLR-4	61	1 (1.6)	4 (6.6)	0	0	5 (8.2)	0	9 (14.8)	4 (6.6)	2 (3.3)	1 (1.6)
	FLR-5	257	7 (2.7)	11 (4.3)	0	0	30 (11.7)	0	13 (5.1)	18 (7.0)	18 (7.0)	2 (.8)
	EL-1	36	1 (2.8)	1 (2.8)	0	0	2 (5.6)	0	7 (19.4)	5 (13.9)	3 (8.3)	0
	EL-2	78	5 (6.4)	0	0	0	6 (7.7)	2 (2.6)	9 (11.5)	10 (12.8)	5 (6.4)	0
	MID-1	154	2 (1.3)	1 (.7)	0	0	13 (8.4)	0	8 (5.2)	9 (5.8)	9 (5.8)	0
	MID-2	19	0	0	0	0	3 (15.8)	0	4 (21.1)	0	0	0
	MID-3	56	0	0	0	0	10 (17.9)	0	2 (3.6)	2 (3.7)	9 (16.1)	0
	MID-4	110	3 (2.7)	0	0	0	13 (11.8)	0	9 (8.2)	16 (14.6)	9 (8.2)	3 (2.7)
	AL-2	103	0	11 (10.7)	0	0	20 (19.4)	1 (.9)	7 (6.8)	13 (12.6)	7 (6.8)	0
	MID-5	117	2 (1.7)	1 (.9)	0	0	13 (11.1)	0	8 (6.8)	15 (12.8)	3 (2.6)	0

Table 7.4. Counts and percentages (in parentheses) for all decorated bowls.

House	Deposit	Tol Poly-chrome B-42	Tol Exterior B-67	Fine Orange B-33	Specular Red Tripod B-38	Red-brown Slip B-31	Possible Tol B-44	Red-tan B-48	Red and Black Incised B-22	Red and Black B-24	Orange-Black Incised B-26	Specular Red and Black Incised B-28	Early Tol B-40	Black on Tan B-46
Late Non-Elite														
STR-1	FLR-1	1 (.6)	0	12 (7.6)	7 (4.4)	2 (1.3)	12 (7.6)	7 (4.4)	0	0	0	0	5 (3.1)	0
	FLR-2	5 (9.8)	0	2 (3.9)	2 (3.9)	2 (3.9)	1 (1.9)	4 (7.8)	0	0	0	0	1 (1.9)	0
STR-2	FLR-1	8 (5.1)	0	2 (1.3)	13 (8.2)	0	9 (5.7)	6 (3.8)	0	0	0	0	0	0
	PFL-1	19 (3.8)	0	1 (.2)	50 (10.1)	8 (1.6)	14 (2.8)	12 (2.4)	0	0	0	0	11 (2.2)	0
	FLR-2	14 (10.9)	2 (1.6)	0	4 (3.1)	9 (7.0)	0	6 (4.7)	0	0	0	0	9 (7.0)	0
	FLR-3	2 (6.7)	0	0	2 (6.7)	2 (6.7)	1 (3.3)	1 (3.3)	0	0	0	0	1 (3.3)	0
	MID-1	0	0	0	1 (5.6)	1 (5.6)	0	0	0	0	0	0	0	0
	MID-2	0	1 (5.6)	0	1 (5.6)	0	0	0	0	0	0	0	1 (5.6)	0
	MID-3	0	0	0	0	0	0	0	0	0	0	0	0	0
	MID-4	6 (4.5)	0	1 (.8)	15 (11.3)	1 (.8)	9 (6.8)	4 (3.0)	0	0	0	0	1 (.8)	0
	MID-5	7 (14.0)	0	1 (2.0)	2 (4.0)	0	2 (4.0)	2 (4.0)	0	0	0	0	0	0
	MID-6	0	0	0	0	0	0	0	0	0	0	0	0	0
	MID-7	5 (5.2)	0	0	5 (5.2)	2 (2.1)	1 (1.0)	1 (1.0)	0	0	0	0	0	0
STR-60	FLR-1	21 (8.3)	0	5 (2.0)	0	12 (4.8)	25 (9.9)	3 (1.2)	0	0	0	0	5 (2.0)	3 (1.2)
	FLR-2	20 (19.1)	0	1 (.9)	0	6 (5.7)	12 (11.4)	2 (1.9)	0	0	0	0	3 (2.9)	1 (.9)
	MID-1	48 (13.4)	0	0	0	15 (4.2)	28 (7.8)	6 (1.7)	0	1 (.3)	1 (.3)	0	13 (3.6)	0
STR-61	FLR-1	0	0	0	0	1 (5.3)	2 (10.5)	0	0	0	0	0	0	0
	FLR-2	0	0	0	0	2 (10.5)	3 (15.8)	0	0	1 (5.3)	0	0	0	0

Table 7.4. Continued.

House	Deposit	Tol Poly-chrome B-42	Tol Exterior B-67	Fine Orange B-33	Specular Red Tripod B-38	Red-brown Slip B-31	Possible Tol B-44	Red-tan B-48	Red and Black Incised B-22	Red and Black B-24	Orange-Black Incised B-26	Specular Red and Black Incised B-28	Early Tol B-40	Black on Tan B-46
	FLR-3	0	0	2 (2.3)	0	4 (4.6)	12 (13.6)	1 (1.4)	0	0	0	0	3 (3.4)	0
	FLR-4	0	0	0	0	0	3 (30.0)	0	0	0	0	0	0	0
	FLR-5	1 (2.3)	0	0	0	12 (27.3)	3 (6.8)	0	0	0	1 (2.3)	0	1 (2.3)	0
Late Elite														
STR-21	FLR-1	2 (4.8)	0	0	7 (16.7)	0	1 (2.4)	0	0	0	0	0	0	0
	FLR-2	0	0	1 (2.9)	1 (2.9)	0	0	2 (5.7)	0	0	0	0	1 (2.3)	0
	FLR-3	0	0	0	0	1 (8.3)	0	0	0	0	0	0	0	0
	FLR-4	1 (10.0)	0	0	0	0	0	0	0	0	0	0	1 (10.0)	0
	FLR-5	0	0	0	1 (11.1)	0	0	1 (11.1)	0	0	0	0	0	0
STR-22	FLR-1	3 (3.2)	0	5 (5.3)	1 (1.1)	0	3 (3.2)	2 (2.1)	0	0	0	0	2 (2.1)	0
	FLR-2	3 (3.2)	0	1 (1.1)	5 (5.3)	2 (2.1)	1 (1.1)	6 (6.3)	0	0	0	0	3 (3.2)	0
	FLR-3	4 (6.9)	0	3 (5.2)	2 (3.5)	0	1 (1.7)	4 (6.9)	0	0	0	0	2 (3.5)	2 (3.5)
STR-23	FLR-1	3 (1.8)	0	6 (3.6)	6 (3.6)	6 (3.6)	0	21 (12.6)	0	0	0	0	0	0
	FLR-2	4 (7.6)	0	2 (3.8)	1 (1.9)	3 (5.7)	0	10 (18.9)	0	0	0	0	1 (1.9)	0
	FLR-3	2 (2.8)	0	1 (1.4)	0	1 (1.4)	0	6 (8.3)	0	0	0	0	0	0
Early Non-Elite														
STR-2	FLR-4	1 (2.9)	0	0	0	1 (2.9)	9 (26.5)	0	0	0	0	0	3 (8.8)	0
STR-60	MID-2&3	6 (4.7)	0	0	0	3 (2.3)	2 (1.6)	1 (.8)	0	0	0	0	1 (.8)	0
	MID-4	4 (6.7)	0	0	0	2 (3.3)	1 (1.7)	0	0	0	0	0	0	0

Table 7.4. Continued.

House	Deposit	Tol Poly-chrome B-42	Tol Exterior B-67	Fine Orange B-33	Specular Red Tripod B-38	Red-brown Slip B-31	Possible Tol B-44	Red-tan B-48	Red and Black Incised B-22	Red and Black B-24	Orange-Black Incised B-26	Specular Red and Black Incised B-28	Early Tol B-40	Black on Tan B-46
Early Elite														
STR-22	FLR-4	5 (8.2)	0	0	1 (1.6)	6 (9.8)	3 (4.9)	4 (6.6)	0	0	0	0	3 (4.9)	3 (4.9)
	AL-1	8 (3.1)	0	1 (.4)	7 (7.2)	31 (12.1)	7 (2.7)	9 (3.5)	1 (.4)	1 (.4)	0	1 (.4)	21 (8.2)	4 (1.6)
	EL-1	0	0	0	0	0	2 (5.6)	3 (3.3)	0	0	0	0	4 (11.1)	0
	EL-2	0	0	0	0	4 (5.1)	1 (1.3)	3 (3.9)	1 (1.3)	0	0	0	13 (16.7)	3 (3.9)
	MID-1	4 (2.6)	0	0	0	24 (15.6)	2 (1.3)	9 (5.8)	2 (1.3)	4 (2.6)	0 (.7)	1 (17.5)	27 (7.1)	11
	MID-2	0	0	0	0	3 (15.8)	0	0	1 (5.3)	1 (5.3)	0	0	0	0
	MID-3	0	0	0	0	3 (5.4)	1 (1.8)	1 (1.8)	3 (5.4)	1 (1.8)	0	2 (3.6)	6 (10.7)	0
	MID-4	1 (.9)	0	0	1 (.9)	11 (10.0)	2 (1.8)	1 (.9)	0	1 (.9)	3 (2.7)	0	3 (2.7)	2 (1.8)
	AL-2	0	0	6 (5.8)	2 (1.9)	4 (3.9)	2 (1.9)	0	0	0	0	0	5 (4.9)	0
	MID-5	0	0	0	3 (2.6)	14 (11.9)	3 (2.6)	3 (2.6)	0	0	1 (.9)	0	12 (10.3)	4 (3.4)

Table 7.5. Counts and percentages (in parentheses) for all plain bowl and all storage jar rim sherds. Also included are various classic period vessels (B-50, B-51, C-52, C-53, C-55).

House	Deposit	Plain Gray Bowl B-30	Plain Orange Bowl B-32	Red-orange Jar J-8	Plain Water Jar J-18	Painted Water Jar J-19	Incised Black-and-red Jar J-16	Painted Black-and-red Jar J-12	Black-on-tan Jar J-70	Various Classic Vessels
Late Non-Elite										
STR-1	FLR-1	3 (1.9)	3 (1.9)	8 (5.0)	3 (1.9)	2 (1.3)	0	0	0	0
	FLR-2	4 (7.8)	2 (3.9)	1 (1.9)	0	0	0	0	0	0
STR-2	FLR-1	3 (1.9)	8 (5.1)	8 (5.1)	2 (1.3)	0	0	0	0	3 (1.9)
	PFL-1	33 (6.7)	48 (9.7)	14 (2.8)	11 (2.2)	1 (.2)	0	0	0	12 (2.4)
	FLR-2	19 (14.8)	9 (7.0)	10 (7.8)	0	0	0	0	0	4 (4.1)
	FLR-3	1 (3.3)	2 (6.7)	0	1 (3.3)	0	0	0	0	2 (6.6)
	MID-1	2 (11.1)	1 (5.6)	0	0	0	0	0	0	1 (5.6)
	MID-2	1 (5.6)	0	0	1 (5.6)	0	0	0	0	0
	MID-3	0	0	0	0	0	0	0	0	0
	MID-4	4 (3.0)	7 (5.3)	4 (3.0)	1 (.8)	0	0	0	0	0
	MID-5	5 (10.0)	3 (6.0)	1 (2.0)	3 (6.0)	0	0	0	0	3 (6.0)
	MID-6	1 (7.1)	6 (42.9)	0	0	0	0	0	0	0
	MID-7	7 (7.3)	7 (7.3)	2 (2.1)	1 (1.0)	0	0	0	0	5 (5.2)
STR-60	FLR-1	14 (5.6)	20 (7.9)	3 (1.2)	4 (1.6)	0	0	0	0	2 (.8)
	FLR-2	3 (2.9)	5 (4.8)	4 (3.8)	1 (.9)	2 (1.9)	0	0	0	1 (.9)
	MID-1	33 (9.2)	12 (3.3)	9 (2.5)	0	4 (1.1)	0	0	0	1 (.3)
STR-61	FLR-1	2 (10.5)	3 (15.8)	0	0	0	0	0	0	0

Table 7.4. Continued.

House	Deposit	Plain Gray Bowl B-30	Plain Orange Bowl B-32	Red-orange Jar J-8	Plain Water Jar J-18	Painted Water Jar J-19	Incised Black-and-red Jar J-16	Painted Black-and-red Jar J-12	Black-on-tan Jar J-70	Various Classic Vessels
	FLR-2	2 (10.5)	1 (5.3)	0	0	0	0	0	0	0
	FLR-3	3 (3.4)	7 (7.9)	0	0	0	0	0	0	0
	FLR-4	1 (10.0)	3 (30.0)	0	0	0	0	0	0	1 (10.0)
	FLR-5	5 (11.4)	2 (4.6)	0	0	0	0	0	0	2 (4.6)

Late Elite

House	Deposit	Plain Gray Bowl B-30	Plain Orange Bowl B-32	Red-orange Jar J-8	Plain Water Jar J-18	Painted Water Jar J-19	Incised Black-and-red Jar J-16	Painted Black-and-red Jar J-12	Black-on-tan Jar J-70	Various Classic Vessels
STR-21	FLR-1	7 (16.7)	0	3 (7.1)	0	0	0	0	0	3 (7.1)
	FLR-2	1 (2.9)	3 (8.6)	0	0	0	0	0	0	1 (2.9)
	FLR-3	0	0	0	0	0	0	0	0	0
	FLR-4	0	1 (10.0)	0	0	0	0	0	0	0
	FLR-5	0	0	1 (11.1)	0	0	0	0	0	0
STR-22	FLR-1	6 (6.4)	7 (7.5)	3 (3.2)	3 (3.2)	1 (1.1)	0	0	0	0
	FLR-2	5 (5.3)	3 (3.2)	4 (4.2)	2 (2.1)	0	1 (1.1)	2 (2.1)	0	2 (2.1)
	FLR-3	4 (6.9)	2 (3.5)	1 (1.7)	1 (1.7)	1 (1.7)	0	2 (3.5)	0	0
STR-23	FLR-1	8 (4.8)	14 (8.4)	4 (2.4)	1 (.6)	0	0	0	0	2 (1.2)
	FLR-2	5 (9.4)	3 (5.7)	3 (5.7)	1 (1.9)	0	0	0	0	0
	FLR-3	1 (1.4)	2 (2.8)	3 (4.2)	0	0	0	1 (1.4)	0	0

Early Non-Elite

House	Deposit	Plain Gray Bowl B-30	Plain Orange Bowl B-32	Red-orange Jar J-8	Plain Water Jar J-18	Painted Water Jar J-19	Incised Black-and-red Jar J-16	Painted Black-and-red Jar J-12	Black-on-tan Jar J-70	Various Classic Vessels
STR-2	FLR-4	3 (8.8)	2 (5.9)	0	1 (2.9)	0	0	0	0	3 (8.8)

Table 7.4. Continued.

House	Deposit	Plain Gray Bowl B-30	Plain Orange Bowl B-32	Red-orange Jar J-8	Plain Water Jar J-18	Painted Water Jar J-19	Incised Black-and-red Jar J-16	Painted Black-and-red Jar J-12	Black-on-tan Jar J-70	Various Classic Vessels
STR-60	MID-2&3	27 (20.1)	8 (6.2)	1 (.8)	0	0	0	0	1 (.8)	1 (.8)
	MID-4	5 (8.3)	9 (15.0)	1 (1.7)	0	1 (1.7)	0	0	0	2 (3.3)
Early Elite										
STR-22	FLR-4	5 (8.2)	3 (4.9)	0	0	0	0	1 (1.6)	0	1 (1.6)
	AL-1	26 (10.1)	10 (3.9)	16 (6.2)	0	3 (1.2)	2 (.8)	1 (.4)	0	9 (3.5)
	EL-1	4 (11.1)	1 (2.8)	3 (8.3)	0	0	0	0	0	0
	EL-2	7 (8.9)	1 (1.3)	1 (1.3)	4 (5.1)	0	1 (1.3)	1 (1.3)	0	1 (1.3)
	MID-1	11 (7.1)	2 (1.3)	0	0	0	0	11 (7.1)	0	4 (2.5)
	MID-2	2 (10.5)	3 (15.8)	0	0	0	0	1 (5.3)	0	1 (5.3)
	MID-3	6 (10.7)	2 (3.6)	3 (5.4)	0	3 (5.4)	0	1 (1.8)	0	1 (1.8)
	MID-4	6 (5.5)	6 (5.5)	7 (6.4)	2 (1.8)	0	1 (.9)	7 (6.4)	0	3 (2.7)
	AL-2	6 (5.8)	6 (5.8)	2 (1.9)	4 (3.9)	0	0	4 (3.9)	0	3 (2.8)
	MID-5	12 (10.3)	5 (4.3)	4 (3.4)	2 (1.7)	0	0	0	0	12 (10.2)

Table 7.6. Counts (#) and ratios of total number to volume excavated (m³)(density=d) for functional groupings of vessesls.

Late Non-Elite

House	Deposit	Total Volume Excavated (m³)	Group 1 Early Cooking Vessels		Group 2 Early and Late Cooking Vessels		Group 3 Late Cooking Vessels		Group 4 Early Serving Vessels		Group 5 Early and Late Serving Vessels		Group 6 Late Serving Vessels		Group 7 Undecorated Serving Vessels		Group 8 Early Storage Jars		Group 9 Early and Late Storage Jars		Total Rim Sherds	
			#	d	#	d	#	d	#	d	#	d	#	d	#	d	#	d	#	d	#	d
STR-1	FLR-1	5.17	3	.6	34	6.6	55	10.6	5	.9	21	4.1	20	3.9	6	1.2	0	0	13	2.5	159	30.8
	FLR-2	5.31	3	.6	18	3.4	6	1.1	1	.2	7	1.3	9	1.7	6	1.2	0	0	1	.2	51	9.6
STR-2	FLR-1	2.29	2	.9	48	20.9	46	20.1	0	0	15	6.6	23	10.0	11	4.8	0	0	10	4.4	155	67.7
	PFL-1	6.41	12	1.9	116	18.1	133	20.8	11	1.7	34	5.3	70	10.9	81	12.6	0	0	26	4.1	483	75.4
	FLR-2	4.62	9	1.9	20	4.3	13	2.8	9	1.9	15	3.3	20	4.3	28	6.1	0	0	10	2.2	124	26.8
	FLR-3	2.01	0	0	9	4.5	6	3.0	1	.5	4	1.9	4	1.9	3	1.5	0	0	1	.5	28	13.9
	MID-1	.11	1	9.1	2	18.2	9	81.8	0	0	1	9.1	1	9.1	3	27.3	0	0	0	0	17	154.6
	MID-2	.18	0	0	6	33.3	7	38.9	1	5.6	0	0	2	11.1	1	5.6	0	0	1	5.6	18	100.0
	MID-3	.26	0	0	0	0	0	0	0	0	0	0	0	0	0	0	0	0	0	0	0	0
	MID-4	1.83	4	2.2	32	17.5	44	24.0	1	.6	14	7.7	22	12.0	11	6.0	0	0	5	2.7	133	72.7
	MID-5	.16	2	12.5	11	68.8	8	50.0	0	0	4	25.0	10	62.5	8	50.0	0	0	4	25.0	47	293.8
	MID-6	.24	1	4.2	4	16.7	2	8.3	0	0	0	0	0	0	7	29.2	0	0	0	0	14	58.3
	MID-7	.42	3	7.1	15	35.7	42	100.0	0	0	4	9.5	10	23.8	14	33.3	0	0	3	7.1	91	216.7
STR-60	FLR-1	8.45	10	1.2	44	5.2	79	9.4	8	.9	40	4.7	26	3.1	34	4.0	0	0	7	.8	248	29.4
	FLR-2	1.48	5	3.4	28	18.9	11	7.4	4	2.7	20	13.5	21	14.2	8	5.4	0	0	7	4.7	104	70.3
	MID-1	4.56	36	7.9	94	20.6	55	12.1	15	3.3	49	10.8	48	10.5	45	9.9	0	0	13	2.9	355	77.9
STR-61	FLR-1	2.52	0	0	5	1.9	6	2.4	0	0	3	1.2	0	0	5	1.9	0	0	0	0	19	7.5
	FLR-2	1.51	0	0	4	2.7	6	4.0	1	.7	5	3.3	0	0	3	1.9	0	0	0	0	19	12.6
	FLR-3	2.99	4	1.3	16	5.4	36	12.0	3	1.0	17	5.7	2	.7	10	3.3	0	0	0	0	88	29.4
	FLR-4	1.03	0	0	2	1.9	0	0	0	0	3	2.9	3	2.9	4	3.9	0	0	0	0	9	8.7
	FLR-5	4.12	4	.9	10	2.4	3	3.8	2	.5	15	3.6	1	.2	7	1.7	0	0	0	0	42	10.2
Subtotals		55.67	99 (4.5%)	1.8	518 (23.0%)	9.3	567 (25.8%)	10.2	62 (2.7%)	1.1	271 (12.0%)	4.9	289 (13.0%)	5.2	295 (13.0%)	5.3	0 (4.6%)		101 (100%)	1.8	2204	39.6

Table 7.6. Continued.

House	Deposit	Total Volume Excavated (m³)	Group 1 Early Cooking Vessels		Group 2 Early and Late Cooking Vessels		Group 3 Late Cooking Vessels		Group 4 Early Serving Vessels		Group 5 Early and Late Serving Vessels		Group 6 Late Serving Vessels		Group 7 Undecorated Serving Vessels		Group 8 Early Storage Jars		Group 9 Early and Late Storage Jars		Total Rim Sherds	
Late Elite																						
STR-21	FLR-1	2.0	2	1.0	3	1.5	14	6.9	0	0	1	.5	9	4.4	7	3.5	0	0	3	1.5	39	19.2
	FLR-2	1.6	0	0	3	1.9	22	13.6	1	.6	2	1.2	2	1.2	1	.6	0	0	0	0	31	19.1
	FLR-3	1.4	0	0	1	.7	10	7.1	0	0	1	.7	0	0	1	.7	0	0	0	0	13	9.2
	FLR-4	.9	1	1.0	3	3.1	3	3.1	1	1.0	0	0	1	1.0	0	0	0	0	0	0	9	9.4
	FLR-5	.8	1	1.3	3	3.8	2	2.5	0	0	1	1.3	1	1.3	0	0	0	0	1	1.3	9	11.3
STR-22	FLR-1	10.3	4	.4	40	3.9	14	1.4	2	.2	5	.5	9	.9	13	1.3	0	0	7	.7	94	9.2
	FLR-2	2.4	3	1.3	35	14.6	17	7.1	3	1.3	9	3.8	9	3.8	8	3.3	3	1.3	6	2.5	93	38.8
	FLR-3	1.9	4	2.1	11	5.7	14	7.3	4	2.1	1	.7	9	4.7	6	3.1	2	1.0	3	1.6	58	30.1
STR-23	FLR-1	2.4	3	1.3	24	10.0	68	28.5	0	0	27	11.3	15	6.3	22	9.2	0	0	5	2.1	164	68.6
	FLR-2	2.9	2	.7	7	2.5	10	3.5	1	.4	13	4.6	7	2.5	8	2.8	0	0	4	1.4	52	18.3
	FLR-3	2.1	1	.5	6	2.9	48	22.9	4	2.1	7	3.3	3	1.4	3	1.4	1	.5	3	1.4	72	34.3
Subtotals		28.8	21	.7 (3.3%)	136	4.7 (21%)	222	7.7 (35%)	12	.4 (2%)	71	2.5 (11%)	65	2.3 (10.5%)	69	2.4 (11%)	6	.2 (1%)	32	1.1 (5%)	634	22.0 (100%)
Early Non-Elite																						
STR-60	M-2&3	1.4	24	17.4	45	32.6	9	6.5	1	.7	6	4.4	6	4.4	35	25.4	1	.7	1	.7	128	92.8
	MID-4	1.9	9	4.6	22	11.3	4	2.1	0	0	3	1.5	4	2.1	14	7.2	0	0	2	1.0	58	29.7
STR-2	FLR-4	.7	2	2.8	7	9.7	2	2.8	3	4.2	10	13.9	1	1.4	5	6.9	0	0	1	1.4	31	43.1
Subtotals		4.0	35	8.6 (16%)	74	18.3 (34%)	15	3.7 (7%)	4	1.0 (2%)	19	4.7 (9%)	11	2.7 (5%)	54	13.3 (25%)	1	.2 (.4%)	4	1.0 (2%)	217	53.6 (100%)

Table 7.6. Continued.

House	Deposit	Total Volume Excavated (m³)	Group 1 Early Cooking Vessels		Group 2 Early and Late Cooking Vessels		Group 3 Late Cooking Vessels		Group 4 Early Serving Vessels		Group 5 Early and Late Serving Vessels		Group 6 Late Serving Vessels		Group 7 Undecorated Serving Vessels		Group 8 Early Storage Jars		Group 9 Early and Late Storage Jars		Total Rim Sherds	
Early Elite																						
STR-22	FLR-4	1.9	7	3.7	14	7.9	5	2.7	6	3.2	13	6.9	6	3.2	8	4.3	1	.5	0	0	60	32.1
	AL-1	2.7	38	14.0	43	15.9	18	6.6	28	10.3	47	17.3	16	5.9	36	13.3	3	1.1	19	7.0	248	91.5
	EL-1	.8	8	9.8	9	10.9	2	2.4	4	4.9	5	6.1	0	0	5	6.1	0	0	3	3.7	36	43.9
	EL-2	1.2	15	12.8	17	14.5	5	4.3	17	14.5	8	6.8	0	0	8	6.8	2	1.7	5	4.3	77	65.8
	MID-1	1.2	18	14.5	21	16.9	3	2.4	45	36.3	35	28.2	4	3.2	13	10.5	11	8.9	0	0	150	120.9
	MID-2	.2	0	0	7	30.4	0	0	2	8.7	3	13.0	0	0	5	21.7	1	4.4	0	0	18	78.3
	MID-3	.2	11	45.8	12	50.0	0	0	12	50.0	5	20.8	0	0	8	33.3	1	4.2	6	25.0	55	229.2
	MID-4	1.8	28	15.9	22	12.5	3	1.7	9	5.1	14	7.9	2	1.1	12	6.8	8	4.6	9	5.1	107	60.8
	AL-2	.5	20	43.5	28	60.9	11	23.9	5	10.9	6	13.0	8	17.4	12	26.1	4	8.7	6	13.0	100	217.4
	MID-5	1.9	18	15.3	21	17.8	3	2.5	17	14.4	20	16.9	3	2.5	17	14.4	0	0	6	5.1	105	88.9
Subtotals		11.7	163	13.9	194	16.6	50	4.3	145	12.4	156	13.4	39	3.3	124	10.6	31	2.7	54	4.6	956	81.8
				(17%)		(20%)		(5.2%)		(15%)		(16%)		(4%)		(13%)		(3%)		(6%)		(100%)

Table 7.7. Ratio of decorated to undecorated bowl rim sherds.

House	Deposit	Decorated Groups 4, 5, & 6	Undecorated Group 7	Ratio of Decorated to Undecorated
Late Non-Elite				
STR-1	FLR-1	46	6	7.7
	FLR-2	17	6	2.8
STR-2	FLR-1	38	11	3.5
	PFL-1	115	81	1.4
	FLR-2	44	28	1.6
	FLR-3	9	3	3.0
	MID-1	2	3	.7
	MID-2	3	1	3.0
	MID-3	0	0	-
	MID-4	37	11	3.4
	MID-5	14	8	1.8
	MID-6	0	7	0
	MID-7	14	14	1.0
STR-60	FLR-1	74	34	2.2
	FLR-2	45	8	5.6
	MID-1	112	45	2.3
STR-61	FLR-1	3	5	.6
	FLR-2	6	3	2.0
	FLR-3	22	10	2.2
	FLR-4	3	4	.8
	FLR-5	18	7	2.6
Subtotals		622	295	2.1
Early Non-Elite				
STR-2	FLR-4	14	5	2.8
STR-60	MID-2&3	13	35	.4
	MID-4	7	14	.5
Subtotals		34	54	.63
Late Elite				
STR-21	FLR-1	10	7	1.4
	FLR-2	5	1	5.0
	FLR-3	1	1	1.0
	FLR-4	2	0	est. (2.0)
	FLR-5	2	0	est. (2.0)

Table 7.7. Continued.

House	Deposit	Decorated Groups 4, 5, & 6	Undecorated Group 7	Ratio of Decorated to Undecorated
STR-22	FLR-1	16	13	1.2
	FLR-2	21	8	2.6
	FLR-3	14	6	2.3
STR-23	FLR-1	42	22	1.9
	FLR-2	21	8	2.6
	FLR-3	14	3	4.7
Subtotals		148	69	2.1
Early Elite				
STR-22	FLR-4	25	8	3.1
	FLR-5	91	36	2.5
	EL-1	9	5	1.8
	EL-2	25	8	3.1
	MID-1	84	13	6.5
	MID-2	5	5	1.0
	MID-3	17	8	2.1
	MID-4	25	12	2.1
	AL-2	19	12	1.6
	MID-5	40	17	2.4
Subtotals		340	124	2.7
Summary Subtotals				
Non-elite		656	349	1.9
Elite		488	193	2.5
Late Period		770	364	2.1
Early Period		374	178	2.1

Table 7.8. Obsidian sources and totals in each deposit.

House	Deposit	Obsidian Sources					
		San Martín Jilotepeque	El Chayal	Ixtepeque	Central Mexican	Pachuca	Total
Late Non-Elite							
STR-1	FLR-1	56	22	1	1	0	80
	FLR-2	57	22	0	1	2	82
STR-2	PFL-1	54	28	3	1	2	88
	FLR-1	23	17	4	2	0	46
	FLR-2	43	22	1	2	0	68
	FLR-3	14	4	0	0	0	18
	MID-1	5	7	1	0	0	13
	MID-2	2	4	0	0	0	6
	MID-3	4	4	0	0	0	8
	MID-4	9	11	1	2	0	23
	MID-5	9	3	0	0	0	12
	MID-6	3	3	0	0	0	6
	MID-7	12	9	0	1	1	23
STR-60	FLR-1	101	57	5	4	1	168
	FLR-2	28	16	1	0	0	45
	MID-1	128	21	2	4	0	155
STR-61	FLR-1	13	5	0	0	1	19
	FLR-2	25	10	3	3	0	41
	FLR-3	57	37	4	0	1	99
	FLR-4	4	7	0	0	0	11
	FLR-5	10	3	1	0	1	15
Subtotals		657	312	27	21	9	1026
(Percent)		(64.0)	(30.4)	(2.6)	(2.0)	(.9)	
Early Non-Elite							
STR-2	FLR-4	10	5	1	0	0	16
STR-60	MID-2&3	50	11	5	2	0	68
	MID-4	25	13	0	1	0	39
SubTotals		85	29	6	3	0	123
(percent)		(69.1)	(23.6)	(4.9)	(2.4)	(0)	
Late Elite							
STR-21	FLR-1	13	6	0	0	1	20
	FLR-2	6	14	2	0	0	22

Table 7.8. Continued.

House	Deposit	Obsidian Sources					
		San Martín Jilotepeque	El Chayal	Ixtepeque	Central Mexican	Pachuca	Total
	FLR-3	7	1	0	0	0	8
	FLR-4	15	6	0	0	0	21
	FLR-5	13	7	0	0	0	20
STR-22	FLR-1	65	38	4	3	1	111
	FLR-2	38	22	2	3	2	67
	FLR-3	30	13	1	1	1	46
STR-23	FLR-1	47	35	4	0	1	87
	FLR-2	26	11	3	0	0	40
	FLR-3	24	2	0	2	0	28
SubTotals		284	155	16	9	6	470
(Percent)		(60.4)	(33.0)	(3.4)	(1.9)	(1.3)	
Early Elite							
STR-22	FLR-4	37	12	2	0	0	51
	FLR-5	162	45	3	3	1	214
	EL-1	20	9	0	1	1	31
	EL-2	26	16	2	1	0	45
	MID-1	70	42	1	1	0	114
	MID-2	8	6	0	1	0	15
	MID-3	47	37	1	1	0	86
	MID-4	117	28	3	2	1	151
	AL-2	173	21	1	6	1	202
	MID-5	115	19	1	0	1	136
SubTotals		775	235	14	16	5	1045
(Percent)		(74.1)	(22.5)	(1.3)	(1.5)	(.6)	
Total in House Deposits		1801	731	63	49	20	2664
(Percent)		(67.6)	(27.4)	(2.4)	(1.8)	(.8)	
Total in Mixed Deposits		533	181	34	7	4	759
(Percent)		(70.2)	(23.8)	(4.5)	(.9)	(.5)	
Overall Total		2334	912	97	56	24	3423
(Percent)		(68.2)	(26.6)	(2.8)	(1.6)	(.7)	

Table 7.9. Ratio of San Martín Jilotepeque obsidain to El Chayal obsidian.

House	Deposit	Total San Martín Jilotepeque	Total El Chayal	Ratio of San Martín to El Chayal
Non-Elite				
STR-1	FLR-1	56	22	2.55
	FLR-2	57	22	2.59
STR-2	FLR-1&PFL-1	77	45	1.71
	FLRS-2&3	57	26	2.19
	FLR-4	10	5	2.00
	MID-1	5	7	.71
	MIDS-2&3	6	8	.75
	MID-4	9	11	.82
	MIDS-5&6	12	6	2.00
	MID-7	12	9	1.33
STR-60	FLR-1	101	57	1.77
	FLR-2&MID-1	156	37	4.22
	MIDS-2&3	50	11	4.54
	MID-4	25	13	1.92
STR-61	FLRS-1&2	38	15	2.53
	FLRS-3,4&5	71	47	1.51
Elite				
STR-21	FLRS-1&2	19	20	.95
	FLRS-3,4&5	37	14	2.64
STR-22	FLR-1	65	38	1.71
	FLRS-2&3	68	35	1.94
	FLRS-4&5	199	57	3.49
	ELS-1&2	46	25	1.84
	MIDS-1&2	78	48	1.63
	MIDS-3&4	164	65	2.52
	AL-2&MID-5	288	40	7.20
STR-23	FLR-1	47	35	1.34
	FLR-2&3	50	13	3.85

Table 7.10. Ratio of total obsidian to volume excavated (m³) and to rim sherds.

House	Deposit	Total Obsidian	Volume Excavated (m³)	Total Rim Sherds	Ratio of Obsidian to Volume Excavated (m³)	Ratio of Obsidian to Rim Sherds
Late Non-Elite						
STR-1	FLR-1	80	5.17	159	15.5	.5
	FLR-2	82	5.31	51	15.4	1.6
STR-2	PFL-1	88	6.41	483	13.7	.2
	FLR-1	46	2.29	155	20.1	.3
	FLR-2	68	4.62	124	14.7	.5
	FLR-3	18	2.01	28	8.9	.6
	MID-1	13	.11	17	118.2	.8
	MID-2	6	.18	18	33.3	.3
	MID-3	8	.26	0	30.8	n/a
	MID-4	23	1.83	133	12.6	.2
	MID-5	12	.16	47	75.0	.3
	MID-6	6	.24	14	25.0	.4
	MID-7	23	.42	91	54.8	.3
STR-60	FLR-1	168	8.45	248	19.9	.7
	FLR-2	45	1.48	104	30.4	.4
	MID-1	155	4.56	355	33.9	.4
STR-61	FLR-1	19	2.52	19	7.5	1.0
	FLR-2	41	1.51	19	27.1	2.2
	FLR-3	99	2.99	88	33.1	1.1
	FLR-4	11	1.03	9	10.7	1.2
	FLR-5	15	4.12	42	3.6	.4
Subtotals		1026	55.67	2204	18.4	.5
Early Non-Elite						
STR-2	FLR-4	16	.72	31	22.2	.5
STR-60	MID-2&3	68	1.38	128	49.3	.5
	MID-4	39	1.95	58	20.0	.7
Subtotals		123	4.05	217	30.4	.6
Late Elite						
STR-21	FLR-1	20	2.03	39	9.9	.5
	FLR-2	22	1.62	31	13.6	.7
	FLR-3	8	1.41	12	5.7	.7
	FLR-4	21	.96	9	21.9	2.1
	FLR-5	20	.80	9	25.0	2.3

Table 7.10. Continued.

House	Deposit	Total Obsidian	Volume Excavated (m³)	Total Rim Sherds	Ratio of Obsidian to Volume Excavated (m³)	Ratio of Obsidian to Rim Sherds
STR-22	FLR-1	111	10.26	94	10.8	1.2
	FLR-2	67	2.40	93	27.9	.7
	FLR-3	46	1.93	58	23.8	.8
STR-23	FLR-1	87	2.39	164	36.4.5	
	FLR-2	40	2.85	52	14.0	.8
	FLR-3	28	2.10	72	13.3	.4
Subtotals		470	28.75	633	16.3	.7
Early Elite						
STR-22	FLR-4	51	1.87	60	27.3	.9
	FLR-5	214	2.71	248	78.9	.9
	EL-1	31	.82	36	37.8	.9
	EL-2	45	1.17	77	38.5	.6
	MID-1	114	1.24	150	91.9	.8
	MID-2	15	.23	18	65.2	.8
	MID-3	87	.24	55	362.5	1.6
	MID-4	151	1.76	107	85.8	1.4
	AL-2	202	.46	100	439.1	2.0
	MID-5	136	1.18	105	115.3	1.3
Subtotals		1046	11.68	956	89.6	1.1
Summary Subtotals						
Non-Elite		1149	59.72	2421	19.2	0.5
Elite		1516	40.43	1589	37.5	1.0
Late Period		1496	84.42	2837	17.7	0.5
Early Period		1169	15.73	1173	74.3	1.0

Table 7.11. Changing obsidian use-wear ratios.

House	Deposit	Number with Light Use-wear	Number with Heavy Use-wear	Ratio of Heavy to Light Use-wear
Non-Elite				
STR-1	FLR-1	71	76	1.07
	FLR-2	81	75	.93
STR-2	PFL-1	67	86	1.28
	FLR-1	31	53	1.71
	subtotal	98	139	1.42
	FLR-2	58	76	1.31
	FLR-3	14	17	1.21
	subtotal	72	93	1.29
	FLR-4	9	21	2.33
	MID-1	8	14	1.75
	MID-2	6	3	.50
	MID-3	5	10	2.00
	subtotal	11	13	1.18
	MID-4	17	27	1.59
	MID-5	9	10	1.11
	MID-6	5	5	1.00
	subtotal	14	15	1.07
	MID-7	18	22	1.22
STR-60	FLR-1	128	172	1.34
	FLR-2	36	54	1.50
	MID-1	113	199	1.76
	subtotal	149	253	1.70
	MID-2&3	59	73	1.24
	MID-4	38	37	.97
STR-61	FLR-1	9	25	2.78
	FLR-2	27	48	1.78
	subtotal	36	73	2.03
	FLR-3	87	85	.98
	FLR-4	7	13	1.86

Table 7.11. Continued.

House	Deposit	Number with Light Use-wear	Number with Heavy Use-wear	Ratio of Heavy to Light Use-wear
	FLR-5	12	18	1.50
	subtotal	106	116	1.09
Elite				
STR-21	FLR-1	13	21	1.60
	FLR-2	13	26	2.00
	subtotal	26	47	1.81
	FLR-3	4	11	2.75
	FLR-4	20	20	1.00
	FLR-5	16	20	1.25
	subtotal	40	51	1.28
STR-22	FLR-1	75	123	1.64
	FLR-2	29	93	3.21
	FLR-3	41	41	1.00
	subtotal	70	134	1.91
	FLR-4	51	48	.94
	FLR-5	218	193	.89
	subtotal	269	241	.90
	EL-1	32	29	.90
	EL-2	35	47	1.34
	subtotal	67	76	1.13
	MID-1	116	96	.83
	MID-2	16	12	.75
	subtotal	132	108	.82
	MID-3	75	87	1.16
	MID-4	159	131	.82
	subtotal	234	218	.93
	AL-2	281	108	.38
	MID-5	157	100	.64
	subtotal	438	208	.47
STR-23	FLR-1	55	86	1.56
	FLR-2	31	36	1.16
	FLR-3	28	25	.89
	subtotal	59	61	1.03

Table 7.12. Obsidian technological categories.

MANUFACTURING BY-PRODUCTS

Core Preparation
> Crested blades
> Percussion blades: whole, proximal, medial, distal
> Macroblades
> Percussion flakes: large, small
> Flake fragments: large, small
> Chunks

Manufacturing
> Exhausted polyhedral cores
> Core fragments

Mistakes
> Hinged prismatic blade
> 2-bulbed, hinged prismatic blade
> "Lip" flakes
> Plunging blades

Core Maintenance
> Core rejuvenation flakes: proximal, distal
> Platform flakes
> Lateral flakes

Bipolar Technique
> Bipolar cores
> Bipolar flakes

BLADES

First series blades
> Whole, proximal, medial, or distal

Prismatic blades
> Whole, proximal, medial, or distal

Table 7.13. Ratio of obsidian manufacturing by-products to blades (fragmentary and whole).

House	Deposit	Number of Manufacturing By-products	Number of Blades	Ratio of By-products to Blades
Late Non-Elite				
STR-1	FLR-1	25	55	.45
	FLR-2	11	71	.15
STR-2	FLR-1	6	40	.15
	PFL-1	11	77	.14
	FLR-2	10	58	.17
	FLR-3	1	17	.06
	MID-1	1	12	.08
	MID-2	3	3	1.00
	MID-3	0	8	0
	MID-4	6	17	.35
	MID-5	1	11	.09
	MID-6	1	5	.20
	MID-7	8	15	.53
STR-60	FLR-1	26	142	.18
	FLR-2	7	38	.18
	MID-1	22	133	.17
STR-61	FLR-1	1	18	.06
	FLR-2	7	34	.20
	FLR-3	15	84	.18
	FLR-4	3	8	.38
	FLR-5	2	13	.15
Subtotals		167	859	.19
Early Non-Elite				
STR-2	FLR-4	4	12	.33
STR-60	MID-2&3	9	59	.15
	MID-4	9	30	.30
Subtotals		22	101	.22
Late Elite				
STR-21	FLR-1	4	16	.25
	FLR-2	1	21	.05
	FLR-3	0	8	0
	FLR-4	0	21	0
	FLR-5	3	17	.18

Table 7.13. Continued.

House	Deposit	Number of Manufacturing By-products	Number of Blades	Ratio of By-products to Blades
STR-22	FLR-1	15	96	.16
	FLR-2	12	55	.22
	FLR-3	10	36	.27
STR-23	FLR-1	12	75	.16
	FLR-2	5	35	.14
	FLR-3	5	23	.22
Subtotals		67	403	.17
Early Elite				
STR-22	FLR-4	9	42	.21
	FLR-5	47	167	.28
	EL-1	6	25	.24
	EL-2	13	32	.40
	MID-1	28	86	.33
	MID-2	3	12	.25
	MID-3	26	60	.43
	MID-4	16	135	.12
	AL-2	29	173	.17
	MID-5	24	112	.21
Subtotals		201	844	.24
Summary Subtotals				
Non-elite		189	960	.20
Elite		268	1247	.22
Late Period		234	1262	.19
Early Period		223	945	.24

Table 7.14. Totals of all types of projectile points combined; ratios of points to total obsidian, rim sherds, and volume excavated (m³).

House	Deposit	Total Obsidian Points	Ratio of Points to Total Obsidian	Ratio of Points to Rim Sherds	Ratio of Points to Volume Excavated (m³)
Late Non-Elite					
STR-1	FLR-1	11	.14	.07	2.1
	FLR-2	6	.07	.12	1.1
STR-2	FLR-1	6	.15	.04	3.1
	PFL-1	10	.11	.02	1.6
	FLR-2	10	.16	.08	2.4
	FLR-3	2	.11	.07	1.0
	MID-1	0	0	0	0
	MID-2	1	.17	.06	5.6
	MID-3	0	0	0	0
	MID-4	4	.17	.03	2.2
	MID-5	1	.08	.02	6.3
	MID-6	0	0	0	0
	MID-7	4	.17	.04	9.5
STR-60	FLR-1	14	.08	.06	1.7
	FLR-2	4	.08	.04	2.7
	MID-1	12	.08	.03	2.6
STR-61	FLR-1	7	.37	.37	2.8
	FLR-2	8	.20	.42	5.3
	FLR-3	13	.13	.15	4.3
	FLR-4	1	.09	.11	1.0
	FLR-5	3	.20	.07	.7
Subtotals		117	.11	.05	2.1
Early Non-Elite					
STR-2	FLR-4	2	.13	.06	2.8
STR-60	MID-2&3	7	.10	.05	5.1
	MID-4	2	.05	.03	1.0
Subtotals		11	.09	.05	2.7
Late Elite					
STR-21	FLR-1	2	.10	.05	1.0
	FLR-2	1	.05	.03	.6

216

Table 7.14.   Continued.

House	Deposit	Total Obsidian Points	Ratio of Points to Total Obsidian	Ratio of Points to Rim Sherds	Ratio of Points to Volume Excavated (m³)
	FLR-3	1	.13	.08	.7
	FLR-4	0	0	0	0
	FLR-5	1	.05	.11	1.3
STR-22	FLR-1	10	.09	.11	1.0
	FLR-2	8	.12	.09	3.3
	FLR-3	3	.07	.05	1.6
STR-23	FLR-1	11	.13	.07	4.6
	FLR-2	4	.10	.08	1.4
	FLR-3	0	0	0	0
Subtotals		41	.09	.06	1.4
Early Elite					
STR-22	FLR-4	5	.10	.08	2.7
	FLR-5	5	.02	.02	1.8
	EL-1	2	.06	.06	2.4
	EL-2	0	0	0	0
	MID-1	2	.02	.01	1.6
	MID-2	1	.07	.06	4.3
	MID-3	1	.01	.02	4.2
	MID-4	3	.02	.03	1.7
	AL-2	3	.01	.03	6.5
	MID-5	3	.02	.03	2.5
Subtotals		25	.02	.03	2.1
Summary Subtotals					
Non-elite		128	.11	.05	2.1
Elite		66	.04	.04	1.6
Late Period		158	.11	.06	1.9
Early Period		36	.03	.03	2.3

Table 7.15. Counts and percentages of obsidian projectile point styles.

| Point Type | Early Postclassic | | | | Late Postclassic | | | | Total |
| | Elite | | Non-elite | | Elite | | Non-elite | | |
	No.	%	No.	%	No.	%	No.	%	
K & L	5	20.0	0	0	2	4.9	3	2.6	10
N	3	12.0	0	0	2	4.9	3	2.6	8
C	2	8.0	1	9.1	2	4.9	4	3.4	9
E	1	4.0	1	9.1	2	4.9	2	1.7	6
H	5	20.0	1	9.1	4	9.8	9	7.8	19
Subtotals	16	64.0	3	27.3	12	29.3	21	17.9	52
B	2	8.0	0	0	0	0	5	4.3	7
J	3	12.0	0	0	2	4.9	8	6.8	13
A	0	0	1	9.1	2	4.9	2	1.7	5
M	2	8.0	4	36.0	7	17.1	25	21.4	38
I	1	4.0	1	9.1	1	2.4	11	9.4	14
Subtotals	8	32.0	6	54.5	12	29.3	51	43.6	77
D	1	4.0	1	9.1	5	12.2	13	11.1	20
F & G	0	0	1	9.1	12	29.3	32	27.4	45
Subtotals	1	4.0	2	18.2	17	41.5	45	38.5	65
TOTALS	25	100.0	11	100.0	41	100.0	117	100.0	194

Table 7.16. Type D and F and G projectile points in the Late Postclassic deposts. Early Postclassic layers shown in parentheses.

House	Deposit	Types D, F and G	Total Points	Percent Types D, F and G
Non-Elite				
STR-1	FLR-1	6	11	54.5
	FLR-2	2	6	33.3
STR-2	PFL-1	3	10	30.0
	FLR-1	3	6	50.0
	Subtotal	6	16	37.5
	FLR-2	1	10	10.0
	FLR-3	0	2	0
	(FLR-4)	1	2	50.0
	Subtotal	2	14	14.3
	MID-4	3	4	75.0
	MID-5	0	1	0
	MID-6	0	0	0
	Subtotal	0	1	0
STR-60	FLR-1	6	14	42.9
	FLR-2	1	4	25.0
	MID-1	3	12	25.0
	Subtotal	4	16	25.0
STR-61	FLR-1	3	7	42.9
	FLR-2	4	8	50.0
	Subtotal	7	15	46.7
	FLR-3	6	13	46.2
	FLR-4	1	1	100.0
	FLR-5	1	3	33.3
	Subtotal	8	17	47.1

Table 7.16. Continued.

House	Deposit	Types D, F and G	Total Points	Percent Types D, F and G
Elite				
STR-21	FLR-1	0	2	0
	FLR-2	0	1	0
	Subtotal	0	3	0
	FLR-3	0	1	0
	FLR-4	0	0	0
	FLR-5	0	1	0
	Subtotal	0	2	0
STR-22	FLR-1	4	10	40.0
	FLR-2	4	8	50.0
	Subtotal	8	18	44.4
	FLR-3	0	3	0
	(FLR-4)	0	5	0
	Subtotal	0	8	0
STR-23	FLR-1	6	11	54.5
	FLR-2	3	4	75.0
	FLR-3	0	0	0
	Subtotal	3	4	75.0

Table 7.17. Spindle whorl distribution by period and by social class: total number, ratio to rim sherds (x1000) and ratio to excavated volume (m³)(x10).

Period	Status	Number of Spindle Whorls	Ratio of Whorls to Rim Sherds (x1000)	Ratio of Whorls to Volume (m³) (x10)
Late Postclassic	Elite	0	0	0
	Non-elite	2	.9	.4
	Sub-totals	2	.7	.2
Early Postclassic	Elite	15	15.7	12.8
	Non-elite	3	13.8	7.4
	Sub-totals	18	15.3	11.1
TOTALS		20	4.9	1.9

Table 7.18. Bone sewing and weaving tools combined with ceramic spindle whorls: ratio of total needles, awls, and spindle whorls to rim sherds (x1000) and ratio to excavated volume (m³)(x10).

House	Deposit	Total Needles and Awls	Total Needles, Awls, and Spindle Whorls	Ratio of Total to Rim Sherds (x1000)	Ratio of Total to Volume Excavated (m³)(x10)
Late Non-Elite					
STR-1	FLR-1	2	2	12.6	3.9
	FLR-2	7	7	137.2	13.2
STR-2	FLR-1	1	1	6.5	4.4
	PFL-1	2	3	6.2	4.7
	FLR-2	5	5	40.3	10.8
	FLR-3	1	1	35.7	4.9
	MID-1	0	0		
	MID-2	0	0		
	MID-3	0	0		
	MID-4	0	0		
	MID-5	0	0		
	MID-6	0	0		
	MID-7	0	0		
STR-60	FLR-1	0	0		
	FLR-2	0	0		
	MID-1	9	9	25.4	19.7
STR-61	FLR-1	2	2	105.3	7.9
	FLR-2	1	2	105.3	13.2
	FLR-3	2	2	22.7	6.7
	FLR-4	0	0		
	FLR-5	1	1	23.8	2.4
Subtotals		33	35	15.9	6.3
Early Non-Elite					
STR-2	FLR-4	0	1	32.3	13.9
STR-60	MID-2&3	0	2	15.6	14.5
	MID-4	3	3	51.7	15.4
Subtotals		3	6	27.6	14.8
Late Elite					
STR-21	FLR-1	0	0		
	FLR-2	0	0		

Table 7.18. Continued.

House	Deposit	Total Needles and Awls	Total Needles, Awls, and Spindle Whorls	Ratio of Total to Rim Sherds (x1000)	Ratio of Total to Volume Excavated (m³)(x10)
	FLR-3	0	0		
	FLR-4	0	0		
	FLR-5	0	0		
STR-22	FLR-1	1	1	10.6	.9
	FLR-2	1	1	10.8	4.2
	FLR-3	0	0		
STR-23	FLR-1	1	1	6.1	4.2
	FLR-2	1	1	19.2	3.5
	FLR-3	0	0		
Subtotals		4	4	6.3	1.4
Early Elite					
STR-22	FLR-4	3	4	66.7	21.4
	FLR-5	7	9	36.3	33.2
	EL-1	0	0		
	EL-2	1	1	12.9	8.5
	MID-1	4	4	26.7	32.3
	MID-2	1	1	55.6	43.5
	MID-3	2	4	72.7	166.7
	MID-4	3	8	74.8	45.5
	AL-2	2	3	30.0	65.2
	MID-5	2	2	19.0	16.9
Subtotals		25	36	37.7	30.8
Summary Subtotals					
Non-elite		36	41	16.9	6.9
Elite		29	40	25.2	9.9
Late Period		37	39	13.7	4.6
Early Period		28	42	35.8	26.7

Table 7.19. Basalt grinding stone fragments: counts, weights, ratio of weight to excavated volume (m^3) and ratio of total number to rim sherds (x100).

House	Deposit	Total Number Manos and Metates	Weight (gm) Manos and Metates	Ratio of Total Weight to Excavated Volume (m^3)	Ratio of Total Number to Rim Sherds (x100)
Late Non-Elite					
STR-1	FLR-1	7	1954	378	4.4
	FLR-2	2	608	115	3.9
STR-2	FLR-1	0	0	0	0
	PFL-1	11	1284	72	.8
	FLR-2	1	146	32	.8
	FLR-3	0	0	0	0
	MID-1	1	359	3264	5.9
	MID-2	1	276	1533	5.6
	MID-3	0	0	0	0
	MID-4	4	908	496	3.0
	MID-5	1	189	1181	2.1
	MID-6	0	0	0	0
	MID-7	1	234	557	1.1
STR-60	FLR-1	3	948	112	1.2
	FLR-2	0	0	0	0
	MID-1	1	463	102	.3
STR-61	FLR-1	2	221	88	10.5
	FLR-2	0	0	0	0
	FLR-3	10	3259	1090	11.4
	FLR-4	0	0	0	0
	FLR-5	10	4762	1156	23.8
Subtotals		55	15611	280	2.5
Early Non-Elite					
STR-2	FLR-4	0	0	0	0
STR-60	MID-2&3	0	0	0	0
	MID-4	3	742	381	5.2
Subtotals		3	742	183	1.4
Late Elite					
STR-21	FLR-1	7	2880	1419	17.9
	FLR-2	0	0	0	0
	FLR-3	0	0	0	0
	FLR-4	0	0	0	0

Table 7.19.   Continued.

House	Deposit	Total Number Manos and Metates	Weight (gm) Manos and Metates	Ratio of Total Weight to Excavated Volume (m³)	Ratio of Total Number to Rim Sherds (x100)
	FLR-5	1	205	256	11.1
STR-22	FLR-1	8	3000	292	8.5
	FLR-2	4	1083	451	4.3
	FLR-3	2	146	76	3.4
STR-23	FLR-1	0	0	0	0
	FLR-2	7	1471	516	13.5
	FLR-3	2	299	142	2.8
Subtotals		31	9084	316	4.9
Early Elite					
STR-22	FLR-4	0	0	0	0
	FLR-5	4	1174	433	1.6
	EL-1	0	0	0	0
	EL-2	0	0	0	0
	MID-1	3	748	603	2.0
	MID-2	0	0	0	0
	MID-3	1	555	2313	1.8
	MID-4	1	395	224	.9
	AL-2	1	259	563	1.0
	MID-5	0	0	0	0
Subtotals		10	3131	268	1.0
Summary Subtotals					
Non-elite		58	16353	274	2.4
Elite		41	12215	302	2.6
Late Period		86	24695	293	3.0
Early Period		13	3873	246	1.1

Table 7.20. Local sandstone manos and metates: counts, weights, ratio of weight to excavated volume (m3) and ratio of total number to rim sherds (x100).

House	Deposit	Total Number Manos and Metates	Weight (gm) Manos and Metates	Ratio of Total Weight to Excavated Volume (m³)	Ratio of Total Number to Rim Sherds (x100)
Late Non-Elite					
STR-1	FLR-1	1	483	93	0.6
	FLR-2	1	565	106	2.0
STR-2	FLR-1	3	1156	505	0.6
	PFL-1	3	2503	390	1.9
	FLR-2	1	153	33	0.8
	FLR-3	0	0	0	0
	MID-1	0	0	0	0
	MID-2	0	0	0	0
	MID-3	0	0	0	0
	MID-4	1	633	346	0.8
	MID-5	1	726	4538	2.1
	MID-6	0	0	0	0
	MID-7	2	3731	8883	2.2
STR-60	FLR-1	1	797	94	0.4
	FLR-2	5	2040	1378	4.8
	MID-1	1	495	109	0.3
STR-61	FLR-1	2	1063	422	10.5
	FLR-2	1	967	640	5.3
	FLR-3	0	0	0	0
	FLR-4	0	0	0	0
	FLR-5	1	798	194	2.4
Sub-totals		24	16110	289	1.1
Early Non-Elite					
STR-2	FLR-4	0	0	0	0
STR-60	MID-2&3	0	0	0	0
	MID-4	0	0	0	0
Sub-totals		0	0	0	0
Late Elite					
STR-21	FLR-1	2	1483	731	5.1
	FLR-2	0	0	0	0.0

Table 7.20.   Continued.

House	Deposit	Total Number Manos and Metates	Weight (gm) Manos and Metates	Ratio of Total Weight to Excavated Volume (m³)	Ratio of Total Number to Rim Sherds (x100)
	FLR-3	1	203	144	8.3
	FLR-4	0	0	0	0.0
	FLR-5	0	0	0	0.0
STR-22	FLR-1	2	1051	102	2.1
	FLR-2	3	6061	2525	3.2
	FLR-3	0	0	0	0
STR-23	FLR-1	0	0	0	0
	FLR-2	0	0	0	0
	FLR-3	0	0	0	0
Sub-totals		8	8798	306	1.3

Early Elite

House	Deposit				
STR-22	FLR-4	0	0	0	0
	FLR-5	1	379	140	0.4
	EL-1	0	0	0	0.0
	EL-2	0	0	0	0.0
	MID-1	2	1519	1225	1.3
	MID-2	0	0	0	0
	MID-3	0	0	0	0
	MID-4	1	1180	670	0.9
	AL-2	0	0	0	0.0
	MID-5	0	0	0	0.0
Sub-totals		4	3078	264	.4

Summary Sub-Totals

Non-elite		24	16110	270	1.0
Elite		12	11876	294	.8
Late Period		32	24908	295	1.1
Early Period		4	3078	196	.3

Table 7.21. Marine shell artifacts: total number, ratio of total to excavated volume (m³), and ratio of total to rim sherds (x100).

House	Deposit	Total Number of Marine shell Artifacts	Ratio of Total to Excavated Volume (m³)	Ratio of Total to Rim Sherds (x100)
Late Non-Elite				
STR-1	FLR-1	1	.19	.63
	FLR-2	4	.75	7.84
STR-2	FLR-1	2	.87	1.29
	PFL-1	1	.16	.21
	FLR-2	2	.43	1.61
	FLR-3	0	0	0
	MID-1	0	0	0
	MID-2	0	0	0
	MID-3	0	0	0
	MID-4	1	.55	.75
	MID-5	1	6.25	2.13
	MID-6	0	0	0
	MID-7	0	0	0
STR-60	FLR-1	0	0	0
	FLR-2	2	1.35	1.92
	MID-1	1	.22	.28
STR-61	FLR-1	1	.40	5.26
	FLR-2	2	1.32	10.53
	FLR-3	0	0	0
	FLR-4	0	0	0
	FLR-5	0	0	0
Subtotals		18	.32	.81
Early Non-Elite				
STR-2	FLR-4	0	0	0
STR-60	MID-2&3	4	2.90	3.13
	MID-4	2	1.03	3.45
Subtotals		6	1.48	2.76
Late Elite				
STR-21	FLR-1	1	.49	2.56
	FLR-2	1	.62	3.23
	FLR-3	0	0	0

Table 7.21. Continued.

House	Deposit	Total Number of Marine shell Artifacts	Ratio of Total to Excavated Volume (m³)	Ratio of Total to Rim Sherds (x100)
	FLR-4	0	0	0
	FLR-5	0	0	0
STR-22	FLR-1	4	.39	4.26
	FLR-2	2	.83	2.15
	FLR-3	0	0	0
STR-23	FLR-1	1	.42	.61
	FLR-2	0	0	0
	FLR-3	0	0	0
Subtotals		9	.31	1.42
Early Elite				
STR-22	FLR-4	1	.53	1.67
	FLR-5	4	1.48	1.61
	EL-1	1	1.22	2.78
	EL-2	0	0	0
	MID-1	1	.81	.67
	MID-2	2	8.70	11.11
	MID-3	4	16.67	7.27
	MID-4	2	1.14	1.87
	AL-2	2	4.35	2.00
	MID-5	1	.85	.95
Subtotals		18	1.54	1.88
Summary Subtotals				
Non-elite		24	.40	.99
Elite		27	.67	1.70
Late Period		27	.32	.95
Early Period		24	1.53	2.05

Table 7.22. Copper and gold artifacts: counts, types, and summary ratios of total number to excavated volume (m³), and total number to rim sherds (x100).

House	Deposit	Type and Number	Ratio of Total Number to Excavated Volume (m³) (x10)		Ratio of Total Number to Rim Sherds (x100)
Late Non-Elite					
STR-60	FLR-2	copper needle (1)			
		copper lump (1)			
Subtotals			2	.34	.09
Early Non-Elite					
STR-60	MID-2&3	copper bell frag. (1)			
Subtotals			1	2.5	.46
Late Elite					
STR-21	FLR-3	copper bell frag. (1)			
	FLR-4	copper bell frag. (2)			
	FLR-5	copper bell rattle ball (1)			
STR-22	FLR-1	copper bi-point (1)			
STR-23	FLR-1	copper bell frag. (1)			
Subtotals			6	2.1	.95
Early Elite					
STR-22	EL-1	gold ornament frag. (1)			
		copper pigment lump (1)			
	MID-1	copper pigment lump (3)			
	MID-3	copper bell (1)			
		copper pigment lump (2)			
Subtotals			8	6.8	.84
Summary SubTotals					
Non-elite			3	.5	.12
Elite			14	3.5	.88
Late Period			8	.9	.28
Early Period			9	5.7	.77

Table 7.23. Distribution of obsidian bloodletters: counts, and summary ratios of total number to excavated volume (m^3), and total number to rim sherds (x100).

House	Deposit	Total Number	Ratio of Total Number to Excavated Volume (m^3) (x10)	Ratio of Total Number to Rim Sherds (x100)
Late Non-Elite				
STR-60	FLR-1	2		
	MID-1	1		
Subtotals		3	.05	.14
Early Non-Elite				
Subtotals		0	0	0
Late Elite				
STR-22	FLR-2	1		
Subtotals		1	.03	.16
Early Elite				
STR-22	FLR-5	3		
	MID-1	1		
	MID-3	1		
	AL-2	1		
	MID-5	2		
Subtotals		8	.68	.84
Summary Subtotals				
Non-elite		3	.05	.12
Elite		9	.22	.57
Late Period		4	.05	.14
Early Period		8	.51	.68

CHAPTER 8

INFANT BURIALS

There were few burials recovered in the excavations, but those that were recovered provide some useful information about Early Postclassic/Late Postclassic change as well as about elite/non-elite social differentiation. I expect changes in mortuary practices to be one of the main symbols of changing relations among households. As with house styles, increasing similarity or differentiation between elite and non-elite households can be traced ultimately to larger intercommunity processes. For example, the extent to which rulers and nobles are able to, and interested in, increasing the degree of differentiation between themselves and commoners, the more likely their social position derives from supra-community alliances. A rapid introduction of new elite mortuary practices could indicate a new set of alliances between the local elite and elite from other centers. Or, it could indicate the immigration of a nonlocal elite.

At Canajasté there was no evidence of within-house group burials during the Early Postclassic, either for elite or non-elite. Although the sample size is admittedly small, I encountered no early burials in the houses or patios, so it seems likely that Early Postclassic mortuary practices took place off-site, outside of the community. More extensive excavation, of course, may have turned up some early burials, but, to date, there is no indication that the Early Postclassic Canajasteños buried their dead within the community. Corroborating this possibility was the fact that many of the main ceremonial mounds at the site had been looted almost a decade earlier, and there was no evidence of human bones or disturbed offerings in the rubble.

At the site of Lagartero, farther to the south, there were some Early Postclassic burials excavated in the main plaza area (Gurr-Matheny

1987; Ekholm n.d. b). At La Libertad, near Lagartero, elaborate Early Postclassic cremation burials were interred in Late Preclassic mounds (Miller n.d. b). Guajilar is another early site farther to the southwest where there were Postclassic burials but little or no evidence of contemporary habitations. This suggests that, during the Early Postclassic period, there was a local tradition of burial in earlier ceremonial centers that must have been considered sacred. If, initially, these sites were not places of the ancestors they certainly became so.

The caves in the limestone cliffs and faces of collapsed cenotes around the Upper Lagartero and Camcum-Canajasté Valley formed the repositories of the ancestors for Postclassic peoples living at Canajasté (Figure 8.1). There may also be, as yet unexcavated, Classic period or earlier sites with Postclassic burials; however, a large portion of the population was cremated and interred in small cave sites.

Archaeologists from the New World Archaeological Foundation explored several of the caves in 1980 hoping to find such remains and, indeed, they found dozens of Late Postclassic dull-paint style "water jars" containing cremated human remains and, in some cases, burial offerings (Lee and Clark 1980). There were also non-cremated burials with offerings. Some of the offerings were clearly Early Postclassic in age—such as Fine Orange mold-made spindle whorls—and have been found at many other sites in this region and throughout southeastern Mesoamerica. Inclusions of these spindle whorl types in burials demonstrates that at least some Early Postclassic people in the upper Grijalva region (probably including those from Canajasté) placed their dead in caves.

Nevertheless, the vast majority of the burials found in the caves are Late Postclassic

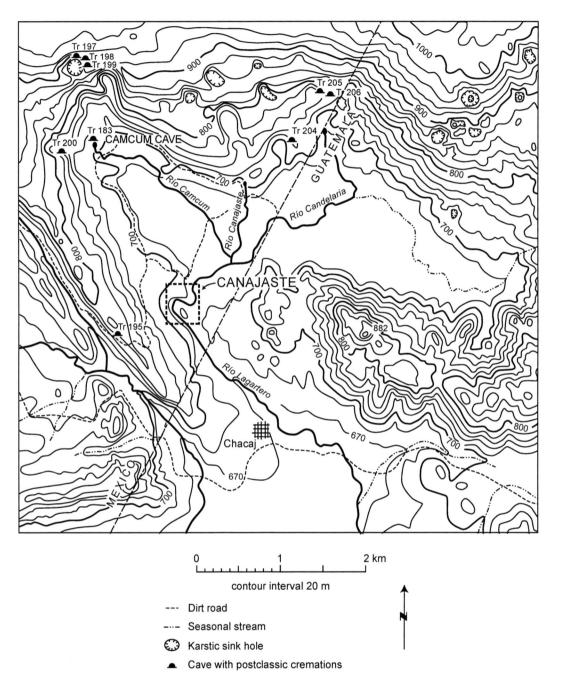

Figure 8.1. Location of known cave sites near Canajasté.

cremations placed in "water jars"—some capped with ceramic discs and sealed with resin. Cave burial, done on a small scale in the Early Postclassic, became even more popular later on (Blom 1954; Thompson 1959:127). Cremations in water jars were common within highland Guatemala (Wauchope 1970; Woodbury and Trik 1953), suggesting that, if people in the upper Grijalva region did not originate the practice themselves, they were probably emulating the Guatemalans. The other possibility is that the practice of cremation was introduced by colonists from Guatemala. Figure 8.2a shows an example of a "cantaro" or water jar cremation vessel recovered from a mound at the site of Guajilar (Co-59), approximately 25 km southwest of Canajasté.

The Late Postclassic pattern of cremation burials in caves is corroborative evidence of a difference in origin for the elite from Canajasté compared with the elite from other upper Grijalva region sites, such as Guajilar and Los Encuentros. I favor this interpretation because, unlike other sites in the upper Grijalva region, Canajasté had no cantaro cremation burials in either its Early or its Late Postclassic deposits. This means that the residents of Canajasté probably expressed their link to the region by association with their ancestors placed in sacred natural locations, such as caves. If they were originally an immigrant colony, they would have no interest or claim to burying their dead, in cremation form or otherwise, in early sites. Using natural instead of cultural burial locations transcends an initial lack of claim to the territory and the centers occupied by the local population. Continued use of a cave or other such location would create a new cultural location that would allow the dead to pass directly into the underworld and link up with their ancestors in faraway locations. Such a conceptual link to the landscape would be much more difficult if burial was in the ceremonial centers of the local indigenous elite.

The Lacandon Maya of the lowland jungles of Chiapas 100 km northeast of Canajasté are now thought to be fairly recent immigrants (Nations 1979; Thompson 1970:67-68; Vos 1980). Villagers living on the shores of Lake

Mensabok place "god pots" (incense burners) in caves or rockshelters overlooking the lake. These caves are full of skulls and long bones lying in piles on the surface. They must predate the missionary era that began in the late 1780s (Nations 1979:88-89) because soon after contact the missionaries encouraged the Indians to bury their dead in cemeteries, after the European fashion. Some of the remains in the caves may date to the Postclassic or even the Classic periods. This pattern of mortuary disposal is what we would expect for communities who would have no direct link to archaeological sites in the region. Caves, and not abandoned temple mounds, are the most sacred locations. This is helped by the fact that all Lacandons can visit the cave and see the actual bones of the ancestors (either theirs or earlier, older, skeletons) right on the surface. Since, in the past, their communities were widely dispersed and shifted location frequently (Nations 1979:105), the permanent mortuary caves would have become a stable symbol of the community and its past.[1]

The practice of similar burial customs near Canajasté has three implications. First, it implies that the community was founded by colonists from outside the region. Even if earlier, during the Classic period, burials were placed in caves, they were seldom cremated. Classic period cremations were extremely rare compared with the prevailing pattern of burial in houses and ceremonial mounds. Second, the Postclassic shift to the placement of all adult burials in caves represents a complete break with the local customs in vogue during the Classic period. Third, some portion of the initial population may have located in small dispersed settlements (which we have not found) and used caves for burials instead of their temporary settlements.

This provides some indication that Early Postclassic Canajasté began as a colony of foreigners migrating into the area. Since the burial customs and vessels are more similar to those in neighboring highland Guatemala (cf. Weeks 1980:235-236) than to those in the surrounding upper Grijalva region, the immigrants may have come from there.

Table 8.1. Distribution of infant burials: olla burials, pit burials, and total number.

House Group	House	*Olla* Burials	Pit Burials	Total
Non-Elite				
1	STR-1	2	1	3
	STR-2	1	0	1
25	STR-60	1	0	1
	STR-61	0	1	1
Test Pit-2	STR-110	2	0	2
Subtotals		6	2	8
Elite				
2	STR-21	0	0	0
	STR-22	0	0	0
	STR-23	0	0	0
Subtotals		0	0	0
TOTALS		6	2	8

Beginning towards the end of the Late Postclassic period there was a shift in burial customs for one segment of the society. Infant burials were found in both non-elite House Groups 2 and 25 (Table 8.1; Figures 8.2b, 6.15, 6.19, 6.46). No infant burials were found in any of the elite houses or in any of the early houses, although the sample of early house floors is very small. The burial of non-cremated, non-elite infants below house floors correlates with the spread of late style rectangular, raised platform house mounds. All the infant burials were placed below the house floors. Some were buried in used and broken pottery vessels (Figure 8.2b), while others were interred in pits beneath the floor.

Table 8.2 summarizes the burial information for all the excavated houses. A 1980 test excavation in one non-elite house recovered one complete infant burial and evidence of a second in house Structure 110 (Test Pit-2) (Figure 6.1). Including those in Structure 110, a total of eight infant burials were discovered. All

non-elite houses had at least one burial, but no elite houses had even a single infant burial.

This is the strongest elite/non-elite dichotomy so far noted in the archaeological record at Canajasté. The most striking thing about it is that it appears to be late, in other words, the pattern is associated with the latest portion of Late Postclassic occupation of each house.

This is exactly the opposite trend compared with that observed in house styles. Whereas the non-elite were able to build houses in styles similar to the elite they were not able to dispose of their deceased infants in the same locations as the elite buried theirs.

Among some contemporary Tzeltal communities cremation and burial in caves were considered rituals restricted only to the highest-ranking members of lineages. Villa Rojas (1969:215) writes that a few generations before he studied various Tzeltal communities in highland Chiapas, "the most distinguished members of each lineage were buried in the

Figure 8.2. Mortuary ceramics. a: cantaro or "water jar" used for a cremation burial (this example is from a temple mound excavation at the site of Guajilar, Co-59); b: an olla covered with a comal, used for an infant burial in Floor 1 of Structure 2 (Lot 5/44) at Canajasté (see Figures 6.15 and 6.16).

Table 8.2. Summary descriptions of Late Postclassic infant burials.

House	Deposit	Burial Number	Associated artifacts and description.
STR-1	FLR-1	4/9 (see Figure 6.18 and 6.19)	The infant was laid in the bottom half of a large undecorated water jar which had been buried beneath the floor. Some large unworked cobbles covered it.
	FLR-2	4/18 (see Figure 6.17)	The infant was buried in a very shallow pit just below the floor. No container was used.
	FLR-2	4/28 (see Figure 6.17)	The infant was placed inside a coarse-temper cooking pot that had been broken. A large sherd was placed over the mouth of the pot. On top of the sherd was a cobble—both the sherd and the pebble had collapsed into the pot.
STR-2	FLR-1	5/44 (see Figure 6.15, 6.16, and 8.2b)	The burial was in a coarse-temper cooking pot with a broken bottom and so a large sherd of another vessel had been placed inside it. The infant was then placed in it and the mouth of the pot sealed with a large comal sherd. On top of the sherd was placed a sandstone metate fragment and another small cobble. The comal sherd had charred spots on the surface as though it had been used to burn some viscous substance before being buried.
STR-60	FLR-1	10/14 (see Figures 6.45 and 6.46	The infant was placed inside a coarse-temper, fillet-banded pot that had been previously broken so that many of its upper parts were missing. Old breaks were rounded from wear. Covering the pot were several large sherds of a comal. One large comal sherd had the same burned spots as the comal covering burial 5/44 in STR-2. Other sherds had a thick carbonized layer on one surface. The burial penetrated an earlier retaining wall beneath the floor.
STR-61	FLR-3	11/16 (see map Figure 6.49)	The infant was placed in a small pit in the floor over top of which were laid a metate fragment and small cobbles.
STR-110	Test Pit	2/4 (see map Figure 6.1)	A large coarse-tempered cooking vessel was used to hold the infant. The mouth of the pot had not been covered. Included was a perforated dog tooth—probably a pendant.
	Test Pit	unexcavated	Another large cooking vessel was noted in the fill next to burial 2/4 but there was not enough time to excavate it. Most likely it, too, was an infant burial.

cave after which the *paraje* was named, the bones and ashes of the dead being placed in large jugs or urns." If burial in particular caves was restricted to high-status lineages then there may have been a hierarchy of caves restricted to members of individual lineages. There are many caves surrounding Canajasté, and it is possible that they were used by different lineages.

One reason for the lack of elite infant burials in houses might be that even very young infants in elite households were of high enough status to warrant burial in caves. In non-elite households perhaps only adults and older children could be buried in caves, while infants simply did not have enough status, by virtue of birth, to warrant the ritual and ceremony that cremation must have entailed.

An important implication of this difference between elite and non-elite is that it indicates an internal social division within the community that was on the increase by the end of the Late Postclassic. In fact, burial patterns for very young infants are evidence of a basic social division between elite and non-elite that superseded attempts to encourage community unity by using community-wide house styles. Both non-elite and elite adults were probably cremated and placed in lineage caves. They may not have been the same caves; nevertheless, the overall ritual would have expressed a commonality between the two classes. The exclusion of non-elite infants from this mortuary treatment would have been a reminder of the differences between elite and non-elite, while at the same time not making the rift too wide to cross, if necessary.

Let me now attempt to summarize the changing mortuary patterns and determine what processes may have influenced them. Although the excavation sample is small for the Early Postclassic, there were no on-site burials encountered. More excavation may reveal some, but it is unlikely since, within the walled zone, at least, the subsurface soil deposits are extremely thin and bedrock underlies what little there is. The elite might have been buried in the ceremonial structures, but there was no evidence that this was the case in the looted structures. During the early part of the Late

Postclassic there was apparently little change in mortuary ritual since no infant burials were found. There is some evidence, however, from the surrounding caves that there were increasing numbers of cremations in "water jars."

By the end of the Late Postclassic period the non-elite began to bury their infants below their house floors, and that is the first and only indication obtained for on-site burial. These burials were all associated with the late-style houses that appear to be emulations of the earlier elite houses at the site. This suggests that by the end of the Late Postclassic, symbolic differences between the elite and non-elite were increasing once more but only in minor ways. A likely explanation for this pattern is that during the Early Postclassic period, both the elite and non-elite colonized the area from another region, founding the new site of Canajasté. Warfare became an increasing pattern of interregional interaction, and several symbolic differences between the two classes were de-emphasized—possibly by allowing the non-elite to emulate the elite. Then, under conditions of continued warfare (but perhaps by now warfare was conducted farther afield), elite/non-elite similarities were maintained in the ritual mortuary treatment accorded adults. However, some differentiation between the two classes was emerging in the treatment of deceased infants. The non-elite began to bury their very young children, non-cremated, beneath the house floors, a custom that the elite never practiced.

If exchange had continued to be as important during the end of the Early and beginning of the Late Postclassic then I would have expected more elite/non-elite differentiation throughout those periods. The increasing similarity through time suggests that community solidarity, as expressed in the manipulation of both mortuary practices and domestic house styles, became more important. There is no evidence for an immigration of nonlocal elite at the beginning of the Late Postclassic, but there is evidence for the process of warfare becoming increasingly important by the end of the Early Postclassic continuing throughout the period. The partial shift to increased elite/non-elite differentiation during the last half of the Late Postclassic suggests that warfare, though probably still important, became an increasingly remote process. That is, the elite may have been successful in using warfare in inter-polity relations and may have been able to invoke some increased degree of symbolic differentiation between themselves and the commoners at Canajasté.

Another possible explanation for the increased number of Late Postclassic infant burials in houses is that the non-elite began to have a higher infant mortality rate than the elite and that this new mortuary practice was related to basic differences between the two classes. Perhaps elite children received better nutrition from an early age and this increased their chances of survival.

Although there was poor plant preservation, there was a good degree of faunal preservation, and the possibility that elite households had a greater access to faunal resources and, thus, were better able to provide the necessary nutrition to reduce infant mortality, can be tested. In the next chapter I explore the evidence for subsistence changes in more detail. For now, let me anticipate the results of the preliminary faunal analysis by saying that, if anything, the early elite had greater access to faunal resources. By the Late Postclassic there was little evidence of differential access to faunal resources for the elite.

ENDNOTES

1   I have not visited the caves, but several anthropologists and archaeologists have shown me photos of them and discussed their implications with me, specifically Jim Nations, John Clark, and Jon McGee.

CHAPTER 9

SUBSISTENCE REMAINS

ANIMALS

The residents of Canajasté consumed the complete range of animals available in the region. Bone preserved relatively well at the site, and so most bone remains could be recovered.[1]

This allows me to answer the following question: how would bone remains vary from house to house and through time given the differing impact of each of the four specific processes?

One fruitful line of inquiry in answering this question should be a study of the differential distribution of species and parts (e.g., Bogan 1980).[2] For the present study, however, I will look at the overall quantity of bone in the deposits and analyze the basic trends. Meat-eating can be expected to be associated more closely with the elite. Therefore, the elite houses should have larger quantities of faunal remains than those of the non-elite. This is especially true if meat-eating was a symbol of status and if the elite consumed more than the non-elite as part of the display of their relatively higher position.

When exchange was the main form of intercommunity relations there should have been a greater difference in meat consumption between the classes. As the importance of exchange declined, there may have been decreasing differentiation between the elite and non-elite. In times of warfare this difference could even be actively downplayed in order to reduce visible class symbols. Therefore, with increased warfare, meat consumption would have either remained high in both social classes or dropped in both so that overall consumption was similar between the two classes.

Of course, some changes in overall meat consumption could be related to environmental changes as well. Over-hunting in times of

population increase could have caused depletion in a wide range of animals and, thus, have led to a decrease in the deposition of bones. This may be an indication of an initial population influx through colonization into an area and the rapid depletion of exploitable animals.

Table 9.1 presents bone weights for all deposits and shows significant variation in the quantity of bone in each deposit. Only one house floor lacked bone. Late Postclassic houses had the least bone, by weight, while the Early Postclassic houses had the most. Table 9.1 also summarizes the bone weights for each social class for each period. In addition, the table provides standardized ratios of bone densities to total excavated volume and to total number of rim sherds collected. Both measures indicate that the quantity of bone in elite houses dropped 15 times (using ratio to volume excavated) and 4 times (using ratio to rim sherds) and in non-elite houses it dropped 4 to 3 times respectively.

Using both ratios I conclude that the consumption of meat, as indicated by bone weight, dropped from the Early to Late Postclassic period. This would be consistent with either of the following two hypotheses. The first is that initial Early Postclassic colonizers of the region encountered plentiful game, both large and small. Faunal resources eventually declined after the population grew throughout the Postclassic period. The second hypothesis is that bone in the later deposits nearer the surface might have been consistently subjected to faster rates of decay and, so, is underrepresented. This latter hypothesis is unlikely since there is not much difference between the depths of the two deposits, and the condition of the bone near the surface was only slightly more decayed. I think the best explanation is that successful hunting actually declined.

Table 9.1. Distribution of animal bone: weight, ratio of weight to excavated volume (m³) and ratio of weight to rim sherds.

House	Deposit	Bone Weight (gm)	Ratio of Weight to Excavated Volume (m³)	Ratio of Weight to Rim Sherds
Late Non-Elite				
STR-1	FLR-1	100.4	19.4	.63
	FLR-2	141.5	26.6	2.77
STR-2	FLR-1	129.4	56.5	.83
	PFL-1	206.3	32.2	.43
	FLR-2	212.1	45.9	1.71
	FLR-3	71.5	35.6	2.55
	MID-1	7.0	63.6	.41
	MID-2	3.3	18.3	.18
	MID-3	6.0	23.1	n/a
	MID-4	24.5	13.4	.18
	MID-5	15.2	95.0	.32
	MID-6	9.1	37.9	.65
	MID-7	24.5	58.3	.27
STR-60	FLR-1	145.4	17.2	.59
	FLR-2	121.9	82.4	1.17
	MID-1	389.5	85.4	1.10
STR-61	FLR-1	3.5	1.4	.18
	FLR-2	36.9	24.4	1.94
	FLR-3	156.2	52.2	1.78
	FLR-4	5.5	5.3	.61
	FLR-5	44.7	10.8	1.06
Subtotals		1854.4	33.3	.84
Early Non-Elite				
STR-2	FLR-4	22.2	30.8	.72
STR-60	MID-2&3	318.1	230.5	2.49
	MID-4	205.0	105.1	3.53
Subtotals		545.3	134.6	2.51
Late Elite				
STR-21	FLR-1	20.4	10.0	.52
	FLR-2	15.4	9.5	.49
	FLR-3	0	0	0
	FLR-4	23.7	24.7	2.63

Table 9.1. Continued.

House	Deposit	Bone Weight (gm)	Ratio of Weight to Excavated Volume (m³)	Ratio of Weight to Rim Sherds
	FLR-5	18.5	23.1	2.06
STR-22	FLR-1	59.4	5.8	.63
	FLR-2	68.7	28.6	.74
	FLR-3	155.8	80.7	2.69
STR-23	FLR-1	110.3	46.2	.28
	FLR-2	48.0	16.8	.32
	FLR-3	28.8	13.7	.19
Subtotals		549.0	19.1	.87
Early Elite				
STR-22	FLR-4	148.3	79.3	2.47
	FLR-5	1210.6	446.7	4.88
	EL-1	104.6	127.6	2.91
	EL-2	336.5	287.6	4.37
	MID-1	394.5	318.1	2.63
	MID-2	17.4	75.6	.97
	MID-3	120.7	502.9	2.19
	MID-4	271.0	153.9	2.53
	AL-2	159.2	346.1	1.59
	MID-5	597.0	505.9	5.69
Subtotals		3359.8	287.7	3.51
Summary Subtotals				
Non-elite		2399.7	40.2	.99
Elite		3908.8	96.7	2.46
Late Period		2403.4	28.5	.85
Early Period		3905.1	241.4	3.33

Looking more closely at the sequences for each house listed in Table 9.1, it appears that the major decline in meat consumption did not take place until after the start of the Late Postclassic. In Structure 22, however, there were some midden deposits with extremely high ratios of bone to excavated volume and to rim sherd counts. But by Floor 4 the downward trend continued essentially unabated. The same trend is present in the Structure 60 sequence, with the largest decline taking place at the end of the Early Postclassic period.

The differences between elite and non-elite are even more striking than the differences between Early and Late periods. In the Early Postclassic, the elite residents of house Structure 22 discarded more bone, of all kinds, than the non-elite of Structures 2 and 60, despite the fact that some Early period middens in Structure 60 had higher densities. Based on the bone-to-rim sherd ratio there were three separate deposits in Structure 22 that had higher densities of bone than did the deposit with the highest density in Structure 60 (Midden 4). Therefore, the Early Postclassic elite had a greater access to meat than did the non-elite. In the Early period meat consumption must have been a symbol of high status; perhaps it was given to the nobles as tribute from commoners at Canajasté.

Meat consumption began to decline first in the non-elite households so that, at the beginning of the Late Postclassic, elite households still consumed more meat than the non-elite. But by the end of the Late Postclassic meat consumption was almost identically low for the two classes (using the bone-to-rim sherd ratio). Using the density measure, the non-elite even surpassed the meat consumption levels exhibited by the elite house deposits, although, in general, consumption declined.

Summarizing the results of this analysis, it appears that meat consumption, at least the quantity consumed, was a symbol of social status distinction between the two classes. If game animals declined because of hunting pressure with population increase, it might partly explain the overall decline from Early to Late Postclassic. Nonetheless, if the social and political processes influencing internal community relations changed, I also expect a shift in the symbols used to distinguish between classes. In spite of the declining availability of meat I would still expect the elite to have greater access to meat than the non-elite, especially if the elite were trying to maintain the visible symbols of their distinct status. But by this time they apparently consumed no more meat than the non-elite. This is the expectation if warfare became more important through time and if the elite encouraged community unity by de-emphasizing social status distinctions.

I had expected that, despite the need to de-emphasize symbolic differences between the elite and non-elite during periods of war, the consumption of meat might have been an ideal symbol for the elite to maintain. Perhaps future analyses will show that the elite consumed different types of animals or more choice parts while not consuming greater quantities. During the Early period, consumption of meat alone obviously was not a distinguishing social status marker since both classes had access to it. The elite, however, did have access to more meat. The method of access could well have been a more important marker than the meat itself. If the Early elite obtained more faunal resources as gifts or as tribute, then it may have been necessary, during the Late period, for them to forego this form of service in order to maintain their control over the community. Faced with declining populations of faunal resources in the Late Postclassic, the gifting of such a transient symbol as meat would have been more divisive than unifying. If the nobility had to count on their commoners to defend the community and follow them into war, they probably did not want to ask too much from them in the way of "luxury" tribute items, such as meat. In times of heightened warfare such forms of tribute exaction would have undermined the community's sense of unity and, eventually, the elite's political control. Instead, they would have been better off limiting tribute to durable and highly visible symbols (i.e., ceremonial structures or their own residences) or in simply underwriting military activity.

One last aspect of the faunal analysis is noteworthy. Comparing the changing frequency of bone deposition to projectile point frequency I find an inverse relationship. Bone deposition and, thus, hunting, became less frequent after the beginning of the Late Postclassic, and projectile points became more frequent. This would tend to confirm that the increase in projectile points was not for hunting purposes. An increase in warfare during the Late Postclassic is indicated by every other source of information examined so far. The patterns of variation in bone deposition also fit the pattern.

One additional pattern alluded to above is the possibility that the community began as a colony in an area of relatively low population density. As the population increased towards the end of the Late Postclassic period faunal resources may have been depleted by over-hunting. This could have led to the observed decrease in bone deposition, if meat consumption declined.

PLANTS

It would have been possible to test the same kinds of hypotheses using botanical remains but, unfortunately, preservation was poor.[3] The most common plant recovered was maize, represented by charred kernels and cob fragments. Also found were several charred beans and a possible piece of squash rind. Several fragments of charred wood and other charred seeds have yet to be identified.

Structures 22 and 60 had most of the preserved materials and, since they both span the Early and Late Postclassic periods, they allow for some comparison between the two periods. Maize and beans were found in the Early deposits, and maize, beans, and squash were found in the Late deposits (Table 9.2). The quantities are too small to compare the frequencies of each or to compare the elite with the non-elite. At present it appears that both classes had access to all three of these staples. Thus, the only possible difference between the classes would have been the relative quantities available.

No evidence has yet been found for tropical fruits, such as zapote, which were grown in the lowlands and may have been traded to the highlands.[4] Nor have cotton seeds been identified. If cotton cloth production was as important as suggested, I would expect some charred seeds to be present.

ENDNOTES

1   Bones from deposits near the surface were slightly less well preserved than those from deeper deposits.

2   The faunal analysis was carried out by Kent Flannery and Patty Wattenmaker of the Museum of Anthropology, University of Michigan. They report that the most common faunal remains in the deposits are brocket deer, dog, and turkey.

3   Paul Minnis of the University of Oklahoma examined the 200 flotation samples that were systematically collected from all provenience units. He found very few identifiable samples in any of the collections. All the flotation samples were collected by using a vat designed by John Rick and made available to the project by Joyce Marcus and Kent Flannery. Fine-mesh chiffon cloth was used to skim the water in collecting the samples.

4   Several types of zapote trees grow in the vicinity of Canajasté. In fact, the Canajasté River, which gives its name to the site, is a Spanish corruption of several Maya words meaning "four zapote colorado trees" (Marcus 1982:243-246, and pers. comm.). *Can* or *kan* is the number four; *jas, haaz, or ha'as* is zapote colorado (*Pouteria sapota*); and *te* or *te'* is tree. The use of *te* for the tree suffix is present in Cholti, Chol, Huastec, Chicomuceltec, and Tzotzil, among others.

Table 9.2. Charred botanical remains in the deposits from Structures 22 and 60.

House	Deposit	Charred plants present
STR-2	FLR-1	unidentified
	FLR-2	unidentified
	CF-2	beans, squash rind
	FLR-3	unidentified
	FLR-4	none
	FLR-5	maize, unidentified
	EL-1	none
	EL-2	unidentified
	MID-1	maize
	MID-2	maize, beans
	MID-3	maize, beans, unidentified
	MID-4	maize, beans, unidentified
	AL-2	maize, beans
	MID-5	maize
STR-60	FLR-1	unidentified (several)
	FLR-2	maize
	MID-1	maize
	MID-2&3	unidentified
	MID-4	maize

CHAPTER 10

REGIONAL SETTLEMENT PATTERNS AND CIVIC-CEREMONIAL ARCHITECTURE

This chapter will attempt to answer the broad question: How did Canajasté fit into its regional political and economic setting? This will be done by examining settlement patterns and civic-ceremonial architecture. In particular, I will examine territorial sizes and locations, settlement distributions, and the range of structures in, and layout of, the centers of Postclassic sites found within the study region

Does Canajasté's position within a regional settlement hierarchy and its internal organization, compared with its neighbors, give any clues as to the importance (and sequence) of processes affecting its evolution? As I argued in Chapter 4, each specific interregional process should have a different impact on changes in the settlement patterns and civic-ceremonial architecture of a community. Some of the patterns, including settlement location and architectural layout, should vary through time in relation to various factors and, therefore, I do not expect a one-to-one correspondence between a given settlement pattern and a particular dominant interregional process. Nevertheless, the discernible patterns should accord, more or less, with those already noted for household architecture and artifacts. If not, the previous conclusions are questionable. The first section of this analysis will look at settlement patterns and the second section will compare the civic-ceremonial architecture.

SETTLEMENT PATTERNS

The community at Canajasté must be placed in its regional political context in order to understand the roles of exchange, warfare, and/or colonization in its development. Since there are no known Preconquest or Early Colonial records discussing the community or its

neighbors, this understanding will have to rely upon information from archaeological survey.

As already noted in Chapter 5, knowledge of sites in the region comes mainly from Thomas Lee's (1975) reconnaissance survey as well as the work of other members of the NWAF during the 1970s and early 1980s. Olivier de Montmollin's intensive surveys of three adjacent valleys within the upper Grijalva region between 1983 and 1990 provide the most comprehensive settlement data collected in this part of Mesoamerica (De Montmollin 1989a, 1989b, 1995). Here, I analyze all the sites that are known to date to the Postclassic period (based on surface ceramic collections and test excavations).[1]

Postclassic Sites

Twenty-six sites have been identified as having Postclassic ceramics or architecture. These are located in the *municipios* (or counties) of La Trinitaria (Tr), Comalapa (Co), Chicomucelo (Ch), and Buena Vista (Bv) (Table 10.1). Sites were assigned a recording number, preceded by the abbreviation for its municipio, and these numbers will be used in the discussion that follows. Canajasté, for example, was recorded as Tr-69. Of the 26 sites only ten are large enough and have high enough densities of Postclassic sherds to be considered as centers. The other 16 sites have little evidence of Postclassic architecture or ceramics, and I estimate that they were relatively small communities during this period. Based on this distinction, I define centers as communities that have a substantial amount of Postclassic architecture, including a civic-ceremonial precinct. In addition, they also have evidence of numerous houses around the ceremonial precinct, and they were the major

Table 10.1. Postclassic sites in the Upper Tributaries Region.

Site Number	Name	Size Class	Earlier Occupation	Topographic Setting	Defensive Features
Tr-13	El Limón	center	Classic (small)	mesa top	slope
Tr-24	El Paraíso	hamlet	Classic (small)	open	none
Tr-68	La Sombra	hamlet	Classic (small)	open	none
Tr-69	Canajasté	center	none	river bend	river, wall, terraces
Tr-73		hamlet	Classic (small)	open	none
Tr-74	Bolsa Platano	hamlet	Classic (large)	open	none
Tr-75		center	none	low hill	slope, swamp
Tr-88		hamlet	Classic (large)	open	none
Tr-94	Los Encuentros	center	Classic (large)	low hill	none
Tr-99	Lagartero	center	Classic (large)	islands	river, walls
Tr-118	Tres Cerritos	hamlet	Classic (large)	open	none
Tr-121		hamlet	none	open	none
Tr-122		hamlet	Classic (large)	open	none
Tr-130	El Salvador	hamlet	Classic (large)	open	none
Tr-157	La Libertad	hamlet, cemetery	Preclassic (large)	open	none
Tr-160	Dolores	hamlet	Classic (small)	open	none
Tr-161	Dolores Puente	center	none	flats	rivers
Tr-227	Aguazarca	center	none	ridge	slopes, walls
Tr-376 Rv-140	La Mesa	center	none	hilltop	slopes
Co-1		hamlet	Classic (small)	open	none
Co-2		hamlet	Classic (small)	open	none
Co-54		center	Classic (large)	open	none
Co-59	Guajilar	center	Preclassic (large)	open	none
Ch-9	Piedra Labrada	hamlet	Classic (large)	open	none
Ch-14		hamlet	Classic (small)	open	none
Bv-8		hamlet	Classic (small)	open	none

sites within the region. No doubt, they would have been politically dominant within their limited territories, a topic I will explore in a later section. The smaller communities, which I am calling hamlets, have little evidence of Postclassic occupation, although in some cases they appear to have been substantial communities during earlier periods (e.g., Tr-74-Bolsa Platano, and Tr-157-La Libertad). In other cases they appear to have been simply small farmsteads consisting of from one to ten houses and lacking ceremonial architecture—either of their own or built by earlier residents. Table 10.1 summarizes the basic characteristics of each site, including its size classification, main period of occupation (in addition to Postclassic), topographic setting, and defensive features.

Site Locations

The sites are located along the many small tributaries of the Grijalva River. The distribution of these sites, as shown in Figure 5.3, is biased by the areas sampled during the reconnaissance. Only roads and river margins were searched and, therefore, it is possible that additional small sites might be found in future, more intensive surveys away from these locations. Despite this, it is likely that all the major Postclassic sites in the study area have been noted because these are only a fraction (roughly 10 percent) of all sites recovered. Interestingly, of the 207 sites recorded by De Montmollin (1989b) in his intensive survey of the Rosario-Santa Inés Valley, only one additional Postclassic site was found—Tr-376 (RV140). Although this proportion of Postclassic to all sites (1:207) is low by comparison to the overall reconnaissance results, it illustrates that (1) there are very few Postclassic sites in the study region and (2) even intensive, systematic survey of the entire region would stand little chance of discovering many more.

In addition to the centers and hamlets, many caves having Postclassic remains were explored. The ones located in the Camcum-Canajasté Valley are plotted in Figure 8.1, but cave sites will be omitted from the analysis that follows since they were not settlements.

Site Chronology

Most Postclassic sites were founded during earlier periods and have evidence of Classic and, sometimes, Late Preclassic occupations. The settlements recorded during Lee's reconnaissance were analyzed in the late 1970s and so the chronological placements were not final at that time. For this study, however, I re-examined the ceramics from each site listed in Table 10.1 and found several temporally diagnostic types characteristic of either the Early or Late Postclassic, or both.[2] The ceramics that were used to assign an Early Postclassic placement included Tohil Plumbate and early-style Tol Polychrome bowls and dishes. Late Postclassic assignment was based on the presence of Tol Polychrome bowls and water jars, large or small-holed colanders, comales, and Gavilan tripod bowls and dishes. Unspecified Early or Late Postclassic placement was based on the presence of thin-walled and coarse-ground calcite-tempered ollas. These diagnostics, of course, do not allow for a detailed chronological breakdown within each period, but they are useful for distinguishing Postclassic components at sites that also had Preclassic or Late Classic components (see Appendix D).

Territorial Organization

This analysis must be considered preliminary for two reasons. First, I have not studied all of the sites in enough detail to be absolutely certain of their size during the Postclassic period, especially the Early Postclassic. For example, without excavation, Canajasté would have been classified as a single component Late Postclassic center since no Early Postclassic artifacts were noted in the extensive surface collections and test excavations. Few of the other sites have been tested by excavation so they too might have Early Postclassic components. Second, the boundaries of the study area are arbitrarily defined by the Guatemalan border, and little is known about the archaeology of the area just inside Guatemala. Where possible I will include fragmentary information from the western portion of the Cuchumatanes (La Farge and Byers 1931; Lovell 1980; Wauchope 1970) but little systematically collected information is available to provide a basis for studying territorial organization of the area.

The starting point for this analysis is to compare the locations of sites presented in Figure 5.3. To facilitate this I have plotted all of the centers and hamlets (excluding the five hamlets recorded for the Tachinula and Blanco Rivers near Chicomucelo) on a map of the river systems in the area (Figure 10.1). Overlaying this I have plotted Thiessen polygons (Haggett 1965:247-248; Hodder and Orton 1976:59-60), which give some indication of the possible extent of each center's territory. Since none

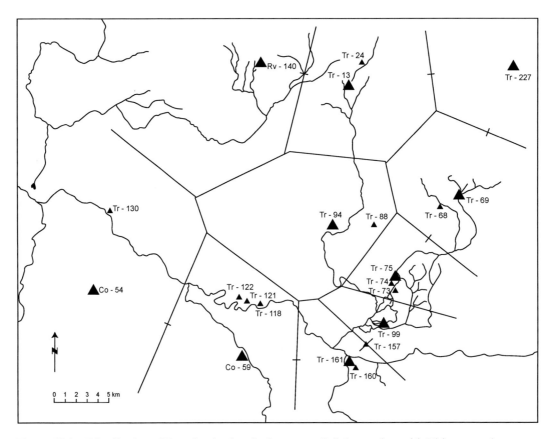

Figure 10.1.   Distribution of Postclassic sites in the upper Grijalva region with Thiessen polygons plotted.

of the centers is clearly dominant over other centers in terms of size, complexity of civic-ceremonial architecture, or other factors, I think it most likely that if there were any very large centers, they must have been located outside the study area. [3]

The purpose of plotting Thiessen polygons in this case is to provide a rough estimate of the possible range of direct territorial control of each center and the size of each territory. Furthermore, the edges of the polygons provide hypothetical locations of boundaries between centers and may ultimately allow an approximation of regional boundaries between groups of interacting centers. The polygons themselves simply provide a geometric statement of the relationship between any point on the map and its nearness to a given center. In the simplest form, any point within a polygon is

closer to that polygon's center than to any other center (Haggett 1967:658). Of course, ancient political boundaries probably did not rely strictly on geometric distance for the definition of a center's control. And it is certainly unlikely that the halfway point between two centers was always used to delimit territorial boundaries. Nonetheless, it is likely that Thiessen polygons will give an accurate approximation of the absolute size of a center's territory, even if the exact location is not the same.

The polygons show (Figure 10.1) that the smallest territories were along the Lagartero River. The overall density of population must have been higher in this zone than in the region to the west. I have calculated the sizes of the territories indicated by the Thiessen polygons, where possible, and present them in Table 10.2. The method used is presented below (and must

Table 10.2. Estimation of territory sizes based on Thiessen polygons.

Site	Half-territory size km²	Estimated territory size (half-territory x 2) km²
Tr-13	83	166
Tr-94	--	166 (whole area)
Tr-69	63	126
Tr-75	30	60
Tr-99	19	38
Tr-161	26	52
Co-59	88	176

be considered only an approximation since all but one territory is left undefined on one side). However, it was possible to estimate the size in most cases by simply marking the halfway point on the perpendicular between each center and its two "outside" neighbors. By outside, I mean the two centers flanking a given center on its territorially open side. For example, in Canajasté's case, Tr-227 and Tr-75 are its outside neighbors. The halfway point between them and Canajasté allow an approximate measure of territorial half-size area. Doubling this gives an estimate of the region's size. The areas were measured from a map using compensating polar planimeter. In the case of sites Tr-227, Co-54, and Tr-376, there is too little known about their surrounding regions to attempt an estimation of their territory sizes.

Calculating the territory size in this manner gives a range of 38–176 km². The three sites without sizes calculated all appear from the map to have territories at least in the upper range of these estimates. Therefore, it is particularly noteworthy that the zone along the Lagartero River has a large number of small territories, compared to the rest of the zone. Because of the unknown territory beyond Tr-99 inside Guatemala, it is quite possible that its size was underestimated. But a more likely explanation is that it was in a more productive zone, and many people could be supported within a smaller region. Furthermore, it is also possible

that Tr-99 had been in a dominant position over other sites along the river. Of importance here is the fact that Tr-157 was the largest site in the region during the Preclassic period, and Tr-99 was probably the most important site during the Classic period. During the Postclassic period, Tr-99 may have continued to be important. Its ceremonial architecture appears to be mostly Classic in age. There is little evidence of Early Postclassic occupation. By the Late Postclassic, it had a dense occupation in this highly defensible location. Significant quantities of decorated Late Postclassic period ceramics were found at Tr-99. Whether it was a center that was able to exact tribute and labor from the surrounding population, such as Tr-75 and Tr-161, remains unknown. The territories of these two sites were also small, much like Tr-99. In fact, their combined estimated sizes (from Table 10.2) add up to 150 km², much closer to the individual sizes of the other four centers' territories

Both Tr-75 and Tr-161 have late architecture and are similar to each other in size and ceremonial construction (see below). They are less defensible than Tr-99, located on a series of islands surrounded by the Lagartero River (Ekholm and Martínez 1983), and this relative openness might itself be a clue to their lower position within the regional hierarchy (J. Marcus 1983b). It is quite possible that they were secondary centers subordinate to Tr-99. If so, the still smaller communities in the settlement system around them, such as Tr-73, Tr-74, Tr-157, and Tr-160, would have been tertiary hamlets in a three-tiered settlement hierarchy. There may even be an as yet undiscovered level below this consisting of a few simple houses with no public architecture.

Upriver, beyond Tr-75, lies Canajasté. Its territorial size is estimated at 126 km^2, two to three times the size of Tr-99 and its possible secondary centers. Canajasté sits on a narrower part of the river surrounded by lands much less fertile and much drier and rockier. It had only one associated hamlet (Tr-68).

Sites, such as Tr-13 and Tr-94, in zones farther away from the Lagartero River, have much larger territories and are spaced farther from their nearest neighbors. These sites are in less productive zones and possibly required larger areas to support a population as large as that of Tr-99. Even farther west, sites such as Co-54, may have had larger territories still. Unfortunately, there is not enough information about their neighbors to be able to calculate territory sizes.

As mentioned, most of the regional centers in the study area are approximately of equal size and architectural complexity. The main difference is that some were built on earlier occupations while others were first-time occupations. This makes comparisons difficult, especially when trying to determine how much of a site's architecture was constructed in the Postclassic period. In the case of El Limón (Tr-13), Canajasté (Tr-69), and Aguazarca (Tr-227), there is little doubt that most of the occupation is Postclassic. Others, such as Lagartero (Tr-99), Guajilar (Co-59), and Co-54, are reoccupations of earlier sites. Without more excavation it cannot be determined which structures were built during the Postclassic reoccupation. In spite of this problem, it is fairly clear that sites with Postclassic reoccupations owe the bulk of their construction to earlier builders. This is primarily because the sites' layout is either like the Preclassic or the Classic pattern. Sites with no evidence of earlier occupation have very different layouts.

Defensive Characteristics

Some sites are located in defensible locations and others are not. What is the main characteristic of this dichotomy of site location with respect to defense? First, I will examine their distribution. The relative defensibility of sites is as follows: Tr-227, Tr-69, and Tr-99 are in defensible topographic locations, i.e., steep hilltops, bends in rivers, and islands; in addition, some have fortification walls. Two other sites, Tr-75 and Tr-161, are located along waterways at locations that only permit access to the sites from one side. But in the case of Tr-161, the river may have made the site more accessible. All the centers west of these sites are minimally protected by topography and have no visible fortification defenses. They may have had wooden palisades that, of course, would not have preserved. Apart from this, they are relatively open, as compared with the sites forming the eastern frontier of the study region.

One of the implications of this distinct regional differentiation in the defensibility of sites is that some sites were under a greater threat of attack than others. If these relatively undefended sites were equally threatened by attack, they may have considered community abandonment or refuge in a redoubt to be more viable alternatives than defending their community. Still, the possibility remains that they were attacked less often.

This leads to the interpretation that the eastern communities were recent immigrants into the region and that they staked out their claim by building or reoccupying fortified centers. The western communities, on the other hand, may have been long-time residents of the region who originally built their communities in indefensible open locations because they were seldom under attack. In fact, they may have been responsible for the attacks upon the eastern zone communities—possibly in attempts to defend their territory.

An alternative explanation is that the eastern communities represent a frontier of the upper Grijalva region with the foothills of the Cuchumatanes. Sites like Canajasté and Lagartero may have been the easternmost outposts of political units occupying the Grijalva Valley and might have been, in fact, in conflict with polities occupying the Cuchumatanes.

Distinguishing between these two alternatives is quite difficult since so little is known about the neighboring sites in Guatemala (Please see note 3). I can say that based on artifact analyses presented in Chapter 7, there is a closer association between the defensible eastern-zone sites and Guatemala, while the relatively indefensible western-zone sites have somewhat different ceramic styles, and they also have much more obsidian, for example, from Mexican sources.

The next section will look at more specific details of civic-ceremonial architecture to ascertain whether the east-zone/west-zone division noted in settlement pattern and territorial organization holds up. Following this, I will explore a model of regional territorial organization that may provide clues to the nature of changing state organization in the region during the Postclassic period.

CIVIC-CEREMONIAL ARCHITECTURE

Just as houses are the physical representation or symbol of the household, public architecture stands for the community as a whole and its relationships with its neighbors. The territorial organization of the upper Grijalva region is comprised of numerous small centers, and, with only a few possible exceptions, each of these is relatively isolated from the others. Certainly none is clearly dominant over the others on a scale similar to the contemporaneous political situation 80 km east at Zaculeu, Guatemala. Still, it may be possible to determine, beyond artifact similarities, if there are stylistically related centers. This is similar to Fox's (1978) approach to determining the extent of the Quiché state's influence on surrounding regions during the Postclassic period. There are several alternatives. If the study region was divided into distinct zones, for example, an eastern zone and a western zone, there should be distinct patterning in the layout of the civic-ceremonial centers and the styles of the structures making up the centers.

Furthermore, if one or another of the zones is closely associated with neighboring states and was organized as a set of bud-off colonies, then that zone should have civic-ceremonial centers similar in layout and building styles to the source state. If, however, the communities in the study region were more or less autonomous, then there should be no such pattern. There would instead be a great deal of variation among the communities, and no zone should have architectural layouts or styles patterned after neighboring states.

Canajasté's Civic-ceremonial Center

The layout of Canajasté's civic-ceremonial center has both similarities to and differences from other Postclassic sites in the study region and beyond. Figure 10.2 maps the civic-ceremonial precinct. Before discussing the details of any one structure I will first describe the overall layout. The main plaza, delineated by Structures 6, 7, 9, 11 and 12, has an inside area of about 375 m². The entire surface of the plaza was plastered at least three times with 1 cm-thick layers of white lime plaster. The plaza is essentially closed. Two of the largest buildings (6 and 7) almost touch, completely blocking the southeast and northeast sides of the plaza. The northwest corner is formed by Structure 9, and the gap between it and Structure 7 is partly blocked by a free-standing stone wall and partly by a terrace drop. The southwest side is formed by the two smallest buildings in the center, Structures 11 and 12. They sit very close to each other and to Structure 9. All of the structures face towards the center of the plaza. The closed nature of the ceremonial center is one very distinctive aspect of the layout. The entire length of the ceremonial zone, from Structure 22 (the elite house) to Structure 5, is blocked by a steep terrace drop of 4 m. Structure 5 and Structure 18 (appended to Structure 6) block off all views and easy access to the ceremonial center from the southeast. The only structures within this blocked-off zone that may have been elite residences and not civic-ceremonial buildings are Structures 15, 16, and 17. They are all low platforms on the terrace just below the level of

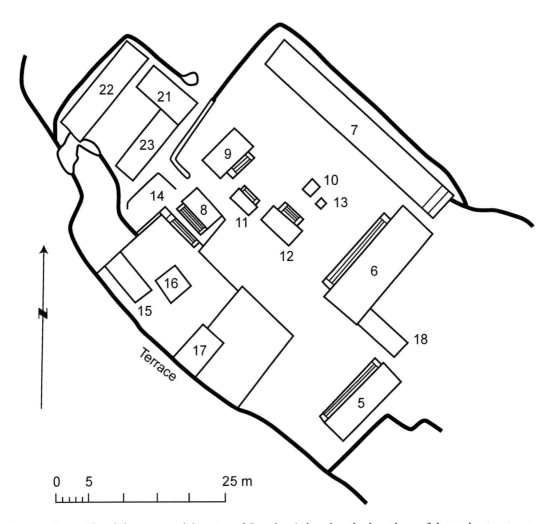

Figure 10.2. The civic-ceremonial center of Canajasté showing the locations of the main structures.

the main plaza. They also gain access to the plaza by an elaborate stairway leading up to Structure 8, which, besides Structure 5, is the only other ceremonial building not facing onto the plaza. If Structures 15 to 17 did comprise an elite residence, access to it was as closed as access to the ceremonial structures themselves. This was the only house group besides House Group 2 (Structure 21 to 23) that had unimpeded access to the plaza.

Inside the plaza area are two small altars that were visible on the surface. Their excavation recovered very few artifacts. Even

though they had been looted in the past, there was no evidence of any caches or features. The three largest structures, Structures 5, 6 and 7, are all quite low. The two with balustraded staircases are only a little more than 1 m tall to the top of the platform. Structure 7 was lower (about 25 cm tall). There was no evidence on the surface of these well-preserved platforms to suggest any stone-walled superstructure. Instead, their surfaces were clear of debris and level, indicating that they had perishable walls—probably of cane-and-daub. In contrast, Structures 9, 11, and 12 had a good deal of

Figure 10.3. Structure 5, south side (away from plaza, facing SW).

collapsed stone debris, plaster from walls, and remnants of floors, suggesting that they were very substantial structures. I will briefly describe each of them to give an indication of the nature of the buildings, even though extensive excavations were only carried out in Structure 9.

Structure 5

This platform faced northwest and was very well preserved (Figure 10.3). Unfortunately, looters had cut holes into two of its corners, pulling them down and exposing the interior core. As a result, it was possible to see that there were no earlier stages of construction; the core was a homogeneous, earth and rubble fill. The exterior of the platform was made of well-squared limestone blocks approximately 10 courses high. They were dry laid (as was all the masonry in the ceremonial buildings'

platforms) with the unworked side of the block placed towards the interior of the structure. Near ground level are remnants of plaster that would have covered the whole building. The staircase was appended onto the front of the structure and consists of five risers and treads. Both ends of the staircase are flanked by sloping stone balustrades (Figure 10.4). The structure's dimensions are 12 m by 4 m (5 m with staircase) and 1 m high.

Structures 6 and 18

Excepting its larger size, this building platform was almost identical to Structure 5. It, too, had a clear surface with no evidence of a stone-walled superstructure. On the front side of the platform it had roughly 10 courses of squared, limestone slabs. On the backside, because of the rising topography, it was only five to six courses high (Figure 10.5). All corners of

Figure 10.4.   Structure 5, showing balustrades on side of staircase (facing NE).

this platform had slumped badly, thus exposing the interior earth and rubble construction fill. No earlier stages of construction were noted. As with Structure 5, it had an appended staircase with balustrades on both ends (in fact, all buildings in the ceremonial center did, except Structure 7). Although the steps were buckled and collapsed to a large extent, I estimate there to have been approximately five risers and treads. Fragments of a plaster coating were visible near the base of the platform where one corner had been badly damaged by looters. The dimensions of this building were 16.5 m by 5 m (6 m including stairs) by approximately 1 m high.

Structure 6 had an additional structure appended to its backside. Structure 18 was a low platform, only 2-3 courses high, of squared limestone blocks. The core was filled with rubble and earth, as was Structure 6. It was added onto Structure 6 in the only exposed and open section between the ceremonial center and the domestic residences to the southeast, thereby blocking off the view of the plaza from the residential zone. The building measured 7 m by 3 m and was 25 to 30 cm high.

Structure 7

This is one of the most distinctive building platforms at the site. It is similar to the long, low "range" structures found throughout the Maya area in the Postclassic period. It alone formed the entire northeast side of the ceremonial center. This platform, although twice as long as the next longest building at the site (Structure 6), was extremely low: only 25 cm high on the side facing the plaza (Figure 10.6). There were only one to two courses of squared limestone slabs visible on the surface. No debris from fallen walls was noted suggesting that Structure 7, like the previous two, was built with cane or cane-and-daub walls.

Figure 10.5.   Structure 6, south side (away from plaza) showing well-preserved courses of stones (facing N).

While the exact functions of all the buildings are unknown, this one is especially enigmatic. These long low buildings only became common in the Postclassic period in the Grijalva Depression, for example, at the Ruíz site near Chiapa de Corzo (Lowe 1959:32). They are unknown in the survey region prior to the Postclassic (Lee et al. n.d.). Similar structures were used as council houses for lineage administration and represent the political activities of the ranking noble lineage at Utatlán (Carmack 1981:159-160). If such was their use, I would expect one for each major lineage. At Canajasté, the presence of only one such structure may indicate that there was only one dominant noble lineage at the site. It is also possible that all major lineages shared the same building, as they did at Potojil and Pismachi in the Quiché region (Carmack 1981:160). I will consider these buildings in more detail when comparing the other sites in the region.

Structure 7 had a single, 3 m long addition made to the northwest end and two, 1 m long additions to the southeast end. Other earlier

constructions may be present below the surface and could be revealed by excavation. The structure is 32.2 m long and 5 m wide.

Structure 8

This building was a low platform located to the southwest of Structures 9 and 11. Its limestone retaining wall was only one to two courses high, and the platform was filled with earth and rubble. The major part of the construction consisted of an elaborate stone staircase with balustrades, similar to the other buildings already described. There was evidence of plaster covering the stones of the staircase. The stairs led down to a level terrace only 1 m wide, whereupon another larger staircase descended to a plaza area containing Structures 15 to 17. Structure 8 and its associated staircases are clearly separate from the main buildings in the plaza. It is 6 m long and 3 m wide (the staircase adds another 80 cm to the width). The lower staircase is 3.4 m long with 1 m long balustrades on either end. The balustrades are

Figure 10.6.   Structure 7 (facing E).

almost vertical, with their tops forming level surfaces. Adjoining the lower staircase, to the west, was a very well-made terrace wall having squared stone blocks, like the ceremonial buildings. The presence of this stairway linking Structure 8 to the lower plaza suggests that the two were integral parts of the same functional unit. Furthermore, it links the whole to the main center, both in terms of physical access and in terms of stylistic unity.

Structure 11

This small temple platform had been badly looted prior to its discovery in 1973 by Thomas Lee (pers. comm.); nevertheless, enough remained to determine its size and type of construction. It was a well-built platform that would have been roughly 1 m high. Pieces of plaster still adhering to stone slabs, as well as the quantity of stone and plaster rubble, suggested that the platform supported a stone-walled superstructure. Unfortunately, no sections of intact wall had survived the looters'

picks. Also badly damaged, but still preserved enough to draw, were the two balustrades and the staircase. They were constructed in exactly the same style as those in Structures 5 and 6. The entire center of the platform and the top courses of its retaining walls had been gutted. This allowed a glimpse into its core, revealing that there were no earlier structural stages of construction. The rubble and earth fill was relatively homogeneous. The overall dimensions of the building were 4 m by 2.2 m with an 80 cm wide staircase. The balustrades were about 50 cm wide. That the entire structure was plastered is indicated by chunks still adhering to the base of the retaining wall.

Structure 12

This building was in the same style as Structure 11 but was even more badly looted. It was an approximately 1 m tall platform made of well-squared limestone slabs encasing an earth and rubble core. The looters had apparently been searching for treasure hidden in the platform because they dug out the entire south half of the building to a depth well below the original ground surface, exposing and even hacking into bedrock. In the looters' rubble in both this building and Structure 11 there was no evidence of smashed pots or other artifacts, so it appears that they were unsuccessful. As in all the other looted buildings, the looters' cuts revealed no earlier substages of architecture.

The toppled and fragmentary remains of walls were common in the debris from this building. As with Structures 9 (see below) and 11, the limestone slabs from the free-standing walls were held together by cement containing carbon flecks and snail shells. They had been plastered on their exterior surfaces with much finer, white lime stucco. There was no evidence of multiple plasterings on the walls in this building, nor had they been painted. The platform was 6 m long by 2.5 m wide. Facing the plaza were the remains of a balustraded staircase, adding an additional meter to the platform's width. Remnants of plaster near the base suggest the whole building had been covered with a coat of white stucco.

Structure 9

This building, of all the structures in the ceremonial center, received the most attention. During Lee's initial reconnaissance in 1973, he found the building to be badly destroyed, with a large pit dug into the center and large slabs of wall toppled in from all directions. Resting on the surface, and still visible on some sections of wall, were fragments of polychrome mural paintings. During investigations in 1980 and 1981-82 many such fragments were recovered, but none were longer than 10-15 cm. In 1982, salvage excavation and consolidation of the structure was initiated in order to find intact sections of murals.[4] Unfortunately, excavations confirmed that the looters had, indeed, destroyed the entire superstructure.

The building was a small platform 6 m long and 4 m wide. It faced southeast, with a well-built stairway descending to the plaza. The stairway was 1 m wide and was flanked by balustrades. In clearing away the considerable

rubble from the looters' pit, the base of the structure was exposed on all four sides. It was preserved well enough to show that the platform retaining walls had been plastered at least three times to form a continuous and rounded join with the plaza surface. This indicates that when the building was replastered, so, too, was the plaza. Perhaps the entire civic-ceremonial center had been refinished at intervals (cf. Guillemin 1959, 1965, 1967, 1977 for similar refinishing at Iximché).

The stucco of the basal platform covered a very well-made retaining wall that consisted of dry-laid limestone blocks carefully squared on their outer surfaces. The inner surface, which was set into the rubble and earth core of the platform, was much less carefully worked. There were no earlier stages of construction visible within the building's core.

Lying atop the heap of debris covering the platform were four large chunks of wall. The wall was constructed of limestone and obdurate sandstone slabs laid on top of each other and cemented together with a coarse mortar. Several of the wall sections were more or less complete. One appeared to be a frontal section. All of the wall segments had been covered with very fine stucco that had been painted with murals on the outside surface. Several wall sections showed, in cross-section, nine very fine layers of white stucco, some barely thicker than a coat of paint, that had been decorated with mural paintings. The tops of the walls were also plastered and had been beveled. Murals were painted on raised panels outlined on the upper half of the walls. One section of wall had in it a 6 cm hole with a molded inset shaped like a "Maltese" cross on the outer surface. This was the only example preserved. It may have formed a curtain rod hole or, perhaps, a hole for making astronomical sightings.

The walls ranged in height from 1.26 m to 1.36 m and in length from 1.38 m to 1.5 m. These measurements, and the combination of shapes, corners, and finished ends, allowed a tentative reconstruction of the building's shape. The walls seem short but sat on slightly raised foundations, approximately 40 cm above the surface of the platform. This would have given

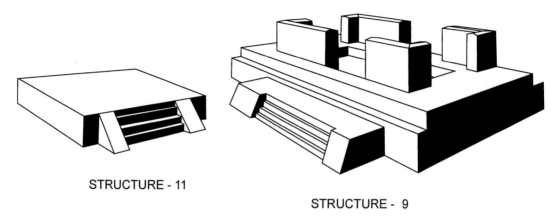

STRUCTURE - 11

STRUCTURE - 9

Figure 10.7.   Reconstruction drawing of Structures 9 and 11 .

the walls an inside height of 1.75 m. Since the wall sections are relatively complete, or have enough finished ends to suggest the building's layout, there are only a few locations where they could have gone. In all cases, it appears that there were openings or doorways on all four sides. They may have been closed in some cases with curtains, and the hole with the Maltese cross may have served this function. The footings for the walls are only preserved along the front, one side, and the back. The front and side footings are molded with plaster to retain the freestanding walls and are only wide enough for the walls. The back footing is almost a meter wide and could have doubled as a back bench. If there was a back bench this makes it difficult to explain a doorway in the back wall, but no section of wall is long enough or broken at the end to suggest that there could have been a wall along the backside of the structure. Two of the wall sections had the same exterior plaster molding panels for murals, and both were recessed to receive a lintel. Neither of the other two sections had these features and, therefore, functioned as side and/or back walls. The portrayal of this structure in Figure 10.7 shows what it would have looked like if there were indeed openings in the walls along the sides and back. The possibility still remains that one or two of these walls were closed along their entire length.

The mural paintings were unfortunately so poorly preserved that it was not possible in most cases to distinguish individual designs. Although one wall end was covered with lichens, a large section of painting was visible (Figure 10.8). It was a standing figure, represented in profile, walking to the left, wearing sandals and a skirt. The figure's torso and head are eroded or covered by lichens and are not visible, but there is some indication of an elaborate "headdress." The figure, which stands about 25 cm high, is painted in red, yellow, and green, and is outlined with fine black lines. The background is blue and yellow. Figure 10.8 presents the remains of the figure as well as a hypothetical sketch (broken line) of its forward leg, torso, and head. The head location is based on the identification of the figure's eye, painted in black, in a style similar to those used in the Santa Rita murals (Gann 1900; Quirarte 1982:fig.26), and the Madrid Codex (Villacorta and Villacorta 1933:280[Madrid 26a]). It is much like a figure depicted on a mural in the Cawek palace at Utatlán (Carmack 1981:297, fig.9.12), and like figures from the room walls of Temple 2 at Iximché (Guillemin 1967:30; Marqusee 1980).

Two to three dozen small fragments of plaster, some with very elaborate but indiscernible designs, were also recovered. They can do little more than give a tantalizing glimpse of how impressive this building must have looked before it was destroyed.

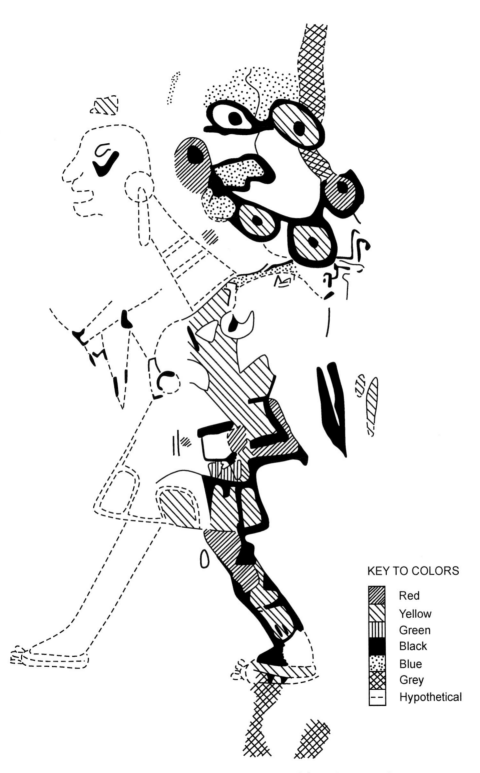

KEY TO COLORS

▨	Red
▨	Yellow
▥	Green
■	Black
⸭	Blue
▩	Grey
--	Hypothetical

Figure 10.8. Tracing of the remnants of a Polychrome mural from Structure 9.

The multiple layers of plaster on the walls may be related to the replastering and repainting ritual described by Carmack (1981:295) for the Quiché. Although he was describing a palace and not a temple, such as Structure 9, the process of replastering and repainting is very important:

> The documents inform us that the palace walls were elaborately adorned with painted frescoes. The paintings are said to have portrayed important events in the lives of past lords. When a lord died, new frescoes were painted over the old ones to honor him.

Guillemin (1967:34) has discussed this matter with reference to Iximché and Carmack (1981:195), citing Tovilla (1965), has written:

> ... when a lord of Utatlán died "they did not knock down his house, but rewhitened all of it, and ingeniously painted some history of his past exploits. When the king died, they rewhitened all the streets and the palaces inside and out, and painted new histories."

If the same reasons prompted the replastering and repainting of the civic-ceremonial structures at Canajasté, then Structure 9 may provide some clues about the length of occupation of the center, or at least the number of successive rulers that may have existed. There appear to have been three major replasterings of the plaza—at least as it was in its final form. Structure 9 was repainted at least nine times. It is impossible to assign an exact time span to a given reign, but if reigns averaged out to 20 years per ruler (one generation), and the temple was repainted upon the death of each new ruler (and only new rulers, not minor functionaries), then the temple may have served for 180 to 200 years (Blake 1984b:13). This would put its original construction at sometime around AD 1300 to 1350, shortly after the beginning of the Late Postclassic period—if the building was used up to the time of the Spanish Conquest. If it was abandoned prior to the Conquest, then it could have been built earlier. In a following section I will explore the implications of this estimated construction date.

There were no caches or other features discovered in the fill of Structure 9; however, near the top of the staircase, between the top tread and the threshold, was a thick deposit of black, ashy soil. The entire contents of the area, which was partly disturbed, were screened and subjected to water flotation. A large number of charred corn kernels were recovered. Also found were three completely unworked obsidian blades that may have been bloodletters. These finds suggest that offerings were made in the temple, and some of the remaining debris found its way into the fill at the top of the stairs. No other domestic artifacts were found on the structure's floor, therefore, it is unlikely that the charred plant remains and obsidian blades were left behind from a post-abandonment reoccupation of the temple.

Structures 10 and 13

These two small structures (10 and 13) were probably altars in the main plaza. Both were excavated as part of the salvage operation associated with Structure 9 because they had been looted. They were both built on top of three layers of plaster flooring and must have been recent additions to the ceremonial center. Although the larger of the two was badly damaged, it appears that it was directly appended onto the smaller altar. There were, at most, two courses high of limestone slabs and were constructed by laying the stones end to end (Figure 10.9). The interiors of the altars were filled with earth. No associated offerings were found. They are almost identical to altars reported by Guillemin at Iximché and Utatlán (1959:34, Altar no. 33). The larger of the two altars was 2.5 m by 1.5 m and the smaller one was 1.6 m by 1.4 m.

Summary of Civic-ceremonial Center

The civic-ceremonial center at Canajasté is remarkable within the study region because it is one of the only ones known that was not built upon earlier structures. The evidence from the looters' pits strongly suggests that there

Figure 10.9.   Structure 10, altar showing looters' pit in its center (facing N).

were no earlier stages of construction below the surface of the platforms—not even Postclassic ones. The cohesive layout of the buildings, their restriction to the Late Postclassic period, and their homogeneous style of construction (except for long, low platform Structure 7) suggest contemporaneity. They were built as one large monument dominating the center of the site. In their prime, and freshly painted, they would have been visible from every location in the valley and a good many kilometers beyond. But one would have to have actually been inside the main plaza to see the façades of any of the buildings, not to mention the people charged with their ongoing use in political and religious activity.

The relative stability of the structures themselves, and their lack of evidence for progressive modification, suggests a constant relationship between the elite and their subordinates. If the buildings were each controlled by a different lineage, or if each

was linked with a particular facet of the polity's organization (e.g., religious, military, or commercial), it seems clear that the balance among them was maintained in stable fashion from the center's inception. In spite of this stability, or perhaps even as a token of it, the buildings, exemplified by Structure 9, were constantly maintained throughout their history, including multiple replasterings and repaintings. As mentioned, the plaza was replastered at least three times. This indicates a considerable time depth for the ceremonial center and reveals a great deal about community-level socio-political dynamics.

The only structure with clear evidence of modification beyond superficial resurfacing is Structure 7. It was lengthened at both ends, adding 5.5 m to its original length. If this building was the leading lineage's "big house," then it is significant that it became "bigger." With little additional labor investment in either materials or construction the building would have been an impressive one to all but those who could actually compare it at close range with the other shorter structures in the ceremonial center. I should also point out that this is exactly the technique used by the members of the elite House Group 2 when they built on to house Structure 22. They sacrificed width and height for length: a strategy that gives the maximum visual impact with the least investment of materials or labor. That Structure 7 also went through this same process suggests that it stood for the extended lineage much as Structure 22 stood for the household. It also suggests that the political or functional social unit associated with Structure 7 was the only one expanding the basic physical symbol of its existence. Of course, only extensive excavations in the ceremonial center would permit a clear definition of the particular social units or political subsystems associated with each structure. Even so, it is likely that Structure 7 played a role in the direct political decision-making by housing council activities and storing the objects associated with political interactions, as Carmack (1981:290) has described for political interaction in the big houses at Utatlán.

The position of Structure 7 with respect to the other buildings is remarkably similar to that of the principal big houses at other sites in highland Guatemala. Likewise, the other civic-ceremonial structures have a layout and relationship with one another that is replicated at many highland sites. It is not possible to specify the symbolic meanings or associations of the structures, but there are distinct parallels with the Mam, Quiché, and Cakchiquel. First, the orientation of the buildings is consistently NW-SE, only a few degrees closer to north than Zaculeu and its satellite communities, Chirijox and Xetenam (Fox 1978). If Structure 9 played a similar role at Canajasté as the major east-facing temple at Utatlán then it could have been associated with Tojil or, more generally, the sun (Carmack 1981:206). Interestingly, Structure 9, like the Tojil temple at Utatlán, is the tallest, and the most elaborate. It is even more closely parallel to the layout of the main buildings at Zaculeu. Structures 5 and 6 at Canajasté could be counterparts of the two long, low platforms

flanking the main temple at Zaculeu (Woodbury and Trik 1953). In comparison with Zaculeu, what is missing from the civic-ceremonial center at Canajasté is the major west-facing temple associated with the flanking structures. Structure 6 may have served this purpose and simply had a perishable superstructure. In either case, this would make the social unit associated with the west-facing ceremonial component (according to Carmack [1981:206] the Awilix, moon, component at Utatlán) subordinate to the group associated with Structure 9. This parallels the relationship between the east-and west-facing temples at various sites in highland Guatemala, including Utatlán, Iximché, Cawinal (Ichon 1981:53), Pueblo Viejo Malacatancito (Fox 1978:133), Xetenam (Fox 1978:152), but not Zaculeu (Fox 1978:145; Woodbury and Trik 1953).

Another similarity is the location of the long low mound on the north or northeast side of the plaza. This is common at almost all of the major sites illustrated by Smith (1955) and Fox (1978) for the Quiché, Mam, and Cakchiquel areas. It also seems to be the case for the site of El Bosque and Chanquejelvé (La Farge and Byers 1931:207-211; Lovell 1980:72-73); both are within 20 km of Canajasté (near Nentón). Cu Manchón and Buena Vista (La Farge and Byers 1931:238; Lovell 1980:72-73), two Postclassic sites nearer to Zaculeu than Canajasté, also have similar layouts and orientations, but architectural details of temple platforms in these latter two sites make them much more similar to Zaculeu than to Canajasté. For example, the main temple platforms at Cu Manchón (Mound F) and Buena Vista (Mound C) both have stairways bisected with a balustrade (La Farge and Byers 1931:238, Fig. 74b). The temple platforms at Chanquejelvé and El Bosque, on the other hand, have stairways and overall shapes much more like the buildings at Canajasté.

At the interregional level, I cannot go much beyond these broad comparisons. None of the sites in western Guatemala between Zaculeu and the Mexican border have been investigated enough to provide the detailed information necessary for finer-scale comparisons. Even so, it is fairly clear that, in spite of the fact that Canajasté is only a small fraction of the size and complexity of the capitals in highland Guatemala, there are basic structural similarities in the layout, orientation, and, probably, the symbolic representation of its ceremonial center. Moving closer to Canajasté from Zaculeu, the site organizational similarities and architectural details of temple buildings between Canajasté and its neighbors increases. For this to have been possible there must have been broad underlying relations between the elite in the two regions.

Unfortunately, there are very few known and excavated Postclassic sites in Chiapas east of Chiapa de Corzo. This paucity of sites is, no doubt, significant. The conquistadors who conquered the region invariably spent their energies overthrowing the largest and most powerful of the native states. When they did not have to overthrow a group militarily, they usually mentioned their alliance with the polity instead. For example, in highland Chiapas, Díaz contrasted the difficult conquest of Chamula with the peaceful submission of Zinacantán (Díaz del Castillo 1912). No such centers of political or economic power drew the attentions of the early Spaniards to the upper Grijalva region of the Grijalva Depression. This suggests that the centers in this zone were either independent but relatively small and harmless, or were politically linked to larger distant centers in Chiapas or Guatemala and collapsed when the Spaniards conquered these centers (e.g., centers such as Utatlán and Zaculeu). In the latter case, they still would have been relatively small and not very powerful. Both possibilities (small independent states or small dependent satellite states) conform with the archaeological record.

ARCHITECTURAL STYLES WITHIN THE UPPER GRIJALVA REGION

During the Late Classic period (ca. AD 800-1000) in the upper Grijalva region there were literally hundreds of settlements. At least 100 of these were much larger and more complex than even the largest of the subsequent Postclassic sites, such as Canajasté. Some of these Classic centers such as Tenam Rosario

(Tr-9), Ojo de Agua (Tr-152), and Lagartero (Tr-99) dwarf Canajasté and were as large as some of the major Postclassic centers in highland Guatemala. This makes it difficult to discern Postclassic reoccupations of many of the Classic sites and, without extensive horizontal and stratigraphic excavation, it would be impossible to pick out the small Postclassic component at a large Classic site. The only sites with mainly Postclassic structures are El Limón (Tr-13), Canajasté (Tr-69), Tr-75, Dolores Puente (Tr-161), Aguazarca (Tr-227), and La Mesa-RV140 (Tr-376). The others are reoccupations of earlier sites. Only one of this latter group, Los Encuentros (Tr-94), had a major Postclassic rebuilding and restructuring of the ceremonial center (in this case, probably because the Classic period occupation was relatively small) (Lee and Bryant 1977).

El Limón, Tr-13

This site is composed of two sections located on separate low hills, approximately 100 m from each other. The larger of the two sections is very similar in layout to Canajasté. The ceremonial center has been badly disturbed by looters, and locals have used it as a stone quarry—stripping the façades of most of the major structures. Even so, the map of the site shows several characteristics in common with Canajasté as well as many differences (Figure 10.10). First, the rectangular-shaped plaza is bounded on the northeast side by a long low mound (Mound B) that may have been a "big house." It is 50 m long, approximately 8 m wide, and 1 m high. Its height and the rounded mound of rubble on the top indicate that it may have had substantial wattle-and-daub or even stone walls, in contrast to the perishable walls for Structure 7 at Canajasté. The length also indicates that the social group responsible for it held a prominent place in the community's social hierarchy.

Mound A sits along the northwest side of the plaza and, like B, is a long low mound. No such structure existed at Canajasté. Its presence at El Limón may indicate a second major lineage. Mounds C and D form the southwest side of the plaza (along with Mound I, which

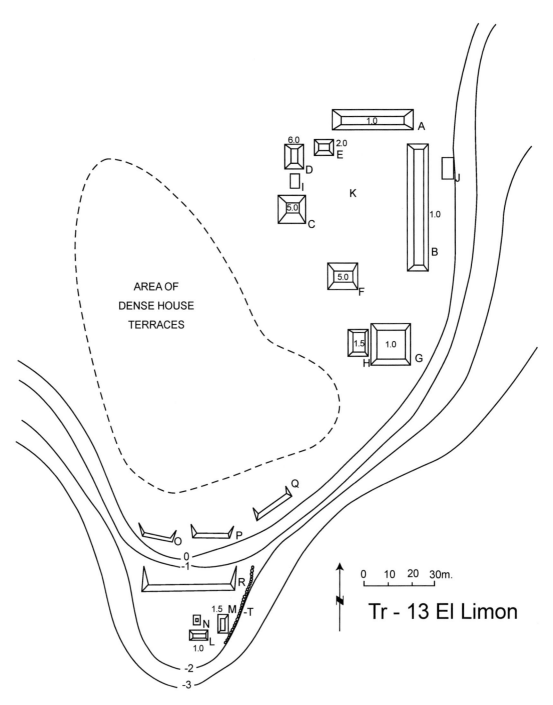

Figure 10.10.   Map of El Limón (Tr-13).

may have been an altar). They are 5 m and 6 m high respectively. They were too heavily covered with debris and rubble to determine the presence or location of stairways. Judging from their location, they most likely faced Mound B, located across the plaza. If so, they were the equivalents of Structures 11 and 12 at Canajasté. Their height, though, means that they were built on earlier structures—a very different situation from that of Canajasté. Mound E, which probably faced southeast, as did Structure 9 at Canajasté, is small by comparison to the other structures at the site. This means that there was a reversal of the importance of Mounds C and D as opposed to E at El Limón compared with Structures 11 and 12 as opposed to 9 at Canajasté

Another key difference is the presence of the 5 m tall, Mound F on the southeast side of the plaza. Its only equivalent at Canajasté would be Structure 5, which was a long low mound. One additional aspect must be mentioned. Surface collections from one of the tall mounds (exact location unknown) recovered a few small pieces of fine stucco painted in red, yellow, and blue, much the same as fragments from Structure 9 at Canajasté. This suggests the presence of elaborate walled temples, even though they were not visible on the surface.

The similarities between the two sites in terms of overall size and complexity are remarkable. El Limón is slightly larger: its buildings longer and taller. In spite of this, there are important structural differences in the layout and positioning of the buildings, indicating that the elites at each site had different ideological/ symbolical emphases. The use of taller buildings at El Limón is similar to the Late Classic pattern in the upper Grijalva region and also is common at a many Postclassic sites in the adjacent zone in Guatemala already mentioned.

Tr-75

This is a minor civic-ceremonial center and habitation area located on a hilltop overlooking a swampy arm of the Lagartero River. Figure 10.11 shows its small size. The layout of the main structures (Mounds A to G) is not at all

in keeping with the Late Postclassic pattern. This leads me to suspect that there is only a small Postclassic habitation zone surrounding buildings that are principally Late Classic. If so, this site would be a small satellite of one of the centers close to it, either Lagartero (Tr-99) or Los Encuentros (Tr-94). In this case, the territory of one or the other of these sites would have been somewhat larger than I have specified in Table 10.2.

Dolores Puente, Tr-161

This site is interesting in its degree of differentiation from the other Postclassic ceremonial centers (Figure 10.12). It has a large open plaza area (N) bounded on the west side by long low Mound A. Although the south and east sides have several mounds, they are relatively open, and the north side has no structures. Mound A is 100 m long, 9 m wide, and 1.5 m high. Its extreme length makes it the longest structure in the study area. If it was a big house, as argued for similar structures at other sites, then a single lineage or group of lineages clearly dominated this site. It would correspond to Mound A at El Limón but has no real counterpart at Canajasté. Facing it (although there are no stairs, so I cannot be certain) across the plaza is Mound E, a 2 m high mound. Its location, shape, and size correspond to Structure 6 at Canajasté and Mound F or G at El Limón.

The overall layout of this site suggests that it represents an individual social segment that is only one of a number of such segments at larger sites. The emphasis on a southeast-facing big house and the lack of small temples clearly distinguishes it from Canajasté. On the other hand, it replicates half the pattern of El Limón. I think this might give a clue to the religious and/ or political functions of some of the Postclassic centers (J. Marcus 1983b). Some sites have both religious functions (temples) and political functions (big houses). Others, such as Dolores Puente, emphasized political functions at the expense of religious functions.

Although it is difficult to be certain without excavations, this site may have also served a prominent role in the economic exchange

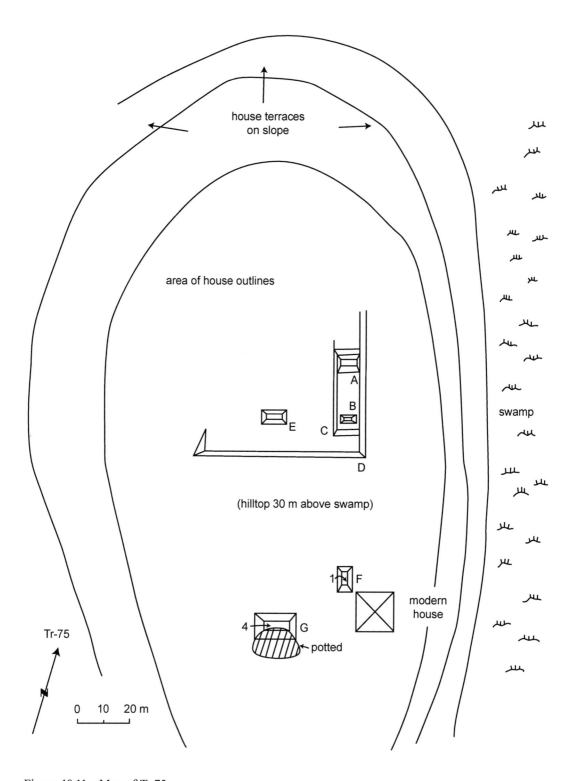

Figure 10.11.   Map of Tr-75.

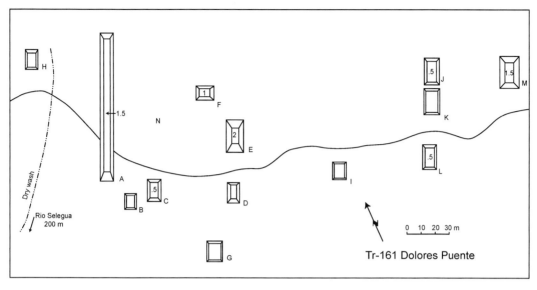

Figure 10.12.   Map of Dolores Puente, (Tr-161).

network, since it is located at the junction of two rivers that were important for canoe trade in the Early Colonial period (Lee 1980a). Just downriver from Dolores Puente is the Colonial site of Aquespala (Co-15) (Figure 5.3) which was known to be a center of canoe traffic and canoe production during the sixteenth and seventeenth centuries (Lee 1980b:21-22; Ximénez 1929-31, II:29). Since Dolores Puente (Tr-161) is on the Camino Real (which extends from Esquintenango [Co-64] up the San Gregorio River, Figure 5.3), and it is the only major Postclassic site known for this zone, it could well have come to serve both economic and political functions.

The site's relatively open, undefended location and its open layout may have been preferred if it served a periodic market function. If so, defense would have been secondary—especially if the elite at the site gave tribute to more important political and religious elites at another site in the region. As Marcus (1983b:210) has pointed out, Mesoamerican regal-ritual cities, where the administrative and religious roles dominate the commercial roles, are "the ones most frequently defended by walls and/or moats." Dolores Puente is one of the least defended of the sites in the region and the one in the most favorable location for commercial

activity. It also has the largest probable "secular" building of all the sites, while at the same time lacking correspondingly large religious structures. I suspect that it was closely linked, if not subservient, to Lagartero (Tr-99)—located only 5 km away. If so, Lagartero's territory (adding in that of Tr-75 and Tr-161) would have been 150 km^2, or roughly on par with the other centers in the region.

Los Encuentros, Tr-94

Los Encuentros was excavated by Lee and Bryant (1977), and their analysis is still in progress. Nevertheless, from my own visits to the site, as well as conversations with Lee, I think there are two major differences between it and other sites in the region. First, it was built upon a Classic period site and seems to have incorporated many earlier temple mounds into its own plan. Several of these mounds are more massive than Postclassic mounds within the study region (Figure 10.13). Second, it has an arrangement of three temples or pyramids side by side along one edge of the plaza (M4, M5, and M6). This is unlike any of the sites in the eastern zone of the region; however, Postclassic sites in the Eastern Mam region and Western Quiché region do have this three

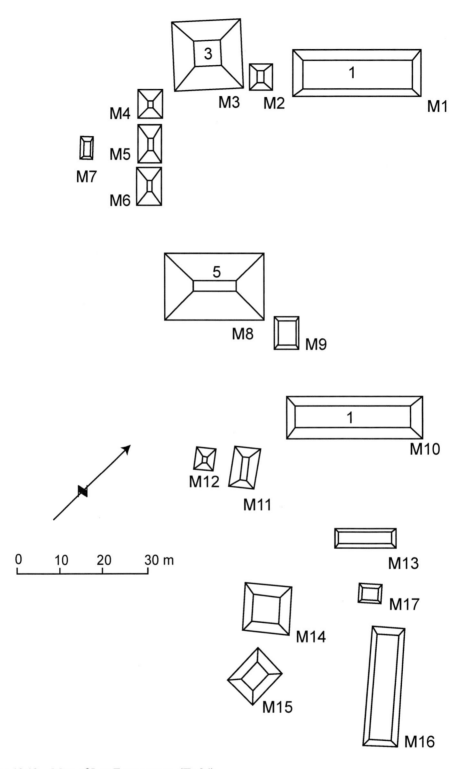

Figure 10.13.   Map of Los Encuentros, (Tr-94).

pyramid configuration. Examples include Pueblo Viejo Malacatancito (Fox 1978:131, Fig.23), Chutinamit-Sacapulas (Fox 1978:77, Fig.12), and Xetenam (Fox 1978:150, Fig.26).

Many of the mounds are quite tall, similar to mounds at El Limón and unlike the low mounds at Canajasté. This may be due to the presence of earlier stages of construction under the Postclassic pyramids. One of the strongest similarities between Los Encuentros and Canajasté is a long low mound (M1—possibly a big house) along the northeast side of the main plaza. It was plastered with a thick layer of white stucco on the sides and floor, but the superstructure must have been made mostly of perishable materials (Lee and Bryant 1977). There is another long low platform (M10) flanking the southeast edge of the plaza.

Unfortunately, there is not enough information about the remaining sites in the upper Grijalva region to understand their Postclassic civic-ceremonial components or to compare them with Canajasté. However, I will briefly mention each in turn.

Lagartero, Tr-99

This site, which was one of the largest Classic centers in the entire region, also accommodated a large Postclassic occupation. There was infrequent use of the main plaza for Early Postclassic burials (Ekholm 1977; Gurr 1979). There were no examples of the wide range of ceramic vessel types or other artifacts common in the Early Postclassic occupation levels at Canajasté (Bryant, Lee, and Blake 2005). Therefore, Lagartero may have been abandoned during the last half of that period. During the Late Postclassic, there was an extensive reoccupation of the site. Since only a small sample of the main pyramids and other structures has been excavated, I cannot determine how much Postclassic modification of the ceremonial center took place. There are no groups of civic-ceremonial buildings at the site that appear to have been built in the Late Postclassic style—known for the study region and in neighboring Guatemala. Prior to recent plowing of the site for agricultural purposes,

numerous low house platforms, almost identical to the many at Canajasté and Dolores Puente, were present (Ekholm, pers. comm.; Rivero Torres 1996, 1999).

Aguazarca, Tr-227

Aguazarca is a highly fortified site. Unfortunately, no map has yet been made of it, and there is only a brief description (Clark and Lowe 1980). It is located on a ridge overlooking a small karstic valley. The site's civic-ceremonial mounds sit on top of the narrow ridge protected by large stone walls that cut off access to the ridge at either end. There is not enough room on the ridge top for many large structures, and it appears there were only three or four. As there is little in the way of house-mound remains on the ridge, people in the surrounding valley may have used the site as a location of religious ceremonies and as a redoubt in times of conflict.

La Mesa, Tr-376 (Rv140)

La Mesa was discovered in 1983 by De Montmollin (1989b) during his Rosario Valley survey. The civic-ceremonial complex sits at the top of Cerro La Mesa and is surrounded by dispersed dwellings covering approximately 10 ha on the site's gentle slopes. De Montmollin (1989b:191-192) records that the main part of La Mesa consists of 55 house groups with 81 dwelling platforms, many of which occur on broad terraces that descend along the northern, western, and southern slopes of the site. The civic-ceremonial plaza covers only 0.36 ha and consists of five public buildings (labeled I-V in Figure 10.14) and four smaller residential platforms (buildings 30-32, and 55). De Montmollin's map of the main plaza shows that the public buildings are oriented approximately 45° from north, similar to Tr-94, Tr-161, and Canajasté, while the residential structures are more haphazardly aligned.

The main structures surrounding the plaza are long, low "range" structures similar to those at other Postclassic sites in the region. La Mesa's Structure II (16 by 6 m) corresponds to

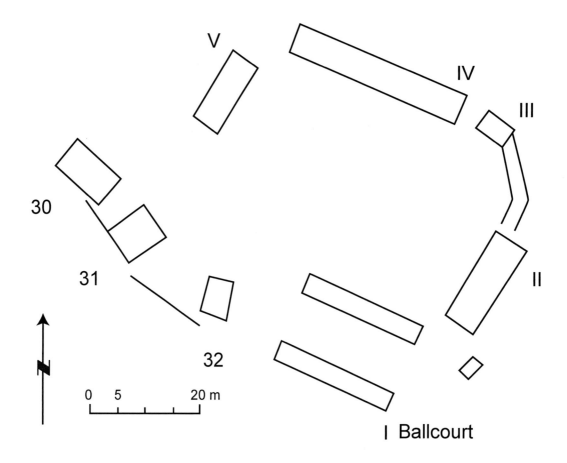

V

IV

III

30

31

II

32

I Ballcourt

Figure 10.14.   Map of La Mesa, Rv140 (Tr-376) (redrawn after De Montmollin 1995: Fig. 191).

Structure 6 at Canajasté, and Structure III (32 by 5 m) corresponds to Canajasté's Structure 7. La Mesa lacks several of the small temple buildings that are found at Canajasté, but it does have two other structures that are not found at any of the other Postclassic sites in the study region. One is a low arcing platform connecting Structures II and III and closing off that end of the patio (unless we consider the low platform, Structure 18 that appears to join Structures 5 and 6 at Canajasté). The other is a well-defined open-ended ballcourt (Structure I) with 22 m long parallel mounds separated by an 8 m wide alleyway. Although ballcourts are very common at earlier sites in the upper Grijalva region (De Montmollin 1995), this is the first one reported at a Postclassic period site.

Co-54

This site was a large Classic Period center, and there is no clear picture of the nature of Postclassic construction. Still, since there was a large amount of both Early and Late Postclassic ceramics (including Tohil Plumbate), it is possible that the site remained an important one within its region.

Guajilar, Co-59

Guajilar was one of the major Preclassic centers within the study region (Clark and Lee 1984; Lee 1976, 1978a). On top of one of the large Preclassic mounds was a Postclassic building containing ceramic types common at Canajasté (e.g., Plumbate) during the Early Postclassic. There were also a number of Late Postclassic "water jar" (cantaro) cremation burials in some of the mounds (see Figure 8.2a) (Bryant 2005). It is not certain how many Postclassic civic-ceremonial structures or domestic residences were present. There was, however, enough Postclassic ceramic debris on the surface of the site to suggest a considerable residential population, and the one building on top of the earlier mound indicates a definite civic-ceremonial focus.

Summary

Moving from east to west, there appears to be a decrease in the formal similarity of the sites to those in neighboring Guatemala. There is also a decrease in the defensibility of sites. All of the centers along the present day Mexico-Guatemala border are located on very well-protected topographic features and make use of natural features to that end. Several employ additional features such as stone walls and terraces to cut off access to the ceremonial centers.

There is also a distinct difference between northern and southern sites. La Mesa (Tr-376) and El Limón (Tr-13) are built in new locations, like Canajasté (Tr-69) and Aguazarca (Tr-227), and are all on low hills, ridges, or mesas. Sites in the southern part of the region are located in the open or on river margins. Residents in this zone appear to have given much less thought to defense when establishing their sites. Instead, they seem to be associated with earlier Classic or Preclassic sites, and they incorporate the earlier architecture into their layout. At the only eastern zone site (Lagartero, Tr-99) to be built on a Classic center, there is no indication yet of Postclassic reuse or incorporation of earlier buildings.

There is little information concerning the layouts of the civic-ceremonial centers for most of the sites in the study region; however, that which is available does suggest a good deal of similarity between the following sites: Canajasté, La Mesa, El Limón, and Dolores Puente. There was also some indication that

the residential architecture of Lagartero was similar to that at Canajasté. Tr-75 has very little civic-ceremonial architecture and was probably a satellite of Lagartero. All of the other sites (except La Mesa) are built on earlier Classic or Preclassic sites and/or have a different layout for their Postclassic civic-ceremonial architecture.

On the basis of this pattern I hypothesize a political boundary between the northern and eastern zone sites of El Limón, La Mesa, Aguazarca, Canajasté, Lagartero, and Dolores Puente and between the southwestern zone sites of Los Encuentros, Guajilar, and Co-54. In the section on obsidian analysis (Chapter 7) I have already mentioned there was a difference between these zones in the proportion of Central Mexican obsidian used. Southwestern zone sites had nearly twice the amount of central Mexican obsidian as did the north and eastern zone sites that had predominantly Guatemalan obsidian. La Mesa differed from sites in both zones in that it had more than 50 percent central Mexican obsidian—five times more than that from the southwestern zone sites. The other pattern, and one which is still tentative, is the distribution of ceramics. Sites in the southwestern zone did not share the same dull paint style bowl types (Tol Polychrome) that were most common in the eastern zone sites. Some did, however, have the Tol Polychrome water jars. These were used in quite different contexts, though; in the north and eastern zone they were used as cremation jars that were placed in caves. In the western zone they were used as cremation jars buried in earlier mounds (Bryant, Lee, and Blake 2005). Not enough is yet known about the other aspects of material culture in these sites to make more detailed comparisons.

The differences that are observable in settlement location and civic-ceremonial plan do, however, point towards the interpretation of the northern and eastern zone sites as intrusions from Guatemala. They do not appear to be the eastern extension of a local, upper Grijalva region tradition. Southwestern zone sites, although they did have trade links with Guatemala, also appear to have had stronger links to the west, down the Grijalva River. As a preliminary hypothesis, the settlement pattern

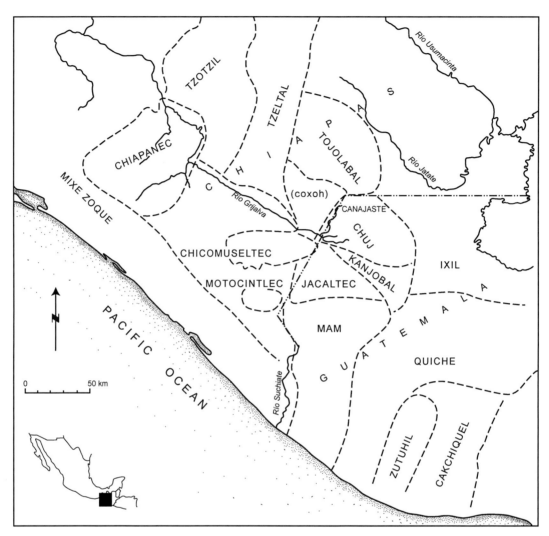

Figure 10.15. Distribution of major language groupings in southeastern Mesoamerica.

distribution and civic-ceremonial layout suggest that the northern and eastern zone was colonized by a stronger state to the east and that there was a definite political and economic boundary between the two zones.

TERRITORIAL ORGANIZATION OF SMALL SECONDARY STATES

The preceding analysis is more subjective than I would have wished, due to the incomplete nature of the settlement pattern data.[5] Nevertheless, here I attempt to synthesize various lines of evidence in determining the political implications of the observable differences in settlement patterns and civic-ceremonial architecture. A useful starting point is with the known, Early Colonial distribution of Maya languages within the region. The border zone of the upper Grijalva region lies within 80 km of at least eight Maya languages. Some questions that can be profitably asked are: (1) why are so many languages found within such a small area? (2) how might these languages relate to the Postclassic territorial organization of the region? and (3) what processes of secondary state development would lead to this situation?

Figure 10.15 shows the distribution of Maya languages in the upper Grijalva region and is based on the work of Campbell (1988) and Miles (1965). In the following discussion, I assume that a distribution of a given language represents a group of communities that interact more with each other than with communities of neighboring zones. By interaction I specifically mean political cooperation. Communities in a region with the same language are more likely to be historically related to each other, to engage in more exchange, and to be linked in the same political organization than they are with communities of different languages.

Five language regions converge on the upper tributaries area of the Grijalva River near the present international border: Chuj, Kanjobal, Jacaltec, Chicomuceltec, and Tzeltal-Coxoh. Each of these languages extends from the lowest elevation at river level (750 m) up into the highlands of the Sierra Madre, the Cuchumatanes, or the Chiapas Highlands (ranging between 1500 and 3000 m in elevation). In other words, each language group extends across the maximum range of altitudinal variation, cross-cutting all environmental zones: *tierra fría,* cold country; *tierra templada*, temperate country; and *tierra caliente*, hot country. Almost all of the other highland Maya language groups— including the Ixil, Tojolabal, Quiché, Mam, Zutuhil, Cakchiquel, Motocintlec, Tzeltal, and Tzotzil, also cross-cut the full range of environmental zones. Since, at the time of the Conquest, each language was not directly equated with a polity, it is not possible to say that this was a conscious policy of the state to attain lands in all environmental zones. Certainly, however, there would be a great deal of advantage in doing so. For one thing, a polity with reliable allies located in neighboring (and different) environmental zones, especially other polities sharing the same language and cultural heritage, would be more readily assured of access to resources in those zones than if they were occupied by polities with a different language and cultural heritage.

This is important, especially with respect to agricultural land. Collier (1975:125-126) reports that highland Zinacantecos in the 1960s derived approximately 80 percent of their maize harvest from the lowlands of the Grijalva Basin. Hot country farming is more productive because the lands are more fertile than the cold country highlands and the growing season longer (Cancian 1965:64). Communities that have access to coastal hot country or to irrigated lowlands can raise two and sometimes three crops per year. Irrigated coastal zones can be planted year-round (McBryde 1947:22). McBryde (1947:23) gives 1300 m elevation as the upper limit of double harvesting for western Guatemala. This would also depend upon the amount of rain: if a given area was too dry then the corn may take too long to grow in time for the second planting. Farmers using both zones have the greatest margin of safety in case either the highland or lowland harvest turns out poorly. This same situation exists for all communities in Chiapas and western Guatemala who have access to both highlands and lowlands.

Beyond these productive differences in maize agriculture there were also other lowland-highland differences that would have encouraged commerce between the regions. The lowlands also produce beans, squash, cotton, tropical fruits, maguey, tomatoes, and chilies in greater abundance than the highlands.

In western Guatemala the Chuj, Kanjobal, and Jacaltec were hemmed in by the Ixil, Quiché, and Mam and, therefore, their only access to hot country was in the upper Grijalva region of the Grijalva Basin. These last three groups had access to the lowland jungle (in the case of the Ixil) and to the Pacific coastal piedmont (in the cases of the Quiché and Mam). The distribution of Chuj, Kanjobal, and Jacaltec speaking groups in the far western highlands of Guatemala, all competing for the relatively little amount of low country land in the upper Grijalva region with the Tzeltal-Coxoh, Chicomuceltec, and, possibly, Tojolabal may have led to a condition of perennial conflict. This conflict could have been related to the initial attempts of each group to obtain a foothold in the lowlands. Conflict would subsequently be maintained by their attempts to protect lowland resources from incursions by other highland-based groups.

This hypothesis would mean that communities located in the upper Grijalva region would have been located near the center of the political, ethnic, and linguistic "pie." Communities close to one another, such as Canajasté and Los Encuentros, could well have been on opposite sides of a political boundary, each representing the limits of their group's penetration into hot country. The Grijalva River itself may have marked a boundary between the Chicomuceltec to the south and the Tzeltal-Coxoh to the north. If this were the case, the southern zone sites (Co-54 and Guajilar) may have been Chicomuceltec (or even Jacaltec) and the northern zone sites (Los Encuentros, La Mesa, and possibly El Limón) may have been Tzeltal-Coxoh.

Sites in each of these different zones may have been linked through elite exchanges, tribute payments, military obligations, and political subordination to other centers in the highlands but not to each other. The lack of large Postclassic sites in the upper Grijalva region, coupled with their obvious affiliation and relations with more distant regions, suggests that the zone was a hinterland divided among outsiders.

DISCUSSION

It should now be possible to provide tentative answers to the questions raised at the beginning of this chapter. First, how did Canajasté fit into its regional-political setting? And second, did Canajasté's position within a regional settlement hierarchy or its layout and internal organization, provide any clues to the importance and sequence of processes affecting its evolution?

The analysis of the territorial organization, although preliminary, indicated that Canajasté was one of a number of equal polities within the upper Grijalva region. It appears to have dominated its small territory (ca. 125 km²) and to have had many smaller hamlets and scattered houses included within its political sphere. Although population estimates cannot be accurately made for the territory, Canajasté's

region of control probably included no more than 2,000 to 4,000 people.

These people appear to have been part of a cultural and political tradition with roots in the neighboring Cuchumatanes region of Guatemala. Canajasté was established in a defensible location upon the arrival of its first colonists, sometime during the 12th century. Settlement location, artifacts, and architectural styles all suggest that the community was colonized by foreigners and not by descendents of the Terminal Classic peoples that once occupied the area. The colony may have started as a bud-off of successful Chuj communities to the east who were attempting to improve their access to hot country resources. The initial mechanism of movement into this region may have been to improve and expand interregional trade. Even so, warfare must have been a consideration early on since the site was originally built with an eye to defense.

The results of analyses in previous chapters suggested that the role of warfare continued to increase, while exchange declined through the Late Postclassic period. Perhaps the local elite at Canajasté found that their need for belligerence to protect their claim to their hot country territory served to maintain political control over the region. Warfare also may have resulted in a revolt against claims to tribute from, or subordination to, their mother-community in Guatemala. Canajasté continued to grow in size during the Late Postclassic period, increasing the role of warfare and decreasing the importation of exotics from outside the region. It is not yet known whether other communities in the Chuj region also went through similar processes of change. If trade declined throughout the Chuj region because of external factors (Quiché expansionism, for example), the elite at Canajasté may have been forced to resort to military interaction to maintain their control of the political system.

Political organization at Canajasté seems to have been a fairly stable adaptation since there is not much evidence for an expansion of the ceremonial center beyond its initial layout. Furthermore, its buildings were not substantially modified. No one polity in the upper Grijalva region, and certainly not Canajasté, was able to expand at the expense of the others or to exert control over the whole area. One possible explanation for this is that they were constantly under the thumb of more powerful highland states that were merely interested in maintaining a foothold in the lowlands. This would have helped them, in turn, to avoid being absorbed by larger, more expansionistic groups such as the Mam and Quiché.

ENDNOTES

1   This analysis includes only the data collected up to 1985.

2   The survey ceramics were originally typed prior to the complete ceramic report (Bryant et al. 2005). However, the Postclassic period ceramics types presented in that report are based largely on collections from Canajasté and Los Encuentros, so we can be reasonably certain that most, if not all of the Postclassic period occupations were correctly identified.

3   Just as this volume was going to press I was informed of an archaeological reconnaissance that had been carried out in 1999 by the NWAF (Clark et al. 2001). The unpublished report, on file with the NWAF, presents the results of a survey of the Huehuetenango region of Guatemala, extending from Huehuetenango westwards and northwards towards the Chiapas border and including many of the Upper Grijalva River tributaries flowing down from the Cuchumatan Mountains. The authors report many sites with evidence of Postclassic ceramics, and in some cases Postclassic architecture, overlying earlier buildings. There are only a few Postclassic period sites reported within 20 km of Canajasté and most of these seem to have been predominately Preclassic or Classic period occupations. There are a few exceptions, such as the site of Yachichin, 19 km from Canajasté, which has both Late Postclassic architecture and nearby mortuary caves.

4   Thomas Lee graciously agreed to conduct the two week operation of salvaging and consolidating Structure 9. The results reported here are from my preliminary investigations of the structure and T. Lee's field notes and drawings, as well as discussions in the field.

5   De Montmollin's intensive and detailed survey work in the late 1980s and early 1990s has shown that the paucity of Postclassic sites is real—more survey, mapping, and artifact collection is unlikely to yield any additional significant Postclassic settlements (De Montmollin 1995:50).

CHAPTER 11

SUMMARY AND CONCLUSIONS

The many lines of information dealt with in this study can be woven together into a coherent prehistory of the foundation and evolution of Canajasté. Four specific political processes were set out at the beginning of this study: exchange, warfare, elite colonization, and complete colonization. These were chosen because they result directly in, and from, internal and external political interaction. They were considered to be distinct, but they are interrelated and can occur either simultaneously or sequentially. My task here is to summarize the evidence presented thus far, and determine what it indicates about the operation and relative importance of each of the four specific interregional processes.

It is certainly not possible to say that one or another of these processes of interregional interaction was always the most important in shaping the developing political organization at Canajasté. Nor is it my goal to go beyond the site and claim that one or another of these processes is always most important in state development in general. Nonetheless, I think these specific processes are clearly interrelated and that there should always be some evidence of their interplay in the history of secondary states, wherever they may be located.

The present study is simply an attempt to unravel the interrelationships among these four specific processes in the prehistory of a particular state. By following the methodology used here, I have been able to study approximately four centuries of Canajasté's prehistory, even though it lacks extant historical records. Admittedly, this archaeological study is not as fine-grained as most historical studies of states; however, it is an attempt at documenting, archaeologically, the detailed evidence of political, social, and economic *changes* during the course of a state's history. The reason for doing this is to study the processes of change at the points where the changes actually occur, rather than looking only at the "before" and "after" reconstructions of a system and then trying to piece together how and why it changed.

INTEGRATING THE PROCESSES

Excavations revealed that the site of Canajasté was founded during the Early Postclassic period in a location that was previously unoccupied. Reconnaissance of the Lagartero Valley, in which the site is located, has yet to reveal any other Early Postclassic occupations; however, there was a substantial Late Classic occupation. Guatemalans, living just across the border, told me of a large, Late Classic site only three kilometers from Canajasté. It sits atop a hill that rises 100 m above the surrounding valley. Of course, inspection is necessary to determine whether this site also had a Postclassic occupation. [1] Assuming that it did not, and assuming that the settlement pattern in the first 30 km within the Guatemalan border is similar to that in Mexico, the founders of Canajasté probably came from some distance away and do not merely represent a reorganization of an earlier population.

If so, the initial founding of the community represented a colonization of a previously unoccupied or a sparsely occupied zone. The exact mechanisms whereby colonization took place are unknown, but I can suggest several plausible alternatives.

In many small secondary states, and certainly among the Postclassic Maya states, it was common for rulers to send out their sons and brothers to conquer and administer new territories and to set up tributary provinces. This is the process of elite colonization (cf. Beattie 1960; Lloyd 1965; and Mair 1962, 1977 for studies of this process in African secondary states). Oral history preserved in the Quiché *Titulo C'oyoi* (Carmack 1973:298) relates that one of the most powerful Quiché Lords, Q'uik'ab, ordered the "younger brothers and sons of the lords, the beloved older and younger brothers":

> You must return, you valiant warriors, you conquerors of the fortified centers, you treaders of the lands; go and be inhabitants of the lands, at the fortified centers of the subject peoples, so that they do not arrive there again ... conquer, you warriors, lancers; likewise go back and forth continually, make many land boundaries for us at each milpa in the canyons of the fortified center, it was said to them; 'Good,' they said to the lord; 'Go with your sons, you, our valiant warriors, our watchmen, be fighters of the subject peoples of the fortified center; with bow and arrow and shield, go and trample them, grab them by the armpits and sacrifice them,' it was said to them, our grandfathers and fathers, and our sons; then indeed we left the Q'uiche mountains and plains and arrived here in the mountains of Xelaju [Quezaltenango].

This was Q'uik'ab's strategy to get potentially powerful and rival military captains to go and take over Quezaltenango, which had previously belonged to their Mam enemies (Carmack 1973:332, note 147). Eventually, during Q'uik'ab's rule, they conquered the Mam capital of Zaculeu and extended the Quiché empire to its maximum size. Still, this strategy was not entirely successful, for the ruler's own "vassal warriors and his sons" eventually led a revolt against him in which they succeeded in increasing their power at the expense of the traditional noble lineages (Carmack 1981:136-137). The stronger, noble warrior class eventually came into conflict with the Cakchiquel lineages at Utatlán and forced them to leave and resettle in their new capital at Iximché (Carmack 1981:137). This is an example of the second kind of colonization: a new community is founded by elites and their commoners in a previously unoccupied location.

In the first case, the relationship between the new colony and its homeland is one of positive interaction, at least until the colony desires or is able to exert some independence. Both the distance of the colony from its homeland and the strength of the homeland would determine its ability to remain dominant and to rely on its colony for protection and resources. In the second case, the colony becomes a distinct political unit because it secedes from the homeland. Relations with the homeland would be expected to be belligerent, especially if conditions leading to the original secession remained operative. If one later conquered the other through warfare, I would expect to see a new set of administrative elite installed who would be able to carry out the policies of the state.

As mentioned earlier it is unknown where the founding Canajasteños came from, but it is most likely, based on their material culture styles (especially architecture and ceramics), that they came from the western Guatemala Highlands. As little is known about the local traditions in Chiapas and, in fact, there is little evidence of strong Early Postclassic polities, it is not yet possible to determine if the founders of Canajasté conquered and reorganized an existing local population and made them vassals. There are indications that distinct differences existed between the Early Postclassic elite and non-elite in their house styles. No other material differences that may have symbolized ethnic differences between the elite and commoners were found. The non-elite had essentially the same styles of ceramics as the elite. A major difference found was that, regardless of the type of artifact, the elite had more than the non-elite. The non-elite apparently were allowed to emulate some limited classes of material goods (excluding houses), but they did not have equal access to imported goods.

There is little relationship between the material culture of Canajasté and that known for Late to Terminal Classic sites in the region. And, for the one known Early Postclassic site, La Mesa (De Montmollin 1984a), there is a remarkable difference between it and Canajasté in terms of the kinds of obsidian present. Over 68% of La Mesa's obsidian came from the central Mexican sources, while only 2% of

Canajasté's Early Postclassic obsidian came from Central Mexican sources. This marked difference in artifacts demonstrates that the two sites, although only 20 km apart, were linked into completely different exchange networks. More importantly, it suggests that they were part of different political spheres. The available evidence indicates that Canajasté began as a colony comprised of foreign elites and non-elites.

In the previous chapter I suggested that the motive for colonizing the upper Grijalva region was partly economic. But, based on what I outlined above, the motive might also have been political. That is, the ruler or class of ruling nobles in the homeland may have encouraged younger nobles and sublineages to venture out into surrounding regions in search of territory and vassals, much as Q'uik'ab did at Utatlán. This would have relieved some of the pressure put on the governing elite to share opportunities for political and economic involvement with younger nobles. At the same time, it would have been advantageous for the rulers to have friendly colonies established in neighboring, yet different, ecological zones. Not only would they have increased their chances of obtaining goods from the new region, but they also could obtain, by way of their contacts with the colony's elite, information crucial to the region's administration. The upper Grijalva region, adjoining the foothills of the Cuchumatanes where a number of powerful states with large centers already existed, would have been to them a particularly attractive zone of *tierra caliente*.

One drawback, however, may have been the extremely low population density in the upper Grijalva region during the Early Postclassic. The lack of Early Postclassic sites does not mean that there were none, but it does mean that they are rare compared with the hundreds of Late Classic and earlier sites. If the Early Postclassic colonists were settling the region in search of land and labor, they would undoubtedly have been disappointed by the low population density. It is clear from ethnohistoric accounts throughout Mesoamerica that the noble class was not wont to bother itself with the actual physical tasks of agriculture (Carmack 1981; Roys 1943; Spores 1967; Whitecotton 1977). If they did not bring their own commoners, the providers of labor with them, then they would have had to round up all available locals in the region. This, judging from the Early Postclassic settlement pattern, would have been extremely difficult, at best. The more likely possibility is that the elite colonists who founded Canajasté brought retainers with them.

The history of Canajasté was a case of state extension or of state formation. If the colony became a regional province of a larger state, then the larger state merely extended its region of political influence. If the colony represented secession from a larger state, then it would have become an independent mini-state. In Chapter 7 (Household Artifacts), I provided evidence that distinguishes between these two alternatives.

If the colony began as a secessionary state, then its relations with the homeland over the next few years, or perhaps a generation or two, would involve little exchange interaction. If, on the other hand, it began as a bud-off colony, then I would expect exchange to flourish between the colony and the homeland, exchange being one of the motives for founding the colony in the first place. Further, if the colony was in a hostile territory, then the direction of exchange would have favored the homeland. There would not be so much exchange with the existing local populations—especially during the initial stages of colonization.

Canajasté's location on a defensible bend in the Lagartero River indicates that the founders had set up residence in hostile territory. During their first few decades of existence, in fact throughout the remainder of the Early Postclassic period, they were heavily engaged in trade with their neighbors, albeit much of this trade was with states in Guatemala. The obsidian trade, mentioned above, is one good example because it can be traced to San Martín Jilotepeque and El Chayal, both Guatemalan sources. Other trade items are more difficult to provenience. Copper artifacts, if they originated in Central America or even the highlands of Guatemala, most likely were obtained through neighboring states in the Cuchumatanes.

One of the copper bells from Canajasté, for example, is of the globular, wirework calyx type (Figure 7.19f) found only at sites in the Maya area, notably Chichén Itzá and Zaculeu (Bray 1977:367-373, type o). Other artifacts, however, such as the ceramic spindle whorls, are common throughout the Maya area and may have originated in Veracruz.

A group of colonizers, such as the first Canajasteños, entering a hostile political environment would not have been excluded from trading with their neighbors, but such trade probably would have been sporadic. It is the continued close trading ties with Guatemala that suggests the colony was a bud-off and not a secessionary state. Any additional trading ties established with existing local polities would have been to Canajasté's advantage. The large quantity of both Guatemalan and non-Guatemalan trade goods indicates that trade was a major part of the community's interregional relations during the Early Postclassic period. The noted emphasis on Guatemalan trade goods allows the interpretation that Canajasté was a bud-off colony from that region. It continued trade relations with a number of communities and was able to obtain goods, mostly for elite consumption, that originated in far-flung regions of Mesoamerica.

The degree of social differentiation within the small community of Canajasté was not remarkable when compared to that which existed in the neighboring capitals of Zaculeu, Utatlán, and Iximché. In the Early Postclassic period there was a substantial occupation at Canajasté, and, as mentioned, this included both elite and non-elite. The differences between the two classes were most marked in the Early Postclassic period. The elite had access to larger, better-made, and stylistically more complex houses; to more of, and a wider variety of, locally-made domestic artifacts; and to imported items such as metal, marine shell ornaments, fancy ceramics, and obsidian. They also ate more meat. Social distinctions between the two classes were clearly marked, from the inception of the community, by differential consumption of goods.

I do not know what the Early Postclassic civic-ceremonial center looked like, but the excavated elite household was located adjacent to what became the most important religious structure during the succeeding Late Postclassic period. In the Early period, the elite occupied an advantageous position with respect to almost all facets of community life. But, more importantly, they maintained this social position throughout most of the Early Postclassic. They were able to do so initially by controlling interregional trade. This does not mean that they lacked control of other resources, in fact, the elite were probably in control of most of the agricultural land and production thereof.

One aspect of the elite's hierarchical position was their ability to control internal political, social, and economic dynamics. The other was their external relations with neighboring polities. There is no evidence that the elite class at Canajasté was divided into opposing lineages. If it was, I would expect to see two or three civic-ceremonial foci at the site; however, the unity of the civic-ceremonial layout (at least in the Late Postclassic) suggests that there was a single ruling social group, possibly a major lineage, and its sublineages. This means that much of the internal political dynamics in the community may have revolved around the relations between the elite and non-elite and the former's ability to dominate the latter. To do this the elite engaged in trade relations with their neighbors and, possibly, formed alliances—including marriage alliances—with the elite at neighboring sites. Such inter-polity elite relations, which are only hinted at by the elite Canajasteños' ability to obtain imported exotics, would have served a dual purpose. The first would have been to keep the Canajasté elite subordinate to the elite in their original homeland—both spatially and socially on the margin of the state. This would have been accomplished by exacting tribute from them and trading exotic items to them. The second would have been to keep the non-elite at Canajasté subordinate to the elite. This internal subordination was symbolized first, by the Canajasté elite's exclusive access to some goods and, second, their greater consumption of other kinds of more generally available goods.

This pattern, however, did not remain static. The Early Postclassic period saw a decline, towards the end of the period, in the degree of material differentiation between the two classes at Canajasté. Elite and non-elite households began to symbolize a greater degree of similarity in the style of the goods they consumed, but the elite maintained a greater scale of consumption. The implications of this for the change in internal and external political relations between the Early and Late Postclassic are quite revealing. Whereas the elite originally controlled both internal relations (symbolized by different styles of goods and greater quantities of goods) and external relations (symbolized by greater quantities of imported goods), they appear to have lost control over the latter in the Late Postclassic. In the Late Postclassic period they allowed, or perhaps even encouraged, the non-elite to share their material symbols (e.g., house styles) at the very time they lost both access to and control over interregional trade.

This change in the relations between elite and non-elite is one that could have been potentially harmful to the structure of the society. If it was sparked by a general, region-wide decline in trade (perhaps for reasons beyond their control), then the Canajasté elite may have been under threat of losing their control over the social, political, and economic hierarchies. The elite probably manipulated trade both to maintain their control of external political relations and to obtain exotic symbols of those relations. If trade relations broke down, the elite would have been faced with a dual problem: first, how to redefine external relations; and, second, how to maintain the existing internal hierarchy. The solution to the first provides a solution to the second, but at the same time, it necessitates a shift in internal hierarchical relations.

This solution is warfare. It is not novel to suggest that warfare benefits some members of society more than others (Service 1975:268-269). As discussed above, it was clearly in the interests of the Quiché rulers to emphasize warfare as a means of extending the size of

their state and of reducing internal conflict. Commoners in the society would also have benefited since warfare was one of the few activities that could lead to an elevation in status (Roys 1943). According to Carmack (1981:152):

> The [Quiché] lords were forced to create a new military rank, which they called *achij* ("military") and to formalize it as part of the lord stratum. The graded titles of the lords (*ajpop, k'alel, utzám*) were given to these new military officers

This would have been in the interests of the commoners and of the particular noble faction who maintained control of the new noble warrior class. Carmack (citing Villacorta and Villacorta 1933:240) says that, in addition to these titles, the new military class was allowed to use "some of the symbols of lordly caste, particularly the sacred benches and chairs upon which they sat during council meetings" (Carmack 1981:153). New warriors were also extended the privilege of setting up residence near the town and participating in what were considered to be noble crafts. This is a clear example of the homogenizing effect that the process of increasing warfare has on a society's internal symbolic differentiation.

At Canajasté, a decline in long-distance trade in exotics and a rise in warfare occurred towards the end of the Early Postclassic period. At the same time, the instruments of warfare, such as projectile points, increased in frequency. Other possible evidence of warfare, such as burned houses, and dense packing of houses within the walled zone, also increased. This evidence complements that of changing relations between elite and non-elite households. Changing relationships between the two social classes were expressed by their material symbolic differences. If the non-elite became more involved in warfare, and if their status was elevated, they would be expected to increasingly adopt elite styles. That is what happened at Canajasté sometime during the Late Postclassic period. The non-elite houses were not built in the same style as elite houses until after the beginning of the Late Postclassic. This pattern was demonstrated by the continued use of the early non-elite house style of Structure 2 well into the Late Postclassic period. Before this stylistic change in non-elite houses, the evidence for increasing warfare had long been visible. During the later part of the period all houses visible on the surface of the site were built in the same general style. There continued to be differences in size and quality of stonework in house platform retaining walls, but the vast difference between the elite and non-elite was no longer present.

The same is also true for projectile point styles; tools directly related to warfare. The elite and non-elite came to share the same point styles, whereas formerly, they used different styles. These patterns of stylistic convergence are expected if warfare was, indeed, responsible for the changing relationships between elite and non-elite.

The case of Canajasté provides evidence that the balance between the processes of warfare and exchange is unstable. Each process is co-opted into internal and external political dynamics, either of which may be beyond the control of any individual group. In fact, the only nonperishable goods that came into the site as part of an interregional exchange system (besides obsidian and vesicular basalt) were used as elite markers. Since they served to reinforce the dichotomy between elite and non-elite, these trade goods would have been most closely associated with the elite.

Of course, many imported, elite-associated goods would have been necessary to effect and maintain intra- and intercommunity class relations. Ritual, knowledge, language, clothing, and a host of other symbols would have marked both classes, in their daily interaction. But, the efficiency of a commodity, such as a copper bell or a shell bracelet, for doing so lies in its ability to stand for and validate the elite's claim to membership in a wider elite class. These exotic imports symbolized the established relationships between distant elite groups (Peebles and Kus 1977). Their *relationship* is difficult to see, but the material symbols of it are not.

If, towards the later end of the Early Postclassic, the elite began to have trouble maintaining external relations with neighboring elite, they would also have had trouble obtaining these symbols of relationships. Without such symbols, the community's entire social order could have been called into question, both by competing elites and by commoners. Warfare would have been an effective way of redefining external relationships upon which an elite's claim to superiority rested, thereby relieving the elite of the burden of trying to obtain exotic goods. I would expect that once warfare becomes more important than trade in maintaining an elite's social hierarchical position, there should be a rapid abandonment of the earlier interregional symbols of nobility.

I argued in an earlier chapter that warfare would have resulted in a symbolic convergence at the community level and a symbolic divergence at the regional level. If this argument is correct, it suggests two important implications for understanding past processes. First, if there were evidence of both rising warfare and trade at the same time, I would expect the elite to control both, on a grand scale. Nobles would take over almost all aspects of warfare since it would be their political domain for maintaining and increasing status. Interregional exchange, also, would be almost exclusively restricted to the elite. In this hypothetical case, the two processes would propel the state beyond a simple, small localized territory, and a conquest or imperialistic strategy would develop.

In the second hypothetical case, if there were rising warfare but declining trade, I would expect the elite to use trade goods to appease the other classes in the society. Although trade goods, especially elite markers, would decline, those that were imported would be used to blur previous social boundaries rather than to maintain them. In this case it would be in the elite's long term interest to engage in warfare and to include as many segments of their community as possible. The community, as a whole, would become the dominant social stratum, ranking above all the other communities it managed to conquer.

If, in a network of warring communities or petty states, none was able to conquer the others, then the cycle of warring interaction would never be able to extend to a regional system. The question then becomes: how would a number of warring states, each with minimal internal stratification and specialization, be able to extend their influence beyond their small territories and become expansionistic? In the case of Canajasté, the community began as part of a larger state in the Early Postclassic. By the Late Postclassic the community was but one of many petty states that relied more on warfare than trade for external relations. It also appears to have grown in size during the Late Postclassic period. But it never grew beyond the size of other centers in the upper Grijalva region. Perhaps it could not do so because the very warfare needed for survival also meant that the elite were unable to establish permanent relations with neighboring elites and could not rise above a homogenizing pattern of internal interaction.

IMPLICATIONS FOR THE STUDY OF PROCESS

Archaeology is unique in that it is the only discipline that can contribute to an understanding of social evolution over long spans of time for which there is no other known record. It does so by studying the material remains of past cultures in a way that no other science can, thereby complementing other sciences of the past, such as history and ethnohistory. Through the study of objects from the past, information about many other aspects of long-dead societies can be gained. One of the most important of these is an understanding of how they evolved.

In recent years, there have been two seemingly related goals in archaeological studies. One is the "reconstruction" of past societies. The other is the "explanation of processes" whereby these societies changed (Binford and Sabloff 1982:137; Renfrew 1973). The question naturally arises: what is the relationship between "reconstructing" the past and "explaining processes" of cultural change? It is a tenuous one at best and one which has its pitfalls. I argue here that the goal of reconstruction can short-circuit our attempts to understand the processes of cultural change. No

amount of reconstruction will explain processual change. As Wright (1980:222) has said,

> Attempts to "make the past live again," to "reconstruct past lifeways," are literary devices useful in stimulating a popular audience, in building a nation's pride in its accomplishments, or in enlivening otherwise dry academic discourse.

It can be argued that the more one attempts to reconstruct a past organization the more one has to ignore the very evidence for change that would lead to an understanding of the processes whereby societies evolve (e.g., Adams 1966:28). This results from the problem discussed by Plog (1973, 1974) where continuous time is made discrete, divided into blocks, and those blocks are characterized by static descriptions. Plog (1977:32) states:

> If diachronic data are necessary to the study of processes, and if we wish to explicate processes, we must begin to focus our investigations on these data rather than continuing to seek synchronic data first and foremost, to infer change from such data, and to defend with tortuous and tenuous arguments the inferences that we have made.

The data presented in this study could have been used to make a detailed synchronic reconstruction of Canajasté's social structure and organization. In fact, they could still be used to do so; however, they were specifically collected and analyzed with the goal in mind of searching for evidence of changes that might reveal process. The key to that search was in focusing on the physical changes in the symbols of past social units. This study grew out of the suggestions by others who reached the conclusion that, if archaeologists are interested in explaining change, they must look for it directly in the archaeological record (Adams 1966:28; Clarke 1968:13; Cordy 1981; Plog 1974:7; Wright 1980). But the central problem remains one of documenting changes between static reconstructions, unless we devise methods that search for evidence of the processes underlying sociopolitical change. The two different theoretical perspectives—

reconstructing the past and explaining processes of change—each require different kinds of archaeological data and lead to different interpretations of the same data. This is because, in reconstructing a past social system, fine-scale change is not a necessary prerequisite to the reconstruction. Conversely, in studying process, these fine-scale changes are essential. Most archaeological studies do not do this. For example, Cordy (1981:6-8), in his study of social change in Hawaiian chiefdoms, has said that societies at successive stages must first be reconstructed before it is possible to determine the changes they underwent. His approach, however, sidesteps the crucial problem of developing archaeological theories and methods useful in studying processes directly.

The main reason that sociopolitical change should not be considered as a series of changes in static reconstructions is that different social subunits of a society may change at different rates. The processes underlying the changes may affect the society's government at one rate, its household interactions at another rate, and inter-sodality relations at yet another rate. Each of these social units has different relational and existential symbols (Cohen 1969, 1979). The symbols of existence and the symbols of relationship will change in different ways and at different rates. These changes, in turn, depend upon the underlying social conditions.

Using the example of Canajasté, it would have been possible to determine that there were two phases, Early Postclassic and Late Postclassic, and then to reconstruct the social, economic, and political structure and organization for each period. Then, by examining the differences between each period, it would have been possible to say that trade was most important during the Early period and that warfare was more important during the Late period. It might also have been possible to ascertain that the community began as a colony. It would not have been necessary to closely examine the layer-by-layer changes in each house in order to come up with these results. But, at the same time, it would not have been possible to determine the changing impacts of these processes throughout the

community's history. Nor would it have been possible to hypothesize the relationship between the interregional political processes and the degree and nature of social differentiation and its changes *within* each period. By avoiding the goal of reconstructing the community's social and political organization first, and by using a method that specifically looked for and incorporated evidence for changing social relations, it was possible to monitor more closely the changing processes. In this way, trajectories of change for the social units of interest (households in this case) became the object of analysis, rather than reconstructed, synchronic sociopolitical hierarchies, collapsed into slices of time.

This approach allowed me to monitor the affects of interregional political processes within periods and not to have to rely only on large-scale changes between periods. In the case of Canajasté, this meant that it was possible to determine that trade was, initially, most important in inter-polity relations, and then, it began to decline *during* the Early period. Warfare then became important at the end of the Early period and continued to increase in importance throughout the Late period. What the analysis shows is important, because it means that, in secondary states—as in all complex societies—the crucial processes affecting inter-polity relations are in a constant state of flux. They are not static during the span of an archaeological phase. And, they should not be assumed to be static for the purposes of reconstructing a synchronic description, akin to a prehistoric ethnography, of a past society.

I think one of the reasons that this "process-first" approach is preferable to a "reconstruction-first" approach is because of the way it influences conceptions of the way time is normally divided up in the archaeological record. In Mesoamerica, particularly, archaeologists use changes in ceramic assemblages to define the broad temporal dimensions of phases. The problem with this approach is that the social and political changes that took place may not necessarily be related to the rates of change in ceramic assemblages. Changes in social relations between households, for example, that could lead to a growth in political power of one social class might be dependent upon its increasing control over trade, warfare, agricultural production, religious ritual, or bureaucratic offices. Important changes in these might not relate directly to the symbolic shifts in ceramic styles, thus, phase-long divisions may miss the crucial period of change. By looking directly at the changing symbols of the social units undergoing change, control over the temporal dimension can be increased. This is where stratigraphy is our greatest ally because it allows us to be virtually certain of the trajectory of change and monitor changes in symbols.

For example, a superimposed sequence of 10 house floors showing continuous expansion might have been laid down during the first half of a 200 year-long phase and then, subsequently, during the last half of the phase, very little building activity took place. This relative chronological control is better than absolute chronological control that Cordy (1981) was attempting obtain with obsidian hydration analysis in his study of emerging Hawaiian chiefdoms. Archaeologists have tended to give priority to ways of establishing contemporaneity across an entire community, as with Cordy's study, and then to look for changes between supposedly synchronic arrays of material culture at the community level. Sometimes, even if 10 superimposed house floors are meticulously excavated, there is little theoretical place for them in "reconstruction-first" studies. They are often collapsed "for the purposes of analysis" and their full potential never realized. This makes for neater synchronic reconstructions, by avoiding within-phase variation.

The present study is a first step towards developing an archaeological method that allows full use of the temporal variation in the material record. This applies to both data collection and analysis. I have tried to apply the "diachronic" approach in examining several interregional political processes that anthropologists have considered important in the development and growth of secondary states. I hope it has been successful in demonstrating that: (1) processes can be studied directly by examining their expected affects on material symbols (such as

houses, household artifacts, mortuary practices, subsistence remains, settlement patterns and civic-ceremonial architecture), (2) changes in the symbols can be monitored over periods of time shorter than the phase—the time period varying with each social unit, (3) change in symbols is dependent upon their roles in maintaining networks of social and political interaction, and (4) it is not necessary to reconstruct a community's sociopolitical structure for a given phase before proceeding to study the underlying mechanisms and processes of change.

This study has not shown that there is one and only one process that is important in the history of secondary states. Instead, it has demonstrated that, at least in the archaeological case of Canajasté, a number of processes interact through time in the ongoing history of a state. This, of course, is not a new idea. What is new is the idea that, using archaeological data, the relative importance of each of the specific processes under consideration can be monitored and linked to the community's internal growth and to its patterns of interregional interactions. By studying a series of such examples, in both historic and archaeological contexts, it may be possible to better understand the relationships among the processes and mechanisms that have led to, and that continue to shape, complex social and political organizations such as secondary states.

ENDNOTES

1   Clark et al. (2001), in their reconnaissance survey of the Huehuetenango region, visited the Lagartero River zone downstream from Canajasté on the Guatemalan side of the border. They provide a description of the main ceremonial complex at Chacaj, consisting of six large platform mounds, probably dating to the Classic period. However there is also ceramic evidence of occupation spanning the Middle Preclassic to the Late Postclassic periods. Even more intriguing is their discovery of a dense area of residential occupation covering at least .5 km2 of the hilltop south of the river on the Guatemalan side of the border. The hill (a long ridge formation) extends

northwest across the international border into Chiapas and forms almost a 5 km long U-shaped rise enclosing the Camcum-Canajasté Valley. Clark et al. (2001: Fig. 3) note that the entire slope is densely covered with residential terraces, very similar to those at Canajasté. If this extensive habitational zone was constructed and occupied during the Postclassic period, then it is surely part of the "greater Canajasté" community. It would mean that Canajasté had many times the population that I have assumed throughout this report, based solely on the tight concentration of settlement behind and adjacent to the walled settlement. Clearly, more testing of both Chacaj, on the Guatemalan side, and the dense habitational terrace zone ringing the Camcum-Canajasté Valley is called for before we can truly understand the social and political significance of this group of settlements within its larger region.

APPENDIX A

RADIOCARBON DATES

Five radiocarbon samples were submitted for analysis to Beta Analytic Inc. All of the samples were from the least disturbed floor or midden deposits. Two samples were selected from House Group 1, two from House Group 2, and one from House Group 25. I attempted to select samples from both the Early Postclassic and the Late Postclassic in each house group. Four of the dates were all statistically indistinguishable from each other at plus or minus 100 years (two standard deviations, 95% probability), even though one (Beta 6112) was associated with Late Postclassic artifacts, and the other three (Beta 6113, 6114, 6115) were associated with Early Postclassic artifacts. The fifth sample (Beta 6116) was also from Early Postclassic deposits and was the earliest of the whole group. Table A.1 presents the age of each sample along with the calibrated date. The dates were calibrated using OxCal 4.0.5 (Bronk Ramsey 2001) and based on IntCal04 (Reimer et al. 2004).

The calibrated dates suggest that the site's occupation span fell (minimally) during the period from about AD 1150 to AD 1635 (Table A.1 and Figure A.1). Since no post-Conquest artifacts of any kind were found at the site it is more likely that the terminal occupation date was in the late 1400s or early 1500s. The two "Early Postclassic" samples from Structure 22 (Midden 3 and Floor 5) were contemporary with the most recent dates at the site from a good Late Postclassic context (Structure 1). I am not certain why they are younger than expected, since they were both from the deposits at the site that were used to define the Early Postclassic occupation. Stratigraphically these deposits underlay sealed floors with no intrusions of later artifacts or features. Therefore, I have to assume that the true age of the deposits is somewhat earlier than these dates would indicate. They

are either contaminated, intrusive (perhaps from underground burning of large tree roots), or their age is actually at the earlier end of their probability range. If the latter is the case, then both dates would slightly overlap with the Early Postclassic sample from Structure 2, Floor 4. This is closer to where they should be; however, all three of the dates from Structures 2 and 22 are later than expected. They should all predate the beginning of the Late Postclassic period which is generally thought to start around AD 1250. Interestingly, the date from Structure 60, Midden 2, was right in this range, where expected.

Unfortunately, the radiocarbon dates do not help greatly in determining the relative ages of each structure, but they do, for the most part, confirm the Postclassic age of the site and show that both the very late end of the Early Postclassic and the Late Postclassic periods are represented. In the upper Grijalva region, the Early Postclassic ceramic phase is named Nichim and dates from approximately AD 900-1250, while the subsequent Late Postclassic ceramic phase is named Tan and dates from 1250-1525 (Clark, Lee, et al. 2005:7). Based on the dates as discussed above, I think it is reasonable to hypothesize that what I have labeled as "Early Postclassic" throughout this report is in fact the last few decades of the Nichim phase and perhaps the first several decades of the Tan phase. The "Late Postclassic," then, refers to the last part of the Postclassic Tan phase—perhaps those deposits dating after about AD 1300.

One line of support for this hypothesis is that Canajasté is lacking many of the Nichim phase (Early Postclassic) ceramic types that have been described for other major centers in the region (especially Guajilar, Los Encuentros, Tenam Rosario, and Lagartero) and vice-versa. Granted, this might have resulted from the possibility that the people who founded Canajasté were originally from the western highlands of Guatemala. But it might also be that they settled the community very late in the Nichim phase and so their ceramic traditions, in addition to generally originating outside of the

region, may also postdate the Early Postclassic ceramic styles from the other upper Grijalva region sites that derive from much longer, local histories. It goes without saying that we need excavations and dates from many more Postclassic sites in region in order to resolve this question.

Table A.1. Radiocarbon dates from Canajaste.

Lab Number	House	Deposit	Radiocarbon Years B.P (±1σ)	Calibrated Date A.D. lower	Calibrated Date A.D. upper	Probability of Range (1σ)
Beta-6112	STR-1	FLR-2	390±50	1443	1521	.745
Beta-6113	STR-2	FLR-4	600±50	1304	1365	.776
Beta-6114	STR-22	FLR-5	470±50	1409	1461	1.0
Beta-6115	STR-22	MID-3	390±50	1443	1521	.745
Beta-6116	STR-60	MID-2	820±50	1179	1263	1.0

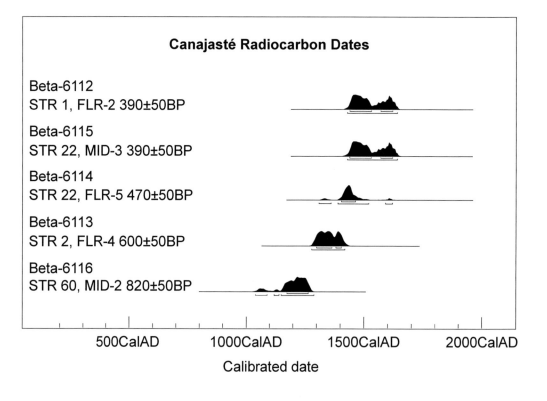

Figure A.1.   Calibrated Radiocarbon Dates Using OxCal 3.10 (Bronk Ramsey 2001) and based on IntCal04 (Reimer et al. 2004).

APPENDIX B

EXCAVATION UNITS

All house structures were excavated as single units. Within each, different deposits, such as floors or construction fill layers, were excavated by means of single or multiple lots. Both horizontal and vertical control was maintained by using excavation lots. Some deposits, such as burials or postholes, were excavated as single lots. Other, more extensive deposits, such as complete house floors, were excavated using multiple lots. Lot size varied depending upon the dimensions of the particular deposit or upon an arbitrary subdivision of the deposit. In general, no lots were larger than about 2 m by 3 m. The depth of the lot always depended upon the thickness of the deposit. Therefore, all excavated units are comprised of natural, not arbitrary, stratigraphic layers. This was relatively easy to do, since the stratigraphy was always clearly defined in the field and there were few deposits thicker than 20 cm.

Tables B.1 to B.7 present the lists of all the excavated deposits for all seven houses and provide a brief description of each. The associated lots for each deposit are given in the "Other lots in deposit" column. Time period designation, excavated volume, and percent of deposit screened are also presented. Abbreviations for all the deposit types are:

AL	Ash lens
BUR	Burial
CF	Construction fill
EL	Earth lens
FLR	Floor
HRT	Hearth
MID	Midden
PFL	Patio floor
PSH	Posthole
ROC	Rock concentration
RWA	Retaining wall
SD	Sterile deposit
SW	Slope wash
TF	Terrace fall
TCF	Terrace construction fill
WF	Wall fall (earth)

Each of these deposits or features was numbered within the excavation unit in order of discovery.

Table B.1. Structure 1, Unit 4, Lots 1 to 30. Excavation units, lots, volume, and percent screening.

Unit/Lot	Deposit[a]	Other lots in Deposit	Time Period	Volume (m^3)	Percent Screened
4/1	FLR-1	4/2	Late	.48	100
4/2	FLR-1	4/1	Late	.60	"
4/3	WF-1	4/4-7, 15, 16	"	.48	"
4/4	WF-1	4/3, 5-7, 15, 16	"	.78	"
4/5	WF-1	4/3, 4, 6, 7, 15, 16	"	.83	"
4/6	WF-1	4/3-5, 7, 15, 16	"	1.32	"
4/7	WF-1	4/3-6, 15, 16	"	1.08	"
4/8	ROC-1	-	"	1.18	"
4/9	BUR-1	-	"	-	"
4/10	SW-1	-	Mixed	1.25	50
4/11	TF-1	4/12, 13	"	.89	100
4/12	TF-1	4/11, 13	"	1.34	75
4/13	SW-1 & TF-1	4/11, 12	"	1.87	100
4/14	ROC-2	-	Late	.32	"
4/15	WF-1	4/3-7, 16	"	.39	"
4/16	WF-1	4/3-7, 15	"	.29	"
4/17	PSH-1	-	"	-	"
4/18	BUR-2	-	"	-	"
4/19	CF-1	-	"	.52	"
4/20	TCF-1	-	Mixed	.40	"
4/21	FLR-2	4/23-27	Late	1.25	"
4/22	SD-1	-	-	1.24	"
4/23	FLR-2	4/21, 24-27	Late	.96	"
4/24	"	4/21, 23, 25-27	"	.58	"
4/25	"	4/21, 23, 24, 26, 27	"	1.25	"
4/26	"	4/21, 23-25, 27	"	.75	"
4/27	"	4/21, 23-26	"	.53	"
4/28	BUR-3	-	"	-	"
4/29	EL-1	-	"	.72	"
4/30	HRT-1	-	"	.01	"

Table B.2. Structure 2, Unit 5, Lots 1 to 56. Excavation units, lots, volume, and percent screening.

Unit/Lot	Deposit[a]	Other lots in Deposit	Time Period	Volume (m³)	Percent Screened
5/1	TF-1	5/2, 7, 12, 13	Late	.94	0
5/2	TF-1	5/1, 7, 12, 13	"	3.12	50
5/3	FLR-1 & CF-1	-	"	.73	100
5/4	FLR-1	5/5, 6, 8, 29, 33	"	.62	"
5/5	"	5/4, 6, 8, 29, 33	"	.45	"
5/6	"	5/4, 5, 8, 29, 33	"	.50	"
5/7	TF-1	5/1, 2, 12, 13	"	3.00	50
5/8	FLR-1	5/4-6, 29, 33	"	.32	100
5/9	CF-1	5/34-43	Mixed	.67	"
5/10	CF-2	5/54	"	.67	"
5/11	TCF-1	-	"	.45	"
5/12	TF-1	5/1, 2, 7, 13	Late	2.74	50
5/13	"	5/1, 2, 7, 12	"	2.27	"
5/14	MID-1	-	"	.11	100
5/15	MID-2	-	"	.18	"
5/16	MID-3	-	"	.26	"
5/17	TF-2	5/18	Mixed	.35	50
5/18	"	5/17	"	.74	"
5/19	TF-3	5/20	"	.65	"
5/20	"	5/19	"	.18	"
5/21	PFL-1	5/22-24, 31, 32	Late	1.60	100
5/22	"	5/21, 23, 24, 31, 32	"	2.18	"
5/23	"	5/21, 22, 24, 31, 32	"	2.00	"
5/24	"	5/21-23, 31, 32	"	.19	"
5/25	MID-4	5/26	"	.29	"
5/26	"	5/25	"	1.54	"
5/27	MID-5	-	"	.16	"
5/28	MID-6	-	"	.24	"
5/29	FLR-1	5/4-6, 8, 33	"	.24	"
5/30	MID-7	-	"	.42	"
5/31	PFL-1	5/21-24, 32	"	.35	"
5/32	"	5/21-24, 31	"	.09	"
5/33	FLR-1	5/4-6, 8, 29	"	.16	"
5/34	CF-1	5/9, 35-43	Mixed	.42	"
5/35	"	5/9, 34, 36-43	"	.90	"
5/36	"	5/9, 34, 35, 37-43	"	.27	"
5/37	"	5/9, 34-36, 38-43	"	.34	0
5/38	"	5/9, 34-37, 39-43	"	1.20	"
5/39	"	5/9, 34-38, 40-43	"	2.05	"

Table B.3. Continued.

Unit/Lot	Deposit[a]	Other lots in Deposit	Time Period	Volume (m³)	Percent Screened
5/40	"	5/9, 34-39, 41-43	"	1.25	100
5/41	"	5/9, 34-40, 42, 43	"	.60	"
5/42	"	5/9, 34-41, 43	"	1.15	"
5/43	"	5/9, 34-42	"	.54	"
5/44	BUR-1	-	Late	-	"
5/45	FLR-2	5/46-48	"	.79	"
5/46	"	5/45, 47, 48	"	.68	"
5/47	"	5/45, 46, 48	"	1.48	"
5/48	"	5/45-47	"	1.67	"
5/49	CF-2 & 3	-	Mixed	3.92	0
5/50	FLR-3	5/51	Late	1.13	100
5/51	"	5/50	"	.88	"
5/52	FLR-4	5/53	Early	.53	"
5/53	"	5/52	"	.19	"
5/54	CF-2	5/10	Mixed	.25	"
5/55	PSH-1	-	Late	-	"
5/56	SW	-	Mixed	.48	"

Table B.3. Structure 22, Unit 7, Lots 1 to 36. Excavation units, lots, volume, and percent screening.

Unit/Lot	Deposit[a]	Other lots in Deposit	Time Period	Volume (m³)	Percent Screened
7/1	FLR-1	7/2-5	Late	2.28	100
7/2	"	7/1, 3-5	"	3.07	"
7/3	"	7/1, 2, 4, 5	"	.96	"
7/4	"	7/1-3, 5	"	1.56	"
7/5	"	7/1-4	"	2.39	"
7/6	CF-1 or FLR-5	-	Early	1.52	"
7/7	FLR-2	7/8, 9	Late	.43	"
7/8	"	7/7, 9	"	.75	"
7/9	"	7/7, 8	"	1.22	"
7/10	CF-2	-	Mixed	1.03	"
7/11	FLR-3	7/12	Late	.71	"
7/12	"	7/11	"	1.22	"
7/13	FLR-4	7/14	Early	.37	"
7/14	"	7/13	"	1.50	"
7/15	FLR-5	7/16, 17, 19, 23	"	.50	"
7/16	"	7/15, 17, 19, 23	"	.47	"
7/17	"	7/15, 16, 19, 23	"	.81	"
7/18	TF-1	-	Mixed	2.11	0
7/19	AL-1	7/15-17, 23	Early	.83	100
7/20	MID-1	7/26	"	1.01	"
7/21	RWA-2	-	Late	.40	0
7/22	EL-1	-	Early	.82	100
7/23	FLR-5	7/15-17, 19	"	.10	"
7/24	MID-2	-	"	.23	"
7/25	EL-2	-	"	1.17	"
7/26	MID-1	7/20	"	.23	"
7/27	MID-3	-	"	.24	"
7/28	CF-3	-	"	2.03	50
7/29	MID-4	-	"	1.76	100
7/30	AL-2	7/33	"	.15	"
7/31	RWA-2	-	Mixed	.76	0
7/32	MID-5	7/34	Early	.89	100
7/33	AL-2	7/30	"	.31	"
7/34	MID-5	7/32	"	.29	"
7/35	SD-1	7/36	Mixed	.39	"
7/36	"	7/35	"	.16	"

Table B.4. Structure 21, Unit 8, Lots 1 to 22. Excavation units, lots, volume, and percent screening.

Unit/Lot	Deposit[a]	Other lots in Deposit	Time Period	Volume (m³)	Percent Screened
8/1	FLR-1	8/2, 3	Late	.69	100
8/2	"	8/1, 3	"	.48	"
8/3	"	8/1, 2	"	.86	"
8/4	CF-1	8/5, 6	Mixed	.69	"
8/5	"	8/4, 6	"	1.20	"
8/6	"	8/4, 5	"	.67	"
8/7	FLR-2	8/8, 9	Late	.89	"
8/8	"	8/7, 9	"	.36	"
8/9	"	8/7, 8	"	.37	"
8/10	SW-1	-	"	.77	0
8/11	FLR-3&4	-	"	1.48	100
8/12	FLR-3	8/13	"	.96	"
8/13	"	8/12	"	.45	"
8/14	FLR-4	8/16	"	.72	"
8/15	HRT-1	-	"	-	-
8/16	FLR-4	8/14	"	.24	100
8/17	FLR-5	8/18, 19	"	.20	"
8/18	"	8/17, 19	"	.36	"
8/19	"	8/17, 18	"	.24	"
8/20	CF-2	-	Mixed	4.31	"
8/21	FLR-6	-	Late	-	-
8/22	CF-3	-	Early	2.66	100

Table B.5. Structure 23, Unit 9, Lots 1 to 16. Excavation units, lots, volume, and percent screening.

Unit/Lot	Deposit[a]	Other lots in Deposit	Time Period	Volume (m³)	Percent Screened
9/1	FLR-1	9/2-4	Late	.73	100
9/2	"	9/1, 3, 4	"	.68	"
9/3	"	9/1, 2, 4	"	.38	"
9/4	"	9/1-3	"	.60	"
9/5	CF-1	9/6-8	Mixed	1.58	"
9/6	"	9/5, 7, 8	"	1.60	50
9/7	"	9/5, 6, 8	"	1.29	"
9/8	"	9/5-7	"	1.73	"
9/9	FLR-2	9/11-13	Late	1.70	100
9/10	CF-2	-	Mixed	1.82	"
9/11	FLR-2	9/9, 12, 13	Late	.46	"
9/12	"	9/9, 11, 13	"	.08	"
9/13	"	9/9, 11, 12	"	.61	"
9/14	FLR-3	9/15, 16	"	.76	"
9/15	"	9/14, 16	"	.99	"
9/16	"	9/14, 15	"	.35	"

Table B.6. Structure 60, Unit 10, Lots 1 to 28. Excavation units, lots, volume, and percent screening.

Unit/Lot	Deposit[a]	Other lots in Deposit	Time Period	Volume (m³)	Percent Screened
10/1	FLR-1	10/2-6	Late	2.16	100
10/2	"	10/1, 3-6	"	1.73	"
10/3	"	10/1, 2, 4-6	"	.84	"
10/4	"	10/1-3, 5, 6	"	1.26	"
10/5	"	10/1-4, 6	"	.72	"
10/6	"	10/1-5	"	1.74	"
10/7	ROC-1	-	"	.29	"
10/8	CF-1	10/11, 13	Mixed	2.37	"
10/9	CF-2	10/10, 12	"	1.55	"
10/10	"	10/9, 12	"	2.52	"
10/11	CF-1	10/8, 13	"	2.94	75
10/12	CF-2	10/9/10	"	1.14	"
10/13	CF-1	10/8, 11	"	3.10	"
10/14	BUR-1	-	Late	-	100
10/15	FLR-2	10/16, 17	"	.64	"
10/16	"	10/15, 17	"	.45	"
10/17	"	10/15, 16	"	.39	"
10/18	MID-1	10/19-23	"	.84	"
10/19	"	10/18, 20-23	"	.71	"
10/20	"	10/18, 19, 21-23	"	.87	"
10/21	"	10/18-20, 22, 23	"	.46	"
10/22	"	10/18-21, 23	"	.76	"
10/23	"	10/18-22	"	.92	"
10/24	MID-2	10/25	Early	.36	"
10/25	"	10/24	"	.42	"
10/26	MID-4	-	"	1.95	"
10/27	MID-3	10/28	"	.22	"
10/28	"	10/27	"	.38	"

Table B.7. Structure 61, Unit 11, Lots 1 to 21. Excavation units, lots, volume, and percent screening.

Unit/Lot	Deposit[a]	Other lots in Deposit	Time Period	Volume (m³)	Percent Screened
11/1	FLR-3	11/2, 10-12	Late	.92	100
11/2	"	11/1, 10-12	"	.84	"
11/3	FLR-1	11/4	"	.96	"
11/4	"	11/3	"	1.56	"
11/5	SW-1	11/6	Mixed	1.35	"
11/6	"	11/5	"	.86	"
11/7	FLR-2	11/8, 9	Late	.80	"
11/8	"	11/7, 9	"	.60	"
11/9	"	11/7, 8	"	.11	"
11/10	FLR-3	11/1, 2, 11, 12	"	.56	"
11/11	"	11/1, 2, 10, 12	"	.54	"
11/12	FLR-3	11/1, 2, 10, 11	Late	.13	100
11/13	FLR-4	11/14, 15	"	.56	"
11/14	"	11/13, 15	"	.36	"
11/15	"	11/13, 14	"	.11	"
11/16	BUR-1	-	Late	-	"
11/17	FLR-5	11/18-21	"	.84	"
11/18	"	11/17, 19-21	"	.86	"
11/19	"	11/17, 18, 20, 21	"	1.28	"
11/20	"	11/17-19, 21	"	.90	"
11/21	"	11/17-20	"	.24	"

APPENDIX C

ETHNOARCHAEOLOGICAL STUDY OF THE CONTENTS OF WATTLE-AND-DAUB WALLS

As a member of the Coxoh Ethnoarchaeological Project during the late 1970s, I had noticed that wattle-and-daub house walls in the Chiapas Highlands often included quantities of durable refuse such as bone, pottery, and glass fragments. This suggested to me that "old" refuse generated prior to the occupation of a house could potentially become incorporated into the mud or daub used to make the dwelling, thereby introducing secondary refuse into the house's archaeological deposits once the house was abandoned and the walls eventually collapsed. The degree to which this might be a problem in the archaeological interpretation of household artifact assemblages depends, to a certain extent, on the frequency of earlier materials incorporated into the house's walls. The problem might be exacerbated by the collapse of wattle-and-daub directly on a house's earthen floor, itself also potentially containing earlier artifacts and debris mixed in.

In order to examine the potential impact of "old refuse" contained within wattle-and-daub walls and the extent to which this material might, if the mixing was undetected during archaeological investigation, impact the overall household artifact assemblage, I decided to carry out a detailed examination of a contemporary wattle-and-daub house. Along with three other members of the Coxoh Ethnoarchaeological Project (Geoff Spurling, Joanna Spurling, and Russell Broulotte) I studied an abandoned house in Aguacatenango, Chiapas, Mexico. The house we studied was only about three years old when it accidentally caught fire and the roof burned. Neighbors told us that the mud used in constructing the walls was obtained from within 25 m of the structure by scraping earth off the ground surface. In Aguacatenango, which is about 400 years old, large quantities of small durable refuse cover the ground. The refuse has accumulated by residents throwing their refuse into their yards and then ploughing it into their yard-gardens. Therefore, the earth used for covering the walls is full of small objects, both organic and inorganic, such as pot sherds, snail shells, glass, charred plant material, etc. The house that we studied was no exception—in fact it was similar to most of the other houses in the community. Houses located closer to the town center, the oldest part of the community, had more material in their walls, while those near the outskirts of the town had less material.

Determination of the frequency and types of "old" refuse incorporated in the house walls was done as follows. We gridded the wattle-and-daub walls into 1m squares and then listed and counted the items visible on the surface of each square. In addition, an estimate of the size range of the items present and the rounding and weathering of the sherds was made. Table C.1 lists the total counts for each class of item observed in the walls. In order to estimate the total contents of the abandoned house walls the thickness of the daub was calculated. The total wall thickness was, on average, 10 cm but this would have been partly made up by the interior wattle and post infrastructure. The canes used for the wattle inside the walls were, on average, about 3 cm thick, leaving a total daub thickness of 7 cm. This estimate is somewhat conservative since the cane is not a solid layer throughout the wall, rather, it is an open lattice.

Using the estimated wall thickness of 7 cm, the total volume of daub for the entire structure is 1.8 m^3 of earth for a total of 25.6 m^2 of surface area. Knowing the thickness of the daub, it is possible to estimate the total contents of the wall by using the following assumption. The counts obtained for the surface represent the artifacts that are found within the top one centimeter of daub only. By multiplying the counts of each item by 7 (the thickness of the daub), an estimate for the total number of items contained within the 1.8 cu m of daub is obtained. Dividing this figure by 1.8 gives a density measurement (number of items per cubic meter of deposit) for each type of refuse.

The estimated figure of over 1000 sherds per cubic meter of wall daub is extremely high. If the walls collapsed on top of the floor, and remained *in situ*, then it is possible that a future archaeologist would find nearly 2000 artifacts in this thin deposit (little more than 10 cm thick)—a deposit that would look strikingly similar to the floor itself. Nonetheless, the artifacts have little to do with the actual function of the structure and many, if not all of them, would have been created before the structure was even built.

Most of the artifacts in the wall daub were much more weathered and had more highly rounded edges than would be expected from artifacts in primary context. The key, then, to avoid incorporating the bulk of the wall-derived artifacts (assuming that they could not be distinguished, using stratigraphic criteria,

from those in the floor deposit) would be to look for a high degree of weathering and rounding. This study shows that not all artifacts found in apparently good house contexts are necessarily related to the house. If the floor material and wall materials are all made from the same sort of earth surrounding the house then they may both look very similar and have roughly the same kinds of secondary refuse items in them. This problem can be expected to be more serious the older the community becomes, since there is likely to be more refuse material surrounding the houses. The solution to avoiding the problem of erroneously including secondary refuse items in an analysis of house deposits is first to carefully look for evidence of wall collapse and then leave that out of the analysis, the same as would be done with any other type of construction material. Second, check the artifacts for signs of excessive weathering and rounding. These steps should prevent the mixing of primary and secondary refuse in the analysis of household artifact assemblages from wattle-and-daub houses.

Table C.1. Surface counts and estimated total numbers of items in the wattle-and-daub walls of a small structure in Aguacatenango, Chiapas

Item	Surface Count	Estimated Total (surface count x 7)	Estimated Total per m³
Sherds	259	1813	1007
Snail Shells	121	847	470
Bone	13	91	51
Tiles	16	112	62
Charcoal	40	280	156
Seeds	3	21	12
Lime	11	77	43
Metal	1	7	4
Glass	3	21	12
Thread	2	14	8

CERAMIC GROUPS AND TYPES

When the original version of this report was written in 1985, the ceramics from Canajasté had all been formally analyzed and provisional labels for each type and form had been assigned (Blake 1985). Subsequently, the provisional labels were replaced with permanent Type-Variety names, and the ceramics were systematically described and compared with other Postclassic sites in the region and beyond. The provisional labels for the ceramic types used in the 1985 analysis are replaced here by the newly published Postclassic ceramic descriptions from the upper Grijalva region provided in Bryant, Lee, and Blake's (2005) Postclassic ceramic report. These updated Type-Variety descriptions for the Canajasté ceramic assemblage are based primarily on type collections from that site and supplemented with detailed descriptions of ceramic samples from Los Encuentros, Guajilar, Coneta, Lagartero, and Tenam Rosario.

Table D.1 presents a concordance of the main ceramic types, varieties, and forms that are defined in the 2005 upper Grijalva region ceramic report and the groups and types originally defined in my 1985 doctoral dissertation. It documents how the types, varieties, and forms used in Chapter 7 are divided into nine groups based on primary vessel function: cooking (C), serving (B), and storage and transport (J) as follows:

(C) cooking wares—including cooking jars, comales (griddles), and pichanchas (colanders),

(B) serving vessels—including plain and decorated bowls and dishes,

(J) storage and transport vessels—including decorated ollas (jars), and cantaros (tall neck jars with strap handles).

Other types that were recovered but are not used in this analysis include ritual vessels, such as censers (including ladles, effigy bowls, and jar-shaped censers) and types that were of Late Classic period origin.

The nine groups in Table D.1 are also based on whether the types in each group were found primarily in Early, Late, or both Early and Late deposits. Therefore, the nine groups, for the purposes of the present analysis, combine various ceramic types into broad functional-chronological categories. These categories are not meant to be definitive, but provide functional-chronological groupings along which the excavated house groups at Canajasté can be compared.

The basic analysis of the Canajasté house group ceramics was carried out as follows. The ceramics from each deposit were washed and labeled with their provenience information and then sorted into piles of rims, identifiable bodies, or unidentifiable bodies. The rims and identifiable bodies of all vessels were further sorted into types based on form/function, decoration, paste, and temper. Only the bodies of decorated vessels and particular bowl/dish types, some cooking vessels such as comales (griddles) or pichanchas (colanders), and ritual vessels (censers) were sorted into types. Most plainware jar and some bowl/dish bodies were not sorted into specific types since it would not have been possible to accurately determine their functional forms, and the likely errors would have outweighed the possible benefits from a attempting such a sort; however, all the counts and weights were recorded for each category of size range for all body sherds.

For the provisional classification, each of the minimal ceramic groups (i.e., a group which could not be subdivided any further) was assigned a unique number, ranging between 1 and 101, and given a descriptive name. When rims and bodies of the same type could be identified, they were each given a separate number. Later, for the purposes of this analysis, these provisional ceramic groups were assigned a capital letter (C, S, or J) indicating the main functional grouping of the type. For example, C-1 consisted of the rim sherds of all plain, unslipped, course-ground calcite temper jars, B-30 was comprised of rims sherds of unslipped, fine-temper dishes and bowls, and J-16 was made up of all rims of fine jars with black and red slip painted in incised zones on the exterior surfaces. In the present analysis 30 such types were defined and used in the house group comparisons.

It is these groupings that were later re-labeled with formal Type-Variety descriptions.

So, for example, group C-1 (plain course calcite temper jars) was renamed Golondrina Unslipped: Calcite Temper Variety, and it includes jar forms 1, 4, and 5, while group C-14 (plain course calcite temper comales) belonged to the same Type-Variety (Golondrina Unslipped: Calcite-temper Variety) but included only comales, form 3 (Bryant, Lee, and Blake 2005:597-602). All of the ceramic types used in the analyses in the present report have been renamed in this fashion, and the concordance between the original 1985 dissertation and the 2005 ceramic report is presented in Table D.1.

Table D.1. Ceramic analytical groups and concordance of ceramic type: variety/form designations (Bryant, Lee and Blake 2005) with provisional type descriptions (Blake 1985).

Groups	Type Labels used in Tables 7.3—7.6	Type: Variety designations in Byrant, Lee and Blake (2005)	Form designations in Byrant et al. (2005)	Pages in Byrant et al. (2005)	Illustrations in Byrant et al. (2005)	Description in Blake (1985)
Group 1: Early Cooking Vessels						
	C-4	Saraquato Unslipped: Saraquato Variety	Jars (forms 1, 3)	594-596	9.24d-e, 9.25j-m	Coarse Rough Jar
	C-7	Golondrina Unslipped: Calcite-temper Variety	Jars (form 1)	597-602	9.29i	Coarse Temper Brushed Neck Jar
	C-20	Chupaflor Red-and-black: Incised Variety	Colander bowls (form 2)	580-584	9.17g-i, 9.19b-d	Decorated Colander
Group 2: Early and Late Cooking Vessels						
2	C-1	Golondrina Unslipped: Calcite-temper Variety	Jars (forms 1, 4, and 5)	597-602	9.29a,h,i	Coarse Temper Jar
2	C-36	Saraquato Unslipped: Saraquato Variety	Bowls (forms 4, 6)	594-596	9.25t-v	Coarse Rough Bowl
2	C-65	Golondrina Unslipped: Red Rim Variety	Colander bowls and jars (form 1)	600-602	9.29j-l	Small-holed Colander
Group 3: Late Cooking Vessels						
3	C-2	Golondrina Unslipped: Golondrina Variety	Jars (forms 7-10)	595-599	9.26-9.27	Fine Temper Jar
3	C-14	Golondrina Unslipped: Calcite-temper Variety	Comales (form 3)	597-602	9.29d-g	Plain Comal
3	C-61	Golondrina Unslipped: Golondrina Variety	Comales (form 3)	595-599	9.26g-h, 9.27h-j	Fillet Rimmed Comal
3	C-63	Golondrina Unslipped: Calcite-temper Variety	Colander bowls and jars (forms 2 and 5)	597-602	9.29b-c	Large-holed Colander

Table D.1. Continued.

Groups	Type Labels used in Tables 7.3—7.6	Type: Variety designations in Byrant, Lee and Blake (2005)	Form designations in Byrant et al. (2005)	Pages in Byrant et al. (2005)	Illustrations in Byrant et al. (2005)	Description in Blake (1985)
Group 4: Early Serving Vessels						
4	B-22	Chupaflor Red-and-black: Incised Variety	Bowls (form 1)	580-584	9.17f, 9.19a	Red-Black Incised Bowl
4	B-24	Chupaflor Red-and-black: Chupaflor Variety	Dishes and bowls (forms 1, 3)	578-580	9.17a-d, 9.18a-g, i-j	Red and Black Bowl
4	B-26	Cacomixtle Red-and-black: Incised Variety	Bowls (form 1)	578	9.12n, 9.16a-b	Orange Black Incised Bowl
4	B-28	Chupaflor Red-and-black: Gouged-incised Variety	Bowls (form 1)	580-583	9.17l, 9.19h	Specular Red-Black Incised Bowl
4	B-40	Tol Polychrome: Wide Band Variety	Dishes and bowls (forms 1-3)	584-586	9.20	Early Tol Polychrome Bowl
4	B-46	Cacomixtle Red-and-black: Cacomixtle Variety	Dishes and bowls (forms 2-3)	575-578	9.12j-h,j, 9.15a-b,e	Black on Tan or Orange Bowl
Group 5: Early and Late Serving Vessels						
5	B-31	Coneta Red: Alan Variety	bowls (form 2, 4)	614-616	9.39q-s, u, 9.40a,d-g	Orange-Red-Brown Slip Bowl
5	B-44	Tol Polychrome: Tol Variety	Bowls (forms 1-4, 6)	619-622	9.42-9.43	Eroded-burned Tol Polychrome Bowl
5	B-48	Choom Red-on-unslipped: Choom Variety	Dishes and bowls (forms 2-3)	575-576	9.14j-l	Red on Tan Bowl
Group 6: Late Serving Vessels						
6	B-33	Tol Polychrome: Tol Variety	Bowls (forms 1-4, 6)	619-622	9.42-9.43	Tol Polychrome-eroded (originally called Fine Orange Bowl)
6	B-38	Gavilan Red: Gavilan Variety	Tripod dishes (form 2)	572-575	9.12a-c, 9.13a-j	Specular Red Tripod Bowl

Table D.1. Continued.

Groups	Type Labels used in Tables 7.3—7.6	Type: Variety designations in Byrant, Lee and Blake (2005)	Form designations in Byrant et al. (2005)	Pages in Byrant et al. (2005)	Illustrations in Byrant et al. (2005)	Description in Blake (1985)
6	B-42	Tol Polychrome: Tol Variety	Bowls (forms 1-4, 6)	619-622	9.42-9.43	Tol Polychrome Bowl
6	B-67	Tol Polychrome: Tol Variety	Bowls (form 3)	619-622	9.42k-m, 9.43a,m-o	Tol Exterior Decorated Bowl
6	B-101	Gavilan Red: Fortress Variety	Tripod dishes (form 2)	616-618	9.41	Specular Red Tripod Bowl
Group 7 Undecorated Serving Vessels						
7	B-30	Golondrina Unslipped: Golondrina Variety	Dishes and bowls (form 4, 6, 11)	595-599	9.27k-m,p-t	Plain Grey Bowl
7	B-32	Golondrina Unslipped: Golondrina Variety	Tripod dishes (form 5)	597	9.27n-o	Plain Orange Bowl
Group 8: Early Storage Jars						
8	J-12	Cacomixtle Red-and-black: Cacomixtle Variety	Jars (form 1)	575-580	9.12k-m, 9.15c-d, f-g	Painted Black and Red Jar (includes J-70)
8	J-16	Chupaflor Red-and-black: Incised Variety	Jars (form 3)	580-584	9.17k, 9.19e-g	Incised Black and Red Jar
Group 9: Early and Late Storage Jars						
9	J-8	Choom Red-on-unslipped: Choom Variety	Jars (form 1)	575-576	9.12d-f, 9.14a-i,	Red-Orange Jar
9	J-18	Xela Polychrome: Xela Variety	Water Jar (form 1)	604-612	9.31-9.38	Polychrome Water Jar (designs mostly eroded)
9	J-19	Coneta Red: Alan Variety	Water Jar (form 1)	614-616	9.39l-p, 9.40c	Red Slipped Water Jar
9	J-68	Xela Polychrome: Xela Variety	Jars (forms 2,3)	604-612	9.31i, 9.32l-m	Polychrome Jar (wide-mouth, short neck, no strap handles)
9	J-82	Golondrina Unslipped: Golondrina Variety	Jars and dish (form 9, 11)	597		Miniature Plain Jar

SOURCE DETERMINATION OF OBSIDIAN USING X-RAY FLUORESCENCE SPECTROMETRY

Fred W. Nelson, of Brigham Young University, analyzed 24 pieces of obsidian from the site in order to determine their sources. The determinations were made by means of X-ray fluorescence spectrometry. The concentrations of the following ten elements were measured: Rb, Sr, Y, ZR, Nb, MnO, Fe_2O_3, TiO_2, Ba, and Na_2O.

Based on the measured concentrations of each element (or compound), the samples were assigned to one of the following source locations: San Martín Jilotepeque (7), El Chayal (8), Ixtepeque (3), Ucareo (3), Zaragoza (1), Pachuca (1), and Unknown (1).

Each of the pieces was selected to represent a larger subgroup of the total sample of obsidian. The pieces in each subgroup shared the same characteristics, such as color, texture, translucency, sheen, and inclusions. Therefore, the X-ray fluorescence determinations of the small sample (only 24 pieces) allowed the visual determination of all but one or two pieces of the entire collection of obsidian.

Table E.1 presents the results of the X-ray fluorescence analysis and shows the amounts of each element.

Table E.1.   X-ray flourescence analysis of obsidian artifacts giving source identification.

Sample No.	Unit/ Lot	Rb ppm	Sr ppm	Y ppm	ZR ppm	Nb ppm	MnO percent	Fe$_2$O$_3$ percent	TiO$_2$ percent	Ba ppm	Na$_2$O percent	Obsidian Source*
1	10/4	162.0	16.9	23.3	142.0	17.5	.026	1.18	.078	135.1	3.23	Uc
2	9/1	154.2	18.6	33.5	142.6	28.3	.026	1.24	.083	144.5	3.81	Uc
3	5/26	150.2	29.2	32.8	220.0	23.0	.038	1.60	.157	480.5	4.02	Za
4	5/2	147.2	19.6	30.0	149.8	23.9	.026	1.23	.085	173.8	3.94	Uc
5	5/22	147.2	143.9	26.1	136.2	19.8	.096	.95	.150	942.8	4.11	EC
6	9/4	146.3	145.7	29.7	136.1	20.4	.094	.94	.149	929.2	4.00	EC
7	7/33	140.3	141.8	30.2	133.1	20.3	.096	.94	.153	944.6	4.15	EC
8	5/51	108.8	185.3	20.9	125.3	14.1	.080	1.05	.157	1102.8	3.80	SMJ
9	7/13	143.3	140.0	30.7	128.1	23.6	.097	.94	.151	950.2	4.16	EC
10	Zn-2	109.7	177.7	26.8	128.9	18.3	.078	1.01	.155	1111.1	3.79	SMJ
11	4/7	95.4	143.8	33.6	192.8	28.1	.067	1.47	.225	1032.3	3.79	Ix
12	9/3	140.4	147.1	25.5	130.2	19.0	.095	.96	.150	935.2	4.07	EC
13	7/15	139.4	138.5	29.5	137.0	23.4	.096	.99	.150	939.7	4.03	EC
14	8/20	140.7	140.7	29.1	129.0	20.8	.096	.98	.150	922.1	4.04	EC
15	7/15	110.2	185.1	19.0	126.9	12.7	.077	1.01	.155	1069.6	3.62	SMJ
16	4/7	93.2	141.6	36.0	192.6	27.1	.066	1.46	.224	1048.1	3.84	Ix
17	5/25	99.5	155.5	20.3	183.2	11.8	.066	1.45	.221	1038.4	3.88	Ix
18	11/2	111.9	186.8	22.7	133.5	17.5	.079	1.06	.158	1095.6	3.84	SMJ
19	5/48	106.4	182.7	23.4	126.4	15.3	.078	.99	.158	1095.4	3.78	SMJ
20	5/30	109.0	183.3	10.5	113.7	6.5	.078	.95	.151	1088.7	3.79	SMJ
21	7/27	138.3	141.6	27.1	127.7	18.0	.096	.93	.150	933.3	4.03	EC
22	11/1	202.2	5.2	118.9	967.6	107.1	.166	2.81	.219	18.0	4.98	Pa
23	10/10	108.4	182.8	23.8	131.3	14.4	.079	1.05	.157	1080.1	3.77	SMJ
24	4/13	107.3	87.2	24.6	167.1	9.6	.083	1.59	.137	1083.2	4.37	Un

* List of abbreviations for Obsidian Sources: Uc=Ucareo, Za=Zaragoza, EC=El Chayal, SMJ=San Martin Jilotepeque, Ix=Ixtepeque, Pa=Pachuca, and Un=Unknown.

REFERENCES

ADAIR, JAMES
1775   *History of the American Indians.*
        Edward and Charles Dilly, London
        [cited in Morgan 1965]

ADAMS, ROBERT MCCORMICK
1961   Changing Patterns of Territorial
        Organization in the Central Highlands
        of Chiapas, Mexico. *American
        Antiquity* 26(3):341-360.

1966   *The Evolution of Urban Society.*
        Aldine, Chicago.

AGRINIER, PIERRE
1983   Tenam Rosario: Una posible
        relocalización del Clásico Maya
        Terminal desde el Usumacinta. In
        *Antropología e historia de los mixe-
        zoques y mayas, homenaje a Frans
        Blom*, edited by Lorenzo Ochoa and
        Thomas A. Lee, Jr., pp. 241-254.
        Universidad Nacional Autónoma de
        México and Brigham Young University,
        Mexico.

n.d.   Late Classic Elite vs. Non-Elite
        Domestic Variations from the Tenam
        Rosario Zone. Paper presented at
        the XLIII International Congress of
        Americanists, Vancouver, Canada,
        1979.

ALVARADO, PEDRO DE
1924   *An Account of the Conquest of
        Guatemala in 1524.* Cortes Society,
        New York.

ÁLVAREZ ASOMOZA, CARLOS
1982   Reconocimiento arqueológico en los
        valles cercanos a Las Margaritas,
        Chiapas. *Estudios de Cultura Maya*
        14:145-177.

ÁLVAREZ DEL TORO, MIGUEL
1952   *Los animales silvestres de Chiapas.*
        Departamento de Prensa y Turismo.
        Ediciones del Gobierno del Estado de
        Chiapas, Tuxtla Gutiérrez.

1971   *Las aves de Chiapas.* Gobierno del
        Estado de Chiapas, Tuxtla Gutiérrez.

1972   *Los reptiles de Chiapas.* Gobierno del
        Estado de Chiapas, Tuxtla Gutiérrez.

1977   *Los mamíferos del estado de Chiapas.*
        Gobierno del Estado de Chiapas, Tuxtla
        Gutiérrez, Chiapas.

ÁLVAREZ, TICUL, PABLO DOMÍNGUEZ, AND JOAQUÍN
ARROYO CABRALES
1984   *Mamíferos de La Angostura, región
        central de Chiapas.* Instituto Nacional
        de Antropología e Historia, Mexico.

ATHENS, J. STEPHEN
1977   Theory Building and the Study of
        Evolutionary Process in Complex
        Societies. In *For Theory Building
        in Archaeology*, edited by Lewis R.
        Binford, pp. 353-384. Academic Press,
        New York.

BATHGATE, DAVID L.
1980   *Cultural-Ecological Adaptations at
        Santa Marta (Tr-19): A Preclassic
        Village in the Upper Grijalva River
        Basin, Chiapas, Mexico.* Unpublished
        M.A thesis, Dept. of Anthropology,
        Brigham Young University, Provo.

Beard, J. S.
1944   Climax Vegetation in Tropical America. *Ecology* 25(2):127-158.

Beattie, John
1960   *Bunyoro: An African Kingdom.* Holt, Rinehart and Winston, New York.

Becquelin, Pierre, and Claude F. Baudez
1979-82 *Tonina, une cité maya du Chiapas (Mexique).* 3 vols. Mission Archeologique et Ethnologique Française au Mexique, Mexico and Paris.

Berlin, Heinrich
1956   *Late Pottery Horizons of Tabasco, Mexico.* Carnegie Institution of Washington, Pub. no. 606. Washington, DC.

Binford, Lewis R.
1981   Behavioral Archaeology and the "Pompeii Premise." *Journal of Anthropological Research* 37:195-208.

Binford, Lewis R., and Jeremy A. Sabloff
1982   Paradigms, Systematics, and Archaeology. *Journal of Anthropological Research* 38(2):137-153.

Blake, Michael
1984a   El estudio de la organización social a través de la arquitectura doméstica. In *Investigaciones recientes en el área maya*, Tomo 1, pp. 471-478. XVII Mesa Redonda de la Sociedad Mexicana de Antropología, Mexico.

1984b   The Postclassic Maya of Canajaste, Chiapas, Mexico. *Masterkey: Anthropology of the Americas* 58(1):9-17.

1985   *Canajaste: An Evolving Postclassic Maya State.* Unpublished Ph.D. dissertation, Dept. of Anthropology, University of Michigan, Ann Arbor.

1988   Household Features and Social Processes in a Modern Maya Community. In *Ethnoarchaeology of the Highland Maya of Chiapas, Mexico*, edited by Thomas A. Lee, Jr. and Brian Hayden, pp. 45-60. Papers of the New World Archaeological Foundation, No. 56. Brigham Young University, Provo.

Blake, Michael, Douglas D. Bryant, Thomas A. Lee, Jr., Pierre Agrinier, and Susanna M. Ekholm
2005   Late Classic Ceramics. In *Ceramic Sequence of the Upper Grijalva Region, Chiapas, Mexico, Part 2*, edited by Douglas D. Bryant, John E. Clark and David Cheetham, pp. 415-547. Papers of the New World Archaeological Foundation No. 67. Brigham Young University, Provo.

Blake, Susan, and Michael Blake
1988   A Regional Study of Household Features in Modern Maya Communities. In *Ethnoarchaeology of the Highland Maya of Chiapas, Mexico*, edited by Thomas A. Lee, Jr. and Brian Hayden, pp. 39-43. Papers of the New World Archaeological Foundation, No. 56. Brigham Young University, Provo.

Blanton, Richard E., Stephen A. Kowalewski, Gary Feinman, and Jill Appel
1981   *Ancient Mesoamerica: A Comparison of Change in Three Regions.* Cambridge University Press, Cambridge.

Blom, Frans
1954   Ossuaries, Cremation and Secondary Burials among the Maya of Chiapas, Mexico. *Journal de la Société des Américanistes* 43 (N.S.):123-136.

1983   Informe preliminar de la John Geddings Gray Memorial Expedition a la América Media, llevada a cabo por la Tulane University de New Orleans, Louisiana, 1928. (Translated by

Thomas A. Lee, Jr.). In *Antropología e historia de los mixe-zoques y mayas: Homenaje a Frans Blom*, edited by Lorenzo Ochoa and Thomas A. Lee, Jr., pp. 103-124. Universidad Nacional Autónoma de México and Brigham Young University, Mexico.

BLOM, FRANS, AND GERTRUDE DUBY
1955-57 *La Selva Lacondona*. 2 Vols. Editorial Cultura, Mexico.

BLOM, FRANS, AND OLIVER LA FARGE
1926-1927 *Tribes and Temples*. 2 Vols. Middle American Research Institute, Pub. 1. Tulane University, New Orleans.

BOGAN, ARTHUR E.
1980 *A Comparison of Late Prehistoric Dallas and Overhill Cherokee Subsistence Strategies in the Little Tennessee River Valley*. Unpublished Ph.D. dissertation, Dept. of Anthropology, University of Tennessee, Knoxville.

BORHEGYI, STEPHEN F.
1956 Settlement Patterns in the Guatemalan Highlands: Past and Present. In *Prehistoric Settlement Patterns in the New World*, edited by Gordon R. Willey, pp. 101-106. Viking Fund Publications in Anthropology, No. 23. Wenner-Gren Foundation for Anthropological Research, New York.

1965 Settlement Patterns of the Guatemalan Highlands. In *Archaeology of Southern Mesoamerica, Part One. Handbook of Middle American Indians, Volume 2*, edited by Gordon R. Willey, pp. 59-94. University of Texas Press, Austin.

BRAY, WARWICK
1977 Maya Metalwork and Its External Connections. In *Social Process in Maya Prehistory: Studies in Honour of Sir Eric Thompson*, edited by Norman Hammond, pp. 365-403. Academic Press, London.

BREEDLOVE, DENNIS E.
1973 The Phytogeography and Vegetation of Chiapas (Mexico). In *Vegetation and Vegetational History of Northern Latin America*, edited by Alan Graham, pp. 149-165. Elsevier, Amsterdam.

BRONK RAMSEY, CHRISTOPHER
2001 Development of the Radiocarbon Program OxCal. *Radiocarbon* 43(2A):355-363.

BROWN, JAMES A. (EDITOR)
1971 *Approaches to the Social Dimensions of Mortuary Practices*. Memoirs of the Society for American Archaeololgy, No. 25. Washington, DC.

BRYANT, DOUGLAS D.
2005 Early Classic Ceramics. In *Ceramic Sequence of the Upper Grijalva Region, Chiapas, Mexico, Part 2*, edited by Douglas D. Bryant, John E. Clark and David Cheetham, pp. 353-399. Papers of the New World Archaeological Foundation, No. 67. Brigham Young University, Provo.

2008 *Excavations at Ojo de Agua, an Early Classic Maya Site in the Upper Grijalva Basin, Chiapas, Mexico*. Papers of the New World Archaological Foundation, No. 69. Brigham Young University, Provo.

BRYANT, DOUGLAS D., AND JOHN E. CLARK
1983 Los primeros mayas precolombinos de la cuenca superior del río Grijalva. In *Antropología e historia de los mixe-zoques y mayas: Homenaje a Frans Blom*, edited by Lorenzo Ochoa and Thomas A. Lee, Jr., pp. 223-239. Universidad Nacional Autónoma de México and Brigham Young University.

2005a Late Preclassic Classic Ceramics. In *Ceramic Sequence of the Upper Grijalva Region, Chiapas, Mexico, Part 1*, edited by Douglas D. Bryant,

John E. Clark and David Cheetham, pp. 265-282. Papers of the New World Archaeological Foundation, No. 67. Brigham Young University, Provo.

2005b   Protoclassic Ceramics. In *Ceramic Sequence of the Upper Grijalva Region, Chiapas, Mexico, Part 1*, edited by Douglas D. Bryant, John E. Clark and David Cheetham, pp. 283-349. Papers of the New World Archaeological Foundation, No. 67. Brigham Young University, Provo.

n.d.   The Late Classic Community at Guajilar. Paper presented at the XLIII International Congress of Americanists, Vancouver, Canada, 1979.

BRYANT, DOUGLAS D., JOHN E. CLARK, AND DAVID CHEETHAM (EDITORS)
2005   *Ceramic Sequence of the Upper Grijalva Region, Chiapas, Mexico, Parts 1 and 2*. Papers of the New World Archaeological Foundation, No. 67. Brigham Young University, Provo.

BRYANT, DOUGLAS D., THOMAS A. LEE, JR., AND MICHAEL BLAKE
2005   Postclassic Ceramics. In *Ceramic Sequence of the Upper Grijalva Region, Chiapas, Mexico, Part 2*, edited by Douglas D. Bryant, John E. Clark and David Cheetham, pp. 549-625. Papers of the New World Archaeological Foundation, No. 67. Brigham Young University, Provo.

BRYANT, DOUGLAS D., AND GARETH W. LOWE
1980   Excavaciones en las ruinas de Ojo de Agua, municipio de La Trinitaria, Chiapas. Report submitted to the Instituto Nacional de Antropología e Historia, Mexico.

CALNEK, EDWARD E.
1973   The Localization of the Sixteenth Century Map Called the Maguey Plan. *American Antiquity* 38:190-195.

1988   *Highland Chiapas before the Spanish Conquest*. In *Archaeology, Ethnohistory, and Ethnoarchaeology in the Maya Highlands*. Papers of the New World Archaeological Foundation, No. 55. Brigham Young University, Provo.

CAMPBELL, LYLE
1988   *The Linguistics of Southeast Chiapas, Mexico*. Papers of the New World Archaeological Foundation, No. 50. Brigham Young University, Provo.

CANCIAN, FRANK
1965   *Economics and Prestige in a Maya Community*. Stanford University Press, Palo Alto.

CARMACK, ROBERT M.
1968   Toltec Influence on the Post-Classic Culture History of Highland Guatemala. In *Archaeological Studies in Middle America*, pp. 49-92. Middle American Research Institute, Pub. 26. Tulane University, New Orleans.

1973   *Quichean Civilizations: The Ethnohistoric, Ethnographic, and Archaeological Sources*. University of California Press, Berkeley.

1981   *The Quiché Mayas of Utatlán*. University of Oklahoma Press, Norman.

CARMACK, ROBERT M., JANINE L. GASCO, AND GARY H. GOSSEN (EDITORS)
2007   *The Legacy of Mesoamerica: History and Culture of a Native American Civilization*, 2nd edition. Prentice Hall, Upper Saddle River, NJ.

CARNEIRO, ROBERT L.
1970   A Theory of the Origin of the State. *Science* 165:733-738.

CARRASCO, PEDRO, AND JOHANNA BRODA
1976   *Estratificación social en la Mesoamérica prehispánica*. Centro de

Investigaciones Superiores, Instituto Nacional de Antropología e Historia, Mexico.

CASO, ALFONSO, AND IGNACIO BERNAL
1965   Ceramics of Oaxaca. In *Archaeology of Southern Mesoamerica, Part Two. Handbook of Middle American Indians, Volume 2*, edited by Gordon R. Willey, pp. 871-895. University of Texas Press, Austin.

CEJA TENORIO, JORGE FAUSTO
n.d.   Preliminary Report on the First Season of Excavations at the Site of Ojo de Agua. In The Upper Grijalva Basin Maya Project: Reports on Fieldwork, 1975-1976, edited by Gareth W. Lowe, pp. 100-111. Ms. on file at New World Archaeological Foundation, San Cristobal de las Casas, Chiapas, 1976.

CHASE, DIANE Z.
1981   The Maya Postclassic at Santa Rita Corozal. *Archaeology* (Jan/Feb): 25-33.

CHÁVEZ, ERNESTO A.
1969   Appendix III: Artifactual and Non-Artifactual Material of the Phyla Mollusca, Arthropoda, and Chordata from Chiapa de Corzo, Chiapas. In *The Artifacts of Chiapa de Corzo, Chiapas, Mexico*, edited by Thomas A. Lee, Jr., pp. 219-220. Papers of the New World Archaeological Foundation, No. 26. Brigham Young University, Provo.

CLARK, JOHN E.
1981   Guatemalan Obsidian Sources and Quarries: Additional Notes. *Journal of New World Archaeology* 4(3):1-15.

1988   *The Lithic Artifacts of La Libertad, Chiapas, Mexico: An Economic Perspective*. Papers of the New World Archaeological Foundation, No. 52. Brigham Young University, Provo.

n.d.   A Brief Note on the Obsidian from Canajasté, Chiapas, Mexico. Ms. on file, New World Archaeological Foundation. San Cristobal de Las Casas, Chiapas, 1980.

CLARK, JOHN E., BARBARA ARROYO, AND DAVID CHEETHAM
2005   Early Preclassic and Early Middle Preclassic Ceramics. In *Ceramic Sequence of the Upper Grijalva Regions, Chiapas, Mexico. Part 1*, edited by Douglas D. Bryant, John E. Clark and David Cheetham, pp. 21-139. Papers of the New World Archaeological Foundation, No. 67. Brigham Young University, Provo.

CLARK, JOHN E., AND DAVID CHEETHAM
2005   Cerámica del Formativo de Chiapas. In *La producción alfarera en el México antiguo I*, edited by Beatriz L. Merino de Carrión and Ángel García Cook, pp. 295-433. Instituto Nacional de Antropología e Historia, Mexico.

CLARK, JOHN E., AND THOMAS A. LEE, JR.
1984   Formative Obsidian Exchange and the Emergence of Public Economies in Chiapas, Mexico. In *Exchange in Early Mesoamerica*, edited by Kenneth Hirth, pp. 235-274. University of New Mexico Press, Albuquerque.

2007   The Changing Role of Obsidian Exchange in Central Chiapas. In *Archaeology, Art, and Ethnogenesis in Mesoamerican Prehistory: Papers in Honor of Gareth W. Lowe*, edited by Lynneth S. Lowe and Mary E. Pye, pp. 109-159. Papers of the New World Archaeological Foundation, No. 68. Provo.

CLARK, JOHN E., LEE, THOMAS A., JR., AND DOUGLAS D. BRYANT
2005   Introducing the Grijalva Maya Project. In *Ceramic Sequence of the Upper*

*Grijalva Region, Chiapas, Mexico.
Part 1*, edited by Douglas D. Bryant,
John E. Clark and David Cheetham,
pp. 1-20. Papers of the New World
Archaeological Foundation, No. 67.
Brigham Young University, Provo.

CLARK, JOHN E., AND RONALD W. LOWE
n.d.   Archaeological Investigations in the
          Morelos Piedmont, Municipio de
          Trinitaria, Mexico. Ms. on file, New
          World Archaeological Foundation. San
          Cristobal de las Casas,1980.

CLARK, JOHN E., MARIO TEJADA BOUSCAYROL,
DONALDO CASTILLO VALDEZ, DAVID CHEETHAM,
DEIRDRE NUTTAL, AND BEATRIZ BALCÁRCEL
2001   *Prospección Arqueológica de la
          Cuenca Superior del Río Grijalva en
          Huehuetenango, Guatemala: Reporte
          Final de la Temporada 1999.* Fundación
          Arqueológica Nueve Mundo, San
          Cristobal de las Casas, Chiapas.

CLARKE, DAVID L.
1968   *Analytical Archaeology.* Methuen,
          London.

COHEN, ABNER
1969   *Custom and Politics in Urban Africa:
          A Study of Huasa Migrants in Yoruba
          Towns.* University of California Press,
          Berkeley.

1974   *Two-Dimensional Man: An Essay
          on the Anthropology of Power and
          Symbolism in Complex Society.*
          University of California Press,
          Berkeley.

1979   Political Symbolism. *Annual Review of
          Anthropology* 8:87-113.

COLLIER, GEORGE A.
1975   *Fields of the Tzotzil: The Ecological
          Bases of Tradition in Highland
          Chiapas.* University of Texas Press,
          Austin.

CORDY, ROSS H.
1946   *A Study of Prehisotoric Social Change:
          The Development of Complex Societies
          in the   Hawaiian Islands.* Academic
          Press, New York.

CORZO, ANGEL M.
1946   *Geografía de Chiapas.* Editorial Protos,
          Tuxtla Gutiérrez, Chiapas.

CULBERT, T. PATRICK
1965   *The Ceramic History of the Central
          Highlands of Chiapas, Mexico.* Papers
          of the New World Archaeological
          Foundation, No. 19. Brigham Young
          University, Provo.

1973   *The Classic Maya Collapse.* University
          of New Mexico Press, Albuquerque.

DE MONTMOLLIN, OLIVIER
1989a   *The Archaeology of Political
          Structure.* Cambridge University Press,
          Cambridge.

1989b   *Settlement Survey in the Rosario
          Valley, Chiapas, Mexico.* Papers of the
          New World Archaeological Foundation,
          No. 57. Brigham Young University,
          Provo.

1995   *Settlement and Politics in Three
          Classic Maya Polities.* Prehistory Press,
          Madison.

n.d.   Dynamic Contentiousness among the
          Late Postclassic Central Quiche of the
          Guatemala Highlands. Ms. on file, New
          World Archaeological Foundation. San
          Cristobal de las Casas, 1983.

DEAL, MICHAEL
1982   Functional Variation of Maya Spiked
          Vessels: A Practical Guide. *American
          Antiquity* 47(3):614-633.

1998   *Pottery Ethnoarchaeology in the
          Central Maya Highlands.* University of
          Utah Press, Salt Lake City.

D<small>ENIS</small>, P<small>IERRE</small>
1982   *Un experimento arqueológico con el fuego en viejo Osumacinta, Chiapas.* Notas Antropológicas, Vol. I, Nota 25. Instituto de Investigaciones Antropológicas, Universidad Nacional Autónoma de México, Mexico.

D<small>ÍAZ DEL</small> C<small>ASTILLO</small>, B<small>ERNAL</small>
1912   *The True History of the Conquest of New Spain.* Translated by Alfred Percival Maudslay. Hakluyt Society, London.

D<small>IEHL</small>, R<small>ICHARD</small> A.
1974   *Studies of Ancient Tollan: A Report of the University of Missouri Tula Archaeological Project.* University of Missouri Monographs in Anthropology, No. 1. Dept. of Anthropology, University of Missouri, Columbia.

D<small>ONLEY</small>, L<small>INDA</small> W<small>ILEY</small>
1982   House Power: Swahili Space and Symbolic Markers. In *Symbolic and Structural Archaeology*, edited by Ian Hodder, pp. 63-73. Cambridge University Press, Cambridge.

D<small>OUGLAS</small>, M<small>ARY</small>, <small>AND</small> B<small>ARON</small> I<small>SHERWOOD</small>
1980   *The World of Goods.* Penguin Books, London.

D<small>ULY</small>, C<small>OLIN</small>
1979   *The Houses of Mankind.* Thames and Hudson, London.

E<small>CHEGARAY</small> B<small>ABLOT</small>, L<small>UIS</small>
1957   *La cuenca del Grijalva-Usumacinta a escala nacional y mundial.* 2nd ed. Secretaría de Recursos Hidrólicos, Mexico.

E<small>KHOLM</small>, S<small>USANNA</small> M.
1979a   The Lagartero Figurines. In *Maya Archaeology and Ethnohistory*, edited by Norman Hammond and Gordon R. Willey, pp. 172-186. University of Texas Press, Austin.

1979b   The Significance of an Extraordinary Maya Ceremonial Refuse Deposit at Lagartero, Chiapas. In *Actes du XLII Congrés International des Américanistes*, Vol. 8, pp. 147-159, Congrés du Centenaire, Paris.

n.d.a   Investigations at Lagartero, Chiapas. In The Upper Grijalva Basin Maya Project: Reports on Fieldwork, 1975-1976, edited by Gareth W. Lowe, pp. 42-48. Ms. on file, New World Archaeological Foundation, San Cristobal de las Casas, 1976.

n.d.b   The Necropolis Burials of Lagartero. Paper presented at the 42nd annual meetings of the Society for American Archaeology, New Orleans, 1977.

E<small>KHOLM</small>, S<small>USANNA</small> M., <small>AND</small> E<small>DUARDO</small> M<small>ARTÍNEZ</small>
1983   Lagartero: Una situación ecológica única de los mayas de la cuenca superior del Grijalva. In *Antropología e historia de los mixe-zoques y maya: Homenaje a Frans Blom*, edited by Lorenzo Ochoa and Thomas A. Lee, Jr., pp. 255-270. Universidad Nacional Autónoma de México and Brigham Young University, Mexico.

E<small>STRADA</small>, J. <small>DE</small>
1955   Descripción de la provincia de Zapotitlán y Suchitepéquez. *Anales de la Sociedad de Geografía e Historia de Guatemala* 28:68-84.

E<small>VANS</small>, S<small>USAN</small> T<small>OBY</small>
2008   *Ancient Mexico and Central America; Archaeology and Culture History*, 2nd edition. Thames and Hudson, London.

F<small>AUVET</small>, M<small>ARIE</small>-F<small>RANCE</small>
1973   Mixco Viejo: Ville Protohistorique de Haute Terres Maya du Guatemala. *Journal de la Société des Américanistes* 62:145-167.

FAUVET-BERTHELOT, MARIE-FRANCE
1981   El Grupo Residencial A. In *Rescate arqueológico en la cuenca del río Chixoy. 2. Cauinal*, edited by A. Ichon, M. F. Fauvet-Berthelot, C. Plocieniak, R. Hill, II, R. Gonzalez Lauck and M. A. Baily, pp. 63-76. Misión Científica Franco-Guatemalteca, Guatemala.

FLANNERY, KENT V.
1969   Appendix II: An Analysis of Animal Bones from Chiapa de Corzo, Chiapas. In *The Artifacts of Chiapa de Corzo, Chiapas, Mexico*, edited by Thomas A. Lee, Jr., pp. 209-218. Papers of the New World Archaeological Foundation, No. 26. Brigham Young University, Provo.

1972a The Cultural Evolution of Civilizations. *Annual Review of Ecology and Systematics* 3:399-425.

1972b The Origins of the Village as a Settlement Type in Mesoamerica and the near East: A Comparative Study. In *Man, Settlement and Urbanism*, edited by Peter J. Ucko, Ruth Tringham and George W. Dimbleby, pp. 23-53. Schenkman, Cambridge.

1976   The Early Mesoamerican House. In *The Early Mesoamerican Village*, edited by Kent V. Flannery, pp. 16-24. Academic Press, New York.

FLANNERY, KENT V., AND MARCUS WINTER
1976   Analyzing Household Activities. In *The Early Mesoamerican Village*, edited by Kent V. Flannery, pp. 34-45. Academic Press, New York.

FOX, JOHN W.
1975   *Centralism and Regionalism: Quiche Acculturation Processes in Settlement Patterning.* Unpublished Ph.D. dissertation, Dept. of Anthropology, State University of New York, Albany.

1978   *Quiche Conquest.* University of New Mexico Press, Albuquerque.

1987   *Maya Postclassic State Formation: Segmentary Lineage Migration in Advancing Frontiers.* Cambridge University Press, Cambridge.

FRIED, MORTON H.
1960   On the Evolution of Social Stratification and the State. In *Culture in History: Essays in Honor of Paul Radin*, edited by Stanley Diamond, pp. 713-731. Columbia University Press, New York.

1967   *The Evolution of Political Society.* Random House, New York.

1983   Tribe to State or State to Tribe in Ancient China. In *The Origins of Chinese Civilization*, edited by David N. Keightley, pp. 467-493. University of California Press, Berkeley.

FRIEDL, ERNESTINE
1964   Lagging Emulation in Post-Peasant Society. *American Anthropologist* 66(3):569-586.

GANN, THOMAS
1900   Mounds in Northern Honduras In *Smithsonian Institution, Bureau of American Ethnology, 19th Annual Report, Part 2*, pp. 655-692. Washington, DC.

GARCÍA SOTO, J. MARIO
1969   *Geografía general de Chiapas.* Imprenta Mexicana, Mexico.

GERHARD, PETER
1979   *The Southeast Frontier of New Spain.* Princeton University Press, Princeton.

GIBSON, CHARLES
1964   *The Aztecs under Spanish Rule: A History of the Indians of the Valley of*

Mexico, 1519-1810. Stanford University Press, Palo Alto.

GILMAN, PATRICIA A.
1983   *Changing Architectural Forms in the Prehistoric Southwest.* Unpublished Ph.D. dissertation, Dept. of Anthropology, University of New Mexico, Albuquerque.

GLASSIE, HENRY
1975   *Folk Housing in Middle Virginia.* University of Tennessee Press, Knoxville.

GODOY, DIEGO DE
1858   Relación hecha a Hernando Cortés, etc. In *Historiadores primitivos de Indias, Vol. 1,* edited by Enrique de Vedia, pp. 465-470. Biblioteca de Autores Españoles, Vol. 22. Imprenta Rivadeneyra, Madrid.

GOLDMAN, E. A.
1951   *Biological Investigations in Mexico.* Miscellaneous Collections, Vol. 115. Smithsonian Institution, Washington, DC.

GOLDMAN, IRVING
1970   *Ancient Polynesian Society.* University of Chicago Press, Chicago.

GÓMEZ-POMPA, ARTURO
1965   La vegetación de México. *Boletín de la Sociedad Botánica de México* 29:76-120.

GORENSTEIN, SHIRLEY
1966   The Differential Development of New World Empires. *Revista Mexicana de Estudios Antropológicos* 20:41-67.

1973   Tepexi el Viejo: A Postclassic Fortified Site in the Mixteca-Puebla Region of Mexico. *Transactions of the American Philosophical Society,* Vol. 63, Part 1.

GUILLEMÍN, JORGE F.
1959   Iximche. *Antropología e Historia de Guatemala* 11(2):22-64.

1965   *Iximche: Capital de antiguo reino cakchiquel.* Tipografía Nacional, Guatemala.

1967   The Ancient Cakchiquel Capital of Iximche. *Expedition* 9(2):22-35.

1977   Urbanism and Hierarchy at Iximche. In *Social Process in Maya Prehistory: Studies in Honour of Sir Eric Thompson,* edited by Norman Hammond, pp. 227-264. Academic Press, London.

GURR-MATHENY, DEANNE L.
1987   *The Northwest Plaza Burials at Lagartero, Chiapas, Mexico.* Unpublished Ph.D. dissertation, Dept. of Anthropology, University of Utah, Salt Lake City.

HAGGETT, PETER
1965   *Locational Analysis in Human Geography.* Edward Arnold Ltd., London.

1967   Network Models in Geography. In *Models in Geography,* edited by Richard J. Chorley and Peter Haggett, pp. 609-668. Methuen & Co Ltd, London.

HAMEL, HENDRIK
1918   The Description of the Kingdom of Corea. *Royal Asiatic Society, Korea Branch, Transactions* 9:92-148.

HAVILAND, WILLIAM A.
1967   Stature at Tikal, Guatemala: Implications for Ancient Maya Demography and Social Organization. *American Antiquity* 32(3):316-325.

HAYDEN, BRIAN, AND MARGARET NELSON
1981 The Use of Chipped Lithic Material in the Contemporary Maya Highlands. *American Antiquity* 46(4):885-898.

HAYDEN, BRIAN, AND AUBREY CANNON
1982 The Corporate Group as an Archaeological Unit. *Journal of Anthropological Archaeology* 1(2):132-158.

1983 Where the Garbage Goes: Refuse Disposal in the Maya Highlands. *Journal of Anthropological Archaeology* 2(2):117-163.

1984 *The Structure of Material Systems: Ethnoarchaeology in the Maya Highlands.* Society of American Archaeology Papers, No. 3. Washington, DC.

HEALAN, DAN M.
1977 Architectural Implication of Daily Life in Ancient Tollan, Hidalgo, Mexico. *World Archaeology* 9(2):140-156.

HEIGHWAY, CAROLYN
1973 Excavation of a Postclassic House: Structure 139, Nohmul. In *British Museum-Cambridge University Corozal Project 1973. Interim Report*, edited by Norman Hammond, pp. 47-55. Centre of Latin American Studies, Cambridge University, Cambridge.

HELBIG, KARL M.
1964 *La cuenca superior del río Grijalva, un estudio regional de Chiapas, sureste de México.* Translated by Félix Heyne. Instituto de Ciencias y Artes de Chiapas, Tuxtla Gutiérrez.

HILL, ROBERT M., II
1980 *Closed Corporate Community and the Late Postclassic Highland Maya: A Case Study in Cultural Continuity.* Unpublished Ph.D. dissertation, Dept. of Anthropology, University of Pennsylvania, Philadelphia.

1982 Ancient Maya Houses at Cauinal and Pueblo Viejo Chixoy, El Quiché, Guatemala. *Expedition* 24(2):40-48.

HODDER, IAN
1979 Economic and Social Stress and Material Culture Patterning. *American Antiquity* 44(3):446-454.

1982 *Symbols in Action, Ethnoarchaeological Studies of Material Culture.* Cambridge University Press, Cambridge.

1984 Burials, Houses, Women and Men in the European Neolithic. In *Ideology, Power and Prehistory*, edited by Daniel Miller and Christopher Tilley, pp. 51-68. Cambridge University Press, Cambridge.

HODDER, IAN, AND CLIVE ORTON
1976 *Spatial Analysis in Archaeology.* Cambridge University Press, Cambridge.

HODGE, MARY G.
1984 *Aztec City-States.* Memoirs of the Museum of Anthropology, No. 18. University of Michigan, Ann Arbor.

HULBERT, HOMER, B.
1906 *The Passing of Korea.* Doubleday, Page, New York.

ICHON, ALAIN
1975 *Organización de un centro quiche protohistórico: Pueblo-Viejo Chichaj.* Instituto de Antropología e Historia, Guatemala.

1981 El Grupo Ceremonial A. In *Rescate arqueológico en la cuenca del río Chixoy. 2. Cauinal*, edited by A. Ichon, M. F. Fauvet-Berthelot, C. Plocieniak, R. Hill, II, R. González Lauk and M. A. Baily, pp. 15-62. Misión Científica Franco-Guatemalteca, Guatemala.

JOHNSON, JAY K.
n.d.   Postclassic Maya Site Structure at
        Topoxte, El Peten, Guatemala. Paper
        presented at the 78th annual meeting
        of the American Anthropological
        Association, Cincinnati, Ohio, 1979.

KANG, YOUNGHILL
1931   *The Grass Roof.* Scribner, New York.

KAPLAN, DAVID
1963   Men, Monuments, and Political
        Systems. *Southwestern Journal of
        Anthropology* 19:397-410.

KEEN, A. MYRA
1971   *Seashells of Tropical West America*,
        2nd edition. Stanford University Press,
        Palo Alto.

KOTTAK, CONRAD P.
1972   Ecological Variables in the Origin
        and Evolution of African States.
        *Comparative Studies in Society and
        History* 14(3):351-380.

KOWALSKI, JEFF, AND CYNTHIA KRISTAN-GRAHAM
(EDITORS)
2007   *Twin Tollans: Chichén Itzá, Tula, and
        the Epiclassic to Early Postclassic
        Mesoamerican World.* Dumbarton
        Oaks Research Library and Collection,
        Washington, DC.

KUBLER, GEORGE
1961   On the Colonial Extinction of the
        Motifs of Pre-Columbian Art. In
        *Essays in Pre-Columbian Art and
        Archaeology*, edited by Samuel K.
        Lothrop and others, pp. 14-34. Harvard
        University Press, Cambridge.

KURJACK, EDWARD B.
1974   *Prehistoric Lowland Maya Community
        and Social Organization--a Case Study
        at Dzibilchaltun, Yucatan, Mexico.*
        Middle American Research Institute,
        Pub. 38. Tulane University, New
        Orleans.

LA FARGE, OLIVER, AND DOUGLAS BYERS
1931   *The Year Bearer's People.* Middle
        American Research Institute, Pub. 3.
        Tulane University, New Orleans.

LEE, THOMAS A., JR.
1975   The Uppermost Grijalva Basin: A
        Preliminary Report of a New Maya
        Archaeological Project. In *Balance
        y perspectiva de la antropología
        de Mesoamérica y del norte de
        México. XIII Mesa Redonda de la
        Sociedad Mexicana de Antropología,
        Arqueología II*, pp. 35-47. Xalapa,
        Veracruz.

1978a   Informe Preliminar de la 2a temporada
        de campo. Febrero-Junio, 1978, del
        Proyecto de la zona Guajilar-Niagara.
        Report submitted to Instituto Nacional
        de Antropología e Historia, Mexico.

1978b   The Origin and Development of
        Plumbate. *Revista Mexicana de
        Estudios Antropológicos* 24(4):287-300.

1979a   Coapa, Chiapas: A Sixteenth-Century
        Coxoh Maya Village on the Camino
        Real. In *Maya Archaeology and
        Ethnohistory*, edited by Norman
        Hammond and Gordon R. Willey, pp.
        208-222. University of Texas Press,
        Austin.

1979b   Early Colonial Coxoh Maya Syncretism
        in Chiapas, Mexico. *Estudios de
        Cultura Maya* 12:93-109.

1980a   Algunos aspectos antropológicos del
        pueblo Coxoh. In *Rutas de intercambio
        en Mesoamérica y el norte de México*,
        Vol. 2, pp. 415-428. XVI Mesa
        Redonda de la Sociedad Mexicana de
        Antropología, Saltillo, Coahila.

1980b   The Long Path to Extinction: Colonial
        Coxoh Maya of Chiapas, Mexico.
        Mexicon 2(2):21-24.

1980c Tercera temporada de campo en Portrero Mango (TR-172), Rancho Entre Ríos, municipio Trinitaria, Chiapas. Report submitted to the Instituto Nacional de Antropología e Historia, Mexico.

1981 New World Archaeological Foundation Obra, 1952-1980. Brigham Young University, Provo.

n.d. A Preliminary Report of the First Phase of Excavations at Guajilar, Chiapas: 1976. In The Upper Grijalva Basin Maya Project: Reports on Fieldwork, 1975-1976, edited by Gareth W. Lowe, pp. 131-145. Ms. on file, New World Archaeological Foundation, San Cristobal de las Casas, 1976.

LEE, THOMAS A., JR., MICHAEL BLAKE, SUSAN BLAKE, BARBARA VOORHIES AND JAMES WHITE
n.d. Archaeological Reconnaissance of the Upper Tributaries Region of the Grijalva Valley, Chiapas, Mexico. In Papers of the New World Archaeological Foundation, [Ms. in Preparation]. Provo.

LEE, THOMAS A., JR., AND DOUGLAS D. BRYANT
1977 A Preliminary Report of the Archaeological Investigations at Los Encuentros, Chiapas (Tr-94). Report submitted to the Instituto Nacional de Antropología e Historia, Mexico.

n.d. Late Postclassic Household Patterns of the Upper Grijalva River Basin. Paper presented at the XLIII International Congress of Americanists, Vancouver, 1979.

LEE, THOMAS A., JR., AND JOHN E. CLARK
1980 Investigaciones arqueológicas en la región Camcum-Canajaste, col. Las Delicias, municipio Trinitaria, Chiapas, México. Report submitted to the Instituto Nacional de Antropología e Historia, Mexico.

1988 Oro, tela y xute: Investigaciones arqueológicas en la región Camcum, Colonia Las Delicias, Chiapas. Arqueología 4:7-46.

LEE, THOMAS A., JR., AND SIDNEY D. MARKMAN
1977 The Coxoh Colonial Project and Coneta, Chiapas, Mexico. A Provincial Maya Village under the Spanish Conquest. Historical Archaeology 11:56-66.

1979 Coxoh Maya Acculturation in Colonial Chiapas: A Necrotic Archaeological-Ethnohistorical Model. In Actes du XLII Congrés International des Américanistes, Vol. 8, pp. 57-66, Congrés du Centenaire, Paris.

LEOPOLD, A. STARKER
1950 Vegetation Zones of Mexico. Ecology 31:507-518.

1959 Wildlife of Mexico: The Game Birds and Mammals. University of California Press, Berkeley.

LLOYD, P. C.
1965 The Political Structure of African Kingdoms: An Exploratory Model. In Political Systems and the Distribution of Power, edited by Michael Banton, pp. 63-112. A.S.A. Monographs No. 2. Praeger, New York.

LOVELL, W. GEORGE
1980 Land and Settlement in the Cuchumatan Highlands (1500-1821): A Study in the Historical Geography of Northwestern Guatemala. Unpublished Ph.D. dissertation, Dept. of Geography, University of Alberta, Edmonton.

LOWE, GARETH W.
1959 Archaeological Exploration of the Upper Grijalva River, Chiapas, Mexico. Papers of the New World Archaeological Foundation, No. 2 (Pub. No. 3). Brigham Young University, Provo.

2007   Early Formative Chiapas: The
        Beginning of Civilization in the
        Central Depression of Chiapas. In
        *Archaeology, Art, and Ethnogenesis
        in Mesoamerican Prehistory: Papers
        in Honor of Gareth W. Lowe*, edited
        by Lynneth Lowe and Mary Pye, pp.
        63-108. Papers of the New World
        Archaeological Foundation, No. 68.
        Brigham Young University, Provo.

LOWE, GARETH W., AND PIERRE AGRINIER
1960   *Mound 1, Chiapa de Corzo, Chiapas,
        Mexico.* Papers of the New World
        Archaeological Foundation, No. 8.
        Brigham Young University, Provo.

LOWE, LYNNETH S., AND CARLOS ÁLVAREZ
ASOMOZA
2007   Recent Explorations at the
        Postclassic Site of Los Cimientos
        de las Margaritas, Chiapas. In
        *Archaeology, Art, and Ethnogenesis
        in Mesoamerican Prehistory: Papers
        in Honor of Gareth W. Lowe*, edited
        by Lynneth S. Lowe and Mary E. Pye,
        pp. 321-335. Papers of the New World
        Archaeological Foundation, No. 68.
        Brigham Young University, Provo.

MACLEOD, MURDO J.
1973   *Spanish Central America: A Socio-
        Economic History 1520-1720.*
        University of California Press,
        Berkeley.

MAIR, LUCY
1962   *Primitive Government.* Penguin Books,
        Baltimore.

MARCUS, GEORGE
1983   *Elites.* University of New Mexico Press,
        Albuquerque.

MARCUS, JOYCE
1976   *Emblem and State in the Classic Maya
        Lowlands: An Epigraphic Approach to
        Territorial Organization.* Dumbarton
        Oaks Research Library and Collection,
        Washington, DC.

1982   The Plant World of the Sixteenth-
        and Seventeenth-Century Lowland
        Maya. In *Maya Subsistence: Studies in
        Memory of Dennis E. Puleston*, edited
        by Kent V. Flannery, pp. 239-273.
        Academic Press, New York.

1983a   Lowland Maya Archaeology at the
        Crossroads. *American Antiquity*
        48(3):454-488.

1983b   On the Nature of the Mesoamerican
        City. In *Prehistoric Settlement
        Patterns: Essays in Honor of Gordon
        R. Willey*, edited by Evon Z. Vogt and
        Richard M. Leventhal, pp. 195-242.
        University of New Mexico Press,
        Albuquerque.

MARQUINA, IGNACIO
1939   *Atlas arqueológico de la república
        mexicana.* Instituto Panamericano de
        Geografía e Historia, Pub. Núm. 41.
        Mexico.

MARQUSEE, STEVEN J.
1980   *An Analysis of Late Postclassic Period
        Quichean Art from the Highlands
        of Guatemala.* Unpublished Ph.D.
        dissertation, Dept. of Anthropology,
        State University of New York, Albany.

MASSON, MARILYN A.
2000   *In the Realm of Nachan Kan:
        Postclassic Maya Archaeology at
        Laguna de On, Belize.* University Press
        of Colorado, Boulder.

MCBRYDE, FELIX WEBSTER
1947   *Cultural and Historical Geography
        of Southwest Guatemala.* Institute
        of Social Anthropology, Pub. No. 4.
        Smithsonian Institution, Washington,
        DC.

MCGUIRE, RANDALL H., AND MICHAEL B. SCHIFFER
1983   A Theory of Architectural Design.
        *Journal of Anthropological
        Archaeology* 2(3):277-303.

McVicker, Donald E.
1974 Variation in Protohistoric Maya Settlement Pattern. *American Antiquity* 39:546-556.

Miles, Suzanne W.
1957 The Sixteenth-Century Pokom-Maya: A Documentary Analysis of Social Structure and Archaeological Setting. *Transactions of the American Philosophical Society* 47:731-781.

1965 Summary of Preconquest Ethnology of the Guatemala-Chiapas Highlands and Pacific Slopes. In *Archaeology of Southern Mesoamerica, Part One. Handbook of Middle American Indians Volume 2*, edited by Gordon R. Willey, pp. 276-287. University of Texas Press, Austin.

Miller, Daniel, and Christopher Tilley (editors)
1984 *Ideology, Power and Prehistory.* Cambridge University Press, Cambridge.

Miller, Donald E.
n.d.a La Libertad, a Major Middle and Late Preclassic Ceremonial Center in Chiapas, Mexico: A Preliminary Report. In The Upper Grijalva Basin Maya Project: Reports on Fieldwork, 1975-1976, edited by Gareth W. Lowe, pp. 8-25. Ms. on file, New World Archaeological Foundation, San Cristobal de las Casas, 1976.

n.d.b La Libertad Burials. Ms. on file, New World Archaeological Foundation. San Cristobal de las Casas, 1979.

Miller, Donald E., Douglas D. Bryant, John E. Clark, and Gareth W. Lowe
2005 Middle Preclassic Ceramics. In *Ceramic Sequence of the Upper Grijalva Region, Chiapas, Mexico. Part 1*, edited by Douglas D. Bryant, John E. Clark and David Cheetham,

pp. 141-264. Papers of the New World Archaeological Foundation, No. 67. Brigham Young University, Provo.

Miranda, Faustino
1952 *La vegetación de Chiapas, segunda parte.* Ediciones del Gobierno del Estado de Chiapas, Tuxtla Gutiérrez.

1975 *La vegetación de Chiapas, primera parte*, 2nd edición. Gobierno del Estado de Chiapas, Departamento de Prensa y Turismo, Tuxtla Gutiérrez.

Moore, Jerry D., and Janine Gasco
1990 Perishable Structures and Serial Dwellings from Coastal Chiapas: Implications for the Archaeology of Households. *Ancient Mesoamerica* 1(2):205-212.

Morgan, Lewis H.
1965 *Houses and House-Life of the American Aborigines.* Reprint of 1881 edition by Phoenix Books. University of Chicago Press, Chicago and London.

Morse, Edward S.
1897 Korean Interviews. *Popular Science Monthly* 51:1-16.

Moseley, Michael E., Robert A. Feldman, and Irene Pritzker
1982 New Light on Peru's Past. *Field Museum of Natural History Bulletin* 53(1):3-11. Chicago.

Müllerried, Frederico K. G.
1957 *La geología de Chiapas.* Ediciones del Gobierno del Estado de Chiapas, Tuxtla Gutiérrez.

Nations, James D.
1979 *Population Ecology of the Lacandon Maya.* Unpublished Ph.D. dissertation, Dept. of Anthropology, Southern Methodist University, Dallas.

NAVARRETE, CARLOS
1962   *La cerámica de Mixco Viejo.*
        Cuadernos de Antropología, No. 1.
        Instituto de Investigaciones Históricas,
        Universidad de San Carlos, Guatemala.

1966   *The Chiapanec History and
        Culture.* Papers of the New World
        Archaeological Foundation, No. 21.
        Brigham Young University, Provo.

1978a   The Prehispanic System of
        Communications between Chiapas
        and Tabasco. In *Mesoamerican
        Communication Routes and Cultural
        Contacts,* edited by Thomas A.
        Lee, Jr. and Carlos Navarrete, pp.
        75-106. Papers of the New World
        Archaeological Foundation, No. 46.
        Brigham Young University, Provo.

1978b   *Un reconocimiento de la Sierra Madre
        de Chiapas.* Centro de Estudios Mayas,
        Universidad Nacional Autónoma de
        México, Mexico.

NELSON, BEN A.
1981   Ethnoarchaeology and
        Paleodemography: A Test of Turner
        and Lofgren's Hypothesis. *Journal of
        Anthropological Research* 37:107-129.

NETTING, ROBERT McC.
1982   Some Home Truths on Household Size
        and Wealth. *American Behavioral
        Scientist* 25(6):641-662.

NETTING, ROBERT McC., RICHARD R. WILK, AND
ERIC J. ARNOULD (EDITORS)
1984   *Households, Comparative and
        Historical Studies of the Domestic
        Group.* University of California Press,
        Berkeley.

OTTERBEIN, KEITH F.
1970   *The Evolution of War: A Cross-
        Cultural Study.* H.R.A.F. Press, New
        Haven.

PAILLÉS H., MARICRUZ
n.d.   Patrones domésticas del Protoclásico
        en Mango Amate. Paper presented at
        the XLII International Congress of
        Americanists, Vancouver, 1979.

PAILLÉS H., MARICRUZ, AND RAÚL AVILA LÓPEZ
1987   Mango Amate, algunas inferencias
        arqueológicas durante el Protoclásico
        en la cuenca superior del río Grijalva.
        *Revista Mexicana de Estudios
        Antropológicos* 33(2):343-356.

PALERM, ÁNGEL
1956   Notas sobre las construcciones
        militares y la guerra en Mesoamérica.
        *Anales del Instituto Nacional de
        Antropología e Historia* 8:123-134.
        Mexico.

PARSONS, JEFFREY R.
1976   The Role of Chinampa Agriculture in
        the Food Supply of Aztec Tenochtitlan.
        In *Cultural Change and Continuity,
        Essays in Honor of James Bennett
        Griffin,* edited by Charles E. Cleland,
        pp. 233-257. Academic Press, New
        York.

PEEBLES, CHRISTOPHER S., AND SUSAN M. KUS
1977   Some Archaeological Correlates of
        Ranked Societies. *American Antiquity*
        42(3):421-448.

PEÑA, MOISES T. DE LA
1951   *Chiapas económica,* Tomo 1.
        Departamento de Prensa y Turismo,
        Gobierno del Estado de Chiapas, Tuxtla
        Gutiérrez.

PIÑA CHAN, ROMÁN
1967   *Atlas arqueológico de la república
        mexicana 3: Chiapas.* Instituto
        Nacional de Antropología e Historia,
        Mexico.

PIRES-FERREIRA, JANE WHEELER
1975   *Formative Mesoamerican Exchange
        Networks with Special Reference to*

the Valley of Oaxaca. Memoirs of
the Museum of Anthropology, No. 7.
University of Michigan, Ann Arbor.

PLOG, FRED
1973   Diachronic Anthropology. In *Research
        and Theory in Current Archeology*,
        edited by Charles L. Redman, pp. 181-
        198. John Wiley and Sons, New York.

1974   *The Study of Prehistoric Change.*
        Academic Press, New York.

1977   Explaining Change. In *Explanation of
        Prehistoric Change*, edited by James
        N. Hill, pp. 17-57. University of New
        Mexico Press, Albuquerque.

POLLOCK, SUSAN M.
1983   *The Symbolism of Prestige: An
        Archaeological Example from the Royal
        Cemetery of Ur.* Unpublished Ph.D.
        dissertation, Dept. of Anthropology,
        University of Michigan, Ann Arbor.

PORTER WEAVER, MURIEL
1972   *The Aztecs, Maya, and Their
        Predecessors.* Academic Press, New
        York.

PRICE, BARBARA J.
1978   Secondary State Formation: An
        Explanatory Model. In *Origins of the
        State: The Anthropology of Political
        Evolution*, edited by R. Cohen and
        Elman R. Service, pp. 161-186. Institute
        for the Study of Human Issues,
        Philadelphia.

PRYOR, FREDERIC L.
1977   *The Origins of the Economy, a
        Comparative Study of Distribution
        in Primitive and Peasant Economies.*
        Academic Press, New York.

QUIRARTE, JACINTO
1982   The Santa Rita Murals: A Review In
        *Aspects of the Mixteca-Puebla Style
        and Mixtec and Central Mexican*

Culture in Southern Mesoamerica,
pp. 43-59. Middle American Research
Institute, Occasional Paper No. 4.
Tulane University, New Orleans.

RANDS, ROBERT L., AND ROBERT E. SMITH
1965   Pottery of the Guatemalan Highlands.
        In *Archaeology of Southern
        Mesoamerica, Part One. Handbook of
        Middle American Indians, Volume 2*,
        edited by Gordon R. Willey, pp. 95-145.
        University of Texas Press, Austin.

RAPOPORT, AMOS
1969   *House Form and Culture.* Prentice-
        Hall, Inglewood Cliffs, NJ.

RECINOS, ADRIÁN, AND DELIA GOETZ
1953   *The Annals of the Cakchiquels.*
        University of Oklahoma Press,
        Norman.

RECINOS, ADRIÁN, DELIA GOETZ, AND SYLVANUS G.
MORLEY
1950   *Popol Vuh.* University of Oklahoma
        Press, Norman.

REDMOND, ELSA M.
1983   *A Fuego y Sangre: Early Zapotec
        Imperialism in the Cuicatlán Cañada,
        Oaxaca.* Memoirs of the Museum of
        Anthropology, No. 16. University of
        Michigan, Ann Arbor.

REIMER, P. J., M. G. L. BAILLIER, E. BARD,
A. BAYLISS, J. W. BECK, C. BERTRAND, P. G.
BLACKWELL, C. E. BUCK, G. BURR, K. B. CUTLER,
P. E. DAMON, R. L. EDWARDS, R. G. FAIRBANKS,
M. FRIEDRICH, T. P. GUILDERSON, K. A. HUGHEN,
B. KROMER, F. G. MCCORMAC, S. MANNING, C.
BRONK RAMSEY, R. W. REIMER, S. REMMELE, J.
R. SOUTHON, M. STUIVER, S. TALAMO, J. VAN DER
PLICHT, AND C. E. WEYHENMEYER
2004   Intcal04 Terrestrial Radiocarbon
        Age Calibration, 0–26 Cal Kyr Bp.
        Radiocarbon 46(3):1029-1058.

REINA, RUBEN, AND ROBERT M. HILL, II
1978   *The Traditional Pottery of Guatemala.*
        University of Texas Press, Austin.

RENFREW, COLIN (EDITOR)
1973   *The Explanation of Culture Change,
        Models in Prehistory.* Duckworth,
        London.

RIBEIRO, DARCY
1968   *The Civilizational Process.* Translated
        by Betty J. Meggers. Smithsonian
        Institution Press, Washington, DC.

RICHARDS, AUDREY I.
1940   The Political System of the Bemba
        Tribe-Northeastern Rhodesia. In
        African Political Systems, edited by
        M. Fortes and E. E. Evans-Pritchard,
        pp. 83-120. Oxford University Press,
        London.

RIVERO TORRES, SONIA E.
1987   *Los Cimientos, Chiapas, Mexico: A
        Late Classic Maya Community.* Papers
        of the New World Archaeological
        Foundation, No. 51. Brigham Young
        University, Provo.

1990   *Patrón de asentamiento rural en la
        región de San Gregorio, Chiapas, para
        el Clásico Tardío.* Instituto Nacional de
        Antropología e Historia, Mexico.

1996   El Juego de Pelota del Sitio
        Lagartero, Chiapas. In *Quinto Foro
        de Arqueología de Chiapas. Serie
        Memorias*, pp. 39-52. Gobierno del
        Estado. de Chiapas, UNICACH, and
        Centro de Estudios Superiores de
        México y Centro América, Tuxtla
        Gutiérrez.

1999   Montículo 1 del Sitio Arqueológico
        Lagartero, Mpio. La Trinitaria,
        Chiapas. *Mexicon* 21:58-61.

RIVERO-TORRES, S., T. CALLIGARO, TENORIO D. AND
M. JIMÉNEZ-REYES
2008   Characterization of Archaeological
        Obsidians from Lagartero, Chiapas,
        Mexico by Pixe. *Journal of
        Archaeological Science* 35(12):3168-
        3171.

ROYS, RALPH L.
1943   *The Indian Background of Colonial
        Yucatan.* Carnegie Institution
        of Washington, Pub. No. 548.
        Washington, DC.

SAHLINS, MARSHALL
1958   *Social Stratification in Polynesia.*
        University of Washington Press,
        Seattle.

1972   *Stone Age Economics.* Aldine, Chicago.

1981   *Historical Metaphors and Mythical
        Realities: Structure in the Early History
        of the Sandwich Islands Kingdom.*
        A.S.A.O. Special Publications, No. 1.
        University of Michigan Press, Ann
        Arbor.

SANDERS, WILLIAM T.
1974   Chiefdom to State: Political Evolution
        at Kaminaljuyú, Guatemala. In
        Reconstructing Complex Societies,
        edited by Charlotte B. Moore, pp.
        97-122. Supplement to the Bulletin
        of the American Schools of Oriental
        Research, No. 20. Cambridge.

SAXE, ARTHUR
1970   *Social Dimensions of Mortuary
        Practices.* Unpublished Ph.D.
        dissertation, Dept. of Anthropology,
        University of Michigan, Ann Arbor.

1971   Social Dimensions of Mortuary
        Practices in a Mesolithic Population
        from Wadi Halfa, Sudan. In
        *Approaches to the Social Dimensions
        of Mortuary Practices*, edited by James
        Brown, pp. 39-57. Memoirs of the
        Society for American Archaeology, 25.
        Washington, DC.

SELER, EDUARD
1901   *Die Alten Ausiedelungen Von Chaculá
        Im Distrikte Nenton des Departments
        Huehuetenango Der Republik
        Guatemala.* Verlag von Dietrich Reimer
        (Ernst Vohsen), Berlin.

SERVICE, ELMAN R.
1971   *Primitive Social Organization*, 2nd
        edition. Random House, New York.

1975   *Origins of the State and Civilization.*
        W. W. Norton, New York.

SHEPARD, ANNA O.
1948   *Plumbate: A Mesoamerican Trade
        Ware.* Carnegie Institution of
        Washington, Pub. No. 573. Washington,
        DC.

SHOOK, EDWIN M.
1952   Lugares arqueológicos del altiplano
        meridional central de Guatemala.
        Antropología e Historia de Guatemala
        4(2):3-40.

SMITH, A. LEDYARD
1955   *Archaeological Reconnaissance
        in Central Guatemala.* Carnegie
        Institution of Washington, Pub. No.
        608. Washington, DC.

SMITH, MICHAEL E., AND FRANCES BERDAN
(EDITORS)
2003   *The Postclassic Mesoamerican World.*
        University of Utah Press, Salt Lake
        City.

SPENCER, CHARLES S.
1982   *The Cuicatlán Cañada and Monte
        Albán.* Academic Press, New York.

SPORES, RONALD
1967   *The Mixtec Kings and Their People.*
        University of Oklahoma Press,
        Norman.

1974   Mixtec Marital Alliance. *American
        Anthropologist* 76(2):297-311.

STEPONAITIS, VINCAS P.
1978   Locational Theory and Complex
        Chiefdoms: A Mississippian Example.
        In *Mississippian Settlement Patterns*,
        edited by Bruce D. Smith, pp. 417-453.
        Academic Press, New York.

SWARTZ, MARC J., VICTOR W. TURNER, AND
ARTHUR TUDEN
1966   Introduction. In *Political Anthropology*,
        edited by Marc J. Swartz, Victor W.
        Turner, and Arthur Tuden, pp. 1-41.
        Aldine, Chicago.

TAUBE, KARL A.
1992   *The Major Gods of Ancient Yucatan.*
        Dumbarton Oaks Pre-Columbian Art
        and Archaeology Studies, No. 32.
        Washington, D.C.

THOMPSON, J. ERIC S.
1930   *Ethnology of the Mayas of Southern
        and Central British Honduras.*
        Anthropological Series, Vol. 17, No. 2.
        Field Museum of Natural History, Pub.
        No. 274. Chicago.

1959   The Role of Caves in Maya Culture.
        In *Mitteilungen Aus Dem Museum
        Fur Volkerkunde in Hamburg, Vol. 25
        (Festband Franz Termer)*, edited by W.
        Bierhenke, W. Haberland, U. Johansen
        and G. Zimmermann, pp. 122-129.
        Museum fur Volkerkunde, Hamburg.

1970   *Maya History and Religion.* University
        of Oklahoma Press, Norman.

TOVILLA, M. A.
1965   *Relación histórica descriptiva de las
        provincias de la del Manche.* Editorial
        Universitaria, Guatemala.

TOZZER, ALFRED M.
1941   *Landa's Relación de las cosas de
        Yucatán, a Translation.* Papers of
        the Peabody Museum of American
        Archaeology and Ethnology, Harvard
        University, Vol. 18. Cambridge.

VILLA ROJAS, ALFONSO
1969   The Tzeltal. In *Ethnology, Part One.
        Handbook of Middle American Indians,
        Volume 7*, edited by Evon Z. Vogt, pp.
        195-225. University of Texas Press,
        Austin.

VILLACORTA, J. ANTONIO AND CARLOS A.
VILLACORTA
1933   *Códices Mayas: Dresdensis,
       Peresianus, Tro-Cortesianus.* La
       Tipografía Nacional, Guatemala.

VIVÓ, JORGE A.
1964   Weather and Climate of Mexico
       and Central America. In *Natural
       Environment and Early Cultures.
       Handbook of Middle American Indians,
       Volume 1*, edited by Robert Wauchope,
       pp. 187-215. University of Texas Press,
       Austin.

VOGT, EVON Z.
1968   Some Aspects of Zinacantan Settlement
       Patterns and Ceremonial Organization.
       In *Settlement Archaeology*, edited by K.
       C. Chang, pp. 154-173. National Press
       Books, Palo Alto.

1969   *Zinacantan.* Harvard University Press,
       Belknap Press, Cambridge.

VOORHIES, BARBARA
n.d.   Vegetation Formations of the Upper
       Grijalva Basin, Chiapas, Mexico.
       Ms. on file, Ms. on file, New World
       Archaeological Foundation. San
       Cristobal de las Casas, 1981.

VOORHIES, BARBARA, AND JANINE L. GASCO
2004   *Postclassic Soconusco Society:
       The Late Prehistory of the Coast
       of Chiapas, Mexico.* Institute for
       Mesoamerican Studies, Mon. 14. State
       University of New York, Albany.

VOS, JAN DE
1980   *La paz de Dios del rey, la conquista
       de la selva lacondona 1525-1821.*
       Gobierno del Estado de Chiapas, Tuxtla
       Gutiérrez.

WAGNER, PHILIP
1964   Natural Vegetation of Middle America.
       In *Natural Environment and Early
       Cultures. Handbook of Middle*

American Indians, Volume 1, edited
by Robert Wauchope, pp. 216-264.
University of Texas Press, Austin.

WAIBEL, LEO
1946   *La Sierra Madre de Chiapas.* Sociedad
       Mexicana de Geografía y Estadística,
       Serie Geografía, No. 2. Mexico.

WASSERSTROM, ROBERT
1983a *Class and Society in Central Chiapas.*
       University of California Press,
       Berkeley.

1983b Spaniards and Indians in Colonial
       Chiapas, 1528-1790. In *Spaniards and
       Indians in Southeastern Mesoamerica,
       Essays on the History of Ethnic
       Relations*, edited by Murdo J. MacLeod
       and Robert Wasserstrom, pp. 92-126.
       University of Nebraska Press, Lincoln.

WAUCHOPE, ROBERT
1934   *House Mounds at Uaxactun,
       Guatemala.* Carnegie Institution of
       Washington, Pub. No. 436. Washington,
       DC.

1938   *Modern Maya Houses: A Study of Their
       Archaeological Significance.* Carnegie
       Institution of Washington, Pub. No.
       502. Washington, DC.

1942   *Notes on the Age of the Cieneguilla
       Cave Textiles from Chiapas.* Middle
       American Research Institute, Pub. 15,
       No. 2. Tulane University, New Orleans.

1970   Protohistoric Pottery of the Guatemalan
       Highlands. In *Monographs and
       Papers in Maya Archaeology*, edited
       by Jr. William R. Bullard, pp. 85-245.
       Papers of the Peabody Museum of
       Archaeology and Ethnology, No. 61.
       Harvard University, Cambridge.

WEBB, MALCOLM C.
1965   The Abolition of the Taboo System in
       Hawaii. *The Journal of the Polynesian
       Society* 74(1):21-39.

1974   Exchange Networks: Prehistory. *Annual Review of Anthropology* 3:356-383.

1975   The Flag Follows Trade: An Essay on the Necessary Interaction of Military and Commercial Factors in State Formation. In *Ancient Civilization and Trade*, edited by J. A. Sabloff and C. C. Lamberg-Karlovsky, pp. 155-209. University of New Mexico Press, Albuquerque.

WEBSTER, DAVID L.
1975   Warfare and the Evolution of the State: A Reconsideration. *American Antiquity* 40:464-470.

1977   Warfare and the Evolution of Maya Civilization. In *The Origins of Maya Civilization*, edited by R. E. W. Adams, pp. 335-372. University of New Mexico Press, Albuquerque.

1978   Three Walled Sites of the Northern Maya Lowlands. *Journal of Field Archaeology* 5:375-390.

1980   Spatial Bounding and Settlement History at Three Walled Northern Maya Centers. *American Antiquity* 45:834-844.

WEEKS, JOHN, M.
1980   *Dimensions of Social Differentiation at Chisalin, El Quiche, Guatemala 1400-1524.* Unpublished Ph.D. dissertation, Dept. of Anthropology, State University of New York, Albany.

WEST, ROBERT C.
1964   Surface Configuration and Associated Geology of Middle America. In *Natural Environment and Early Cultures. Handbook of Middle American Indians, Vol. 1*, edited by Robert West, pp. 33-83. University of Texas Press, Austin.

WHITE, JAMES M.
1976   *The Cultural Sequence at Chicomucelo,*

Chiapas. Unpublished M.A. thesis, Dept. of Archaeology, Simon Fraser University, Burnaby.

WHITECOTTON JOSEPH W.
1977   *The Zapotecs: Princes, Priests, and Peasants.* University of Oklahoma Press, Norman.

WILK, RICHARD R.
1983   Little House in the Jungle: The Causes of Variation in House Size among Modern Kekchi Maya. *Journal of Anthropological Archaeology* 2:99-116.

1984   Households in Process: Agricultural Change and Domestic Transformation among the Kekchi Maya of Belize. In *Households, Comparative and Historical Studies of the Domestic Group*, edited by Robert McC. Netting, Richard R. Wilk and Eric J. Arnould, pp. 217-244. University of California Press, Berkeley.

WILK, RICHARD R., AND WILLIAM L. RATHJE
1982   Household Archaeology. *American Behavioral Scientist* 25(6):617-639.

WINTER, MARCUS C. AND JANE W. PIRES-FERREIRA
1976   Distribution of Obsidian among Households in Two Oaxacan Villages. In *The Mesoamerican Village*, edited by Kent Flannery, pp. 306-311. Academic Press, New York.

WOBST, H. MARTIN
1977   Stylistic Behavior and Information Exchange. In *For the Director. Research Essays in Honor of James B. Griffin*, edited by Charles E. Cleland, pp. 317-342. Museum of Anthropology, Anthropological Papers, No. 61. University of Michigan, Ann Arbor.

WOODBURY, NATALIE F. S.
1953   The History of Zaculeu. In *The Ruins of Zaculeu, Guatemala, Volume 1*, edited by Richard B. Woodbury and Aubry S.

Trik, pp. 9-20. United Fruit Company, New York.

WOODBURY, RICHARD B., AND AUBRY S. TRIK
1953   *The Ruins of Zaculeu, Guatemala,* 2 Vols. United Fruit Company, New York.

WOOLRICH, B., AND A. MANUEL
1948   Parte III: Hidrología. In *Enciclopedia Chiapaneca,* pp. 169-280. Sociedad Mexicana de Geografía y Estadística, Mexico.

WRIGHT, HENRY T.
1977   Recent Research on the Origins of the State. *Annual Review in Anthropology* 6:375-397.

1980   Past Mastery: A Review Article. *Comparative Studies in Society and History* 22:222-226.

WRIGHT, HENRY T., AND GREGORY A. JOHNSON
1975   Population, Exchange, and Early State Formation in Southwest Iran. *American Anthropologist* 77(2):267-289.

WRIGHT, HENRY T., NAOMI MILLER, AND RICHARD REDDING
1980   Time and Process in an Uruk Rural Center. In *L'Archeologie de l'Iraq: Perspectives et limites de l'Interpretation Anthropologique des Documents,* edited by M.T.Barrelet, pp. 265-282. Colloques Internationaux du Centre National de la Recherche Scientifique, No. 580. Editions du CNRS, Paris.

XIMÉNEZ, FRANCISCO
1929-31 *Historia de la Provincia de San Vicente de Chiapa y Guatemala.* 3 Vols. Biblioteca "Goathemala" de la Sociedad de Geografía e Historia, Guatemala.

YELLEN, JOHN E.
1977   *Archaeological Approaches to the Present.* Academic Press, New York.